WEB LAW
A Field Guide to
Internet Publishing
2004 Edition

D1314277

Web Law: A Field Guide to Internet Publishing
By Jonathan D. Hart

"Jonathan Hart's *Web Law* is a rare blend of scholarship and clarity, invaluable not only to the legal community but to anyone engaged in—or contemplating engaging in—online publishing. *Web Law* maps the still-evolving legal landscape of the Internet with information, perspective and wisdom on issues including intellectual property, free speech, privacy and electronic commerce. It is, quite simply, an indispensable resource for the Internet."

> — Rich Jaroslovsky, former Managing Editor of *The Wall Street Journal Online* and founding President of the Online News Association.

"The legal system on a national and international scale moves very slowly in contrast to developments of information storage, retrieval and distribution on the Internet which all is on fast forward. Therefore, the *Web Law: A Field Guide to Internet Publishing* is a very much needed and timely guide and reference source on the legal issues for publishers and lawyers. The comprehensive text is supported and supplemented with an excellent choice of case summaries that help the reader understand the principles of the law in e-publishing. From the basic copyright issues through to defamation, trademark, jurisdiction through to such key topics as commercial email, data collection, privacy, and commercial code for computer information transactions are all supported by case studies which makes this volume an essential and appropriate resource. It is indeed THE legal guide to Internet publishing."

> — Robert E. Baensch
> Director, Center for Publishing
> School of Continuing and Professional Studies
> New York University

"Thorough and thoughtful, the Field Guide captures both settled and emerging legal issues surrounding Internet publishing. Lawyer and layman alike will want it close at hand."

> — Andy Merdek, General Counsel, Cox Enterprises, Inc.

"*Web Law* is a valuable resource for any journalist attempting to sort through the body of new law developing around news as it is distributed on the Internet instead of through your father's newspaper or television set. Jon Hart guides us ably through case after hazy case with clarifying explanations."

> — Doug Feaver, Executive Editor
> washingtonpost.com

"Jon Hart has produced a tremendous resource text for anyone interested in knowing what are the important cases and controversies presented by the Internet. This well-indexed compendium allows the user to get a handle on the issues that need to be addressed in operating on the web."

> — Sandy Baron, Executive Director of the Media Law Resource Center

WEB LAW
A Field Guide to Internet Publishing
2004 Edition

Jonathan D. Hart

Dow, Lohnes & Albertson, PLLC
1200 New Hampshire Avenue, N.W.
Suite 800
Washington, D.C. 20036-6802
(202) 776-2819
jhart@dowlohnes.com
www.dowlohnes.com

BRADFORD PUBLISHING COMPANY
Denver, Colorado

APR 0 8 2005

This book, *Web Law: A Field Guide to Internet Publishing, 2004 Edition,* is intended to provide general information with regard to the subject matter covered. It is not meant to provide legal opinions or offer professional advice, nor to serve as a substitute for advice by licensed, legal or other professionals. This book is sold with the understanding that Bradford Publishing Company and the author, by virtue of its publication, are not engaged in rendering legal or other professional services.

Bradford Publishing Company and the author do not warrant that the information herein is complete or accurate, and do not assume and hereby disclaim any liability to any person for any loss or damage caused by errors, inaccuracies or omissions, or usage of this book.

Laws, and interpretations of those laws, change frequently and the subject matter of this book contains important legal consequences. It is the responsibility of the user of this book to know if the information contained in it is applicable to his situation, and if necessary, to consult legal, tax, or other counsel.

Library of Congress Cataloging-in-Publication Data

Hart, Jonathan D.
  Web law : a field guide to Internet publishing / Jonathan D. Hart.-- 2004
ed.
      p. cm.
  Includes bibliographical references and index.
  ISBN 1-932779-00-0
  1. Internet publishing--Law and legislation--United States. I. Title.

  KF2750.H37 2004
  342.7308'53--dc22

2004013764

Cover design by Brent Beltrone
ISBN: 1-932779-00-0
Published 2004 by Bradford Publishing Company
1743 Wazee Street, Denver, Colorado 80202

Dedication

For Meg, Peter, Molly and Sam, on whose time this book was written.

Acknowledgments

This volume is the work of many: Tracy M. Benjamin, Kathleen E. Fuller, Michael Heath, Todd B. Klessman, Mira J. Koplovsky, Michael Kovaka, Kevin J. Kuzas, Carolyn Wimbly Martin, Matthew V. Munro, Jennifer A. Ness, Karen A. Post, Michael D. Rothberg, Prabha R. Rollins, David M. Rudin, Marc S. Sher, Briana E. Thibeau, Heather B. Sachs, Mitchell H. Stabbe, and Kristi Thompson, all lawyers at Dow, Lohnes & Albertson, at one time or another, made substantive contributions. Pat Dawson, my assistant at DL&A, managed the manuscript ably. I am grateful to them all. Any errors are my own. Special thanks to Holly Brady, director of the Stanford Professional Publishing Courses, for inviting me to teach, year after year, in the publishing programs for which this volume was originally prepared, and to Robert Baensch, director of the Center for Publishing at New York University, and Charlene Gaynor, executive director of the Association of Educational Publishers, for persuading me there was a market for it. Thanks also to Lexis/Nexis and Westlaw for providing computer-assisted legal research services.

Table of Contents

Over the last two decades, the Internet has grown from a novel means of communication among research scientists into a tool of mass communication essential to the daily lives of millions of people. The Internet is now widely used to send and receive correspondence, to access and disseminate information, and to buy and sell goods and services.

A body of law is taking shape. Perhaps most significantly, the United States Supreme Court has made clear that there is "no basis for qualifying the level of First Amendment scrutiny that should be applied to [the Internet]." *Reno v. American Civil Liberties Union*, 521 U.S. 844, 897, 117 S. Ct. 2329, 2344 (1997). In other words, for purposes of applying First Amendment speech protections, speech on the Internet is treated like the printed speech in newspapers, books, and magazines, as opposed to speech broadcast on radio or television, which the government has more latitude to regulate.

Not surprisingly, many of the legal issues that have been addressed to date involve how traditional bodies of law in areas such as trademark, copyright, libel, and privacy apply in this new medium. This volume tracks the case law, legislation, and proposed legislation that have developed around Internet publishing and raises various issues that are likely to become increasingly significant in the coming years.

This 2004 edition expands upon the previous edition, titled *Law of the Web*, in several ways. Not only does it present the results of legislation and decisions that were not yet completed at the time of publication of the last edition, it also introduces all of the new legislation that arose during calendar year 2003. The larger format allows about 25 percent more material to be presented in a manageable number of pages.

The importance of the issue of domain names warrants an entire chapter in this edition. In addition, a new chapter on advertising and marketing adds to the previous edition's chapter that concentrated solely on spam by presenting new topics related to Internet advertising, such as contextual marketing, pop-ups, fraudulent marketing, Internet gambling, and Internet pharmacies, among other timely topics.

The major user-friendly addition that this edition offers is the presentation of end-of-chapter summaries of the law. By using these summaries, the reader can determine the relevance of each chapter to the case at hand. The comprehensive table of centents and index also aid the user in finding pertinent information.

FREEDOM OF SPEECH

The First Amendment to the Constitution of the United States guarantees that "Congress shall make no law . . . abridging the freedom of speech, or of the press; or the right of the people peaceably to assemble, and to petition the government for a redress of grievances."

Although the First Amendment expressly limits Congressional action (that is, it prohibits the enactment of federal laws that improperly limit speech), courts have long applied the protections of the First Amendment to limit state action, as well, through the Due Process Clause of the Fourteenth Amendment. The Fourteenth Amendment prohibits states from depriving anyone of "life, liberty or property" without due process of law. Nearly all the guarantees of the Bill of Rights, including the First Amendment guarantee of freedom of speech, have been found by the Supreme Court to be aspects of "liberty."

First Amendment Basics

Content-based or Content-neutral

In determining whether a particular restriction on speech is permissible despite the First Amendment, the courts have distinguished between restrictions based on the content of the affected speech (which are generally prohibited) and restrictions that are content-neutral (which may, under certain circumstances, be permissible). A restriction on speech is deemed content-based if the restriction is aimed at the communicative impact of the expression. If a restriction is aimed at something other than the communicative impact of expression, even if it has the effect of burdening some expression, it is deemed content-neutral.

A content-based regulation is constitutional only if the government can show that it is "necessary to serve a compelling state interest and that it is narrowly drawn to achieve that end." *Perry Education Association v. Perry Local Educators' Association*, 460 U.S. 37, 45 (1983). If a restriction is content-neutral, it will generally be found constitutional if it serves an "important or substantial" governmental interest, is crafted as narrowly as possible to address the interest, and leaves alternative channels of communication open to those whose speech the law restricts. *Id.*

The Supreme Court has also identified categories of speech that it deems generally unprotected by the First Amendment: child pornography; speech that advocates imminent lawless action; speech meeting the constitutional test for obscenity; and certain speech that is shown to be false, defamatory, and uttered, depending on the circumstances, either with knowledge of its falsity, with reckless indifference to its truth or falsity, or negligently. See *Ashcroft v. Free Speech Coalition*, 535 U.S. 234, 245-46 (2002); *New York v. Ferber*, 458 U.S. 747, 765 (1982). Speech not falling into one of these categories is generally deemed protected and restrictions are presumed to be unconstitutional.

Overbreadth

Laws that ban a substantial amount of protected speech along with speech that may be regulated may be found unconstitutionally "overbroad." For example, a Massachusetts statute that prohibited adults from posing or exhibiting minors "in a state of nudity" was found overbroad until it was amended to exempt family photos of naked infants. *See Commonwealth v. Oakes*, 401 Mass. 602, 518 N.E.2d 836 (1988), *overbreadth found moot based on revision of statute, Massachusetts v. Oakes*, 491 U.S. 576 (1989).

Vagueness

A law is unconstitutionally vague if the conduct forbidden is defined so unclearly that a reasonable person would have difficulty understanding the difference between legal and illegal conduct. For example, a state law prohibiting public school teachers from engaging in "seditious" utterances was found unconstitutionally vague because it did not distinguish between statements about doctrine and statements intended to incite action in furtherance of that doctrine. *See Keyishian v. Board of Regents*, 385 U.S. 589 (1967).

Print Media Versus Broadcast Media

The Supreme Court has determined that "differences in the characteristics of news media justify differences in the First Amendment standards applied to them." *Red Lion Broadcasting Co. v. FCC*, 395 U.S. 367, 386-87 (1969). In *Red Lion*, the Court ruled that because there are a limited number of broadcast frequencies available, a broadcaster does not have an "unabridgeable First Amendment right to broadcast comparable to the right of every individual to speak, write, or publish." *Id.* at 388. Accordingly, the Court held that the FCC could require broadcasters to make time available to the public to reply to personal attacks and political editorials. Similarly, in *FCC v. Pacifica Foundation*, 438 U.S. 726 (1978), the Court upheld the FCC's authority to regulate the use of nonobscene "adult language" on the radio, at least in certain circumstances.

By contrast, in *Miami Herald Publishing Co. v. Tornillo*, 418 U.S. 241 (1974), the Supreme Court made clear that the right of a newspaper editor to choose what to publish cannot be circumscribed in the interest of permitting public access to the paper. The Court rejected the notion that a state can require a newspaper to provide free space in the paper for political candidates to reply to personal attacks printed in the paper. The Court justified treating the print media differently from the broadcast media because there is no limit to the number of newspapers that can be published; anyone can publish a newspaper, but only a finite number of broadcast frequencies are available and a would-be broadcaster must obtain a governmental license to use one.

Speech on the Internet Is Entitled to Full First Amendment Protection

In the first major decision of the Internet era, the Supreme Court ruled in *Reno v. ACLU*, 521 U.S. 844 (1997), that speech on the Internet is entitled to the full First Amendment protection afforded to newspapers and other print publications.

The Communications Decency Act

In *Reno v. ACLU*, 521 U.S. 844 (1997), the U.S. Supreme Court found unconstitutional certain provisions of the Communications Decency Act of 1996 (CDA) that aimed to protect minors from harmful material on the Internet. One such provision, 47 U.S.C. § 223(a)(1)(B)(ii), prohibited transmission of "obscene or indecent" communications to any recipient under 18 years of age, if the sender had knowledge that the recipient was a minor. Another provision, § 223(d), prohibited transmission or display to a minor of any message that was "patently offensive" as measured by community standards. The CDA provided two defenses: one available to persons who used "good faith, reasonable, effective and appropriate actions under the circumstances to restrict or prevent access by minors"; and the other available to persons who restricted access to communications by using a verified credit card or other adult identification number. Violation of either § 223(a) or § 223(d) was criminally punishable by a fine or imprisonment for up to two years, or both.

The Court found that speech on the Internet was entitled to the full First Amendment protection afforded newspapers and other print publications, and held the CDA to be an unconstitutional "content-based blanket restriction on speech." The Court concluded that the CDA lacked the precision required in a statute that regulates the content of speech. To deny minors access to potentially harmful speech, the CDA effectively suppressed speech that adults have a constitutional right to receive and to address to one another. The Court noted that in evaluating the free-speech rights of adults, existing precedent has clearly established that "[s]exual expression which is indecent but not obscene is protected by the First Amendment." The Court then dismissed the government's argument that restricting transmissions to minors would not interfere with adult-to-adult communication.

Critical to the Court's analysis was the trial court's finding that at the time of trial there was no technology available to allow senders to avoid sending messages to minors without also restricting access by adults. For the same reason, the Court also rejected the government's argument that the CDA was not overbroad because its prohibition on indecent communications was limited to persons known to be under 18 years of age.

The Court also found that the CDA's vague definitions of "indecent" and "offensive" communications were problematic under the First Amendment. The use of an indecency standard in one section of the statute and a prohibition in another section against speech that "in context, depicts or describes, in terms patently offensive as measured by contemporary community standards, sexual or excretory activities or organs," created uncertainty about how the standards related to each other and just what they meant. The Court also found that this inconsistency in the legal standard to be applied made it unlikely that the CDA was narrowly tailored to achieve Congress' interest in protecting children from harmful material. The inconsistency was particularly troubling to the Court because a violation of these vague standards was punishable as a crime, creating a further chilling effect on free speech.

The CDA's affirmative defenses did not protect the statute from an overbreadth challenge, either. First, with respect to the defense of "good faith, reasonable, effective, and appropriate actions" to prevent transmissions to minors, the Court held that the requirement that the action be *effective* made the defense "illusory." Although the government suggested that such actions could include "tagging" communications to identify their content, the Court pointed out that the sort of screening software described by the government did not then exist and that even if it did, there would be no way to know whether a particular covered communication would actually be blocked so as not to reach a particular underage recipient. The Court found the second affirmative defense, available to sites that require credit card or other forms of adult identification verification, to be too broad a burden on noncommercial speech because it would not be economically feasible for most noncommercial speakers to use verification procedures. Finally, the Court rejected the argument that, aside from the interest in protecting children, the government's interest in fostering the growth of the Internet provided sufficient justification for upholding the CDA. The Court found this argument unpersuasive in light of the already rapid growth of the Internet and held that the interest in encouraging freedom of expression was greater than any possible benefits from limiting speech.

In December 2001, the National Coalition for Sexual Freedom (Coalition), a separate group called The National Coalition for Sexual Freedom Foundation (Foundation) and photographer Barbara Nitke, who publishes sadomasochistic photos on the Internet, filed suit in federal court, seeking to overturn the obscenity-related provisions of the Communications Decency Act that had not already been struck down. The original complaint charged that the remaining CDA provisions were unconstitutionally overbroad and vague because they do not specify which "community standards" apply for purposes of defining obscenity. Plaintiffs sought a preliminary injunction prohibiting enforcement of the CDA; the government moved to dismiss the case on the grounds that the plaintiffs lacked standing and that there was no basis for the overbreadth and vagueness claims.

The U.S. District Court for the Southern District of New York agreed that Nitke and the Foundation lacked standing, but ruled that the Coalition did have sufficient standing to sue. On the substantive elements of the lawsuit, the trial court dismissed the vagueness claim, noting that for purposes of a vagueness challenge, Supreme Court precedent established that "community standards" do not have to be defined with precision. However, the court authorized the plaintiffs to continue to press their overbreadth claim as it relates to the definition of "community standards" in the context of the worldwide reach of the Internet. The plaintiffs' motion for a preliminary injunction was denied because the plaintiffs had not shown a likelihood of irreparable harm. *Nitke, et al. v. Ashcroft*, 253 F. Supp. 2d 587 (S.D.N.Y. Mar. 24, 2003). For a discussion of this case in the context of applying "community standards" to the Internet, see page 10, below.

The Child Online Protection Act

In October 1998, Congress enacted the Child Online Protection Act, 47 U.S.C. § 231 (COPA, sometimes referred to as CDA II), an attempt to achieve the CDA's objective of protecting children while addressing the Supreme Court's concerns. COPA is more limited than the CDA in two basic ways. First, COPA prohibits the distribution of material that is "harmful to minors" rather than material that is "obscene or indecent." Second, COPA only applies to communications for commercial purposes. The statute provides that a communication is for a commercial purpose only if the speaker devotes time, labor, and attention to the communication as part of his or her business, and tries to profit from it. COPA also provides a defense for any speaker who has restricted access to material harmful to minors by requiring a credit card or other adult identification number, accepting a digital certificate that verifies age, or through other reasonable means using available technology. The statute restricts the disclosure of information collected while establishing these procedures.

The ACLU filed suit shortly after COPA was enacted. The trial court issued a preliminary injunction prohibiting enforcement of COPA on February 1, 1999, finding that COPA imposed significant burdens on protected speech in violation of the First Amendment. *ACLU v. Reno*, 31 F. Supp. 2d 473 (E.D. Pa. 1999). On June 22, 2000, the United States Court of Appeals for the Third Circuit upheld the trial court's decision, holding that the statute was unconstitutionally broad because, among other things, it affected even nonpornographic websites. *ACLU v. Reno*, 217 F.3d 162 (3d Cir. 2000).

On May 13, 2002, the Supreme Court vacated the judgment and sent the case back to the Third Circuit. The Supreme Court held that the COPA's reliance on community standards to identify what material is harmful to minors does not by itself render the statute substantially overbroad (and therefore unconstitutional) under the First Amendment. The Court remanded the case with instructions to the Third Circuit to evaluate other constitutional challenges to the statute that it had not addressed. The Third Circuit then found COPA to be unconstitutionally overbroad because it prohibited a wide range of constitutionally protected speech. The court focused, in particular, on the expansive definitions of "material harmful to minors" and "for commercial purposes," and the burdensome requirements of the statutory defenses. *ACLU v. Ashcroft*, 322 F.3d 240 (3d Cir. 2003). On October 14, 2003, the Supreme Court agreed to review the Third Circuit's latest decision. *Ashcroft v. ACLU*, U.S. No. 03-218, *cert. granted* (Oct 14, 2003). The case was scheduled to be argued before the Supreme Court on March 2, 2004.

The Child Pornography Protection Act

In 1996, Congress enacted the Child Pornography Protection Act (CPPA), 18 U.S.C. § 2252A, which criminalized the transmission or possession of digital child pornography, whether the pornographic image is computer-generated or an actual photograph. The statute was directed at conduct intrinsically related to the sexual abuse of children.

The constitutionality of the CPPA has been challenged in several federal courts, resulting in conflicting decisions. *United States v. Hilton*, 167 F.3d 61 (1st Cir. 1999), *cert. denied*, 528 U.S. 844 (1999) (CPPA's definition of child pornography comports with the First Amendment); *United States v. Fox*, 248 F.3d 394 (5th Cir. 2001) (CPPA survives strict scrutiny and is neither overbroad nor vague), *vacated by Ashcroft v. Free Speech Coalition*, 122 S. Ct. 1602 (2002); *United States v. Acheson*, 195 F.3d 645 (11th Cir. 1999) (upholding CPPA); *Free Speech Coalition v. Reno*, 198 F.3d 1083 (9th Cir. 1999) (ruling CPPA unconstitutionally vague and overbroad, in part because the definition of child pornography could include otherwise protected speech).

On April 16, 2002, in *Ashcroft v. Free Speech Coalition*, 535 U.S. 234, 122 S. Ct. 1389 (2002), the Supreme Court overturned the provisions of CPPA that made it a crime to possess or distribute any sexually explicit image that appears to be, or gives the impression of, a minor engaged in sexual acts. These provisions applied to both depictions of youthful-looking adults and computer-generated images of children. The court held that CPPA "prohibits speech that records no crime and creates no victims by production." Moreover, the statute did not incorporate the community standards test of obscenity or require the artistic merit of a work be judged considering the work as a whole. The government cannot ban protected speech as a means to ban unprotected speech. The court determined that these provisions of the act were overbroad and therefore unconstitutional.

The Children's Internet Protection Act

In December 2000, Congress enacted the Children's Internet Protection Act (CIPA), Pub. L. No. 106-554, tit. XVII, 114 Stat. 2763A-335 (2000), which requires schools and libraries that receive funds under the E-rate program and the Library Service and Technology Act to install "technology protection measures" on all their Internet access terminals, regardless of whether federal programs paid for the terminals or the Internet connections.

On May 31, 2002, in a unanimous decision, a three-judge panel found CIPA invalid under the First Amendment because it requires libraries to use filtering technology that inadvertently blocks access to thousands of legitimate websites while allowing access to some pornographic sites. The panel stated that less restrictive means, such as enforcement of Internet use policies in libraries, would accomplish the underlying purpose while allowing access to websites containing protected speech. *American Library Association v. United States*, 201 F. Supp. 2d 401 (E.D. Pa. 2002). On June 23, 2003, the U.S. Supreme Court reversed. The Supreme Court stated that just as a library exercises judgment in making traditional collection decisions, it may exercise similar judgment when it collects material from the Internet. Accordingly, laws regulating content in libraries do not have to use the least restrictive means of achieving the government's goal. In addition, the Court noted that adult patrons can have Internet sites unblocked by asking a librarian to disable the filter. Thus, according to the Court, filtering does not present any insurmountable constitutional difficulties. *United States v. American Library Association*, 123 S. Ct. 2297, 2003 U.S. LEXIS 4799 (2003).

The effectiveness of filtering software has been the subject of much debate. One study, from the Berkman Center at Harvard University, notes that filtering software inevitably produces "overblocking," denying access to some sites even though they comply with the stated filtering rules. Benjamin Edelman, "Web Sites Sharing IP Addresses: Prevalence and Significance," Berkman Center for Internet & Society, Harvard Univ. (Feb. 2003), *available* at http://cyber.law.harvard.edu/people/edelman/ip-sharing/; Declan McCullagh, "Net Blocking Threatens Legitimate Sites," CNET News.com (Feb. 19, 2003), *available at* http://news.com.com/2100-1023-985216.html. Another study, from the Kaiser Family Foundation, reports that most of the popular filtering programs block health-related websites, including the website of the Centers for Disease Control and Prevention. WSJ.com, "Web Filters Are Blocking Health Sites, Report Finds" (Dec. 11, 2002), *available* at http://online.wsj.com/article_print/0,,SB1039556006230825993.html. A study from the Electronic Frontier Foundation and Online Policy Group also indicates that some filtering software may have the unintended result of blocking access to information related to topics that are included in state-mandated curricula in public schools. "Internet Blocking in Public Schools: A Study on Internet Access in Educational Institutions," Electronic Frontier Foundation and Online Policy Group (June 3, 2003), *available at* http://www.eff.org/Censorship/Censorware/net_block_report/; Electronic Frontier Foundation Press Release, "Study Released on Internet Blocking in Schools" (June 23, 2003), *available at* http://www.eff.org/Censoship/Censorware/net_block_report/20030623_eff_pr.php.

The Child Abduction Prevention Act

In April 2003, Congress enacted the Child Abduction Prevention Act (CAPA). Lawmakers originally conceived of this law to strengthen federal penalties for pedophilia and to provide funding for a child abduction notification system known as the Amber Alert. Two provisions relate to the Internet. The first criminalizes the use of a misleading domain name with intent to deceive a minor into viewing material that is harmful to minors. The second amendment criminalizes computer-generated child pornography regardless of whether a child, instead of a computer-generated image that looks like a child, is actually used to create the pornography. CAPA was signed into law by the President on April 30, 2003. 18 U.S.C. §§ 2252B, 2256(8)(B), Pub. L. No. 108-21, 117 Stat. 650 (2003).

Reviewing or Downloading Obscene Material

In Stanley v. Georgia, 394 U.S. 557 (1969), the Supreme Court held that the Constitution prohibits making mere possession of obscene material a crime. Nevertheless, in United States v. Reilly, 2003 WL 1878308 (S.D.N.Y. Apr. 14, 2003) (*unpublished opinion*), a federal trial court found that Congress can prohibit an individual from receiving obscene material over the Internet. An employee of the U.S. Department of Labor was found downloading from the Internet what appeared to be child pornography. The government prosecuted the employee under 18 U.S.C. § 1462, a statute criminalizing the electronic transportation and receipt of obscene material. The defendant moved to dismiss the charge, arguing that the statute is unconstitutionally overbroad. The court held that the statute is not overbroad because it is sufficiently related to the goal of prohibiting interstate trafficking in, not mere possession of, obscene materials, and denied the motion to dismiss.

Obscenity and "Community Standards" Online

Part of the legal test for obscenity, established by the Supreme Court in *Miller v. California*, 413 U.S. 15 (1973), asks whether "the average person applying contemporary community standards would find that the work, taken as a whole, appeals to the prurient interest." *Miller* established as a general principle that in cases involving interstate transportation of obscene material, juries are properly instructed to apply the community standards of the geographic area where the materials are sent. *Miller*, 413 U.S. at 30-34. Because the legal definition of obscenity is determined with reference to the community standards of a particular community, courts must figure out where obscene materials are "sent" on the Internet to determine which community's standards apply.

U.S. v. Thomas, 74 F.3d 701 (6th Cir. 1996), *cert. denied*, 519 U.S. 820 (1996).

A couple in California operated a computer bulletin board service (BBS). They purchased sexually explicit magazines and scanned the images onto a computer for downloading by BBS members. The couple was convicted of knowingly transporting obscene files in interstate commerce under a federal obscenity statute, 18 U.S.C. § 1465. The appellate court affirmed that "the venue for federal obscenity prosecutions lies in any district from, through, or into which the allegedly obscene material moves." *Id.* at 709 (quoting federal jurisdictional statute 18 U.S.C. § 3237). Because the BBS user who complained was in the Western District of Tennessee, venue there was proper.

The court found that because the images in question had been purposely sent to Tennessee, the community standards of Tennessee were properly applied. *Id.* at 711. The court refused to consider a new definition of "community," under which offenses allegedly committed online would be measured against the standards of the online community, in part because the BBS operators in the case had a mechanism for tailoring content offerings to varying community standards depending on the location of users. The court specifically found that, through its membership process, the BBS operators had knowledge of and control over the jurisdictions from which their materials were being accessed. *Id.* at 711-12.

Ashcroft v. American Civil Liberties Union, 535 U.S. 564 (2002); *remanded to* 322 F.3d 240 (3rd Cir. 2003); *cert granted*, U.S. No. 03-218 (Oct 14, 2003).

The Supreme Court overturned a Third Circuit decision that the Child Online Protection Act's reliance on community standards to identify material "harmful to minors" made the law overbroad. Justices Thomas, Scalia, and Rehnquist ruled in a plurality opinion that the use of the community standards test "does not *by itself* render the statute substantially overbroad for the purposes of the First Amendment." 535 U.S. 564 at 585. The plurality rejected the argument that because Internet publishers are unable to limit the geographical reach of their materials, the use of the community standards test burdens protected speech. The Third Circuit ruled that the function of COPA in conjunction with variations in local community standards would force publishers to self-censor their works to meet the standards of the least tolerant community reachable through the Internet. The plurality relied on earlier cases upholding the community standards test in the context of mail-order and telephone pornography, which had held that if a speaker's audience happened to include different communities with different standards, the burden was on the speaker to tailor the message accordingly. The fact that Internet publishers cannot restrict their messages by location was no excuse, according to the plurality; rather, the burden must be on publishers to choose whether to use the Internet at all given its widespread reach. The Court sent the case back to the Third Circuit to consider whether the CDA was unconstitutional for any other reason. Although eight justices ultimately concurred in the judgment, five justices expressed separate opinions disagreeing with the plurality's application of the community standards test to the Internet. These justices agreed with the Third Circuit that the community standards test would burden too much speech, even if that factor alone was not sufficient to strike the law. Justices Breyer and O'Connor went so far as to say that the concept of "community" should be defined by a national standard rather than by separate local standards.

On remand, the Third Circuit reaffirmed its earlier decision that the use of the "community standards" test was overbroad. The Court also found various other constitutional defects in the statute. The Supreme Court agreed to review the Third Circuit's latest decision. Oral argument is scheduled for March 2004.

Barbara Nitke, et al. v. Ashcroft, 253 F. Supp. 2d 587 (S.D.N.Y. 2003).

Only a few weeks after the Third Circuit issued its decision on remand of *Ashcroft v. ACLU*, the District Court for the Southern District of New York denied the government's motion to dismiss this case (discussed above at page 6). Nitke and her fellow plaintiffs argued that the CDA is overbroad because it forces Internet publishers to self-censor their content to meet the standards of the least tolerant community in the nation. The court declined to accept the government's contention that the Supreme Court's opinion in *Ashcroft* had definitively rejected this argument, noting that under Supreme Court precedent, the three-Justice plurality decision was not binding precedent. The court went on to conclude that the plaintiffs presented a valid overbreadth challenge, authorizing the plaintiffs to continue the suit. As of December 31, 2003, the case remained pending.

Use of Zoning Law to Restrict Access to Internet Content

The government attempted to defend the CDA by analogizing it to zoning law. In *Reno v. ACLU*, 521 U.S. 844 (1997), discussed above at page 4, Justice Stevens, writing for the majority, rejected the government's "cyberzoning" analogy, which compared the CDA to ordinances such as those that bar adult theatres from residential neighborhoods (upheld in *Renton v. Playtime Theatres*, 475 U.S. 41 (1986)). Justice Stevens characterized the CDA as an invalid content-based restriction, rather than a permissible content-neutral restriction such as a zoning ordinance. However, in a concurring opinion, Justice O'Connor disagreed, saying she would have upheld the CDA by analogy to zoning law if adults had been able to obtain access to the regulated speech. Justice O'Connor noted that online speakers have already begun to "zone" cyberspace through the use of technology that requires users to enter information about themselves before they can access certain areas, much like a bouncer checks a person's driver's license before he admits him or her to a nightclub in the physical world. Despite what Justice O'Connor characterized as the promising prospects for the eventual zoning of the Internet, she agreed with the court that, as of 1997, technology was not yet advanced enough to allow zoning-like content restrictions on the Internet.

Voyeur Dorm L.L.C. v. City of Tampa, 265 F.3d 1232 (11th Cir. 2001), *cert. denied*, 122 S. Ct. 1172 (2002).

The City of Tampa alleged that Voyeur Dorm was violating a local zoning ordinance by operating its voyeurdorm.com website from a Tampa residence. The zoning ordinance prohibits property owners in residential areas from "offer[ing] [] adult entertainment to members of the public." *See* Tampa, Fla., Code § 27-523. Voyeur Dorm's website provides subscribers with a 24-hour-a-day video transmission portraying the lives of young women living together in a Tampa home. Subscribers pay a monthly fee for access to the website and opportunities to "chat" with the women living in the house. The women in the house are employees of Voyeur Dorm and are compensated for their entertainment services. The house from which the images are filmed is located in a residential neighborhood within a restricted zoning area. The trial court upheld application of the zoning restrictions, finding that the residential house was a "premises on which is offered to members of the public for consideration entertainment featuring specified sexual activities within the plain meaning of the City Code." *Voyeur Dorm v. Tampa*, 121 F. Supp. 2d 1373 (M.D. Fla. 2000).

The court of appeals reversed because it agreed with Voyeur Dorm that the Tampa zoning ordinance applies to locations at which adult entertainment is actually available to the public. Voyeur Dorm's entertainment exists wholly on the Internet. The public cannot physically visit the Voyeur Dorm house to observe the adult entertainment: "The offering occurs when the videotaped images are dispersed over the internet and into the public eye for consumption. The City Code cannot be applied to a location that does not, itself, offer adult entertainment to the public." *Voyeur Dorm*, 265 F.3d at 1236. Therefore, the court held that the Voyeur Dorm house was not subject to regulation as an adult entertainment establishment under Tampa's zoning ordinance.

The U.S. Supreme Court declined to review the appellate court's decision.

Dot-Kids Implementation and Efficiency Act of 2002

On December 4, 2002, President Bush signed legislation (Pub. L. 107-317) creating a new second-level Internet domain that is intended to be a safe haven for online material for children and families. The new domain, ".kids," will be within the U.S. country code domain; domain names will appear as "www.website.kids.us." Internet sites using .kids in their addresses will not be permitted to link to other websites and may not offer chat or instant messaging features. All content must be suitable for children under the age of 13.

The law defines two standards for allowable content: not harmful to minors and suitable for minors. Mirroring the three-prong test for obscenity established by the Supreme Court in *Miller v. California*, discussed above at page 9, "harmful to minors" is defined as material (1) that the average person, applying contemporary community standards, would find, taking the material as a whole and with respect to minors, is designed to appeal to, or is designed to pander to, the prurient interest; (2) that depicts, describes, or represents, in a manner patently offensive with respect to minors, an actual or simulated sexual act or sexual contact, or a lewd exhibition of the genitals or post-pubescent female breast; and (3) that, taken as a whole, lacks serious, literary, artistic, political, or scientific value for minors. "Suitable for minors" means material that is psychologically or intellectually appropriate for minors and that serves the educational, informational, intellectual, social, emotional, entertainment, or cognitive needs of minors. The bill states that the domain-name registry of the ".kids.us" domain would provide written content standards and would promulgate rules and procedures for enforcement and oversight that "minimize the possibility" that the new domain would provide access to content that is inconsistent with these standards. The registry would also create a process for removing content that violates the articulated standards, as well as a process for resolving disputes over the exclusion of particular material.

For discussion of .kids in the context of domain names, *see* Chapter 3, page 55.

State Laws Restricting Online Content

Despite the Supreme Court's ruling in *Reno v. ACLU* that speech on the Internet is entitled to the highest level of First Amendment protection, states continue to pass Internet censorship laws. Many of these state statutes have been found unconstitutional.

The Commerce Clause of the U.S. Constitution reserves to Congress the regulation of interstate commerce and prevents a state from imposing laws outside its territory. Because the Internet transcends state boundaries, state attempts to regulate online content often impose restrictions on content providers or users outside the state's jurisdiction, and are therefore found to be violations of the Commerce Clause as well as the First Amendment.

ACLU of Georgia v. Miller, 977 F. Supp. 1228 (N.D. Ga. 1997).

The plaintiffs filed suit for declaratory and injunctive relief challenging a Georgia statute that criminalized computer communications knowingly made using a false name. The statute also criminalized the knowing transmission on a computer network of a trade name, registered trademark, logo, legal or official seal, or copyrighted symbol in a manner that stated or falsely implied that the speaker was authorized to use the mark when no such permission had been obtained. The court granted a preliminary injunction against the enforcement of the statute and held that the statute was a content-based restriction on speech, subject to strict scrutiny because the identity of a speaker is part of the content of his speech. Although the Georgia legislature's purpose of fraud prevention was compelling, the court found that the statute was not narrowly tailored to achieve this goal. Instead, the statute had an impact on innocent speech as well as fraudulent speech, because several terms of the statute were not well defined. The court also held that the plaintiffs were likely to succeed on claims of overbreadth and unconstitutional vagueness.

The court later made the temporary injunction permanent, effectively putting an end to enforcement of the law. *ACLU of Georgia v. Miller*, 1997 U.S. Dist. LEXIS 14972 (Aug. 7, 1997). The state of Georgia did not appeal the court's decision.

American Library Ass'n v. Pataki, 969 F. Supp. 160 (S.D.N.Y. 1997).

New York made it a crime for an individual intentionally to use a computer to initiate or engage in communication with a minor, knowing that the communication depicted nudity, sexual conduct, or sadomasochistic abuse and would be harmful to minors. N.Y. Penal Law § 235.21. The statute defined "harmful to minors" as any representation or description of nudity, sexual conduct or excitement, or sadomasochistic abuse when it (1) considered as a whole, appealed to the prurient interest in sex of minors; (2) was patently offensive according to prevailing standards in the adult community regarding suitable material for minors; and (3) considered as a whole, lacked serious literary, artistic, political, and scientific value for minors. N.Y. Penal Law § 235.20(6).

Several individuals and organizations filed suit to prevent the state from enforcing the statute, claiming that it violated the Commerce Clause and the First Amendment. The U.S. District Court granted a preliminary injunction because the plaintiffs had shown a likelihood of success on the merits of the Commerce Clause claim. The court found that the statute clearly involved interstate commerce because the legislative history demonstrated the intent to reach citizens of other states, and because the nature of the Internet makes it impossible to determine where a communication originates. The Commerce Clause, the court noted, applies even to activities that are not motivated by profit. Direct state regulation of interstate commerce is a per se violation of the Commerce Clause. The court also found that the burden on interstate commerce outweighed any local benefit of the law. While the objective of protecting children from sexual exploitation was valuable, the law would only have limited effect. For example, it would not reach any communications from outside the United States. The burden, however, would be great, as it would chill communications nationwide or even worldwide. Finally, the court found that this law subjected Internet communication to inconsistent regulations, since each state could develop its own laws. The court noted that the Internet, as an important tool for commerce, has an even greater need for consistency than other channels of commerce. The court did not consider the First Amendment claim because the Commerce Clause claim supported the injunction.

Mainstream Loudoun v. Board of Trustees of the Loudoun County Library, 24 F. Supp. 2d 552 (E.D. Va. 1998).

A library board of trustees passed a policy restricting Internet access at public libraries in a Virginia county. Under this policy, libraries were required to install software to block child pornography, obscene websites, and other material deemed harmful to juveniles. The court held that the policy was subject to strict scrutiny because it was a content-based regulation of speech and the libraries were limited public forums. The court found that the asserted state interest in minimizing access to illegal pornography and avoiding the creation of a sexually hostile environment was compelling. However, the court found insufficient evidence to demonstrate that such a policy was necessary and determined that other less restrictive means were available to serve the compelling interest without infringing the rights of adult patrons. The court also held that the policy was a prior restraint on speech in violation of the First Amendment because it blocked material without a prior judicial decision on whether the material was constitutionally protected and because it did not include adequate procedural safeguards. The Loudoun County Library Board decided not to appeal the court's decision. *See* Mainstream Loudoun litigation archive website, *available at* http://loudoun.net/mainstream/Library/Internet.htm.

This case is discussed further in Chapter 5, at page 145.

ACLU v. Johnson, 194 F.3d 1149 (10th Cir. 1999).

In 1998, New Mexico enacted a statute that prohibited dissemination by computer of material harmful to minors. A person would be guilty of a misdemeanor if he or she "knowingly and intentionally" initiated or engaged in computer communication with a minor when the communication depicted nudity or any sexual conduct. N.M. Stat. 30-37-3.2(a). The statute also provided for defenses where the speaker took certain steps to restrict access to indecent material. The ACLU and other organizations filed suit to prevent enforcement of the statute. The district court granted a preliminary injunction. The Court of Appeals for the Tenth Circuit affirmed, relying heavily on the Supreme Court's reasoning in *ACLU v. Reno*, 521 U.S. 844, discussed above at page 4. The court found that the statute was an unconstitutional burden on adult speech. That the statute prohibited only knowing and intentional conduct did not effectively limit the burden because the definition of "knowing" only required general knowledge, reason to know, or belief that necessitated inquiry into the age of the minor. Therefore, given the lack of any age verification mechanism on the Internet and the size of the audience, almost all communication would be subject to the statute. The court observed that the Internet should be subject to national regulation, rather than inconsistent state laws.

Cyberspace Communications, Inc. v. Engler, 55 F. Supp. 2d 737 (E.D. Mich. 1999), *aff'd and remanded*, 238 F.3d 420 (6th Cir. 2000); *aff'd on remand*, 142 F. Supp. 2d 827 (E.D. Mich. 2001).

In 1999, the Michigan legislature amended a statute that prohibited the distribution of obscene materials to children to add Internet communications to the prohibition, and to change the language of the statute so that it prohibited dissemination of sexually explicit, rather than obscene, materials. Mich. Comp. Laws § 722.675 (1999).

The trial court entered a preliminary injunction on First Amendment and Commerce Clause grounds. Although the Supreme Court had held in *Ginsberg v. New York*, 390 U.S. 629 (1968), that states could prohibit the dissemination of sexually explicit materials to minors, even where the materials would not be obscene as to an adult, the court found that this analysis did not apply based on the unique nature of the Internet. Because a speaker on the Internet cannot reliably know to whom he or she is speaking (or whether the recipient is a minor), such a prohibition would require that all speakers use language suitable for children. In analyzing the content-based restriction, the court acknowledged that the state's interest in protecting children was compelling, but found that the statute was not necessary to further that interest and, in fact, could stifle important discussion about issues such as public health. The court also found that the statute was not narrowly tailored, and identified other measures that would accomplish the same goal, such as blocking software and parental supervision.

The court also found a likelihood of success as to the Commerce Clause claim. Because the Internet does not recognize geographical boundaries, the impact of the statute could not realistically be limited to Michigan and the burdens on interstate commerce (chilled speech and inconsistent regulation) would exceed any local benefits from the statute.

The Court of Appeals for the Sixth Circuit affirmed the preliminary injunction, but remanded the case for further proceedings before the trial court after deciding that the district court's final conclusions were premature. *Cyberspace Communications, Inc. v. Engler*, 238 F.3d 420 (6th Cir. 2000). On remand, the court found the statute violated both the First Amendment and the Commerce Clause for the same reasons as articulated in its decision to grant the injunction. *Cyberspace Communications, Inc. v. Engler*, 142 F. Supp. 2d 827 (E.D. Mich. 2001). Michigan's attorney general elected not to appeal the court's decision.

People v. Wheelock, No. 990875-7 (Cal. Super. Ct. Jan. 3, 2000).

The Contra Costa County California Superior Court found unconstitutional a California statute that made it illegal to transmit sexual material over the Internet knowing that the recipient is a minor (California Penal Code § 288.2(b)). The court held that the statute was overbroad in violation of the First and Fourteenth Amendments and the Commerce Clause. The supreme court of California declined to review this decision. *People v. Wheelock*, Case No. 01-10-2001, 2001 Cal. LEXIS 62 (Cal. Jan 10, 2001).

People v. Foley, 709 N.Y.S.2d 467 (N.Y. 2000), cert. denied, 531 U.S. 875 (2000).

The defendant was convicted under a New York statute that barred the invitation or inducement of a minor to engage in sexual activity through the knowing transmission of indecent materials (defined as materials that are harmful to a minor) to a minor by computer (New York Penal Code § 235.22). The defendant asserted that the statute was unconstitutionally overbroad and vague, and a content-based restriction inconsistent with the First Amendment.

The court held that the statute did not violate the First Amendment because it was precisely drawn to serve a compelling state interest, and was neither overbroad nor vague; the statute would not chill adult speech because it requires intent to lure a minor to engage in sexual conduct for the sender's benefit. Additionally, the court noted that, unlike the CDA, the New York statute clearly defined the "harmful to minors" standard.

The court also held that the statute did not violate the Commerce Clause because the effects on commerce would be small compared to the benefit of protecting children. The statute was not designed to regulate commerce and was narrow enough (due to the requirement that the person invite or induce a minor to engage in sexual activity) to limit any potential burden on commerce.

People v. Hsu, 99 Cal. Rptr. 2d 184 (Cal. Ct. App. 2000).

In August 2000, a California court of appeal upheld a conviction under the same statute found unconstitutional by a trial court in *People v. Wheelock*, discussed above (§ 2882.2(b) of the California Penal Code). The statute makes it illegal to transmit sexual material over the Internet knowing that the recipient is a minor, with intent to appeal to the sexual desires of the minor and with intent to seduce the minor.

The court found that the statute targeted speech based on its content and was therefore subject to strict judicial scrutiny. But the court concluded that the statute was narrowly tailored and represented the least restrictive means available to achieve the state's compelling interest. To violate the statute, the sender must have knowledge that the recipient is a minor, must know that he or she is sending harmful material, must intend to excite the sexual desires of the minor, and must intend to seduce the minor. The double-intent requirement, the court reasoned, distinguishes the California statute from the CDA and the similar Michigan statute struck down in *Cyberspace Communications, Inc. v. Engler.*

The court also stated that the statute did not suffer from the overbreadth problems associated with COPA, noting that the definition of "harmful matter" includes a reference to contemporary statewide community standards (as discussed in *Miller v. California*, 413 U.S. 15 (1973)). The statute's built-in affirmative defenses also narrow its scope.

In response to the defendant's Commerce Clause challenge, the court simply stated that the proscription against use of the Internet for the statute's specifically defined purposes (knowing and intentional arousal and seduction of minors) does not burden interstate commerce. The court reasoned that the knowledge and intent requirements distinguished this statute from the New York statute struck down in *American Library Association v. Pataki*. Additionally, the court noted that when harmonized with the rest of the California Penal Code, the statute does not have the effect of regulating activity outside of the state; California only prosecutes criminal acts occurring within the state. The California state supreme court declined to review the decision. *People v. Hsu*, No. S091535, 2000 Cal. LEXIS 9303 (Cal. Nov. 29, 2000).

PSINet, Inc. v. Chapman, 167 F. Supp. 2d 878 (W.D. Va. 2001), *questions certified to Supreme Court of Virginia*, 317 F.3d 413 (4th Cir. 2003).

Virginia enacted a law prohibiting the knowing display, for commercial purposes, of images harmful to minors in a place where children may be able to access the material. In 1999, the statute was amended to include electronic media. Va. Code Ann. § 18.2-391 (1999). In addition to requiring newsstands, for example, to obscure the covers of pornographic magazines displayed on their shelves, the statute specifically applied to electronic files and messages.

In *PSINet*, the court permanently prohibited the defendants from enforcing the statute to the extent it barred the "sale, rental, loan, or display of an 'electronic file or message containing an image' or an 'electronic file or message containing words' that is harmful to minors." The court agreed that the Virginia statute sought to achieve a compelling state interest (*i.e.*, protecting the Commonwealth's minors from exposure to indecent and harmful materials); however, the statute failed because of its overly broad scope. The statute, as it applied to electronic files and messages, was likely to result in an undue burden on commercial websites, as well as on the rights of adults seeking to access electronic materials that fall within the reach of the statute. Citing the indefinite language of the statute and the lack of defenses available to potential violators (*e.g.*, legitimate steps taken to screen consumers, such as requiring credit cards or personal identification numbers for access to electronic files), the court indicated that compliance with the statute would be overly difficult and that the statute imposed significant burdens on electronic bulletin boards, newsgroups, and websites that feature material that is not harmful to minors. Finally, the court commented that even if the statute were upheld, it would not be effective in protecting minors because current technology cannot prevent content originating abroad from being accessed in the U.S. Therefore, because the statute could not effectively support the compelling state interest, the court found its burden on protected speech to be unconstitutional.

Virginia appealed. On Jan 28, 2003, the United States Court of Appeals for the Fourth Circuit concluded that before it could address the constitutionality of the statute, certain questions concerning the scope and requirements of the statute should be decided in Virginia's state court system. Accordingly, the Fourth Circuit "certified" these questions to the Virginia Supreme Court. The Virginia Supreme Court declined to answer the certified questions because it concluded that disposition of the case would not turn on how they answered the questions. Accordingly, answering would be tantamount to issuing an improper advisory opinion. As of December 31, 2003, the case was again pending before the Fourth Circuit. For a history and timeline of the case, see the Media Coalition's case update website, *available at* http://mediacoalition.org/legal/psinet/.

American Booksellers Foundation for Freedom of Expression v. Dean, 342 F.3d 96 (2nd Cir. Aug. 27, 2002).

American Booksellers Foundation (along with the ACLU and other plaintiffs) challenged a Vermont statute that criminalized the distribution to minors of any image or written material in an electronic format that is sexually explicit and found to be "harmful to minors." The trial court invalidated the statute because it restricted constitutionally protected adult speech in an effort to protect minors. The court also took issue with the fact that the definition of a violation "forces every speaker on the Internet in every state or community in the United States to abide by Vermont's standards, even if the online speech would not be found 'harmful to minors' in any other location." The statute also lacked practical safe harbors or exceptions for web publishers.

The United States Court of Appeals for the Second Circuit affirmed the trial court's finding that the statute violated the First Amendment and the Dormant Commerce Clause. The court found that, like the statute at issue in *ACLU v. Reno* (discussed at page 4, above), the Vermont statute restricted too much speech in its effort to protect children from harmful materials. The court also found that the statute was a per se violation of the Dormant Commerce Clause, as it would apply to virtually any offending conduct originating anywhere on the planet.

Bookfriends, Inc. et al. v. Taft, 223 F.Supp.2d 932 (S.D. Ohio 2002).

Bookstores, publishers, and video software dealers have had some success challenging Ohio's revised "harmful-to-juveniles" law, which expanded the definition of harmful material to include material displayed electronically, including via the Internet. On August 2, 2002, the U.S. District Court issued a temporary restraining order to block enforcement of the statute, stating that the law was too broad and appeared to violate First Amendment rights of free speech. In December 2002, the Ohio state legislature amended the statute to clarify the definition of "harmful to juveniles" but left unchanged the provisions applicable to the Internet. In June 2003, the Sixth Circuit sent the case back to the trial court to consider the constitutionality of the law in light of the legislature's changes. As of December 31, 2003, the trial court had not yet issued a decision. *See* Media Coalition website, http://mediacoalition.org/legal/bookfriends (cataloging progress of the lawsuit).

Southeast Booksellers Association v. Condon, No. 02-CV-3747 (D.S.C., filed Nov. 6, 2002); *motion to dismiss denied*, 282 F. Supp. 2d 389 (D.S.C. July 25, 2003).

In 2001, the South Carolina legislature amended S.C. Code Ann. § 16-15-375 to criminalize the distribution to minors of digital electronic files that are "harmful to minors." A coalition of organizations representing artists, writers, booksellers and publishers sued, seeking a permanent injunction against enforcement of the statute. The plaintiffs assert that the amendment unconstitutionally restricts free speech because it has the effect of prohibiting adults from viewing and transmitting a wide range of constitutionally protected images. In addition, the plaintiffs claim that the law violates the Commerce Clause by regulating speech outside the borders of South Carolina. The state moved to dismiss the case on the grounds that the suit lacked merit and that plaintiffs lacked standing to sue. The trial court denied both motions in July 2003. As of December 31, 2003, the case was still pending before the trial court.

New Jersey v. May, 362 N.J. Super. 572 (N.J. Super. Ct. App. Div., Aug. 18, 2003).

A New Jersey state appeals court upheld that state's anti-child pornography statute, finding that the law did not contain the same unconstitutional provisions struck down by the Supreme Court in *Ashcroft v. Free Speech Coalition*. New Jersey's statute only criminalizes real images (as opposed to computer-generated images) of child pornography. The court also interpreted the statute to require the state to prove that the images are real rather than computer generated.

Sheehan v. Gregoire, 272 F. Supp. 2d 1135 (W.D. Wash. May 22, 2003).

The plaintiff, William Sheehan, operated a watchdog website devoted to fostering accountability of police departments, particularly in cases involving allegations of misconduct on the part of police officers. The state of Washington passed a law that prohibited publishing the names, addresses and telephone numbers of police officers and other law enforcement agents "with the intent to harm or intimidate" such officers. To help facilitate legal actions brought by citizens complaining of police abuse, Sheehan's website archived lawfully obtained, publicly available names, addresses, phone numbers and Social Security numbers of police officers. Sheehan sought to have the law invalidated as an abridgment of his right to free speech. The court struck down the law, stating that the law improperly restricted the publication of lawful, publicly available information, and rejected the state's argument that the statute only applied to "true threats" to·the lives and safety of law enforcement officials. The court disagreed with the state's contention that publication of names and contact information was equivalent to expressing an intent to do violence to law enforcement officers, noting that the free speech of law-abiding citizens cannot be squelched to deter the actions of third-party lawbreakers.

Center for Democracy and Technology v. Fisher, No. 03-5051 (E.D. Penn., Sept. 9, 2003).

In February 2002, the Pennsylvania legislature enacted Pa. Cons. Stat. § 7662, a law imposing criminal liability on Internet service providers for providing access to child pornography on the Internet. Under this law, an Internet service provider may be prosecuted for failing to remove or disable child pornography that resides on, or can be accessed through, its servers. To avoid criminal liability, an Internet service provider (ISP) must block access to a website that contains child pornography within five days of receiving notice of the offending material from the Pennsylvania attorney general. The nonprofit group the Center for Democracy and Technology (CDT) and the ACLU filed suit in federal court both challenging the law and petitioning to enjoin Pennsylvania from sending any more takedown notices to ISPs. The court granted a preliminary injunction in favor of the plaintiffs pending discovery in the case. CDT has created a web page to explain its side of the case and archive the pleadings and motions, *available at* http://www.cdt.org/speech/pennwebblock/. Both sides filed briefs in December 2003. A hearing is scheduled for January 2004.

Liability of Public Libraries for Providing Unrestricted Internet Access

In addition to various attempts by Congress and various states to regulate online speech deemed harmful to children, at least one lawsuit has attempted (unsuccessfully) to hold a public library accountable for providing children access to unsuitable online speech.

Kathleen R. v. City of Livermore, 87 Cal. App. 4th 684 (Cal. Ct. App. 2001).

Several individuals and organizations, led by a mother of a 12-year-old boy who was able to download pornography at a library in Livermore, California, brought a suit that included causes of action for waste of public funds, nuisance, premises liability, and denial of due process. A California court of appeal held that libraries cannot be sued for damages for providing unfettered access to the Internet, even if it means that children might be able to view pornography on library computers. The court specifically found that as long as the library is simply providing computer access and is not assisting children in viewing particular material, it cannot be held liable for failing to police the content available over the Internet.

The court of appeal affirmed the trial court's dismissal of the suit and held that the state government has no "constitutional duty" to protect minors from harmful materials available over the Internet. The library's alleged awareness that minors were being exposed at library computers to obscenity and harmful matter from the Internet was insufficient to establish liability.

Unwelcome Exposure to Pornography

Another suit, brought on behalf of library employees, claims that library patrons accessing pornography on the Internet create a hostile work environment.

Adamson v. Minneapolis Public Library, No. 03-CV-2521 (D. Minn., filed Mar. 24, 2003).

In March 2003, a group of Minneapolis library employees filed suit claiming that the Minneapolis Public Library's policy of prohibiting restrictions on Internet access created a hostile work environment. The librarians alleged that ever since the library began providing patrons with free Internet access in 1997, pornographic images on computer screens have bombarded library patrons and employees. Certain patrons allegedly started accessing pornographic sites on an increasingly regular basis and interacted with library patrons and staff in a threatening manner. The librarians claimed that the lack of restrictions caused an "intimidating" and "hostile" work environment under the Minnesota Human Rights Act, Minn. Stat. § 363.03 *et seq.* and Title VII of the Equal Employment Opportunity Act, 42 U.S.C. § 2001 *et seq.* In August 2003, the library announced that it had settled the case, paying the library employees $435,000 in damages and agreeing to maintain its internal security force, enhance penalties for violations of the library's Internet use policy, undertake an examination of filtering technology, and manage the location of computer terminals designated for children's use. *See* Statement of Minneapolis Library Board of Trustees, Settlement of *Adamson, et al. v. Minneapolis Public Library*, Aug. 15, 2003, *available at* http://www.mplib.org/settlement_030815.asp; Gary Young, "No Smut at Work, Please", NATIONAL LAW JOURNAL, Sept. 15, 2003, *available at* http://www.law.com/jsp/nlj/PubArticleNLJ.jsp?id=1063212018621.

Discovery of the Identities of Anonymous Internet Users

Online message boards have provided a forum for Internet users to speak out on issues, companies, and individuals, often cloaked in apparent anonymity. The targets of disparaging comments have sometimes responded by filing lawsuits against various unidentified "John Doe" defendants claiming, among other things, libel, breach of confidentiality agreement, or violation of securities laws. In these lawsuits, subpoenas are issued to the message board hosts in an effort to obtain identifying information about the authors. The courts have varied in their treatment of these subpoenas. *See generally* J. Hart & M. Rothberg, "Anonymous Internet Postings Pit Free Speech Against Accountability," WSJ.com (March 6, 2002), *available at* http://online.wsj.com/public/resources/documents/SB1015261972510360720.htm.

Columbia Insurance Co. v. Seescandy.com, 185 F.R.D. 573 (N.D. Cal. 1999).

The plaintiff attempted to sue anonymous defendants for registering the plaintiff's trademark as the defendants' domain name. The court would not issue a temporary restraining order against the defendants until the complaint was properly served on them. Balancing the public interest in providing injured parties with a forum to seek redress for grievances against the legitimate and valuable right to participate in online forums anonymously, the court formulated a four-part test for deciding when to permit discovery to uncover the identity of an anonymous defendant before a complaint has been served. The plaintiff (1) must identify the missing defendant with sufficient specificity to allow the court to determine that the defendant is a real person or entity that could be sued in federal court; (2) must identify all previous steps taken to locate the elusive defendant; (3) must establish to the court's satisfaction that the plaintiff's suit against the defendant has sufficient merit to withstand a motion to dismiss; and (4) must file a request for discovery with the court, along with a statement of reasons justifying the specific discovery requested, and must identify a limited number of persons or entities from which the plaintiff could take discovery that might lead to identifying information making service of process on the defendant possible. *Columbia Insurance Co.*, 185 F.R.D. at 578-580.

In re Subpoena Duces Tecum to America Online, Inc., 52 Va. Cir. 26 (Va. Cir. Ct. 2000).

An anonymous plaintiff company filed suit in Indiana alleging that five John Doe defendants published in Internet chat rooms defamatory material, misrepresentations, and confidential inside information concerning the plaintiff. Four of the defendants were AOL subscribers and, upon a motion by the plaintiff, the Virginia trial court was asked by the Indiana trial court to issue a subpoena ordering AOL to produce documentation from which the identities of the four AOL subscriber defendants could be ascertained. AOL moved to quash the subpoena.

The plaintiff argued that AOL lacked standing to quash the subpoena and that the John Does were the proper persons to seek such relief. The court held that AOL had standing because (1) if AOL does not keep confidential the identities of its subscribers, subscribers would look to AOL's competitors for anonymity, and thus the subpoena would have an oppressive effect on AOL; (2) the John Does may not have actual notice of the proceedings; and (3) forcing the John Does to respond would nullify the anonymity that the motion to quash was seeking to protect.

The trial court held that it will "only order a nonparty Internet Service Provider to provide information concerning the identity of a subscriber (1) when the court is satisfied by the pleadings or evidence supplied to that court that the party requesting the subpoena has a legitimate, good faith basis to contend that it may be the victim of conduct actionable in the jurisdiction where suit was filed; and (2) the subpoenaed identity information is centrally needed to advance that claim." *Id.* at 37. The court denied AOL's motion to quash the subpoena.

The Virginia Supreme Court overturned the trial court's order, stating that the anonymous plaintiff company had to reveal its identity if it wished to proceed further with the case, including to subpoena AOL documents. For more discussion on this case, *see AOL Inc. v. Anonymous Publicly Traded Co.*, 542 S.E.2d 377 (Va. 2001), discussed in Chapter 5, at page 151.

Doe a/k/a Aquacool_2000 v. Yahoo!, Inc., Case No. CV 00-04993 WMB (RZx) (C.D. Cal. filed May 11, 2000).

On May 11, 2000, a complaint was filed in the U.S. District Court for the Central District of California alleging that Yahoo Inc. violated the right to privacy guaranteed by the California constitution and its contract with its message-board users by turning over to a company bringing a defamation action identifying information about a user posting messages critical of the company. This case was settled on June 1, 2001, pursuant to a confidentiality agreement.

Irwin Toy Ltd. v. Doe, 99 A.C.W.S. (3d) 399, 2000 CarswellOnt 3164 (Ont. Super. Ct. Sept. 8, 2000).

The plaintiffs, a corporation and its president, applied to the court for an order forcing an ISP to provide the identity of a subscriber who sent emails containing allegedly defamatory material. The Ontario Superior Court of Justice ordered the ISP to reveal the information, holding that when a plaintiff has established a *prima facie* case against the anonymous defendant, as was the case here, the ISP must release the identity of the maker of the allegedly defamatory statements.

Doe v. 2TheMart.com, 140 F. Supp. 2d 1088 (W.D. Wash. 2001).

An anonymous plaintiff moved to quash 2TheMart.com's subpoena requesting disclosure of the identity of 23 anonymous speakers who participated on Internet message boards. The court granted the plaintiff's motion and established a four-part test for evaluating a civil subpoena that seeks the identity of an anonymous Internet user who is not a party to the underlying litigation. The court said it would consider (1) whether the subpoena seeking the information was issued in good faith and not for any improper purpose; (2) whether the information sought relates to a core claim or defense; (3) whether the identifying information is directly and materially relevant to that claim or defense; and (4) whether the information sought to establish or to disprove the claim or defense is unavailable from any other source. The court held that 2TheMart.com had not demonstrated that the identity of the anonymous Internet message posters was directly and materially relevant to the core defense in its underlying securities litigation.

Dendrite International Inc. v. Doe, 775 A.2d 756 (N.J. Super. Ct. App. Div. 2001).

The plaintiff, Dendrite, a publicly traded New Jersey corporation, filed suit against numerous anonymous individuals alleging that postings made by one of the defendants, John Doe No. 3, on a Yahoo message board were libelous. Yahoo maintains a message board for every publicly traded company, including Dendrite, on which Internet users post comments related to the company's stock performance. These messages are usually posted anonymously, but Yahoo requires all users to provide identifying information before using its message boards. Yahoo guarantees in its privacy policy that such user information will remain confidential unless Yahoo believes that disclosure "is necessary to identify, contact or bring legal action against someone who may be violating Yahoo's Terms of Service or may be causing injury to . . . anyone . . . that could be harmed by such activities." *Dendrite* at 762. Dendrite sought discovery of the identities of all the defendants, including John Doe No. 3, whose postings included accusations that Dendrite inflated earnings by changing the way it recognized revenue and that the president wanted to sell the company but was finding no takers.

The trial court granted Dendrite's motion to conduct limited discovery to ascertain the identities of John Doe defendants Nos. 1 and 2, but denied the motion as to John Doe defendants Nos. 3 and 4. Dendrite appealed only as to John Doe No. 3, and the appellate court affirmed the trial court's decision denying discovery of John Doe No. 3's identity. The court outlined four requirements that it stated must be met before a plaintiff can compel discovery of the identity of an anonymous Internet poster: (1) the plaintiff must attempt to notify the anonymous poster, by posting a notice in the forum where the offending comment was made, that a disclosure of his or her identity is being sought; (2) the plaintiff must identify the specific statements that are allegedly actionable; (3) the plaintiff must proffer evidence supporting each element it would have to establish to prove its claim; and (4) the court must balance the anonymous poster's First Amendment right of anonymous free speech against the strength of the plaintiff's case and the necessity of the disclosure to allow plaintiff to proceed. *See id.* at 767-768.

In affirming the trial court's denial of discovery of the identity of John Doe 3, the appellate court, while acknowledging that Dendrite had stated a defamation claim sufficient to survive under a traditional motion-to-dismiss standard, focused on the third requirement, above. It stated that a higher level of scrutiny is required when a case involves the right to anonymous speech. The court reasoned that this more exacting test can be satisfied by showing a nexus between the anonymous speaker's comments and the harm alleged by the plaintiff. However, the court found that Dendrite had failed to establish that it was harmed by John Doe No. 3's statements because the company's stock value had not decreased in value in the wake of the allegedly injurious statements.

Immunomedics, Inc. v. Doe, 775 A.2d 773 (N.J. Super. Ct. App. Div. 2001).

A publicly held New Jersey corporation brought a breach of contract action against an anonymous Internet poster who had posted information that the company alleged was confidential and proprietary. The court reiterated the four-part test it set forth in *Dendrite* and held that disclosure of the defendant's identity was warranted because there was evidence that defendant was an employee or former employee bound by the company's confidentiality agreement, and the content of the Internet postings provided evidence of breach of that agreement. The court distinguished this case from *Dendrite*, a libel action where the plaintiff failed to demonstrate that it suffered damages, because Immunomedics established a *prima facie* cause of action for breach of the confidentiality agreement.

America Online, Inc. v. Nam Tai Electronics, Inc., 571 S.E.2d 128 (Va. 2002).

Nam Tai Electronics filed a libel and unfair business practice suit in California against 51 anonymous bulletin-board posters who criticized the company and its directors on a Yahoo message board. One of the anonymous posters accessed the Internet through AOL. Nam Tai subpoenaed Virginia-based AOL to identify the anonymous poster. AOL moved to quash the subpoena, citing the poster's First Amendment right to speak anonymously; the California court denied AOL's motion. AOL then asked a Virginia court to quash the subpoena, again arguing the poster's right to speak anonymously. Nam Tai argued that the Virginia court should not revisit issues that had already been decided by the California court. The Virginia trial court agreed with Nam Tai, and the Supreme Court of Virginia affirmed: principles of "comity" prevented the Virginia court from quashing a subpoena already reviewed by the California court under substantially the same standard Virginia would have applied.

Melvin v. Doe, 2003 WL 22724628 (Pa. 2003).

The creators of a website posted messages on the site claiming that plaintiff Melvin, a superior court judge, had lobbied then-governor Tom Ridge to appoint a friend to a vacant county judgeship. Pennsylvania law prohibits judges from engaging in such political activities. Melvin denied the allegations and sued her critics for libel in 1999. The ACLU challenged a trial court order requiring AOL to disclose the identities of 13 "John Doe" defendants who had posted anonymous messages criticizing the plaintiff on a message board. The case has not progressed beyond addressing whether Melvin has a right to know the identities of the authors of the critical postings. The Supreme Court of Pennsylvania most recently sent the case back to the trial court for disposition of the ACLU's constitutional argument—that is, whether the public figure plaintiff in a defamation case should be required to establish actual economic harm prior to obtaining discovery of an anonymous defendant's identity.

California Assemblyman S. Joseph Simitian proposed the Internet Communications Protection Act, A.G. 1143, to address concerns arising out of the use of the discovery process to identify otherwise anonymous Internet users. This bill would require ISPs to provide notice to a subscriber when the ISP is served with a subpoena ordering it to reveal the subscriber's identity. Such notice would provide the subscriber an opportunity to move to quash the subpoena before the ISP reveals his identity. Yahoo and the Recording Industry of America Association (RIAA) oppose the bill, citing the administrative burden it could place on ISPs. As of December 31, 2003, the bill was pending in the California legislature.

Penalties for Posting Personal Information of Others

In addition to the cases described above addressing anonymous speech on the Internet, recent cases have considered whether posting material that discloses *others'* personal information without their consent is protected by the First Amendment.

Mitchell v. Trummel, No. 01-2-04698-5 (Wash. Ct. App. 2001), *petition for review granted*, 147 Wn. 2d 1002 (Wash. 2002).

Paul Trummel, a resident of Council House, a federally subsidized retirement home in Seattle, spent 3½ months in jail for refusing to comply with an anti-harassment order prohibiting him from contacting, or listing on his website, the addresses and phone numbers of any past, present, or future residents or managers at Council House. Trummel accused staff and residents of bigotry, violations of housing laws, and conspiring to keep him awake at night. Trummel was released from jail only after agreeing to remove the information from his website. Trummel appealed the trial court's order and punishment; the Washington Court of Appeals heard oral argument on the appeal in November 2003. As of December 31, 2003, the appeals court had not yet issued a decision.

Planned Parenthood of the Columbia/Willamette, Inc., et al. v. American Coalition of Life Activists, et al., 290 F.3d 1058, (9th Cir. en banc, May 16, 2002); *reh'g denied*, 2002 U.S. App. LEXIS 13829 (9th Cir. July 10, 2002); *cert. denied*, 123 S. Ct. 2637 (2003).

The defendant, American Coalition of Life Activists, created "wanted-style" posters containing the names and addresses of, and other personal information about, several abortion providers. (Doctors have been murdered in the past after being the subject of similar posters.) The distribution of the posters, both in paper form and electronically on an anti-abortion website called the Nuremberg Files, was found to meet the definition of a "threat of force" under the Freedom of Access to Clinics Entrances Act (FACE), 18 U.S.C. § 248. Despite the fact that the speech could be characterized as being political and taking place in a public forum, the court declared it unprotected by the First Amendment.

Johnson v. Tucker, No. CA-00-4867 (Fla. Cir. Ct., filed May 5, 2003).

On his personal website, Tucker Max posted pictures of his former girlfriends and descriptions of his relationships with them. In particular, Max described his relationship with Katy Johnson, a former Miss Vermont, who founded anti-alcohol abuse groups Say Nay Today and the Sobriety Society. Max's description portrayed Johnson as vapid, promiscuous, and fond of consuming alcoholic beverages. Johnson sued Max, and a Florida court ordered him to remove all information about Johnson from his website regardless of whether the information was true. In addition, the order forbade Max to post any future information about Johnson, including links to her website. A court order prohibiting future publication—often termed a "prior restraint"—is highly unusual. *See* NYTimes.com, "Internet Battle Raises Questions about the First Amendment" (June 5, 2003), *available at* http://www.nytimes.com/2003/06/02/national/02INTE.html. In July

2003, Ms. Johnson voluntarily dismissed her suit against Max, and the restraining order dissolved. Max continues to host pages about Johnson on his website.

Anti-Teacher Speech in Cyberspace

Harm resulting from allegedly defamatory speech on the Internet may be redressed through litigation. When the source of the online speech is a student and the target a school official or a member of the school community, the student may also be subject to discipline by the school.

Schools maintain some control over speech and displays on school property, but many schools attempt to assert disciplinary jurisdiction over Internet speech that originates and is accessed wholly off campus. Some courts have held that a school may discipline a student for off-campus activities where the activities substantially interfere with the educational process.

J.S. v. Bethlehem Area School District, 757 A.2d 412 (Pa. Commw. Ct. 2000), *aff'd*, 807 A.2d 847 (Pa. 2002).

A Pennsylvania middle school student created a website containing derogatory statements about, and pictures of, his teachers and school principal. On his "Teacher Sux" website, created at home on his personal computer, the student depicted his teacher's likeness morphing into an image of Adolph Hitler, called his teacher a "fat bitch," displayed a picture of her severed head dripping with blood, accused the school principal of having an extramarital affair, and solicited donations for hiring a hit man to kill his teacher. The teacher and principal pursued civil remedies against the student. The school permanently expelled him.

The student and his family filed suit against the school for violating his constitutional rights of free expression, privacy, and equal protection. The Pennsylvania court held in favor of the school, stating that the website hindered the educational process sufficiently to warrant a school disciplinary response. The court reasoned that the website's effect on the teacher's ability to continue educating, as well as its effect on the school community in general, constituted material interference with the educational process outside the scope of constitutional protection.

In affirming the trial court's decision, the Pennsylvania Supreme Court indicated that the website included "on-campus" speech because the site was accessed at school and was aimed at the specific audience of people affiliated with the school. The school was therefore permitted to discipline the student for his speech without infringing his First Amendment rights.

Emmett v. Kent School District No. 415, 92 F. Supp. 2d 1088 (W.D. Wash. 2000).

Nick Emmett, an 18-year-old high school student in Kent, Washington, created from his home the "Unofficial Kentlake High Home Page," a website; he did not use any school resources, time, or materials. The website included disclaimers indicating that the school was not affiliated with the site and that it was for entertainment purposes only. The site included satire about the school, its faculty, and students. One feature of Emmett's website drew particular attention from the school: mock obituaries of Emmett's fellow students. The website was accessible over the Internet for four days. Though no one reported feeling threatened or intimidated by the obituary parodies, the school expelled Emmett for, among other things, intimidation, harassment, and disruption to the educational process. Emmett's expulsion was reduced to a five-day suspension.

Emmett successfully secured an injunction to prevent the school from enforcing its suspension. The court found that Emmett was likely to succeed in showing that it is not within the school's purview to limit speech that is wholly outside school supervision and control, particularly where there is no evidence that the site intended to, or did, threaten anyone.

Emmett's case eventually settled out of court.

In re I.M.L., a minor v. State of Utah, 61 P.3d 1038 (Utah 2002).

On his home computer, a 16-year-old student at Utah's Milford High School created a website displaying disparaging comments about his school, his teachers, the principal, and other students, including a list of classmates with descriptions of their sexual histories. The website did not contain any violent content or threats of any kind. The student was charged with criminal libel. He moved to dismiss the charges, asserting that Utah's criminal libel statute was unconstitutional because it unfairly burdened his freedom of speech. The juvenile court denied the motion, but the Utah Supreme Court reversed the ruling, dismissed the case, and declared the statute unconstitutional because it would have permitted conviction without the constitutionally required showing that the defendant knew the statements he published were false or that he had published them with reckless disregard for whether they were true. The statute was also deemed unconstitutionally overbroad because it did not provide for truth as an absolute defense. In January 2003, the juvenile court dismissed all remaining charges at the request of the county attorney. The student was not sued civilly for defamation of those he featured on his website.

Muss v. Beaverton School District, No. CV-02-1706-AA (D. Or., filed Dec. 17, 2002).

On a website he created at home, middle school student Carlson Muss posted derogatory comments about Canadians, lesbians, albino florists, classmates, and teachers. In addition, Muss proposed a death sentence for eight of his classmates and others who did not show him proper respect. Despite the fact that a psychologist interviewed Muss and concluded that he posed no threat to school safety, Highland Park Middle School expelled Muss for violating district policies prohibiting disruptive conduct, harassment, and threats. A year later, the school district denied Muss' application for admission to the Arts & Sciences Magnet Academy. In December 2002, the ACLU filed suit on Muss' behalf in federal court, seeking $101,800 in damages for violation of Muss' right to free speech. The case was settled in September 2003, with Muss and his mother reportedly receiving $20,000 from the school district. *See* Kevin Harden, "Free-speech Law Suit Settlement Costs School District $20,000," BEAVERTON VALLEY TIMES (Sept. 11, 2003), *available at* http://www.beavertonvalleytimes.com/article/578.

The ACLU recently filed suit in federal court on behalf of two students from Atlanta's Brookwood High School who were suspended from school after they posted comments criticizing one of their teachers on a website maintained off-campus by a different student. According to the complaint, the comments that led to the suspensions were not violent in nature, nor did they endorse any disruptive action against the teacher or the school. The postings were made off-campus after school hours and without using any school equipment. The plaintiffs seek a ruling that the school policy is unconstitutional and are asking for a court order directing the school to remove the suspension from the disciplinary records of the two students. *See* Bill Rankin, "Suit Filed Over Brookwood Students' Suspensions," THE ATLANTA JOURNAL-CONSTITUTION (Oct. 28, 2003), *available at* http://www.ajc.com/metro/content/metro/gwinnett/1003/28suspensions.html.

Online Vote Trading

Porter v. Jones, 319 F.3d 483 (9th Cir. 2003).

In the fall of 2000, the California Secretary of State sent cease and desist letters to operators of websites that allowed voters in different states to "swap" votes, threatening criminal prosecution for violations of the state's election code. The operators of these websites filed suit against the Secretary of State for violations of their First Amendment rights to freedom of expression. By using the plaintiffs' websites to communicate with people across the country, voters could make informal voting arrangements with each other. The purpose of these arrangements was generally to generate a large number of Democratic votes in crucial swing states while enabling third-party candidates to get enough votes to become eligible for federal funding in future elections. The federal trial court abstained from deciding the freedom of speech issues, relying on the "Pullman Doctrine." The Pullman Doctrine allows a federal court to refrain from deciding a controversy that is otherwise properly before it if the case involves sensitive social issues that might be resolved in another forum, such as a state court, thus making it unnecessary for the federal court to decide the issues. The trial court dismissed the plaintiffs' claims for damages. On appeal, the U.S. Court of Appeals for the Ninth Circuit found that the trial court's refusal to rule on the First Amendment issue was an improper application of the Pullman Doctrine, and that federal courts are generally well-suited to resolve challenges to violations of the constitutional right of free expression. The appellate court stated that the trial court's failure to consider the issue could result in the chilling of free speech. Accordingly, the appellate court reversed and remanded the case to the trial court for a decision on the First Amendment issues. As of December 31, 2003, no further action had been taken at the trial court level.

Advertising for Internet Gambling

In June 2003, the U.S. Department of Justice (DOJ) sent a letter to the Newspaper Association of America and the National Association of Broadcasters, warning the associations and their members that the DOJ considers it unlawful to publish advertisements for Internet gambling, whether in print, over radio or television, or on the Internet. The letters stated that advertisements for gambling may violate various state and federal laws, and that entities and individuals accepting and running such advertisements may be aiding and abetting illegal activities. See, for example, Letter from John G. Malcolm, Deputy Assistant Attorney General, U.S. Department of Justice, to Newspaper Association of America (June 11, 2003). The letter pointed out that under federal criminal law, any person who aids or abets illegal Internet gambling activities is punishable as a principal. 18 U.S.C. § 2.

Internet Search Engines

 Search King Inc. v. Google Technology, Inc., 2003 WL 21464568 (W.D. Okla., May 27, 2003).

On May 27, 2003, a federal trial court in Oklahoma ruled that page rankings resulting from the use of an Internet search engine constitute protected speech. The plaintiff, Search King, claimed Google had injured it by maliciously and purposefully reducing Search King's search results ranking. Google ranks its search results according to an algorithm that takes into account a number of factors, including text-matching and the number of links to the ranked site from other websites that are themselves frequently linked to by others. Search King argued that Google's ranking process is objective in nature, but the court concluded that Google rankings are subjective and emphasized there is no way to prove that a search ranking is false. Because, in the court's view, a Google search-results ranking constitutes opinion, protected under the First Amendment, the court found that Search King's claims were without merit and dismissed the case.

U.S. First Amendment Protections in the International Context of the Internet

One of the most complex issues raised by online speech is that the Internet does not recognize geographic boundaries. This worldwide reach not only raises complicated jurisdictional questions (discussed in more detail in Chapter 9, pages 293 to 297) but also raises significant questions as to how other countries will deal with the unique speech protections provided under the First Amendment to the U.S. Constitution.

 Yahoo!, Inc. v. La Ligue Contre Le Racisme et L'Antisemitisme, 169 F. Supp. 2d 1181 (N.D. Cal. 2001).

In November 2000, a French court held Yahoo auctions in violation of a French law prohibiting exhibition for sale of Nazi propaganda and artifacts. The French court ordered Yahoo to eliminate French citizens' access to the prohibited material. Yahoo France barred the sale of Nazi memorabilia, but a French user could still access Yahoo.com, where such items were listed for sale. Yahoo contended that banning Nazi-related material from Yahoo.com would infringe impermissibly on its rights under the First Amendment. Accordingly, Yahoo asked a U.S. court for a declaratory judgment that the French court's order was not enforceable.

A federal court in California framed the issue as "whether it is consistent with the Constitution and laws of the United States for another nation to regulate speech by a United States resident within the United States on the basis that such speech can be accessed by Internet users in that nation." *Id.* at 1186. "Although France has the sovereign right to regulate what speech is permissible in France, this Court may not enforce a foreign order that violates the protections of the United States Constitution by chilling protected speech that occurs simultaneously within our borders." *Id.* at 1192. Summary judgment was granted for Yahoo, and defendants appealed the judgment. Although the Ninth Circuit heard oral argument on the appeal in November 2002, as of December 31, 2003, the case was still pending. Yahoo has since banned the sale of Nazi memorabilia on its auction sites.

In a separate action, French prosecutors filed criminal charges against Yahoo and its former CEO, Timothy Koogle, on the grounds that the auctions of Nazi memorabilia constitute acts condoning crimes against humanity, which is itself a crime in France. On February 11, 2003, a French criminal court ruled that neither Yahoo nor its former CEO is guilty of condoning or justifying war crimes or crimes against humanity. *Association L'Amicale des Deportes d'Auschwitz v. Societe Yahoo Inc., Tribunal Correctionnel de Paris*, case number unavailable, (Feb. 11, 2003). *See* Jon Henley, "Yahoo Cleared in Nazi Case," THE GUARDIAN (Feb. 12, 2003), *available at* http://www.guardian.co.uk/international/story/0,3604,893642,00.html.

Google, a widely used Internet search engine, has deleted more than 100 controversial sites from search result listings customized for the French and German markets. The deleted sites are generally anti-Semitic, pro-Nazi, or related to white supremacy. These sites still appear on search result listings displayed in response to searches conducted from the main Google.com website. For discussion of this case in the context of enforcement of foreign judgments, *see* Chapter 9, page 297. For a discussion of international forum shopping in libel cases, *see* Chapter 9, page 293.

In July 2003, the United States House of Representatives passed a bill that would allocate funds for the development of technological means for citizens of foreign countries to defeat their respective nations' Internet censorship schemes. The proposed "Global Internet Freedom Act" was incorporated into an appropriations bill, the Millennium Challenge Account, Peace Corps Expansion, and Foreign Relations Authorization Act of 2003 (H.R. 1950). The Act would create a new governmental department, called the "Office of Global Internet Freedom." The office would be charged with the task of aiding in the development of technology to prevent other nations from blocking or otherwise restricting Internet access. The bill's sponsors state that censorship is widespread in China, Cuba, Vietnam, Saudi Arabia and other nations. The bill would encourage the development of mechanisms to help ordinary citizens in those nations defeat firewalls and other protection measures used by their governments to block access to news and information from around the world. *See* Declan McCullagh, "Bill Aims to Curb Net Censorship," CNET News.com (July 17, 2003), *available at* http://news.com.com/2102-1029_3-1026690.html. The bill was received in the Senate for consideration on July 17, 2003. No further action on the proposed measure has been reported.

Chapter 1: Freedom of Speech
Summary of the Law

- The U.S. Supreme Court has held that speech on the Internet is subject to the highest level of First Amendment protection, the same level of protection afforded books, newspapers, and magazines. (The government has somewhat broader latitude to regulate broadcast speech.)

- All speech is protected by the First Amendment, except for speech that falls within several narrowly defined categories: child pornography; speech that advocates imminent lawless action; speech meeting the constitutional test for obscenity; and certain speech that is shown to be false, defamatory, and uttered, depending on the circumstances, with knowledge of its falsity, with reckless indifference to its truth or falsity, or negligently.

- The First Amendment prohibits governmental restrictions on speech. The First Amendment directly limits the power of the federal government to impose restrictions on speech. The First Amendment applies to state governments through the Fourteenth Amendment.

- The First Amendment does not prohibit private entities from prohibiting or regulating speech in places, or through media, they control.

- Restrictions that are based on the content of protected speech are generally pro-hibited. A restriction is considered content-based if it is aimed at the communicative impact of expression. A content-based regulation will be found constitutional only if the government can show that it is necessary to serve a compelling governmental purpose and that it is narrowly drawn to achieve that end.

- Restrictions that are content-neutral may be permissible. A restriction is deemed content neutral if it is aimed at something other then the communicative impact of expression, even if it has the effect of burdening some expression. A content-neutral restriction may be found constitutional if it serves an important or substantial governmental interest, is crafted as narrowly as possible to address that interest, and leaves alternative channels of communication open to those whose speech the law restricts.

- A law that bans a substantial amount of protected speech along with speech that may be regulated may be found unconstitutionally "overbroad." A law may be found unconstitutionally vague if the conduct forbidden is defined so unclearly that a reasonable person would have difficulty understanding the difference between legal and illegal conduct.

- Courts have recognized that the right to speak anonymously is a component of the First Amendment right to free speech. Accordingly, courts have been reluctant to require Internet service providers to identify users who have posted messages anonymously unless the party seeking to identify the anonymous speaker can make a case for why identification is warranted. Where the plaintiff sues a "John Doe," the court will ordinarily require the plaintiff to establish a good-faith basis for bringing the suit before it will compel an ISP to identify the anonymous-speaker defendant. Where the anonymous speaker is not a party to the case, the court is likely to require the party seeking the speaker's identity to demonstrate that identifying the speaker is essential if the party is to establish its claims or defenses.

- No other country protects speech as vigorously as the United States. Speech on the Internet that is protected under U.S. law may well be illegal or unprotected in other countries.

TRADEMARKS

Trademark Basics

Trademark law has played a significant role in the development of the Internet. Most Internet-related trademark disputes (whether between parties with competing trademark rights or between a trademark owner and a "cybersquatter") center on the desire of trademark owners to establish or maintain online brand recognition and associated brand loyalty through the use of domain names. Trademarks and domain names, however, are not one and the same. This chapter examines traditional trademark law as it has been applied to the Internet, as well as laws and policies designed specifically to protect trademark rights online. Chapter 3 addresses domain names, the application of trademark law to domain names, and other issues unique to domain name administration and oversight.

Definition of a Trademark

A trademark is a designation that is used to identify the source of goods and to distinguish that source from other sources. A service mark is a designation that is used to identify the source of services and to distinguish that source from other sources. A mark (whether a trademark or service mark) can consist of a word or words, a stylized rendition of a word or words, a number or numbers, a design, a color, a sound, or any combination of these elements. *See* 15 U.S.C. § 1127. The term "trademark" is frequently used to encompass both trademarks and service marks, and the law applicable to each is essentially the same. The principal U.S. law governing trademarks and the rights associated with trademark is the Lanham Act, 15 U.S.C. § 1051 *et seq.*

Rationale behind Trademark Protection

Protection of marks serves the interests of both trademark owners and consumers. Trademark owners do not want others to use marks that would be confusingly similar to their marks for two reasons. First, they do not want to lose to competitors sales they would otherwise make to consumers who mistakenly believe they are purchasing goods or services from the trademark owner. Second, trademark owners do not want consumers to mistakenly believe that inferior goods or services sold under a mark identical or similar to the trademark owner's mark are associated with the trademark owner's goods or services. When consumers make purchasing decisions, they want to be able to rely on marks as an indication of the source of a product or service.

Indication of Origin

Not all marks are protectable. To create trademark rights, a mark must identify the source of a product and distinguish it from other sources. If a mark does not serve as an indication of origin (for example, because the mark is merely descriptive of or generic for the goods or services), the law does not protect it.

Obtaining Trademark Rights

Common Law. Common-law rights in a trademark are established by a history of exclusive use in connection with a particular product. The protection extended to the owner of a common law mark is limited to the geographical area in which the mark is used. *See, e.g., Union National Bank v. Union National Bank*, 909 F.2d 839 (5th Cir. 1990).

Registered. A trademark owner can register a trademark with the U.S. Patent and Trademark Office. Federal registration of a mark provides the owner with benefits not extended to owners of common law marks, such as presumed validity and presumed exclusive nationwide rights in the mark. *See* 15 U.S.C. § 1057(b) (2001).

Famous. Under § 43(c) of the Lanham Act, and many parallel state statutes, the owner of a "famous" mark is entitled to protection from dilution. Whether a mark qualifies as "famous" depends on numerous factors, including degree of recognizability, extent and duration of use, advertising of the mark, and geographical scope of use. *See Lexington Management Corp. v. Lexington Capital Partners*, 10 F. Supp. 2d 271, 288 (S.D.N.Y. 1998).

Trademark Ownership Actions and Remedies

Infringement

Registered Marks. A registered trademark is infringed when a person uses "in commerce any reproduction, counterfeit, copy, or colorable imitation of a registered mark in connection with the sale . . . or advertising of any goods or services on or in connection with which such use is likely to cause confusion, or to cause mistake, or to deceive." Lanham Act § 32(1)(a), 15 U.S.C. § 1114(1)(a).

Common Law Marks. Section 43(a) of the Lanham Act prohibits the use of "any word, term, name, symbol, or device, or any combination thereof . . . which is likely to cause confusion, or to cause mistake, or to deceive as to the affiliation, connection, or association of such person with another person, or as to the origin, sponsorship, or approval of his or her goods, services, or commercial activities by another person." 15 U.S.C. § 1125. All states have parallel statutes or recognize similar claims under common law.

Prevailing Test. Once a plaintiff has demonstrated ownership of a mark, the ultimate test under a claim of trademark infringement is likelihood of consumer confusion (such as confusion as to sponsorship, origin, or endorsement).

Dilution

Dilution of a famous trademark is actionable under the Lanham Act, 15 U.S.C. § 1125(c), and many state laws as well. Under the federal statute, dilution is defined as the "lessening of the capacity of a famous mark to identify and distinguish goods or services, regardless of the presence or absence" of competition between the parties or likelihood of confusion. 15 U.S.C. § 1127. Dilution can occur as a result of "blurring" (when customers see the mark used to identify goods or services not produced by the trademark owner) or "tarnishment" (unauthorized trademark use that taints or degrades the owner's mark). *See Intermatic Inc. v. Toeppen*, 947 F. Supp. 1227 (N.D. Ill. 1996); *Hasbro, Inc. v Internet Entertainment Group, Ltd.*, 40 U.S.P.Q.2d (BNA) 1479, No. C96-

130WD, 1996 U.S. Dist. LEXIS 11626 (W.D. Wash. February 9, 1996); *Kraft Foods Holdings, Inc. v. Helm*, 2002 U.S. Dist. LEXIS 10258 (N.D. Ill. June 7, 2002) (finding that the defendant's use of "King VelVeeda" on website containing pornographic material diluted Kraft's famous "Velveeta" mark).

Difference between Dilution and Infringement

In contrast to the plaintiff in a trademark infringement action, the plaintiff in a dilution action does not need to prove likelihood of confusion to prevail. Instead, a dilution plaintiff must show that its mark is famous and that the defendant is engaged in a commercial use that will cause dilution of the trademark by blurring its distinctiveness or tarnishing or disparaging it. A trademark not famous to the general public may still qualify as "famous" where "both the plaintiff and defendant are operating in the same or related markets, so long as the plaintiff's mark possesses a high degree of fame in its niche market." *See Times Mirror Magazines, Inc. v. Las Vegas Sports News, L.L.C.*, 212 F.3d 157 (3d Cir. 2000) (holding that "The Sporting News" mark was entitled to protection from dilution because it was famous in the sports periodicals market).

Statutory Remedies

Trademark Infringement. The remedies a plaintiff may obtain for trademark infringement include injunctive relief, damages (including the defendant's profits, damages sustained by the plaintiff, and the costs of the action), and, in some cases, attorney fees. 15 U.S.C. §§ 1116, 1117. Injunctive relief is an important remedy in trademark infringement cases because the nature of the injury often makes it difficult to assess money damages. In relatively rare cases, the court may also order impoundment and destruction of the infringing goods. 15 U.S.C. § 1118.

Dilution. A plaintiff may obtain injunctive relief barring any conduct that "dilutes" a "famous" trademark. In exceptional cases in which willful intent is proved, the owner of a famous mark may also be entitled to the infringement remedies set forth above. 15 U.S.C. § 1125.

First Amendment Issues in Trademark Disputes

Use of Trademarks as Communicative Speech

Trademark owners have sometimes attempted to use trademark law to prevent the communication of unflattering messages about the trademark owner or its products. However, trademark law recognizes a "fair use" defense if the trademark is used only "to describe the goods or services of [a] party, or their geographic origin." 15 U.S.C. § 1115(b)(4). The First Amendment right to free speech is also a potential bar to such claims. In other words, a trademark owner cannot ordinarily use trademark law to prevent third parties from using the trademark owner's mark to identify the trademark owner's own goods or services. Rather, trademark law prevents third parties from using the trademark owner's mark, or a confusingly similar mark, to identify the third party's goods or services or falsely to imply an association between the trademark owner and the third party.

Bally Total Fitness Holding Corp. v. Faber, 29 F. Supp. 2d 1161 (C.D. Cal. 1998).

The prominent appearance of "Bally Sucks" on a website criticizing the chain of Bally health clubs was not found to constitute trademark infringement or dilution because the "Bally" trademark was being used for noncommercial expression and was therefore not being "used in commerce" as required for a dilution claim. Furthermore, this use of the "Bally" trademark for critical commentary was protected speech under the First Amendment, as it was crucial to identifying the services that were the subject of constitutionally protected speech.

Playboy Enterprises., Inc. v. Terri Welles, Inc., 7 F. Supp. 2d 1098 (S.D. Cal.), *aff'd*, 162 F.3d 1169 (9th Cir. 1998), *summary judgment granted by* 78 F. Supp. 2d 1066 (S.D. Cal. 1999), *aff'd*, 279 F.3d 796 (9th Cir. 2002).

Playboy sued former Playboy Playmate Terri Welles for her use of the terms "Playmate" and "Playboy" on her website and in metatags. (For discussion of use of trademarks in metatags generally, see pages 39 to 42.) In April 1998, a federal trial court held that Welles' use of the terms was a descriptive or nominative fair use of the marks to describe her career, which could not be accomplished without the use of Playboy's marks. Playboy's request for a preliminary injunction was denied.

In December 1999, the trial court granted summary judgment for Welles on all trademark, dilution, and unfair competition counts, finding that she made descriptive and fair uses of Playboy's marks and did not act in bad faith.

On February 1, 2002, the U.S. Court of Appeals for the Ninth Circuit ruled that use of the trademarks "Playboy," "Playmate," and "Playmate of the Year 1981," was permissible "nominative fair use" of the marks: "There is simply no descriptive substitute for the trademarks used in Welles' metatags. Precluding their use would have the unwanted effect of hindering the free flow of information on the internet, something which is certainly not a goal of the trademark law." The appeals court sent the case back to the trial court to decide whether the repeated use of the phrase "PMOY'81" as website wallpaper qualified as nominative fair use of a trademark, or was, instead, an infringing use of plaintiff's marks.

See also Bihari v. Gross, 119 F. Supp. 2d 309 (S.D.N.Y. 2000) (declining to issue an injunction prohibiting use of plaintiff's mark in metatags because (1) defendant did not use plaintiff's mark to trick users into visiting his websites, but rather as a means of cataloging thoses sites; and (2) defendant did not use plaintiff's mark as a trademark, but only in a descriptive sense permissible under the doctrine of "fair use").

J.K. Harris & Co., LLC v. Kassel, 253 F. Supp. 2d 1120 (N.D. Cal. 2003).

Plaintiff and defendant were competitors in the tax representation business, and each had a website. Plaintiff filed a complaint in federal court alleging that defendant had infringed plaintiff's trademark rights by using plaintiff's "J.K. Harris" trademark on defendant's website. Defendant argued that its use was a nominative fair use and did not amount to infringement. An unauthorized use of another's mark may be defensible as a "nominative fair use" when (1) the mark is the only word that can identify a particular product or service; (2) only so much of the mark is used as is necessary to identify the product or service; and (3) the mark is not used in a way that would suggest endorsement or sponsorship by the trademark owner.

Initially, the trial court granted plaintiff's request for a preliminary injunction against defendant's use of plaintiff's "J.K. Harris" trademark on, and in metatags for, defendant's website that contained information critical of plaintiff. The court found the second prong of the nominative fair use defense lacking because plaintiff used the mark 75 times, frequently in a prominent fashion, such as in a large or underlined font or at the top of various web pages. Upon further reflection and review of *amicus* briefs, the court vacated its earlier ruling, and found defendant's use satisfied the nominative fair use test. Defendant, the court determined, used the plaintiff's "J.K. Harris" mark only as much as was reasonably necessary to identify the mark holder's product or services. While frequent and prominent, the uses were not in the stylized form used by plaintiff. The court determined that defendant's "referential use" of plaintiff's mark was precisely the type of use the nominative fair use defense is intended to allow. Thus, the court denied a preliminary injunction limiting defendant's use of the "J.K. Harris" mark.

For a discussion of First Amendment issues arising out of domain name registrations incorporating others' trademarks, please see Chapter 3, pages 90 to 93.

Linking and Framing

Linking

Linking from one website to another website (or to particular pages within such a website) may raise intellectual property questions. A hyperlink alone is not generally understood to imply sponsorship or endorsement of the linking site by the linked-to site. However, it is possible to imagine circumstances where the use of a word or design mark associated with the linked site could create confusion regarding origin, affiliation, endorsement, or sponsorship in violation of the Lanham Act or state laws regulating unfair competition.

For discussion of linking in the context of copyright infringement, *see* Chapter 4, pages 102 to 104.

Linking Cases

 Ticketmaster Corp. v. Microsoft Corp., No. 97-3055 (C.D. Cal. filed Apr. 28, 1997).

Microsoft deep-linked from its "Seattle sidewalk" website, where events were described, to the pages on the Ticketmaster site on which tickets to those events could be purchased, bypassing the Ticketmaster home page and the various pages users would otherwise have to click through before reaching a page on which tickets could be purchased. Ticketmaster objected, claiming that the deep-linking infringed Ticketmaster's trademark, diluted the mark's value, and violated state and federal laws prohibiting unfair competition. This lawsuit was settled in February 1999 and resulted in no substantive rulings.

 Ticketmaster Corp. v. Tickets.Com, Inc., 2000 U.S. Dist. LEXIS 4553, 54 U.S.P.Q.2d (BNA) 1344 (C.D. Cal. March 27, 2000), *preliminary injunction denied*, 2000 U.S. Dist. LEXIS 12987 (C.D. Cal. Aug. 10, 2000).

Ticketmaster sued Tickets.com, alleging that it had provided false and misleading information and illegally linked to the Ticketmaster website. Among other claims, Ticketmaster complained that Tickets.com was "deep-linking" to its website, that is, linking not to the homepage of the Ticketmaster website, but to internal pages, several clicks into the site. On the defendant's motion, the court dismissed several of the plaintiff's claims. Although the court did not dismiss the copyright infringement, passing-off, reverse passing-off, or false advertising claims, the court concluded that "deep-linking by itself (*i.e.*, without confusion of source) does not necessarily involve unfair competition." On August 10, 2000, the court denied Ticketmaster's request for a preliminary injunction, taking into account, but not specifically relying on, the implementation by Ticketmaster of technology that prevented deep-linking to its interior pages.

For discussion of this case in the context of trespass, *see* Chapter 10, page 383.

 Voice-Tel Enterprises, Inc. v. Joba, Inc., 258 F. Supp. 2d 1353 (N.D. Ga. 2003).

The plaintiff, which sold voice messaging products and services, entered into a franchise agreement with the defendant. The defendant operated a website that promoted the plaintiff's company, which included several links to external websites. Unbeknownst to the defendant, one of the hyperlinks pointed to a domain name that had been taken over by a company that operated a pornography and gambling website. Plaintiff notified the defendant about this hyperlink and website, and the defendant removed the link from its website. The plaintiff then sued to terminate the franchise agreement because, it argued, the "offensive" link tarnished and diluted the plaintiff's trademark in breach of the agreement. The court granted the defendant's motion for summary judgment as to whether the agreement could be terminated based on material impairment of the mark. The court found that evidence of a hyperlink to a pornography website was not enough to presume harm to the mark. The court also granted the defendant's motion for summary judgment regarding the plaintiff's claim that the defendant diluted the plaintiff's mark. The court stated that extending a dilution claim to a use of a hyperlink would exceed the purpose of the Lanham Act's anti-dilution provision.

Hyperlink Patent Dispute

A federal court has ruled that British Telecommunications (BT) does not hold a patent on hyperlinking. The U.K. phone company claimed it had held the patent for linking online documents since 1989, but only discovered it owned the patent in 1996. The patent, which details a method for accessing documents by hyperlinking "from a central location," was discovered, BT said, during a routine check. In December 2000, BT filed a patent infringement complaint in the United States District Court for the Southern District of New York against Prodigy, a U.S. Internet service provider, asserting that Prodigy infringed BT's patent by using the hyperlinking method and by allowing its customers to use the hyperlinking method on the Internet. In March 2002, the court issued its decision defining the scope of the patents and ordered the parties to file motions for summary judgment based on its ruling on the scope of the patents. The court held that the patents described a system in which documents were retrieved from a central computer, a single device in one location. *British Telecommunications PLC v. Prodigy Communications Corp.*, 189 F. Supp. 2d 101 (S.D.N.Y. 2002).

In August 2002, the court granted Prodigy's motion for summary judgment, finding that no jury could reasonably find patent infringement because the Internet is a decentralized network, not a system centralized around a single device. Therefore, the court concluded, BT does not hold a patent on the process of hyperlinking via the Internet. *See* 217 F. Supp. 2d 399 (S.D.N.Y. 2002).

Better Business Bureau Controversy

The Better Business Bureau (BBB) has announced a linking policy that prohibits nonmembers (except government agencies, search engines, directory services, and news organizations) from linking to the BBB website. The BBB says it may grant websites the right to link to the BBB website if they demonstrate that the link will not reflect unfavorably on the BBB, that the company has a clean record with the BBB, that the public interest is served by allowing the link, and that the link is limited to the context of general resource information. The BBB's linking policy is available at http://www.bbb.org/about/terms.asp. As of December 31, 2003, the BBB has not attempted to take legal action against those who have failed to comply with its linking policy.

Framing

The practice of framing, in which one website displays the content of another site within its own pages, is discussed in the context of copyright in Chapter 4, pages 147 to 150. Framing, like linking, can potentially infringe a trademark where the use of the frame creates confusion as to origin, affiliation, endorsement, or sponsorship.

Washington Post Co., et al. v. Total News, Inc., et al., No. 97 Civ. 1190 (PKL) (S.D.N.Y., filed Feb. 20, 1997) *Stipulation & Order Of Settlement & Dismissal* (S.D.N.Y. June 5, 1997).

The Washington Post and other news organizations filed suit in February 1997 to stop the defendant online news services from framing their websites. The plaintiffs alleged that the defendants had designed a parasitic website: instead of creating its content, Total News and other similar online services simply "republished" the news and editorial content of other web publishers within a frame. Among other causes of action, the plaintiffs asserted federal trademark dilution, claiming that the defendants' actions diluted and detracted from the distinctiveness of the plaintiffs' famous trademarks. The case settled when the defendants agreed to remove their frames and the plaintiffs allowed access to their websites through simple hypertext links, without any framing.

Metatags and Hidden Code

To achieve favorable positioning in lists of search results displayed to users of search engines, many websites place key words in data fields invisible to users but routinely surveyed by the search engines.

Courts have grappled with the question of whether the inclusion of a competitor's trademark in such "metatags" violates federal trademark law.

Oppedahl & Larson v. Advanced Concepts, No. C-97-Z-1592 (D. Colo., filed July 23, 1997).

The plaintiff, a patent law firm, filed suit claiming that the five defendants' use of the plaintiff's marks as metatags infringed and diluted the value of those marks. The case settled with an agreement that precluded further use of the plaintiff's marks in the defendants' metatags.

See also Playboy Enterprises, Inc. v. Calvin Designer Label, 985 F. Supp. 1220 (N.D. Cal. 1997) (ordering the defendant to cease use of the trademarks "Playmate" and

"Playboy" in its metatags, as well as the registered mark "Playmate" as part of its domain name).

 The New York State Society of Certified Public Accountants v. Eric Louis Assocs., 79 F. Supp. 2d 331 (S.D.N.Y. 1999).

The plaintiff, a nonprofit organization for certified public accountants, has been using the common law service mark "NYSSCPA" since 1984 and registered the domain name nysscpa.org in 1994. The defendant operates a placement firm for accountants and other financial professionals. It registered the domain name nysscpa.com in 1999, along with two other domain names. Each of these three sites used the term "NYSSCPA" in its metatag field so that the defendants' sites would be listed among the search results when those using search engines searched the term "NYSSCPA." The court found that the defendant's domain name and use of metatags constituted trademark infringement and dilution; the court found that the use of domain name NYSSCPA.com and use of NYSSCPA in metatags created "initial interest confusion." Although the defendant's website included a notice that it was not affiliated with NYSSCPA, the court found that the user's momentary initial confusion was sufficient to establish a likelihood of confusion and was also relevant in showing dilution.

 Brookfield Communications, Inc. v. West Coast Entertainment Corp., 174 F.3d 1036 (9th Cir. 1999).

Brookfield Communications, a movie-industry vendor and operator of the website located at moviebuffonline.com, filed suit against video rental chain West Coast Entertainment Corp. to prevent its planned launch of a website at moviebuff.com. The court found Brookfield to be the senior user of the mark, and the defendant was enjoined from using the "moviebuff" trademark in either a domain name or in metatags. The court commented that "using another's trademark in one's metatags is much like posting a sign with another's trademark in front of one's store."

 Bihari v. Gross, 119 F. Supp. 2d 309 (S.D.N.Y. 2000).

The defendant registered several domain names, which he used to criticize the plaintiff's interior design business. The defendant voluntarily relinquished the two domain names that included the plaintiff's service marks, but continued to use the plaintiff's marks in the metatags of the remaining sites. The court rejected the plaintiff's trademark infringement claim holding that defendant used plaintiff's marks in the metatags of his websites as a fair description of the content of those sites, not as marks.

 Nissan Motor Co. v. Nissan Computer Corp., 204 F.R.D. 460 (C.D. Cal. 2001).

The plaintiff, Nissan Motor, has held several U.S. registered trademarks including the word mark "Nissan" since 1959. The defendant, Nissan Computer Corp., was founded in 1991 by Uzi Nissan, who had used his name in connection with several businesses since 1980. In the mid-1990s, Nissan Computer registered its logo as a trademark in North Carolina and registered the domain names nissan.com and nissan.net, which resolved to Nissan Computer's website. Nissan Motor "purchased" the search terms "nissan" and "nissan.com" from various search engine operators to ensure that users searching for such terms would be directed to its website rather than the website of Nissan Computer. The court found that because Nissan Motor had a "valid, protectable trademark interest in the 'Nissan' mark," Nissan Motor could not be held liable for purchasing these search terms even though Nissan Computer held the rights to the nissan.com and nissan.net domain names.

⚖ *Trans Union LLC v. Credit Research, Inc.*, 142 F. Supp. 2d 1029 (N.D. Ill. 2001).

The plaintiff, Trans Union, succeeded on a number of trademark infringement claims involving the defendant's use of domain names and logos that infringed Trans Union's trademark rights. The court, however, found that the use of the "Trans Union" mark in a single metatag constituted fair use of the trademark. The court distinguished this case, in which there was only one such metatag, from "cyber-stuffing," the practice of repeating a term numerous times in a website's metatags in order to lure the attention of Internet search engines. Such cyber-stuffing is not fair use, the court said, because it serves to misdirect the user to the stuffer's page rather than the page that the consumer was initially seeking.

⚖ *Promatek Industries Ltd. v. Equitrac Corp.*, 300 F.3d 808 (7th Cir. 2002), *reh'g denied* (Oct. 18, 2002).

The U.S. Court of Appeals for the Seventh Circuit ruled that a company may not include a competitor's trademark in metatags when such use will cause users initial confusion. The plaintiff, Promatek, and the defendant, Equitrac, compete in the cost-recovery equipment market. Equitrac provides services for "Copitrak" equipment, for which Promatek owns the trademark. Equitrac included the word "Copitrack" in the metatags field on its website, prompting Promatek to file suit. Equitrac subsequently removed the "Copitrack" metatags from its website, but Promatek persisted in its suit, seeking an injunction to prevent Equitrac from using the term "Copitrack" on its site in the future. The trial court granted the injunction and ordered Equitrac to include language on its website (1) indicating that it is not affiliated Copitrack, and (2) directing users seeking Copitrak to Promatek's website via a link. Although the trial court found it likely that Equitrac did not intend to confuse or mislead consumers, it nevertheless found a strong likelihood that the Copitrack metatag would lead to initial confusion. This potential confusion was actionable under the Lanham Act. The court of appeals affirmed the injunction, but added that the use of another party's metatags may be permissible if undertaken in a legitimate and nondeceptive way.

⚖ *Mark Nutritionals Inc. v. FindWhat Services Inc.*, No. SA-02-CA-0085-OG (W.D. Tex. filed Jan. 31, 2002); *Mark Nutritionals Inc. v. Overture Services Inc.*, No. SA-02-CA-0086-OG (W.D. Tex. filed Jan. 31, 2002); *Mark Nutritionals Inc. v. Alta Vista Co.*, No. SA-02-CA-0087-EP (W.D. Tex. filed Jan. 31, 2002); *Mark Nutritionals Inc. v. Innovative Marketing Solutions Inc. d/b/a Kanoodle.com*, No. SA-02-CA-0088-OG (W.D. Tex. filed Jan. 31, 2002).

Mark Nutritionals, the company that markets the Body Solutions weight-loss program, filed suit against multiple search engines claiming that their practice of allowing advertisers to purchase the rights to have their websites listed first when users enter the search terms "body" and "solutions" violates the Lanham Act (§§ 1114 and 1125). As of December 31, 2003, the court has yet to consider the merits of the case.

⚖ *PACCAR, Inc. v. TeleScan Technologies., LLC*, 319 F.3d 243 (6th Cir. 2003).

PACCAR manufactures trucks and truck parts under various trademarks, including "Peterbilt" and "Kenworth." TeleScan operates several websites that provide databases of trucks that are available for sale, including Peterbilt and Kenworth trucks. TeleScan incorporated the marks "Peterbilt" and Kenworth" into some of its domain names and in metatags, and displayed the marks on its websites. TeleScan filed suit, seeking declaratory judgment that it was not infringing PACCAR's rights. PACCAR filed a counterclaim, alleging trademark infringement, unfair competition, trademark dilution, and false designation of origin under the Lanham Act.

The trial court enjoined TeleScan from using PACCAR's marks in any of its domain names, webpages, or metatags. The U.S. Court of Appeals for the Sixth Circuit affirmed the trial court's injunction with respect to the use of the marks in domain names and on web pages, but vacated and sent back to the trial court the portion of the injunction concerning metatags. The court held that the trial court erred because it did not conduct a separate analysis of whether TeleScan's use of PACCAR's trademarks in its websites' metatags was likely to cause consumer confusion regarding the origin or affiliation of the websites.

 Horphaf Research Ltd. v. Pellegrini, 337 F.3d 1036 (9th Cir. 2003).

Plaintiff owned the federal registration for the trademark "Pycnogenol," the name of the product it produced. Defendant sold this product from its website, and used the mark "Pycnogenol" on the site and in its metatags. Plaintiff filed several claims against defendant, including a claim for trademark infringement based on defendant's use of the mark in metatags without permission. Defendant conceded that it used the mark in its metatags, but argued that its use qualified as a fair use. In affirming the trial court's finding of trademark infringement, the court found that defendant did not qualify for a fair use defense because defendant used the mark to cause confusion and to capitalize on the goodwill associated with the "Pycnogenol" mark.

Spam

Several suits have been filed to prevent companies and individuals from sending out "spam," or junk email, with another company's trademark as a return address. Through this practice, known as "spoofing," "spammers" avoid detection and prevent their own Internet service providers' systems from being clogged by returned email. Some companies have successfully sued spammers on the ground that forging a return address constitutes trademark infringement.

In December 2003, Congress enacted the first federal law regulating spam. Among other things, the law prohibits falsifying the return address on an email. For a more detailed discussion of spam and spam laws, see Chapter 8.

Hotmail Corp. v. Van$ Money Pie, Inc., 47 U.S.P.Q.2d (BNA) 1020, 1998 U.S. Dist. LEXIS 10729 (N.D. Cal. April 16, 1998).

A "forged header" suit was filed seeking injunctive relief and damages against spammers, alleging trademark infringement and dilution, as well as computer fraud and abuse claims, and trespass. The court entered a preliminary injunction on April 16, 1998. On June 16, 1998, the court issued a permanent injunction against three of the eight spammers named as defendants in the suit, finding that their use of the plaintiff's "Hotmail" mark in the false spam email headings violated the plaintiff's trademark rights in the mark.

Contextual Marketing: Paid Search and Targeted Pop-Up Ads

Trademark owners have challenged the unauthorized use of their marks to identify and target online advertising to potential consumers for competing products and services. Some advertising services run software that triggers the appearance of advertisements for goods and services related to the sites an Internet user visits or to search terms an Internet user types into a search engine. Trademark owners have argued that such use of their marks violates their rights.

Paid Search

Search engine companies have been accused of improperly exploiting the trademarks of others by selling companies the right to have their banner advertisements served up to users who include the trademarks of other companies in their search queries.

Estee Lauder, Inc. v. Fragrance Counter, Inc. & Excite, 189 F.R.D. 269 (S.D.N.Y. 1999).

Estee Lauder sued the Excite portal, alleging that users who searched for "Estee Lauder" on Excite's WebCrawler service were presented with banner ads for retailers The Fragrance Counter and Cosmetics Counter, and that Estee Lauder's name was used in the banner advertisements without the company's permission. Neither The Fragrance Counter nor Cosmetics Counter is licensed to sell Estee Lauder merchandise. The case was dismissed without prejudice on August 16, 2000, after the defendants agreed to stop "keying" their banner ads to searches for the plaintiff's trademarks.

Playboy Enterprises., Inc. v. Netscape Communications Corp., 55 F. Supp. 2d 1070 (C.D. Cal. 1999) (denying injunction), *aff'd*, 202 F.3rd 278 (9th Cir. 1999), No. SA CV 99-320 AHS, 2000 U.S. Dist. LEXIS 13418 (C.D. Cal., Sept. 14, 2000) (granting defendant's motion for summary judgment).

Playboy alleged that Excite and Netscape were violating its trademark rights by displaying banner ads for other companies to users who run searches for "Playboy." On June 24, 1999, the U.S. District Court for the Central District of California refused Playboy's request for a preliminary injunction. The court ruled narrowly that the terms "playboy" and "playmate" are generic, that Playboy Enterprises has no monopoly on those words in all forms, and that the sale of those search keywords to third-party advertisers who operate adult-entertainment sites is not likely to be found to constitute trademark infringement or dilution. The Ninth Circuit affirmed the trial court's denial of a preliminary injunction. Subsequently, in September 2000, the trial court granted summary judgment for the defendants, finding no dilution, no likelihood of confusion, and no use of the plaintiff's marks to identify the defendants' goods. As of December 31, 2003, the Court of Appeals for the Ninth Circuit was considering Playboy's appeal.

Washingtonpost.newsweek Interactive Co., LLC, et al. v. Gator Corp., C.A. No. 02-909-A, 2002 U.S. Dist. LEXIS 20881 (E.D. Va. 2002).

The plaintiff news organizations complained that Gator infringed their trademarks by displaying pop-up format ads to computer users who were visiting the plaintiffs' websites. Gator had developed and deployed software that would track a user's Internet activity and deliver pop-ups that Gator determined would be of interest to the user based on the user's past Internet usage. The publishers claimed that Gator violated their trademark rights because computer users saw Gator's pop-ups at the same time as they saw the publishers' trademarks on their respective websites and were therefore confused about the source of the pop-ups. A federal judge concluded that the plaintiffs had established a likelihood of prevailing on the merits of their claims; he entered a preliminary injunction prohibiting Gator from displaying ads to users visiting the plaintiffs' websites. The case was settled in February 2003 without any written opinion evaluating Gator's conduct or the plaintiffs' legal theories. The terms of the settlement were not disclosed.

A number of lawsuits challenging Gator's practices have been consolidated for discovery in federal court in Atlanta, Georgia. *Gator Corp. v. Gator Corp.*, No. 1:03md01517 (N.D. Ga., filed Aug. 20, 2003), consolidating for discovery: *United Parcel Service v. Gator Corp.*, No. 1:02cv02639 (N.D. Ga., filed Sept. 26, 2002); *Six Continents Hotel v. Gator Corp.*, No. 1:02cv03065 (N.D. Ga., filed Nov. 12, 2002); *Gator Corp. v. L.L. Bean, Inc.*, No. 1:03cv01198 (N.D. Ga., filed May 2, 2003); *Gator Corp. v. PriceGrabber.com*, No. 1:03cv01302 (N.D. Ga., filed May 2, 2003); *Lendingtree, Inc. v. Gator Corp.*, No. 1:03cv01224 (N.D. Ga., filed May 6, 2003); *Extended Stay America v. Gator Corp.*, No. 1:03cv01225 (N.D. Ga., filed May 6, 2003); *Gator Corp. v. Tiger Direct, Inc.*, No. 1:03cv01260 (N.D. Ga., filed May 8, 2003); *Gator Corp. v. Extended Stay America*, No. 1:03cv01303 (N.D. Ga., filed May 8, 2003); *Tigerdirect, Inc. v. Gator Corp.*, No. 1:03cv01273 (N.D. Ga., filed May 9, 2003); *Hertz Corp. v. Gator Corp.*, No. 1:03cv01973 (N.D. Ga., filed July 14, 2003); *True Communication v. Gator Corp.*, No. 1:03cv02297 (N.D. Ga., filed July 30, 2003); *Gator Corp. Wells Fargo & Co. v. Gator Corp.*, No. 1:03cv02709 (N.D. Ga., filed Sept. 11, 2003); *Overstock.com v. Gator Corp.*, No. 1:03cv02810 (N.D. Ga., filed Sept. 17, 2003).

Societe Luteciel v. Societe Google France, No. 03/00051 (Tribunal de Grande Instance de Nanterre, Oct. 13, 2003).

A French court found Google France liable for trademark infringement when it sold the French-language terms "bourses des voyages" (travel market) and "bourses des vols" (flight market) to online travel agencies so that when users of the Google search engine type in these phrases, the travel agencies' advertisements will appear on the webpage near the search results. Plaintiff, the operator of a travel site located at www.bourse-des-voyages.com, argued that Google's sale of the search terms to competing travel agencies, and the display of advertisements for such agencies near the search results, infringed its trademark rights. The court determined that such use unlawfully traded off the goodwill of the plaintiff, constituting infringement. The court rejected Google's argument that its search engine was incapable of differentiating a request for generic terms "bourse" (market), "vols" (flights), and "voyages" (travel) from a request for the plaintiff's "Bourse des Voyages" mark, and ruled in favor of plaintiff.

In a similar action against Google, French company Louis Vuitton SA, maker of shoes, handbags and other high-end accessories, filed suit in August 2003 against the search engine for selling advertising to Louis Vuitton's competitors and displaying such advertisements next to the search results when a Google user typed the word "Vuitton." *See* "Handbag Maker Vuitton Sues Google, Trademark Infringement Alleged," CNN.com (Oct. 24, 2003), *available at* http://www.cnn.com/2003/TECH/biztech/10/24/france.google.ap/.

U-Haul International, Inc. v. WhenU.com, et al., 279 F. Supp. 2d 723 (E.D. Va. 2003).

Defendant WhenU.com developed and deployed software that monitors the activity within a user's web browser and serves advertisements to the user's computer desktop based on the URL's of the web pages visited by the user, the search terms the user types in search engine queries, and the content of the web pages the user views. U-Haul sued WhenU on federal copyright infringement, trademark infringement, and unfair competition theories, and on various related state-law theories, based on ads for a U-Haul competitor that WhenU served to users who were visiting the U-Haul website. In granting WhenU's motion for summary judgment on all of U-Haul's federal claims, the court emphasized that: the WhenU ads are served only to users who have installed the WhenU software pursuant to When U's license agreement consistent with the user's right to control his/her own computer display; and that the ads open "in a WhenU-branded window that is separate and distinct from the window in which the U-Haul website appears." The court found that the appearance of a WhenU-branded pop-up ad to a user viewing the U-Haul website does not constitute a trademark use of any U-Haul mark because WhenU does not use U-Haul's "trademarks to identify the source of its goods or services." The court analogized the simultaneous appearance of the WhenU and U-Haul marks to comparative advertising, which "does not violate trademark law, even when the advertising makes use of a competitor's trademark." U-Haul dismissed the related state claims, but appealed the trial court's grant of summary judgment for WhenU on its trademark and copyright claims. However, U-Haul dismissed its appeal before the case was briefed or argued in the Court of Appeals.

 Wells Fargo & Co., et al. v. WhenU.com, No. 03-71906, 2003 U.S. Dist. LEXIS 20756 (E.D. Mich., preliminary injunction denied Nov. 19, 2003).

Wells Fargo and Quicken Loans, which marketed the availability of mortgages on their respective websites, sued WhenU.com for serving pop-up ads for competing mortgage lenders to users who were visiting the plaintiffs' websites. Plaintiffs alleged trademark and copyright infringement and sought a preliminary injunction. In a detailed opinion accompanied by extensive factual findings, the trial court denied plaintiffs' request for an injunction, finding that plaintiffs had failed to establish a likelihood that they would succeed on the merits of their claims. Like the *U-Haul* court, the court found that the plaintiffs had failed to establish that WhenU "used" plaintiffs' trademarks in any manner actionable under trademark law and analogized the pop-ups to permissible comparative advertisements.

 1-800 Contacts, Inc. v. WhenU.com, et al., No. 02 CIV 8043, 2003 U.S. Dist. LEXIS 22932 (S.D.N.Y., preliminary injunction granted, Dec. 22, 2003).

1-800 Contacts, a retailer of contact lenses, sued WhenU.com and its advertiser, Vision Direct, complaining of pop-up ads for Vision Direct that WhenU displayed to users who were visiting the 1-800 Contacts website. Like the plaintiffs in the *U-Haul* and *Wells Fargo* cases, discussed above, 1-800 Contacts complained of trademark and copyright infringement. Plaintiff sought a preliminary injunction. Like the *U-Haul* and *Wells Fargo* courts, the trial court rejected 1-800 Contact's copyright claim, finding that the plaintiff was not likely to prevail on its derivative work theory: "to hold that computer users are limited in their use of plaintiff's website to viewing the website without any obstructing windows or programs would be to subject countless computer users and software developers to liability for copyright infringement and contributory copyright infringement." 2003 U.S. Dist. LEXIS 22932 at *43. But unlike the *U-Haul* and *Wells Fargo* courts, the court found that the pop-up ads infringed 1-800 Contacts trademarks. The court found that WhenU "used" plaintiff's trademark in two ways: "First, in causing pop-up advertisements for Defendant Vision Direct to appear when [WhenU] users have specifically attempted to access Plaintiff's website—on which Plaintiff's trademark appears—Defendants are displaying Plaintiff's mark 'in the . . . advertising of' Defendant Vision Direct's services." 2003 U.S. Dist. LEXIS 22932 at *54. Second, "Defendant WhenU.com includes Plaintiff's URL . . . in the proprietary WhenU.com directory of terms that triggers pop-up advertisements on [WhenU] user's computers. In doing so, Defendant WhenU.com 'uses' Plaintiff's mark to advertise and publicize companies that are in direct competition with Plaintiff." 2003 U.S. Dist. LEXIS 22932 at *55. The U.S. Court of Appeals for the Second Circuit granted expedited review of the trial court's decision. *1-800 Contacts, Inc. v. WhenU.com, Inc.*, Nos. 04-0026-cv & 04-0446-cv (2d Cir., filed Jan. 7, 2004).

Other courts have considered whether using another's trademark in keyword search terms constitutes trademark infringement.

 Google, Inc. v. American Blind & Wallpaper Factory, Inc., No. 5:03-CV-05340-JF (N.D. Cal. filed Nov. 26, 2003).

Google, the Internet search engine, filed a claim in November 2003 seeking a court declaration that allowing Google's advertisers to include trademarks of the advertisers' competitors in keyword search terms to trigger their own advertisements in Google search results does not constitute trademark infringement in violate of the Lanham Act.

For discussion of these cases in the context of marketing and advertising, see Chapter 8, pages 245 to 246.

Liability of Internet Service Providers

Liability for Third-Party Trademark Infringement

There is no explicit "safe-harbor" immunity for Internet service providers (ISPs) with regard to third-party trademark infringement (as there is for third-party copyright infringement under the Digital Millennium Copyright Act (DMCA), *see* Chapter 4, page 107). Some ISPs have attempted to claim immunity from trademark infringement liability for a third party's infringing activities under the DMCA's safe-harbor provision. Courts have been reluctant to apply the safe-harbor provision to ISPs in trademark infringement cases.

 Gucci America, Inc. v. Hall & Assoc., 135 F. Supp. 2d 409 (S.D.N.Y. 2001).

The defendant, Internet service provider Mindspring, operated the goldhaus.com website on behalf of its client, Hall & Associates. The plaintiff, Gucci, informed Mindspring that the material posted on Hall's website infringed Gucci's trademark rights and demanded removal of the material. When Mindspring failed to remove the material, Gucci sued both Hall and Mindspring. The court denied Mindspring's motion to dismiss, holding that an ISP may be liable for contributory trademark infringement where the ISP exercised "direct control and monitoring of the instrumentality used by a third party to infringe the plaintiff's mark." The court declined to extend the ISP immunity that is available for contributory copyright infringement under the Digital Millennium Copyright Act to cases involving trademark infringement. The court noted that the plaintiff would have a high burden of proof to establish that the defendant had sufficient knowledge of the infringement for the plaintiff to prove a claim of contributory infringement.

See also Ford Motor Co. v. GreatDomains.com, Inc., 60 U.S.P.Q.2D (BNA) 1446, No. 00-CV-71544-DT, 2001 U.S. Dist. LEXIS 24780 (E.D. Mich., Sept. 25, 2001) (denying ISP GreatDomains.com's supplemental motion to dismiss pursuant to the DMCA provision of immunity from contributory infringement liability, citing the *Gucci* court's interpretation that the provision does not apply to trademark claims).

Chapter 2: Trademarks
Summary of the Law

- A trademark is a designation that identifies the source of goods, and distinguishes that source from other sources. Trademark rights can be acquired through common law, through registration of a trademark, or through the "fame" of the mark. Trademarks are governed by federal and state statutes, and by common law.

- The federal law that governs trademarks is the Lanham Act. Under the Lanham Act, to prevail on a trademark infringement claim, a plaintiff must demonstrate ownership of the mark, and a likelihood of consumer confusion resulting from another's use of the mark.

- Remedies for trademark infringement include injunctive relief, disgorgement of defendant's profits from use of the trademark, damages to the plaintiff, and costs incurred in bringing the action.

- Most Internet-related trademark disputes reflect a trademark owner's desire ·to establish or maintain online brand recognition and loyalty. A website operator may be liable for trademark infringement for displaying another's trademark on a website, without permission, in a way that implies an association between the website and the trademark owner.

- An Internet service provider (ISP) may be liable for contributory trademark infringement for infringing material posted by a third party on a website that is under the ISP's control.

- Linking from one website to another website, by itself, does not amount to trademark infringement. Linking may present trademark infringement questions if the link implies an endorsement or association to the linked-to site. "Deep-linking" (that is, linking directly to particular pages within a website rather than the website's home page) may also raise trademark infringement issues if the deep-link leads consumers to believe there is an association between the sites.

- Framing a website (that is, displaying another's website within the pages of one's own website) can potentially constitute trademark infringement, if the frame confuses website visitors into believing there is an affiliation or association between the websites.

- A metatag is a word or code embedded in a data field on a website that is not normally part of any publicly viewable web page. Search engines read a website's metatags to determine the subject(s) addressed on the site so that the search engine can determine whether the site is responsive to a search query input by a user. Some website operators include on their sites metatags that incorporate the trademarks of their competitors, so that when a user searches for a competitor, the search results include the website operator's site. Courts have found that using a competitor's trademark in metatags may constitute trademark infringement when such use causes users confusion about the origin or affiliation of the website. In some instances, use of metatags will not amount to trademark infringement if the use is not intended to deceive or confuse consumers.

- Contextual marketers monitor the Internet activity of computer users (analyzing the search terms they include in search engine queries, the URLs of web pages they visit and/or the words that appear on these pages) and target contextually relevant advertising to users based on their apparent interests as reflected in their Internet activity. Various trademark owners have brought suit against contextual marketers, claiming that their monitoring practices and/or the appearance of their pop-up ads on users' computer screens constitute trademark infringement. Federal trial courts have split on whether this activity is infringing; the first court of appeals ruling could come as early as the summer of 2004.

DOMAIN NAMES

Domain-Name Registration

Background

Until 1998, the Department of Commerce exercised exclusive control over the domain name system, and it contracted with a private company, Network Solutions, Inc., to be the exclusive registrar of second-level domain names (*e.g.,* the "amazon" in amazon.com, the "npr" in npr.org) in the top-level domains (TLDs) ".com," ".org," ".net," and ".edu." Network Solutions was therefore at the center of early disputes. In 1998, the Department of Commerce decided to move the noncompetitive, government-funded, domain-name registration system into the private sector. In November 1998, the Department of Commerce entered into a Memorandum of Understanding with the nonprofit Internet Corporation for Assigned Names and Numbers (ICANN), under which ICANN assumed responsibility for management of much of the domain name system. Since then, ICANN has approved and accredited almost 200 companies, including Network Solutions, to offer domain-name registrations in ten of the TLDs (.aero, .biz, .com, .coop, .info, .museum, .name, .net, .org, and .pro). One hundred seventy-four of these companies were operational as of December 2003. ICANN does not accredit registrars for TLDs that are restricted to specific entities and purposes. These TLDs include ".edu" (educational institutions), ".gov" (U.S. government entities), and ".mil" (U.S. military sites).

In July 2003, a coalition of domain name registrars sued ICANN for breach of contract when ICANN initiated a plan giving VeriSign, a domain name registrar, control over a waiting list to obtain expired .com or .net domain names. The plaintiff domain registrars argued that the waiting list violated their agreements with ICANN, and gave VeriSign an unfair advantage by allowing VeriSign to reserve registrations for domain names that other registrars had previously administered. The plaintiff's request for a preliminary injunction was denied in November 2003, but the case remains pending. *Dotster, Inc. et al. v. ICANN*, No. CV 03-5045, 2003 U.S. Dist. 22634 (C.D. Cal., Nov. 10, 2003) (denying preliminary injunction).

Adding Top-Level Domain Names

On November 16, 2000, ICANN announced seven new top-level domain names. Four of these domain names are "unsponsored" names for use by broad segments of the Internet community: ".biz" (for use by businesses), ".info" (unrestricted use), ".name" (for use by individuals), and ".pro" (for use by accountants, lawyers, physicians, and other professionals). The other three approved TLDs are "sponsored" TLDs, which are defined as specialized TLDs, each of which has a sponsoring organization representing the narrower community most affected by the TLD. These three are: ".aero" (air transport industry), ".coop" (cooperatives), and ".museum" (museums).

An agreement was reached in May 2001 to allow any company currently accredited by ICANN as a domain-name registrar to begin registering ".biz" and ".info" domain names upon completion of the required registry documents, and a similar agreement was reached in July 2001 for the ".name" domain. Under that agreement, distribution of the ".biz," ".info," and ".name" domain names provides some form of preferential treatment to existing trademark holders.

Unsponsored TLDs

- *Status of the ".biz" Domain*. ".biz" domain names became available for registration beginning November 7, 2001. NeuLevel is the overseeing registry. Registration information for the ".biz" domain can be obtained at www.neulevel.com. NeuLevel has been attacked for allegedly running an illegal lottery. In *Smiley v. ICANN*, No. BC-254659 (Cal. Super. Ct. July 23, 2001), the plaintiffs filed a class-action suit against ICANN, NeuLevel, and several agents, alleging that NeuLevel's practice of selling applications that provided the chance to win the right to register a domain name constituted an illegal lottery under California law. On October 11, 2001, a California state court ordered a temporary injunction, finding that NeuLevel's decision to charge a $2.00 fee for processing certain ".biz" domain name applications might violate California's lottery law. However, that injunction was dissolved on October 23, 2001, when the plaintiffs failed to post the appropriate bond. On December 13, 2002, the trial court approved the public release of a proposed settlement. Under the proposed settlement, those who applied for a ".biz" domain name before September 25, 2001 may be eligible for a refund of the $2.00 fee and may be able to retain their domain names.

- *Status of the ".info" Domain*. ".info" domain names became available for registration on a first-come, first-served basis beginning October 1, 2001. The overseeing registry for ".info" is a consortium of domain-name registrants called Afilias. Registration information for the ".info" domain can be obtained at http://www.afilias.com/.

- *Status of the ".name" Domain*. ".name" domain names "went live" on January 15, 2002. The overseeing registry is a privately held company called Global Name Registry. Registration information for the ".name" domain can be obtained at http://www.nic.name.

  According to a study by Ben Edelman at Harvard's Berkman Center For Internet & Society, thousands of registrations for ".name" domain names apparently violate ICANN regulations, either by not adhering to the prescribed format "firstname.lastname.name" or by not being a person's real name (or a name by which the person is commonly known). In May 2002, an arbitration panel ordered that two such domain names, "aim5.instantmessenger.name" and "instant.messenger.name," be canceled for failure to comply with these requirements. *America Online, Inc. v. AD 2000 D.Com*, Claim No. FA0203000108377 (NAF May 6, 2002).

- *Status of the ".pro" Domain*. The ".pro" domain registry established a sunrise period for companies to register their domain names. This allowed registered trademark holders to secure .pro domain names using their marks before the registry opened to the public. Public registration of .pro domain names began in 2003. The overseeing registry is Registry/Pro. Registration information for the ".pro" domain can be found at http://www.registrypro.com.

Sponsored TLDs

- *Status of the ".aero" Domain*. The ".aero" domain name is administered by the aviation industry, and managed by SITA, a nonprofit cooperative representing the aviation industry. The TLD is available only for use by members of the aviation community, subject to verification by SITA. Eligible registrants may reserve domain names using the ".aero" TLD, but as of December 31, 2003, the domain names were not affiliated with a registrar and remained inactive. Registration information is available at http://www.nic.aero.

- *Status of ".museum" Domain*. The ".museum" domain is sponsored by MusaDoma, which administers and verifies the eligibility of prospective registrants to register a ".museum" domain name. Once ICANN approved the new TLD in 2000, eligible museums were able to reserve domain names with MusaDoma. In 2003, museums with reserved names were able to register their domain names with one of four ".museum" domain name registrars recognized by ICANN. MusaDoma continues to administer the eligibility of entities to register a ".museum" domain name. Information concerning the ".museum" TLD is available at http://about.museum/.

- *Status of ".coop" Domain*. The domain name sponsor, DotCoop, ensures that applicants to register ".coop" domain names are cooperatives, cooperative service organizations and wholly owned subsidiaries of cooperatives. The ".coop" TLD was launched on January 30, 2002, with several accredited registrars working with DotCoop to maintain the domain name registrations. Information about the ".coop" TLD is available at http://www.nic.coop/.

Restrictions on Pre-registration. No organization is authorized to "pre-register" domain names in the new TLDs. Domain names may only be assigned pursuant to the procedures authorized by ICANN for each TLD. Persons who attempt to pre-register do so at their own risk and with no assurance from ICANN that they will receive the pre-registered names once the TLDs become operational.

Country Code Top-Level Domain Names

ccTLDs are two-letter combinations that are obtained by host countries, or dependent areas not directly bordering their parent countries, from the Internet Assigned Numbers Authority (IANA). The actual code formulations are determined by the ISO 3166 Maintenance Agency. These domain names can only be procured in accordance with IANA rules and procedures. The IANA provides a database of assigned ccTLDs, as well as the procedures and restrictions for obtaining secondary domain names for each, at http://www.iana.org/cctld/cctld-whois.htm.

Some countries have entered into agreements under which they license the right to use ccTLDs for purposes other than to suggest an affiliation with the host country. Under an agreement with the Laotian government, for example, a Los Angeles-based company, dotLA, has purchased the right to market ".la" domain names to companies and organizations in Los Angeles, Latin America, and Louisiana. Another company, dotTV, has made a similar agreement to market ".tv" domain names for purposes unrelated to the nation of Tuvalu, the country that owns the right to that TLD. As of December 31, 2003, ICANN had yet to take a position on the propriety of such arrangements, but its former president and CEO, Michael Roberts, asserted that it is legal for a country to license the control of its top-level domain to a private company. *See* Todd R. Weiss, "Laos Licenses .la for Corporate Sites," *Computerworld*, December 18, 2000, at 24.

The status of a ccTLD after the host country ceases to exist is unclear. ICANN announced that the former Soviet Union's ".su" ccTLD will be discontinued sometime in 2004, prompting negative reactions among some Russian Internet activists. Registration of domain names using .su had ceased, but registration re-opened in December 2002 to trademark holders and in June 2003 to the public. "The Supervising Council of the Foundation Approved Open Registration of Domain Names in the .SU Registry," Foundation for Internet Development (June 21, 2003), *available at* http://www.fid.su/ engl/news/news030621.html.

The ".us" Domain

The U.S. Department of Commerce has entered into an agreement with NeuStar to commercialize and administer the ".us" TLD. (NeuStar is the parent of NeuLevel, the company that is the registry for the ".biz" top-level domain.) The ".us" TLD is being marketed as "America's Internet Address."

Applications for ".us" domain names can be submitted through any U.S.-accredited registrar. There was a sunrise period for ".us" top-level domain names. On April 24, 2002, registrations became available to owners of marks that were the subject of U.S. registrations or applications for registration on file with the Patent and Trademark Office as of July 27, 2001. The remaining ".us" domain names are being assigned on a first-come, first-served basis. A challenge to a ".us" domain-name registration is made through the "usTLD DRP," similar to the UDRP discussed at page 75. The usTLD DRP was approved by the Department of Commerce on February 21, 2002, and is available online at http://www.nic.us/policies/docs/usdrp.pdf.

Only American citizens, residents, people who are domiciled in the United States, entities incorporated under U.S. law, and entities that have a bona fide presence in the United States may secure ".us" domain names.

Top-Level Domain Names and the First Amendment

Though it is conceivable that future top-level domain names may be sufficiently expressive to receive First Amendment protection, restrictions limiting the availability of top-level domain names that existed as of 2000 were found not to violate the First Amendment. The restrictions were found to be reasonable "time, place, and manner" restrictions on speech. *Name.space, Inc. v. Network Solutions, Inc.*, 202 F.3d 573 (2d Cir. 2000). For a discussion of constitutional limitations on restrictions on freedom of speech generally, *see* Chapter 1.

Unauthorized Top-Level Domain Names

Some Internet companies have attempted to circumvent ICANN by setting up unsanctioned TLDs, such as ".xxx." The companies that run these TLDs would make websites in these domains accessible to the public by entering into agreements with individual ISPs to make such sites available to their subscribers. This approach has created concern that, in the future, multiple registrars might register duplicative names. This development also might serve to limit the TLDs that could ultimately be made available through ICANN, or alternatively, might force ICANN either to accept these pre-registered names or to take away existing domain names from website operators as it establishes new official TLDs.

Domain-Name Legislation

Congress has taken steps to create legislation addressing certain perceived problems relating to domain names and domain-name registration.

Dot-Kids Implementation and Efficiency Act of 2002. In December 2002, President Bush signed a statute creating a second-level Internet domain, dot-kids, in the .US registry. The dot-kids.us domain is to be used for sites featuring material that promotes positive experiences for children. The new domain is intended to prevent children from being exposed to harmful material on the Internet. The Act established guidelines for content targeted to children under the age of 13. The initial sunrise period for organizations to register dot-kids domain names using their existing or pending registered trademarks and service marks in this new domain ended on August 15, 2003. General registration began on September 4, 2003. 47 U.S.C. §§ 902(b)(3) & 941 (2003).

For a discussion of this legislation in the context of freedom of speech, *see* Chapter 1, page 12.

Truth in Domain Names Act (18 U.S.C. § 2252B). In April 2003, President Bush signed a statute that prohibits knowingly using a misleading domain name with the intent to attract a minor to view on the Internet a visual depiction of sexually explicit conduct. The penalties for violating this act include fines and imprisonment up to four years.

United States v. Zuccarini, No. 03-MAG-1701 (S.D.N.Y., Dec. 10, 2003)

Infamous cybersquatter and typosquatter John Zuccarini was arrested under the Truth in Domain Names Act and charged with creating misleading domain names to deceive children into viewing websites containing content that is harmful to minors. The U.S. Attorney for the Southern District of New York charged Zuccarini with creating more than 3,000 misleading domain names, including Dinseyland.com, bobthebiulder.com, and teltubbies.com, which are misspellings of legitimate domain names for websites that are targeted to children. Minors who type in these misspellings are led to pornography sites.

On December 10, 2003, Zuccarini pled guilty to 49 counts of creating misleading domain names in violation of the Truth in Domain Names Act. The trial court is scheduled to sentence Zuccarini on February 20, 2004. Zuccarini faces up to four years in prison and a $250,000 fine for each violation of the Act. (Additionally, Zuccarini pled guilty to one count of possession of child pornography, for which he faces up to 10 years imprisonment and a $250,000 fine.)

Criminalizing False Registration Information (H.R. 4640). In May 2002, legislation was introduced that would have imposed criminal penalties, including a maximum of five years' imprisonment, on anyone who knowingly provided "material and misleading false contact information" when registering a domain name. This bill was referred to House Subcommittee on Crime, Terrorism, and Homeland Security, where it stalled. The bill has not been reintroduced.

Is a Domain Name a Trademark?

A registered domain name is not automatically entitled to trademark protection. Simply registering the name does not constitute "use" or establish priority in the mark under federal trademark law. *See Brookfield Communications, Inc. v. West Coast Entertainment Corp.*, 174 F.3d 1036 (9th Cir. 1999). A domain name is protectable as a trademark only if the domain name is also used to brand the website located at that address (*e.g.*, amazon.com, washingtonpost.com, AutoTrader.com). *See* U.S.P.T.O., "Marks Composed, in Whole or Part, of Domain Names" (Sept. 29, 1999) available at http://www.uspto.gov/web/offices/tac/notices/guide299.htm. Trademark registration will not be granted where the domain name is merely being used as an address for the applicant's website. *Id.* Simply registering a domain name can, however, constitute trademark infringement if it creates a likelihood of confusion. *See Panavision International, L.P. v. Toeppen*, 141 F.3d 1316 (9th Cir. 1998).

Use of another's trademark in the post-domain path of a web page's URL (that is, everything in the URL after the TLD) has led to at least one trademark dispute.

Interactive Products. Corp. v. A2Z Mobile Office Solutions, 326 F.3d 687 (6th Cir. 2003).

The plaintiff developed a portable computer stand under the trademark "Lap Traveler." Defendant A2Z, with the plaintiff's consent, sold the Lap Traveler from its webpage, located at the URL: http://a2zsolutions.com/desks/floor/laptraveler/dkfl-lt.htm. Plaintiff eventually terminated its relationship with A2Z, and demanded that A2Z cease all uses of the "Lap Traveler" mark on its website. Defendant then began selling a competing product, "Mobile Desk," from the same webpage, but did not change the URL. When users sought the "Lap Traveler" through various search engines, A2Z's "Mobile Desk" webpage appeared in the search results. The plaintiff filed a claim against A2Z for trademark infringement. The trial court denied relief. Affirming the trial court, the U.S. Court of Appeals for the Sixth Circuit defined the differences between a website's domain name and the post-domain path of a URL. The court held that while a domain name may be an important identifier of a website's source, the post-domain path in the URL merely reflects the organization of data on a computer. Including a trademark in a domain name can be infringing if it creates consumer confusion regarding the origin of the goods. However, the court noted, because the post-domain path does not signify source, it is unlikely that a consumer would be confused by the presence of a trademark in the post-domain path of the URL.

Applying Trademark Licenses to Domain Names

A trademark licensee with distribution and marketing rights to a protected trademark does not necessarily obtain the right to use the mark in a domain name in connection with its online business. In *Creative Gifts, Inc. v. UFO*, 235 F.3d 540 (10th Cir. 2000), the defendant purchased and distributed anti-gravity "Levitron" tops manufactured by the plaintiff. Although the parties had no written licensing agreement, the court recognized that the defendant had a license to use the plaintiff's trademark in conjunction with its advertising to the extent that it promoted the Levitron tops with the knowledge and approval of the plaintiff. However, it rejected the defendant's assertion that the right to use the domain name Levitron.com was within the scope of that license. The court also found that it would be inequitable to allow the defendant to assert a "naked licensing" defense, which is essentially a claim of trademark abandonment, because the defendant had continued to recognize the validity of the plaintiff's trademark by securing a license. *See also SARL Alifax v. Sony Corp.*, Cours d'Appel de Versailles, September 14, 2000.

Extra-Statutory Relief in Domain Name Cases

The most common judicial remedy in trademark infringement cases and dilution cases is the issuance of an injunction prohibiting future infringement of the mark. But an injunction does little to help the owner of a trademark secure a domain name containing its trademark where that domain name has been registered to another. For domain name cases, courts have gone beyond traditional injunctive relief and ordered the transfer of domain names from the domain name owners to the trademark owners. *See, e.g., ActMedia, Inc. v. Active Media International*, No. 96C3448, 1996 WL 466527, 1996 U.S. Dist. LEXIS 20814 (N.D. Ill. July 17, 1996); *Intermatic Inc. v. Toeppen*, 947 F. Supp. 1227 (N.D. Ill. 1996); *PACCAR, Inc. v. TeleScan Technologies, LLC*, 115 F. Supp. 2d 772 (E.D. Mich. 2000), *aff'd in part*, 319 F.3d 243 (6th Cir. 2003); *Trans Union LLC v. Credit Research, Inc.*, 142 F. Supp. 2d 1029 (N.D. Ill. 2001).

Domain Names Used in Competition with Trademark Owner

Domain-name disputes in which the operator of a website uses a domain name that is identical to a competitor's trademark are analyzed under the usual principles of trademark infringement and dilution, discussed in further detail in Chapter 2, pages 34 and 35.

 Brookfield Communications, Inc. v. West Coast Entertainment Corp., 174 F.3d 1036 (9th Cir. 1999).

Brookfield Communications, a movie industry vendor and operator of the website moviebuffonline.com, filed suit against video rental chain West Coast Entertainment Corp. to prevent its planned launch of moviebuff.com. Even though West Coast had registered the domain name almost two years before Brookfield had first used the moviebuff name on the Internet, the Court of Appeals for the Ninth Circuit held that West Coast's registration of the domain name did not by itself constitute "use" for purposes of trademark priority, and that Brookfield's use of the mark in commerce since 1993 qualified it as the senior user. The court further stated that the senior user of a mark is the legitimate owner of the mark, and enjoined the defendant from using the "moviebuff" trademark either in a domain name or in metatags. (For discussion of this case in the context of metatags, *see* Chapter 2, page 40.)

In reaching its conclusion, the court recognized "initial interest confusion" (the possibility of customers inadvertently finding a site and becoming interested in the services offered there instead of the services they were initially seeking) as sufficient to constitute the confusing similarity necessary to support a trademark infringement claim. Though no such showing was explicitly required in *Brookfield*, a number of courts have required a showing that defendant designed the site in bad faith to create initial interest confusion. *See Interstellar Starship Services, Ltd. v. Epix, Inc.*, 125 F. Supp. 2d 1269 (D. Or. 2001); *Bigstar Entertainment Group, Inc. v. Next Big Star, L.L.C.*, 105 F. Supp. 2d 185 (S.D.N.Y. 2000).

 Washington Speakers Bureau, Inc. v. Leading Authorities, Inc., 33 F. Supp. 2d 488 (E.D. Va. 1999), *aff'd*, Nos. 99-1440 and 99-1442, 2000 U.S. App. LEXIS 14669 (4th Cir. June 27, 2000).

In March 1998, Leading Authorities registered the domain names washingtonspeakers.com, washingtonspeakers.net, washington-speakers.com, and washington-speakers.net, along with other names incorporating the word "speakers." The

Washington Speakers Bureau, which had represented many well-known speakers for nearly two decades, sued its rival for infringement and dilution of its common law mark. The court found a likelihood that consumers would be confused by the defendant's use of a "colorable imitation" of the plaintiff's mark and that Leading Authorities had registered the domain names in a bad-faith effort to attract its competitor's business. Leading Authorities was directed to relinquish rights to those names.

PACCAR, Inc. v. TeleScan Technologies, LLC, 115 F. Supp. 2d 772 (E.D. Mich. 2000), *aff'd in part*, 319 F.3d 243 (6th Cir. 2003).

PACCAR, a manufacturer of heavy trucks and truck parts under the "Peterbilt" and "Kenworth" trademarks, filed suit against TeleScan Technologies, the operator of several websites that allow consumers to locate new and used heavy truck dealers. TeleScan had registered domain names that incorporated PACCAR's trademarks (peterbilttrucks.com, kenworthtrucks.com, peterbiltnewtrucks.com, kenworthdealers.com, and others).

The trial court issued a preliminary injunction, ordered TeleScan to transfer registration of the challenged domain names to PACCAR, and enjoined TeleScan from using any PACCAR mark or colorable imitation of any such mark in any domain name, metatag, or portion of a web page (such as "wallpaper") if such use would cause consumers to associate the Peterbilt or Kenworth marks with TeleScan. The court also ordered TeleScan to post the order on its website.

The trial court applied traditional analysis to PACCAR's claims of trademark infringement and dilution under the Lanham Act. The trial court rejected TeleScan's argument that its use of the PACCAR marks in its domain names was akin to the use of a manufacturer's marks to identify a vehicle in a classified ad or to identify merchandise for the purpose of stocking, displaying, or reselling. The trial court stated, "[A] classified advertisement communicates information as to the source of the truck, not information as to the seller of the truck. Words in domain names, however, do communicate information as to the nature of the entity sponsoring the website." Because the domain names identified the websites, not the trucks that TeleScan advertised via those websites, the court found trademark infringement and dilution.

The U.S. Court of Appeals for the Sixth Circuit affirmed the injunction, except to the extent that it had enjoined TeleScan from using PACCAR marks in its metatags. The appellate court rejected TeleScan's argument that its disclaimer disavowing affiliation with the trademark owner corrected any initial interest confusion caused by TeleScan's use of PACCAR's marks in its domain names.

For discussion of this case in the context of metatags, *see* Chapter 2, page 41.

Trademark Owners with Competing Claims to a Domain Name

Courts have also applied traditional trademark analysis to cases involving competing trademark interests in domain names.

Virtual Works, Inc. v. Network Solutions, Inc., 106 F. Supp. 2d 845 (E.D. Va. 2000), *aff'd sub nom. Virtual Works, Inc. v. Volkswagen of America, Inc.*, 238 F.3d 264 (4th Cir. 2001).

The defendant, Virtual Works, an Internet service provider, registered the domain name vw.net in 1996. In 1999, Volkswagen requested that Network Solutions, Inc. (NSI) place the domain name on hold pursuant to its dispute resolution policy. In response, Virtual Works filed suit against NSI and Volkswagen claiming that Volkswagen's attempts to claim vw.net amounted to tortious interference with a registered domain name. Volkswagen counterclaimed for trademark infringement, dilution, and cybersquatting. Both parties moved for summary judgment; the court denied Virtual Works' motion and granted Volkswagen's motion.

With respect to the cybersquatting claim, the court retroactively applied the Anticybersquatting Consumer Protection Act (discussed at page 63, below) and found that Virtual Works "attempted to profit from the trafficking of a domain name of a previously trademarked name." The court based its finding on the fact that Virtual Works did not have any rights in, and had never conducted business using, the initials "VW." It found that Volkswagen is the only entity with any intellectual property rights in the VW mark, that use of vw.net had already caused confusion, that Volkswagen's VW mark is famous, and that Virtual Works had attempted to sell the domain name for financial gain.

The court also found that Virtual Works infringed and diluted Volkswagen's trademark. It noted that "the holder of a domain name should give up that domain name when it is 'an intuitive domain name' that belongs to another" and that VW is the intuitive domain name of Volkswagen. The court discounted the fact that the companies offered different products because both used the same channel of commerce, the Internet.

WWF Worldwide Fund for Nature (Formerly World Wildlife Fund), World Wildlife Fund Inc. v. World Wrestling Federation Entertainment, Inc., Neutral Citation No.: [2002] EWCA Civ 196, available at http://www.courtservice.gov.uk/judgmentsfiles/j1056/civil_wwf.htm.

A United Kingdom appeals court decided on February 27, 2002, that the World Wrestling Federation must give up its WWF.com address and curtail use of the WWF logo outside of the United States. A lawsuit brought by the World Wildlife Fund in Switzerland ended in a 1994 agreement in which the wrestling federation, which holds U.S. trademarks containing the initials "WWF," would cancel pending applications for additional WWF trademarks and curtail use of the letters in broadcasting and print outside of the United States. The court found that the website was more than a technical infringement of that agreement. In May 2002, the wrestling organization agreed to change its name to World Wrestling Entertainment to end the dispute.

Entrepreneur Media Inc. v. Smith d/b/a EntrepreneurPR, 279 F.3d 1135 (9th Cir. 2002).

The plaintiff, Entrepreneur Media Inc., had published Entrepreneur Magazine since 1978, and operated a website available at the domain names entrepreneur.com and entrepreneurmag.com.

In 1987, the plaintiff registered the trademark "Entrepreneur" for magazines, books, publishing reports, and computer programs. Since 1995, the defendant had operated a public relations company using the name Icon Publications. In 1997, the defendant changed the name of the company to EntrepreneurPR and changed the name of a periodical that it published to Entrepreneur Illustrated. At that time, he registered the domain name entrepreneurpr.com.

The court held that a domain name does not infringe a descriptive trademark when the domain name is not exactly the same as the mark. In this case, the small difference in the letters "pr" between the mark Entrepreneur and the domain name entrepreneurpr.com precluded a finding that the domain name was infringing. The court said that, because of the need for economy of language in domain names, "very small differences matter."

Interstellar Starship Services, Ltd. v. Epix, Inc., 304 F.3d 936 (9th Cir. 2002)

The defendant, Epix, Inc., held the trademark EPIX, which it used to identify its hardware and software products related to imaging. The plaintiff registered the domain name epix.com to establish a website featuring personal photographs and promoting video imaging hardware and software design services. The plaintiff brought suit seeking declaratory judgment that its epix.com domain name did not infringe Epix's trademark. The defendant counterclaimed under federal and state trademark law. The court of appeals upheld the trial court's ruling that the plaintiff's use infringed Epix's mark, but only to the extent the website promoted similar products and services. Interstellar was permitted to retain the domain name and continue to use if for noninfringing purposes.

Visa International Services Association v. JSL Corp., No. CV-S-01-0294 2002 U.S. Dist. LEXIS 24779 (D. Nev. Oct. 22, 2002).

A federal court in Nevada enjoined a company that operated language schools in Japan from using the domain name evisa.com because it diluted the famous VISA credit card trademark. Although the court acknowledged that the word "visa" has ordinary meaning beyond the credit card company's commercial use, it said that trademark dilution was likely because use of the evisa.com domain name increases the possibility of customer confusion when searching for the Visa credit card company website. The court granted Visa International's motion for summary judgment with respect to the trademark infringement claim. However, the court denied plaintiff's motion for summary judgment with respect to its cybersquatting claim, finding that factual questions remained concerning whether the language school acted in bad faith in registering the domain name.

See also Gateway 2000, Inc. v. Gateway.com, Inc., 1997 U.S. Dist. LEXIS 2144 (E.D.N.C. Feb. 6, 1997) (denying computer manufacturer Gateway's request to enjoin consulting company Gateway from continued use and registration of the gateway.com domain name on the ground that it had only registered the "Gateway 2000" mark and not the "Gateway" mark); *Hasbro, Inc. v. Clue Computing, Inc.*, 66 F. Supp. 2d 117 (D. Mass. 1999), *aff'd*, 232 F.3d 1 (1st Cir. 2000) (granting summary judgment for defendant in dispute over the domain name clue.com where plaintiff asserted rights in the CLUE mark based on its popular board game because there was no likelihood that consumers would confuse plaintiff's game with defendant's services); *Network Network v. CBS, Inc.*, 2000 U.S. Dist. LEXIS 4751 (C.D. Cal. Jan. 19, 2000) (rejecting plaintiff's assertion that defendant's use of the TNN.com domain name for its television programming service, The Nashville Network, infringed plaintiff's rights on the ground that the goods and services offered by the companies were "wholly distinct.")

Domain Names Used for Harmful Purpose

Domain-name disputes in which the domain name has allegedly been used for a harmful purpose are analyzed under the usual principles of trademark infringement and dilution. Trademark dilution by tarnishment is often claimed in domain name disputes when a website sponsor offers, for example, pornographic material through a domain name that is the same as or similar to a trademark held by a business. Trademark dilution by blurring is often alleged when a website operator's use of a domain name that is the same as or similar to a business's trademark lessens the capacity of the business's mark to identify and distinguish the business's goods.

Domain Name Identical to Another's Trademark

Hasbro, Inc. v. Internet Entertainment Group, Ltd., 1996 U.S. Dist. LEXIS 11626 (W.D. Wash. Feb. 9, 1996).

Internet Entertainment Group (IEG) registered candyland.com for its adult entertainment site. Hasbro, Inc., the makers of the game "Candy Land," sought a preliminary injunction claiming that IEG's use created a negative image in connection with the Candy Land trademark. The U.S. District Court for the Western District of Washington found that the defendant's use of candyland.com had been "diluting the value of Hasbro's Candy Land mark" in violation of both the Washington State anti-dilution law and the Federal Trademark Dilution Act.

Planned Parenthood Federation of America, Inc. v. Bucci, 1997 U.S. Dist. LEXIS 3338 (S.D.N.Y. Mar. 24, 1997).

Planned Parenthood, an organization that provides reproductive health care information, sued the defendant for trademark infringement when the defendant registered the domain name plannedparenthood.com for his anti-abortion website. The court enjoined defendant's use of plannedparenthood.com, finding that there was a likelihood of confusion with the "Planned Parenthood" trademark. The court provided relief even though the defendant asserted he was using the domain name for a legitimate exercise of his First Amendment right to free speech.

Domain Name Similar, But Not Identical, to Another's Trademark

Toys "R" Us, Inc. v. Akkaoui, et al., 40 U.S.P.Q.2d 1836, 1996 U.S. Dist. LEXIS 17090 (N.D. Cal. Oct. 29, 1996).

Defendants registered adultsrus.com and used it to operate a website through which they sold "a variety of sexual devices and clothing" over the Internet. The court issued a preliminary injunction, finding that "'Adults R Us' tarnishe[d] the 'R Us' family of marks by associating them with a line of sexual products that are inconsistent with the image Toys 'R' Us has striven to maintain for itself."

Peterson Publishing Co. v. Blue Gravity Communications, 2000 U.S. Dist. LEXIS 6966 (D.N.J., Jan. 21, 2000).

The owner of *Teen Magazine* obtained a temporary restraining order against the operator of the website teenmagazine.com, a pornographic site. The temporary restraining order enjoined the defendants from using or transferring teenmagazine.com and required the defendants to turn over the domain name to the plaintiff.

 *Ty, Inc. v. Perryman*, 306 F.3d 509 (7th Cir. 2002), *cert. denied*, 123 S. Ct. 1750 (2003).

Ty, Inc., manufacturer of the well-known beanbag animals "Beanie Babies" and holder of the "Beanie Babies" trademark, sued Perryman, the owner of a second-hand beanbag plush toy retailer operating under the domain name bargainbeanies.com. The suit alleged trademark infringement under the Lanham Act. The trial court granted Ty, Inc.'s request for an injunction, but the Court of Appeals for the Seventh Circuit reversed the injunction, with one exception. Because the defendant, Perryman, was in the business of selling the very product to which the trademark attached, it would be illogical to prohibit her from using the mark: it would be like "forbidding a used car dealer who specializes in selling Chevrolets to mention the name in his advertising." *Ty, Inc. v. Perryman*, 306 F.3d at 509. The court allowed Perryman to continue using the domain name, operating her website, and referring to "Beanies," except when referring to beanbag plush toys that were not manufactured by Ty, Inc.

Domain Name Unlawfully Appropriated

Not surprisingly, a court found liability where defendant fraudulently transferred a domain name to himself and then used the domain name to operate a profitable website.

Kremen v. Cohen, 337 F.3d 1024 (9th Cir. 2003).

The plaintiff, Kremen, registered sex.com with Network Solutions (NSI) on May 9, 1994, in the name of a fictitious business, Online Classified, Inc. (OCI). In October 1995, the defendant, Cohen, forged a letter to NSI in the name of Kremen's housemate, Sharon Dimmick, that asserted that she was president of OCI and that she wished to transfer the domain name to Cohen. NSI transferred the name, and the defendant began operating a pornographic site at sex.com. The court found that the defendant, whose sex.com website generated substantial revenue, had used fraud to obtain the name from Network Solutions. Therefore, the court granted summary judgment for the plaintiff, holding that a domain name is a form of intangible property and thus the transfer was invalid under the property rule that a "forged document is void *ab initio* and constitutes a nullity." The court ordered the domain name to be returned immediately to its rightful owner and froze $25 million in the defendant's assets.

On appeal, the Court of Appeals for the Ninth Circuit considered whether NSI could be liable for its role in transferring the sex.com domain name to Cohen based on a claim of unlawful "conversion" of property. (In tort law, "conversion" is wrongfully possessing or disposing of another's personal property as if it were one's own.) The court concluded that a domain name is properly subject to the law of "conversion," likening a registrar's transfer of a domain name without the registrant's authorization to a corporation's giving away someone's shares under similar circumstances. The court remanded to the trial court the question of whether NSI improperly disposed of Kremen's property: the sex.com domain name.

Cybersquatting and Typosquatting

The term "cybersquatting" describes the act of obtaining a trademark-associated domain name with the aim of benefiting from the association with the mark. "Typosquatting" is the registration of a domain name that is similar to another's for the purpose of capitalizing on typos that may lead the user to the squatter's website rather than the site the user intends to locate. Cybersquatter and typosquatter motivations may include a desire to market a competing or entirely different product or service or to sell the domain name back to the trademark owner for a profit.

Prior to the 1999 enactment of the Anticybersquatting Consumer Protection Act (ACPA), discussed below, cybersquatting and typosquatting cases were analyzed under the traditional principles of trademark infringement and dilution.

Pre-ACPA Cases

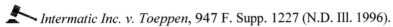 *Intermatic Inc. v. Toeppen*, 947 F. Supp. 1227 (N.D. Ill. 1996).

Dennis Toeppen registered the domain name intermatic.com, based on the plaintiff's "Intermatic" trademark for electrical and electronic products. The court found that the Intermatic mark was "famous" and that Toeppen's registration of the intermatic.com domain for the purpose of selling it to Intermatic was "sufficient to meet the 'commercial use' requirement of the Federal Dilution Act." The court found that Toeppen had lessened the capacity of Intermatic to identify and distinguish its goods and services by means of the Internet, and had diluted the Intermatic mark.

Panavision International, L.P. v. Toeppen, 141 F.3d 1316 (9th Cir. 1998).

Toeppen registered the domain name Panavision.com, used it to display an aerial view of Pana, Illinois, and offered to release it to the owner of the "Panavision" trademark for $13,000. The Court of Appeals for the Ninth Circuit affirmed the entry of summary judgment against Toeppen, finding that his actions violated California and federal trademark dilution laws and that his use of Panavision on the website diluted the distinctive quality of the trademark.

Microsoft Corp. v. Karr, et al., No. 98-4245 (S.D. Tex. 1998).

Microsoft filed suit against two Texans, Kurtis Karr and Kenny Brewer, who had registered microsoftwindows.com and nine other domain names, allegedly with the intent to sell them to Microsoft. Microsoft alleged trademark infringement and misleading the public. The court ordered the domain names to be relinquished to Microsoft.

PaineWebber v. Fortuny, No. 99-0456-A, 1999 U.S. Dist. LEXIS 6552 (E.D. Va. Apr. 9, 1999).

The court issued a preliminary injunction against a Miami man who allegedly linked the address wwwpainewebber.com to a pornographic website. The defendant allegedly sought to capitalize on typographical errors and lure people to his pornographic sites. The court held that, "Paine Webber is a famous mark that will be diluted . . . by being linked with pornography." Network Solutions was ordered to place the domain name on "hold."

The Anticybersquatting Consumer Protection Act

Enactment of the ACPA. The Anticybersquatting Consumer Protection Act (ACPA) became effective on November 29, 1999, as an addition to the federal Lanham Act. *See* 15 U.S.C. § 1125(d). The ACPA was enacted to address perceived deficiencies under traditional law that limited the ability of trademark owners to stop others from registering and using domain names that were intended to trade off the goodwill developed in their marks. For example, a claim of trademark infringement or dilution under the Lanham Act requires "use" of a mark. Courts have generally found "use" to exist where the defendant had an active website or offered to sell the registration for the domain name to the trademark owner. Where the cybersquatter simply registered the domain name and did nothing more, the courts could not find "use" and therefore there was no remedy for the trademark owner. *See Juno Online Services L.P. v. Juno Lighting, Inc.*, 979 F. Supp. 684, 691-92 (N.D. Ill. 1997) (no remedy under the Lanham Act for "warehousing" a domain name). In addition, if the cybersquatter used the domain name for a website but not for one in a field similar to that of the trademark owner, there might not be a likelihood of consumer confusion as required for a finding of trademark infringement. In such instances, the only remedy might lie in a cause of action for dilution of a famous mark. The new law was written to overcome such problems.

The ACPA imposes liability on a person who registers, traffics in, or uses a domain name that is identical or confusingly similar to a distinctive mark or dilutes a famous mark, and has a bad-faith intent to profit from the domain name.

The ACPA outlines nine factors that a court may consider in determining whether bad faith exists: (1) the intellectual property rights that the defendant has in the domain name; (2) the extent to which the domain name is the same as the defendant's name or nickname; (3) the defendant's prior lawful use of the domain name in making an offer of goods or services; (4) the defendant's noncommercial or fair use of the mark in the website; (5) the defendant's intent to divert customers to a website that could harm the goodwill of the mark; (6) whether the defendant has offered to assign the domain name for monetary gain without use or whether the defendant intended to use the name; (7) whether the defendant provided false contact information when applying for the domain name; (8) whether the defendant registered multiple domain names that are confusingly similar to distinctive marks or dilute famous marks; and (9) whether the mark is famous or distinctive.

Remedies. The owner of the mark may seek actual or statutory damages (from $1,000 to $100,000 per domain name) and a court order requiring the forfeiture, cancellation, or transfer of the domain name. (Actual damages are damages awarded to compensate the plaintiff for demonstrable injury. Statutory damages can be awarded by a court without regard to whether they are commensurate with any injury actually suffered by the plaintiff.)

In rem Action. The ACPA allows the owner of a mark to bring an action against the domain name itself, rather than the domain-name registrant, if the registrant cannot be located. (An action brought against personal, real, or intellectual property is referred to as *in rem*, as distinguished from an action brought against a person or other entity, which is referred to as *in personam*). The relevant provision of the ACPA states that the owner of a mark may maintain an *in rem* action against an infringing domain name if (1) the action is brought in the jurisdiction where the registrar or registry of the infringing domain name is located, or where the owner of the mark has deposited with the court documents sufficient to establish "control and authority regarding the disposition of the registration;" and (2) *in personam* jurisdiction over the registrant does not exist. 15 U.S.C. § 1125(d)(2)(A),(C). *See Mattel Inc. v. Barbie-club.com*, 310 F.3d 293 (2d Cir. 2002) (holding that an *in rem* action may only be filed in the district where the registrar or other domain name authority is located, despite statutory language suggesting that jurisdiction could be created by depositing documents establishing control and authority of the domain name with a court in another district); *Fleetboston Financial Corp. v.*

Fleetbostonfinancial.com, 138 F. Supp. 2d 121 (D. Mass. 2001) (stating that *in rem* actions may only be filed "in the judicial district in which the domain name registry, registrar, or other domain name authority is located.").

Although the element of bad faith is discussed solely in the *in personam* section of the ACPA, some courts have held that bad faith is a substantive element of *in rem* ACPA actions, as well. *See Hartog & Co., AS v. SWIX.com*, 136 F. Supp. 2d 531 (E.D. Va. 2001); *Harrods Ltd. v. Sixty Internet Domain Names*, 110 F. Supp. 2d 420 (E.D. Va. 2000); and in a related case, *Harrods Ltd. v. Sixty Internet Domain Names*, 157 F. Supp. 2d 658 (E.D. Va. 2001), *aff'd in part, rev'd in part, remanded by* 302 F.3d 214 (4th Cir. 2002); *BroadBridge Media, LLC v. Hypercd.com*, 106 F. Supp. 2d 505 (S.D.N.Y. 2000). However, the U.S. Court of Appeals for the Fourth Circuit has held that a plaintiff does not need to establish bad faith to prevail in an *in rem* trademark infringement and dilution action. *Cable News Network v. Cnnews.com*, No. 02-1112, slip op. (4th Cir. Jan. 23, 2003). See page 74 for further discussion of this case.

A plaintiff may not proceed simultaneously *in personam* and *in rem*, but may amend its complaint or re-file if unable to sustain the claim initially pled. *See Alitalia-Linee Aeree Italiane S.p.A. v. CASINOALITALIA.COM*, 128 F. Supp. 2d 340 (E.D. Va. 2001); *V'soske, Inc. v. vsoske.com*, No. 00-CIV-6099 (DC), 2001 WL 546567 (S.D.N.Y. May 23, 2001) (granting plaintiff leave to amend its complaint to include an *in rem* action against defendant domain name).

The *in rem* provisions of the ACPA have been found Constitutional by the U.S. Court of Appeals for the Fourth Circuit. The court concluded that domain names are property; by registering the domains within a state's jurisdiction, a registrant exposes the domain names to the state's jurisdiction—at least for the purpose of determining proper ownership. *See Porsche Cars North America, Inc. v. Porsche.net*, 302 F.3d 248, No. 01-2703 (4th Cir. Aug. 23, 2002); *Harrods Ltd. v. Sixty Internet Domain Names*, 302 F.3d 214, No. 00-2414 (4th Cir. Aug. 23, 2002).

Jurisdiction of ACPA

Jay D. Sallen d/b/a J.D.S. Enterprises v. Corinthians Licenciamentos LTDA, 273 F.3d 14 (1st Cir. 2001).

The defendants asserted that they had rights in Brazil to the name "Corinthiao," which is the name of a popular soccer team in Brazil and the Portuguese equivalent of "Corinthians." Sallen was the initial registrant of the corinthian.com domain name. An arbitration panel originally ordered the domain name transferred to the soccer team under the UDRP (discussed later in the chapter at page 75). Sallen appealed to federal court. The trial court declined to rule on the case, saying that there was no actual controversy because the defendants never claimed that Sallen had violated the ACPA. The Court of Appeals for the First Circuit overturned the decision, finding that a registrant who has lost a domain name under the UDRP has a right to sue in court for an injunction ordering return of the domain name if the registrant can show that the registration and use of the domain name was not unlawful under the ACPA. The case was sent back to the trial court, but the parties apparently settled before the trial court rendered a decision.

Dluhos v. Strasberg, 321 F.3d 365 (3rd Cir. 2003).

The parties were embroiled in a dispute over the domain name leestrasberg.com. The owner of the trademark "Lee Strasberg" (the name of the well-known acting teacher), seeking to have the domain name transferred, filed a claim with an arbitration panel of the National Arbitration Forum (NAF), under the UDRP, discussed at page 75. The domain name registrant submitted a letter to the NAF panel stating he would not submit to the UDRP. Thereafter, the domain name registrant filed a complaint in a federal court in New Jersey challenging the constitutionality of the UDRP. Before resolution of the federal suit, the UDRP panel found in favor of the complainant and ordered transfer of the domain name. The federal trial court then dismissed the suit for failure to state a claim. The plaintiff/domain name registrant appealed the dismissal. On appeal, the U.S. Court of Appeals for the Third Circuit considered whether losing the UDRP proceeding provided the plaintiff with a federal cause of action under the ACPA. The court determined that the ACPA provides registrants with a federal cause of action when a registrant loses a domain name in a UDRP proceeding. (For a discussion of this case in connection with the standard of review a federal court should apply in reviewing a UDRP decision, see page 76.)

Globalsantafe Corp. v. globalsantafe.com, 250 F. Supp. 2d 610 (E.D. Va. 2003).

An individual in South Korea registered the domain name globalsantafe.com one day after the plaintiff's announcement of a corporate merger that created the entity Global Santa Fe. The domain name was registered via a South Korean registrar, through a U.S. registry. The plaintiff filed an *in rem* action under the ACPA in a U.S. court seeking transfer of the domain name, and, following completion of the merger, filed an application to register the trademark "Globalsantafe." When the registrant did not respond to the complaint, the trial court entered a default judgment that the domain name registration violated the ACPA, and ordered the domain name registry to transfer the domain name to the plaintiff. That order was subsequently extended to the South Korean registrar. The defendant/registrant filed an action in a South Korean court to stop the transfer of the domain name. The South Korean court held that the U.S. court lacked jurisdiction to extend the order to a South Korean entity and entered an injunction prohibiting the South Korean registrar from transferring the domain name. On plaintiff's motion to order the U.S. registry to cancel the domain name registration, the trial court agreed with the plaintiff that it could exercise jurisdiction over the U.S. registry under the ACPA to order the cancellation of the domain name, and that the domain name registration violated the ACPA. The ACPA authorized the court to grant plaintiff's request to order the American registry to cancel the domain name registration. In the court's view, applying the ACPA to achieve this end was the least intrusive means of canceling the domain name registration without the South Korean registrar's cooperation in transferring the domain name.

America Online, Inc. v. aol.org, 259 F. Supp. 2d 449 (E.D. Va. 2003).

An earlier judgment by the federal trial court (*see America Online, Inc. v. aol.org*, No. 02-1116-A (E.D. Va. Nov. 15, 2002) (Judgment Order)) had directed a domain name registrar, headquartered in China, to transfer the domain name aol.org to the plaintiff America Online. Instead, at the registrant's request, the domain name registrar transferred the domain name to another foreign registrar, located in South Korea. America Online requested that a U.S. trial court direct the .org domain name registry to transfer the disputed domain name to AOL. The trial court first noted that the court that issued the initial order had jurisdiction, and that America Online had established a claim of trademark infringement. The court found that ordering the .org registry to transfer the domain name when the foreign registrar refused to do so was an appropriate remedy under the ACPA. According to the court, international comity did not proscribe ordering the transfer because the location of the .org registry in Virginia was sufficient to establish presence in the jurisdiction. According to the court, the transfer order would not be an extraterritorial application of the Lanham Act, and it would not be unfair to exercise jurisdiction over foreign registrants who chose to register domain names in the U.S. .org registry rather than in a foreign top-level domain registry or country code domain registry.

The ACPA Can Apply Retroactively

Minarik Electric Co. v. Electro Sales Co., No. 2001-12352-RBC (D. Mass. Sept. 26, 2002).

A prior judgment under trademark law does not bar a later claim of infringement and cybersquatting. The plaintiff, Minarik Electric, had failed in its 1996 trademark infringement suit against the defendant, Electro Sales, complaining that Electro Sales had improperly registered and used the domain name minarik.com. At the time of the original suit, Electro was an authorized distributor of Minarik's products. A federal court in California granted the defendant's motion for summary judgment because the use of Minarik's mark was in furtherance of the distribution contract. The contractual arrangement expired in 1997. In December 2001, Minarik brought suit again, complaining of Electro's continued use of the MINARIK trademark. Due to the change in the business relationship between the parties and the enactment of the ACPA, the U.S. District Court for the District of Massachusetts held that the 1996 suit did not bar the 2001 action.

Ford Motor Co. v. Catalanotte, 342 F.3d 543 (6th Cir. 2003)

Catalonotte, a former employee of the Ford Motor Company who knew that Ford published an employee newspaper called *Ford World*, registered the domain name fordworld.com. Catalonotte registered the domain name in 1997, prior to the 1999 enactment of the ACPA. In October 2000, Catalonotte contacted Ford officers with an offer to sell the fordworld.com domain name to Ford. Ford brought a claim against Catalonotte, claiming trademark infringement and cyberpiracy under the ACPA. The trial court awarded Ford injunctive relief and statutory damages for Catalonotte's trafficking of the domain name in bad faith in contravention of the ACPA. On appeal, Catalonotte argued that he could not be required to pay statutory damages because he registered the domain name before the ACPA's enactment. The appellate court disagreed, concluding that liability can be based on trafficking of a domain name that occurred after the ACPA's enactment, regardless of when the domain name was registered.

Liability of Domain-Name Registrars under the ACPA

Lockheed Martin Corp. v. Network Solutions, Inc., 141 F. Supp. 2d 648 (N.D. Tex. 2001).

Plaintiff owns several federal registrations for famous marks. The defendant domain name registrar permitted a third party to register domain names that were identical or confusingly similar to the plaintiff's marks. The plaintiff sued the defendant domain name registrar, claiming that the registrations were obtained in violation of the ACPA. A federal judge in Texas dismissed the action, holding that domain name registrars have no duty to perform gatekeeper functions when registering domain names; the ACPA was not intended to impose liability on the registrars. The court held that the language in the ACPA that prohibits improper "registration" was intended only to apply to the party *obtaining* the domain name.

Hawes v. Network Solutions, Inc., 337 F.3d 377 (4th Cir. 2003)

Hawes filed an action in a federal court against Network Solutions after Network Solutions transferred his domain name, lorealcomplaints.com, to L'Oreal, the owner of the "Loreal" trademark. Initially, L'Oreal filed a trademark infringement suit against Hawes in a French court seeking cancellation of the domain name. Upon learning of that action, Network Solutions transferred the disputed domain name to L'Oreal. Hawes brought suit in a U.S. District Court, alleging that Network Solutions breached the Domain Name Registration Agreement when it transferred the disputed domain name to L'Oreal, and that his registration and use of the domain name did not violate the Lanham Act. The trial court dismissed Hawes' claims and the U.S. Court of Appeals for the Sixth Circuit affirmed. The court stated that although the domain name registrar was generally exempt from trademark liability under 15 U.S.C. § 1114(2)(D)(i)(II)(bb), the statute imposes potential liability on a registrar when the registrar transfers a domain name during the pendency of a court action without permission from the court. Here, the court held, the French proceeding did not qualify as an "action" for purposes of the statute because it was not an ACPA action. Accordingly, the domain name registrar was exempt from liability for transferring the domain name.

Liability of Domain Name Registrars for "Coming Soon" Pages

Domain name registrars often link registered domain names to a placeholder page that announces that the registrant's site is under construction and will be "Coming Soon." These "Coming Soon" pages may include banner advertisements for the registrar's services, as well as advertisements for the registrar's sponsors. Some domain name registrants may not be aware that registrars engage in this practice.

Zurakov v. Register.com, No. 600703/01 (N.Y. Sup. Ct. July 25, 2001).

Zurakov had registered the domain name www.laborzionist.org with Register.com, and while Zurakov was constructing his site, Register.com set up the domain name to resolve to a "Coming Soon" page containing banner advertisements for Register.com and its sponsors. Zurakov claimed that his domain-name registration gave him an exclusive property right in the domain name and that the "Coming Soon" page interfered with that right and deprived him of the benefits of the parties' service contract. The court held that Zurakov only had a contract right, not a property right, in www.laborzionist.org because the domain name was merely a product of the service contract with Register.com and was not a registered patent or trademark. Because the service agreement governed the parties' contract rights, it alone governed Zurakov's rights in the domain name. The court found that Zurakov "received everything he bargained for under the service contract" because the contract explicitly provided that "register.com may suspend, cancel, transfer or modify [Zurakov's] use of the services at any time, for any reason, in register.com's sole discretion." *Zurakov*, No. 600703/01 at 4-5. Further, the court noted that Register.com fully disclosed its practice of displaying a "Coming Soon" page in both the "Frequently Asked Questions" and the "Help" sections of the Register.com website, and Zurakov had the ability to delete the "Coming Soon" page by following the instructions set forth in those sections. Accordingly, the court granted Register.com's motion to dismiss.

Cybersquatting Cases under the ACPA

For the most part, courts have found violations of the ACPA where a similar domain name was registered for purposes of sale, or where the defendant was a competitor of the trademark owner or was aware of the trademark owner's prior rights in the mark. The ACPA might not apply, however, to Internet sites specializing in auctioning domain names. *See Bird v. Parsons*, 2002 U.S. App. LEXIS 9543 (6th Cir. May 21, 2002) (finding that domain-name registrars and companies that provide an auction site for registered domain names are not liable for third-party infringement); *Ford Motor Co. v. Greatdomains.com*, No. 177 F. Supp. 2d 656 (E.D. Mich. 2001) (finding that an Internet auction site cannot be held liable for third-party violations of the ACPA when the site offered for auction domain names that incorporated plaintiff's trademarks, including fordtrucks.com, jaguarcenter.com, and lincolntrucks.com).

Sporty's Farm LLC v. Sportsman's Market, Inc., 202 F.3d 489 (2d Cir.), *cert. denied*, 530 U.S. 1262 (2000).

The ACPA was enacted while this case was on appeal. The U.S. Court of Appeals for the Second Circuit used the new act to affirm an award of injunctive relief. The trial court had decided the case based on the Federal Trademark Dilution Act. Sportsman's Market, Inc., a catalog company known for selling aviation products, had been using the mark "sporty's" to identify its products since the 1960s. Omega Engineering, Inc., a mail-order catalog company that primarily sold scientific process instruments, formed a subsidiary, Pilot's Depot, LLC, in late 1994 or early 1995 to sell aviation-related products by mail order. Omega then registered the domain name sportys.com. Nine months later, Omega formed another subsidiary, Sporty's Farm, to sell Christmas trees, and transferred the rights to the domain name to that subsidiary. The Second Circuit found that "sporty's" was a distinctive mark owned by Sportsman's Market, and that sportys.com was confusingly similar to the mark. The court also found "more than enough evidence" to find bad faith. First, neither Sporty's Farm nor Omega had any intellectual property rights in sportys.com when Omega registered the domain name. Second, the domain name was not the legal name of the party that registered it. Third, Sporty's Farm did not use the website until after the lawsuit had been filed. Fourth, Omega planned to enter into direct competition with Sportsman's Market, Inc. and Omega's owners were fully aware of Sportsman's Market's rights in the "sporty's" mark. Finally, no credible explanation was given for Omega's registration of sportys.com.

Northern Light Technology, Inc. v. Northern Lights Club, 97 F. Supp. 2d 96 (D. Mass. 2000), *aff'd*, 236 F.3d 57 (1st Cir. 2001), *cert. denied*, 121 S. Ct. 2263 (2001).

Northern Light Technology, Inc., owner of northernlight.com, brought suit against the owner of northernlights.com alleging trademark infringement and violation of the ACPA. The defendant used the northernlights.com domain to run a website for the Northern Lights Club, a club with no actual members, and allegedly had offered to sell the domain name to Northern Light Technology. The court found that the defendant demonstrated bad faith by registering the domain name in question, as well as other domain names of known trademarks (*e.g.,* yankees1.com, rollingstones.com, evinrude.com), by disregarding numerous cease-and-desist letters and by its willingness to sell the northernlights.com domain name. The court also compared the ACPA's "confusingly similar" standard to the traditional trademark infringement "likelihood of confusion" test and stated, "for purposes of [the ACPA], Congress intended simply a comparison of the mark and the allegedly offensive domain name." Therefore, the court concluded that the plaintiff was likely to succeed on its ACPA claim, and issued a preliminary injunction accordingly.

But see Mattel, Inc. v. Internet Dimensions, Inc., 2000 U.S. Dist. LEXIS 9747 (S.D.N.Y. July 13, 2000) (finding defendant had acted in bad faith in registering barbiesplaypen.com and noting that the ACPA's "confusingly similar" standard is different from the "likelihood of confusion" standard for trademark infringement).

E.&J. Gallo Winery v. Spider Webs Ltd., 129 F. Supp. 2d 1033 (S.D. Tex. 2001), *aff'd*, 286 F.3d 270 (5th Cir. 2002).

Spider Webs registered nearly 2,000 domain names, based on the names of famous places, people, and companies, including the domain name ErnestandJulioGallo.com. The company spent an average of $70 per domain name, but offered the domain names for sale on eBay.com and on its own website for substantially higher prices, seeking millions of dollars for some. The defendant admitted that it intended to sell the Gallo domain name to the famous wine maker. The lower court rejected the defendant's claims that the ACPA was unconstitutional as overbroad or as an unconstitutional taking, explaining that the law is not retroactive in application, even though it had been enacted after the defendant had registered the Gallo name, because cybersquatting is a continuing wrong. The defendant was enjoined from using the domain name as well as from registering any domain name containing the name "Gallo" or a combination of the names "Ernest" and "Julio."

On April 3, 2002, the Court of Appeals for the Fifth Circuit affirmed the trial court's ruling, stating that defendant's plan to maintain the domain name registrations with the intent to sell them to trademark owners in the event the ACPA is declared unconstitutional was a basis for a finding of bad-faith use of the domain name.

Victoria's Cyber Secret v. Victoria's Secret Catalogue, Inc., 161 F. Supp. 2d 1339 (S.D. Fla. 2001).

The defendant, the lingerie manufacturer and retailer Victoria's Secret, had filed an administrative action under the UDRP in January 2001 contesting plaintiff's right to own victoriassexsecret.com, victoriassexysecret.com, victoriasexsecret.com, and victoriasexysecret.com. The domain names were not associated with any websites, but the plaintiff asserted that its domain names were going to be used for websites devoted to former Playboy Playmate of the Year Victoria Silvstedt. An arbitrator ordered the domain names transferred to the defendant, and the plaintiff then brought this action requesting a declaratory ruling that it could retain ownership of the names. The defendant counterclaimed, alleging trademark infringement and dilution, unfair competition, and cybersquatting.

The court granted the defendant's motion for summary judgment on all of its counterclaims. Regarding the ACPA claim, the court held that the plaintiff's registration and use of the domain names constituted a violation of the ACPA because the plaintiff had no valid trademark rights in the Victoria's Secret mark and none of the plaintiff's domain names bore a relation to the adult entertainment websites that the plaintiff proposed to create. Further, the plaintiff had previously agreed to transfer the domain names to the defendant but rescinded its promise. Therefore, the court concluded that the plaintiff registered the names with a bad-faith intent to trade upon the fame of the Victoria's Secret mark.

The court dismissed the plaintiff's complaint and issued a permanent injunction against the plaintiff, prohibiting it from using the Victoria's Secret trademarks and registering domain names incorporating a mark similar or identical to Victoria's Secret's marks. The court ordered the domain names transferred to the defendant, and awarded the defendant treble damages calculated on the basis of $10,000 in statutory damages for each bad-faith domain-name registration. The court also found that the circumstances of this case were "exceptional" such that the defendant was entitled to reasonable attorney fees and costs under the ACPA.

Caterpillar Inc. v. Telescan Technologies., LLC, No. 00-1111, 2002 U.S. Dist. LEXIS 3477 (C.D. Ill. Feb. 13, 2002).

The plaintiff, Caterpillar, Inc., a manufacturer of heavy equipment, brought suit against Telescan Technologies, LLC, charging trademark infringement, trademark dilution, and cybersquatting. Telescan had registered at least six domain names incorporating Caterpillar's mark, such as caterpillarusedequip.com, caterpillarequipment.com, and caterpillardealers.com.

The court found that Telescan's use of the mark was likely to cause confusion under 15 U.S.C. §§ 1114 and 1116 and that adding words to the marks, such as "dealers," did not lower the risk that Internet users would assume that the sites were sponsored by Caterpillar. Moreover, Telescan's listing of Telescan's affiliated heavy-equipment dealers increased the likelihood of confusion. These facts led to a determination that the defendant's site was designed to direct traffic to Telescan's own dealers, who were in the same market as the plaintiff. The court held that Telescan's use of the mark diluted Caterpillar's marks and that Telescan's registration of the domain names was in violation of the ACPA.

See also Saturn Corp. v. Saturn Service, Inc., No. 01-6939 (S.D. Fla. Sept. 13, 2001) (finding that defendant violated the ACPA by using the "Saturn" trademark in its domain name, www.saturnusedparts.com where defendant was in no way affiliated with Saturn, and was not authorized to use the Saturn name or marks in association with its businesses. Accordingly, the court issued a permanent injunction against defendant and ordered the infringing domain name transferred to Saturn.); *E-Stamp Corp. v. Lahoti*, No. 00-9287 (C.D. Cal. July 31, 2000) (enjoining registration and use of estamps.com and estampsnow.com, which defendant had offered to sell to E-Stamp Corporation); *Spear, Leeds & Kellogg v. Rosado*, 122 F. Supp. 2d 403 (S.D.N.Y. 2000) (ordering the transfer of several domain names incorporating plaintiff's "Redibook" mark and enjoining defendant from using marks similar to plaintiff's mark).

 Eurotech, Inc. v. Cosmos European Travels, 213 F. Supp. 2d 612 (E.D. Va. 2002).

Bad faith can also be evidenced by a failure to conduct a trademark search before establishing a domain name. The plaintiff, Eurotech, registered the domain name cosmos.com with the apparent intent to sell space on the site to the trademark holder, Cosmos. A World Intellectual Property Organization (WIPO) proceeding led to an order to transfer the domain name to the trademark holder. Eurotech brought suit in federal court under the ACPA seeking a declaration legitimizing the domain name and preventing the transfer. The court concluded that Eurotech was not an ongoing business and it did not have a legitimate purpose in securing the domain name. The court also found that Eurotech registered the domain name in bad faith, in part because it did not conduct a trademark search prior to registering the disputed domain name. The court therefore refused to declare that Eurotech had a legitimate right to the domain name.

Typosquatting Cases Under the ACPA

As discussed above at page 62, typosquatting is the registration of a domain name that differs from another domain name by only one or a few characters in the hope that users looking for a website will mistype the domain name and arrive accidentally at the typosquatter's site. While the ACPA does not address the practice of typosquatting specifically, courts have generally held that typosquatting is actionable as a form of cybersquatting under the ACPA.

 Bargain Bid v. Ubid & Belcher, 2000 U.S. Dist. LEXIS 3021 (E.D.N.Y. Jan. 3, 2000).

The plaintiff operated an online auction site at bargainbid.com. The defendant, Belcher, registered a misspelling, barginbid.com, and operated a site at that address that provided users with a link to an online auction site called "Ubid," a competitor of Bargain Bid. Belcher was a Ubid affiliate and received a fee for providing the link to the Ubid site. The court granted the plaintiff's request for a preliminarily injunction under the ACPA enjoining the defendants from using the marks and names Bargain Bid and Barginbid, and from indicating sponsorship or affiliation with the plaintiff.

 Shields v. Zuccarini, 254 F.3d 476 (3d Cir. 2001).

The plaintiff owned the trademark "Joe Cartoon" and used the name professionally for several years to identify his cartoons and related products. He also registered and used the domain name joecartoon.com. In 1999, the defendant registered the domain names joescartoon.com, joecarton.com, joescartons.com, joescartoons.com, and cartoonjoe.com. The plaintiff filed suit under the ACPA alleging that the defendant had registered the domain names in bad faith.

The court found that the registration of purposeful misspellings of a trademark does fall within the scope of the ACPA. The court stated that the plain meaning and the purpose of the ACPA encompass registering misspellings to increase website traffic. The court also rejected the defendant's fair-use argument because the defendant had added text to the sites criticizing the plaintiff's cartoons only after this suit was filed. Therefore, the court upheld the district court order granting a permanent injunction, statutory damages of $10,000 for each of the five domain names, and attorney fees.

In 2002, the Federal Trade Commission won a $1.9 million judgment against Zuccarini for his cybersquatting and typosquatting practices, as well as an order barring Zuccarini from diverting or obstructing consumers on the Internet and from participating in online "affiliate marketing programs" (defined by the court as revenue-sharing arrangements between online merchants and online content providers who market goods and services using ads and text links posted on websites). *Federal Trade Commission v. Zuccarini*, No. 01CV4854 (E.D. Pa. Apr. 9, 2002); *see also Electronic Boutiques Holdings Corp. v. Zuccarini*, 2000 U.S. Dist. LEXIS 15719 (E.D. Pa. Oct. 30, 2000) (imposing a total of $500,000 in damages for other violations of ACPA).

Toronto-Dominion Bank v. Karpachev, 188 F. Supp. 2d 110 (D. Mass. 2002).

The plaintiff brought suit under the ACPA against Boris Karpachev, a disgruntled former customer of the online brokerage services of TD Waterhouse Group, Inc., a subsidiary of the Toronto-Dominion Bank. Karpachev had registered 16 domain names that incorporated misspellings and alternative spellings of TD Waterhouse's domain name. The domain names linked to a site featuring criticism and disparaging remarks about TD Waterhouse. The court held that the intentional use of confusingly similar domain names to draw customers to a critical website was a bad-faith act under the federal anticybersquatting statute.

Foreign Nationals Under the ACPA

Courts in the United States have generally found that the ACPA applies equally to foreign nationals and extends to foreign websites that have sufficient contacts within the United States. (For discussion of international jurisdictional issues that apply to websites generally, *see* Chapter 9, pages 293 to 297.)

Barcelona.com, Inc. v. Excelentisimo Ayuntamiento de Barcelona, 330 F.3d 617 (4th Cir. 2003).

A Spanish citizen, Joan Cobo, registered the domain name barcelona.com with the registry Network Solutions. He developed a business plan to design a website for tourists in Barcelona, Spain, but he never received enough financing to develop the website. The city of Barcelona filed a UDRP complaint demanding that he transfer the domain name. A WIPO panel ordered the domain name transferred to the city. The panel concluded that the potential for consumer confusion when users visited the site expecting the official homepage of Barcelona constituted sufficient bad faith to warrant a transfer of the domain name. Cobo appealed to a federal trial court. The court ruled that the domain name should be transferred.

The U.S. Court of Appeals for the Fourth Circuit reversed the trial court's ruling based on its determination that the trial court had incorrectly applied Spanish law instead of U.S. law. The appellate court found that the ACPA requires application of the Lanham Act, not foreign law. Applying the Lanham Act, the court ruled that the domain name should not be transferred. Barcelona is a descriptive geographical designation, and thus warrants no trademark protection under the Lanham Act. Accordingly, the court ruled that Cobo's registration and use of the domain name Barcelona.com did not infringe the city's trademark rights.

Cable News Network v. Cnnews.com, 162 F. Supp. 2d 484 (E.D. Va. 2002), *aff'd in part*, No. 02-1112, slip op. (4th Cir. Jan. 23, 2003).

The plaintiff, Cable News Network, filed suit against an English-language site, based in Hong Kong, over the use of the cnnews.com domain name. The court ruled that use of the domain name in connection with the Hong Kong-based website was a use in commerce under the ACPA, and that the U.S. court had jurisdiction over the Hong Kong registrar in asking for the transfer of the domain name. The court found that the defendant had acted in bad faith in registering the domain name. The Fourth Circuit affirmed the trial court's exercise of *in rem* jurisdiction and its holding that the domain name should be transferred. The court held that an *in rem* trademark action does not require proof of bad faith, and vacated the portion of the lower court's opinion discussing bad faith.

Schmidheiny v. Weber, 164 F. Supp. 2d 484 (E.D. Pa. 2002), rev'd, 319 F.3d 581 (3d Cir. 2003).

Schmidheiny, a Swiss national, filed suit against Weber, who had registered the domain name Schmidheiny.com. The trial court held that the ACPA extended standing to foreign nationals to sue in the United States under the ACPA to protect use of surnames. This finding was not appealed. The trial court granted summary judgment to Weber, holding that the ACPA did not apply because the domain name was registered before the ACPA was enacted. The appellate court reversed, holding that the ACPA applied because Weber had re-registered the domain name, using a different registrar and under a different registrant name, after the ACPA had passed. The court held that "registration" is not limited to the initial registration of a domain name, but also covers "a new contract at a different registrar and to a different registrant." The court held that any other conclusion would allow a potentially infringing domain name to be sold repeatedly without the trademark owner's consent, if the domain name had been initially registered before enactment of the ACPA.

Domain-Name Dispute Resolution—Arbitration

In addition to remedies under the ACPA and trademark law, a party who wishes to obtain the transfer of a domain name may choose to initiate an arbitration proceeding. Domain-name registrants are required to submit to these arbitration proceedings under the terms of their agreements with their registrars.

Former Policy: The NSI Policy

The NSI dispute resolution policy allowed the owner of a federally registered trademark or a foreign trademark owner to register a complaint with NSI if its trademark was registered as a domain name by someone else. If the owner of the mark was able to demonstrate that it had a prior trademark registration, NSI would place the domain name "on hold."

NSI's dispute resolution policy provided no relief to the owner of a trademark that was substantially similar, but not identical, to the disputed domain name, or to owners of common law trademarks or state-registered trademarks. The policy also did not address concurrent uses of the same trademark in different lines of commerce, or conflicts between U.S. and foreign trademarks. *See Roadrunner Computer Systems, Inc. v. Network Solutions, Inc.*, No. 96-413-A (E.D. Va. June 21, 1996) (NSI refused to allow plaintiff to keep roadrunner.com, despite receipt of foreign trademark registration, after Warner Brothers, Inc., owner of "Road Runner" trademark in the United States, complained to NSI).

The Current Domain-Name Dispute Policy: Uniform Dispute Resolution Policy (UDRP)

Effective January 3, 2000, the Uniform Dispute Resolution Policy (UDRP), adopted by ICANN, governs disputes concerning all ".com," ".net," ".org," ".aero," ".biz," ".coop," ".info," ".museum," and ".name" domain names. The registrars for a number of country-code top-level domains (*e.g.*, ".nv" (Niue), ".tv" (Tuvalu), ".ws" (Western Samoa), ".ac" (Ascencion Island), ".gt" (Guatemala), ".sh" (St. Helena), and ".tt" (Trinidad and Tobago)) have also agreed to be bound by the UDRP.

Under the UDRP, a complainant can challenge a domain-name assignment by bringing a complaint before an authorized administrative dispute resolution service provider. A domain-name holder is not allowed to transfer the name to a new holder or to change registrars during administrative proceedings, or for 15 days after a proceeding is concluded. There are currently three authorized dispute resolution service providers:

- World Intellectual Property Organization (WIPO) (which is the sole dispute resolution service for ".edu" domain names). WIPO decisions are available at http://www.wipo.int/search/en/. In May 2003, WIPO received its 5,000th domain name dispute filed under the UDRP; at that time, it was averaging receipt of three new complaints each day.

- National Arbitration Forum (NAF). NAF decisions are available at http://www.arb-forum.com/domains/decisions.asp.

- CPR Institute for Dispute Resolution. These decisions are available at http://www.cpradr.org/ICANN_Cases.htm.

To prevail in a UDRP dispute in any of these fora, a complainant must establish three elements at an administrative proceeding:

1. that the domain name is identical or confusingly similar to a trademark or service mark in which the complainant has rights;

2. that the domain-name registrant has no rights or legitimate interests with respect to the name; and

3. that the domain name was registered and is being used in bad faith. The UDRP sets forth four nonexclusive factors that, if found, will be evidence of bad faith: (i) whether the domain name was registered primarily for the purpose of selling it for profit to a trademark owner or its competitors; (ii) whether the name was registered to prevent the trademark owner from using the mark in its domain name, provided the registrant has engaged in a pattern of this behavior; (iii) whether the registration was intended primarily to disrupt the business of a competitor; or (iv) whether the registrant used the domain name in an intentional attempt to attract users to a site, for commercial gain, by creating a likelihood of confusion as to the source of the site or a product on the site.

Remedies available under the UDRP include cancellation of the domain name or transfer to the complainant. Decisions are stayed for ten days to allow a losing party to file a complaint in court challenging the arbitration panel's findings. If such a complaint is filed, the administrative decision is stayed. A WIPO panel has held that the UDRP could not be used to resolve factual disputes over oral communications. *TAM Communications Inc. v. 3DNet Inc.*, Case No. D2002-1136 (WIPO Feb. 10, 2003) ("The conflicting versions of the parties' relationship and of the Respondent's right to use and Complainant's opposition to or acquiescence in such use is better left to the courts, with all the resources at their disposal, to resolve.").

Over 8,900 complaints involving nearly 15,000 domain names had been filed under the UDRP as of December 31, 2003. Of the cases decided through November 14, 2003, the trademark owner or complainant prevailed in 5,925 out of 7,455 cases. An additional 57 decisions had split results, with some of those decisions leading to the transfer of additional domain names. Over 10,200 domain names have been transferred or cancelled as a result of UDRP proceedings. The most recent statistics can be found at http://www.icann.org/udrp/proceedings-stat.htm.

The UDRP was challenged in a case brought against the Department of Commerce for promulgating the UDRP. In *Bord v. Banco de Chile*, Civ. Action No. 01-1360A (E.D. Va. May 15, 2002), a plaintiff who had a domain name transferred under the URDP argued that the Department of Commerce had unlawfully delegated policymaking authority to ICANN and that the UDRP is void because it is unconscionable. However, the court rejected the claim on the ground that the plaintiff was not able to show that he had standing to sue the Department of Commerce.

At least one federal appellate court has held that UDRP arbitrations do not constitute arbitrations within the meaning of the Federal Arbitration Act of 1925 (FAA), and are not entitled to judicial deference.

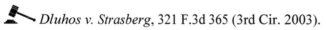 *Dluhos v. Strasberg*, 321 F.3d 365 (3rd Cir. 2003).

The parties were involved in a domain name dispute. The trademark owner brought the dispute to the National Arbitration Forum, pursuant to the UDRP. The domain name registrant filed a complaint in federal court challenging the constitutionality of the UDRP process. In the meantime, the UDRP panel ruled against the domain name registrant and ordered the domain name transferred to the trademark owner. The federal trial court reviewed the UDRP panel's decision, and, applying the FAA's deferential standard of review, upheld the panel's decision. On appeal, the U.S. Court of Appeals for the Third Circuit held that UDRP decisions do not fall under the FAA; federal courts are not bound to apply the FAA's deferential standard of review when reviewing a UDRP panel's decision. (The case also addressed whether the loss of a domain name in a UDRP proceeding provides a federal cause of action under ACPA. See page 66.)

UDRP Decisions

As discussed above, a complainant in a UDRP proceeding must prove that the registered domain is identical or confusingly similar to the complainant's protected trademark, that the registrant has no legitimate rights or interests in the domain name, and that the domain name has been registered and used in bad faith. If the complainant fails to prove one of these elements, the contested domain name will remain with the current registrant. The determination of these three issues is often quite fact-specific, and panels are not bound by precedent of prior panel decisions. Accordingly, generalizing from these decisions is difficult.

Element 1: Domain Name is Identical or Confusingly Similar to Trademark in Which Complainant Has Rights

Generally, any domain name that includes the trademark, or a "confusingly similar approximation," will be considered identical or confusingly similar to the trademark. *See e.g., The Rival Co. v. DVO Enterprises*, Case No. D2002-0265 (WIPO Aug. 2, 2002) (ordering transfer of crockpotrecipes.net domain name to the owner of Crock-Pot trademark); *Wal-Mart Stores, Inc. v. Richard MacLeod*, Case No. D2000-0662 (WIPO Sept. 19, 2000) (finding walmartsucks.com confusingly similar to "Wal-Mart"); *see also Dell Computer Corp. v. Farmi Phull*, Case No. D20001-0285 (WIPO Apr. 11, 2001) (finding dellonline.net and dellonline.org confusingly similar to "Dell"); *Adaptive Molecular Technologies, Inc. v. Woodward*, Case No. D2000-0006 (WIPO Feb. 28, 2000) (finding militec.com confusingly similar to trademarks "MILITEC (& design)" and "MILITEC-1"); *Ingersoll-Rand Co. v. Gully*, Case No. D2000-0021 (WIPO March 9, 2000) (finding ingersoll-rand.net, ingersoll-rand.org, and ingersollrand.org identical or confusingly similar to "Ingersoll Rand"). *But see A & F Trademark, Inc. v. Nestor*, Case No. D2003-0260 (WIPO May 24, 2003) (finding aberzombie.com not confusingly similar to the mark "Abercrombie," despite the phonetic and visual similarities, because Abercrombie is a surname used in a trademark whereas "zombie" has its own meaning).

In some instances, the inclusion of a registered trademark in a domain name was insufficient to render the domain name confusingly similar to such trademark. *See AT&T Corp. v. Gormally*, Case No. D2002-0738 (WIPO Oct. 2, 2002) (finding that the domain name attelephone.com was not confusingly similar to complainant's AT&T trademark because the website did not mislead consumers, the domain name was more likely to be conceptualized as "at telephone" than related to "AT&T," and the respondent never offered to sell the domain name). *Twentieth Century Fox Film Corp. v. Risser*, Case No. FA 0002000093761 (NAF May 18, 2000) (finding the domain names foxfashion.com, foxfashion.net, foxforfun.com, foxdownload.com, and tcfhv.com were deemed not to be confusingly similar to the "Fox" and "Twentieth Century Fox" trademarks, because the domain names were not suggestive of segments of the entertainment industry in which Fox participates. However, as discussed at page 102, the panel found that other domain names registered by the respondent, including foxnewsnetwork.com, foxvideos.com, and foxflicks.com, were confusingly similar to the "Fox" mark, and ordered their transfer.)

The tribunal's decision on this first UDRP factor, confusing similarity, may turn on the rights of the complainant in the trademark:

Bryant v. Yerke, AF-0315 (eResolution October 15, 2000).

The complainant had registered the mark AS SEEN ON THE INTERNET with the U.S. Patent and Trademark Office in conjunction with his Internet advertising company. The respondent registered the name Asseenontheinternet.com, but had not posted a website at that address and was allegedly attempting to sell the domain name. Despite these allegations of cybersquatting, the arbitrator declined to order transfer of the domain name, holding that the complainant had not established a trademark interest in the phrase despite the formal registration. This phrase was deemed to be merely descriptive and not to have acquired the distinctiveness in the marketplace as a source identifier required to justify trademark protection.

<u>Element 2: Lack of a Legitimate Right or Interest in the Domain Name</u>

There is no uniform definition of what constitutes a legitimate right or interest in a domain name for purposes of evaluating the registrant's rights in a trademark used as a domain name. Because the complainant has the burden of proving that the registrant of the domain name does not have a legitimate right in the name (as opposed to the registrant being required to prove that it has a legitimate right in the name), UDRP panels will find either that respondent has no legitimate right or interest in the disputed name, or that the complainant has failed to prove that the respondent lacks a legitimate interest.

For example, speculation in domain names has been determined not to be a legitimate right or interest. *See J.Crew International, Inc. v. crew.com*, Case No. D2000-0054 (WIPO Apr. 20, 2000) ("Speculation is not recognized by the Policy as a legitimate interest in a name, and the Policy should not be interpreted to hold that mere speculation in domain names is a legitimate interest."). (This case is also discussed at page 83.) Also, there is no legitimate right in using a domain name to "damage" the trademark owner. *Reg Vardy PLC v. Wilkinson*, Case No. D2001-0593 (WIPO July 3, 2001). (This case is also discussed at page 83.)

In *Digitronics Inventioneering Corp. v @Six.Net Registered*, a WIPO panel concluded that the complainant had failed to prove that the registrant lacked a legitimate interest in the domain name because the registrant had operated a business for five years under a name similar to the trademark and had registered domain names incorporating that business name. *Digitronics Inventioneering Corp. v. @Six.Net Registered*, Case No. D2000-0008 (WIPO March 1, 2000) (finding that the complainant could not prove that the respondent did not have a right or legitimate interest in sixnet.com and six.net, even though the complainant owned trademark "Sixnet"). Other examples that demonstrate when complainant failed to prove that the respondent did not have a legitimate right or interest in the domain name include:

Adaptive Molecular Technologies, Inc. v. Woodward, Case No. D2000-0006 (WIPO Feb. 28, 2000).

The complainant has trademarks in "Militec" (& design) and "Militec-1." The respondent had registered the domain name militec.com for a website that sold the complainant's Militec-1 product. The arbitration panel found that although there was "confusing similarity," questions as to whether the complainant acquiesced in use of domain name or whether use and registration of domain name constituted fair use, precluded a finding that the respondent had no "rights or legitimate interests" in the domain name.

Pearson v. Byers Choice, File No. FA92015 (NAF March 9, 2000).

The respondent, Byers Choice, registered the domain names byerschoice.com and buyerschoice.com with the intention of linking the names to the Byers Choice website. The respondent registered buyerschoice.com to ensure that customers who misspelled the Byers Choice name would nevertheless be able to locate the respondent's website. The complainant, who operated a real estate business under the trademark Buyers Choice, contested the respondent's right to own the buyerchoice.com domain name. The arbitration panel found that the complainant had failed to prove (1) that the respondent did not have a legitimate interest in the domain name, and (2) that the respondent had registered the domain name in bad faith.

Amazon.com, Inc. v. Amazonpic, Case No. D2002-0330 (WIPO July 22, 2002).

A South Korean company operated under the name amazonpic.com, and holds the trademark in the name in South Korea. Amazonpic.com sold DVDs via its website at the domain name. Amazon.com, the U.S.-based retailer, filed a complaint with WIPO to compel transfer of the name. A divided panel transferred the domain name despite the South Korean trademark registration and evidence that Amazon.com is not well-known in South Korea. The dissenters cautioned that this decision might preclude anyone from registering a domain name that includes "Amazon" because of Amazon.com's trademark.

Miller Brewing Company v. The Miller Family, File No. FA0201000104177 (NAF Apr. 15, 2002).

A UDRP panel ordered the domain name "Millertime.com" to be transferred to Miller Brewing Company. The name had been in use by the Miller family of San Mateo, California, who used the website to post family photos and also to offer educational services and to sell computer software. The panel found that there was no evidence that the family was ever commonly known by the domain name "millertime," and that the fact that the site was used for commercial purposes precluded a finding of noncommercial fair use.

Microsoft Corp. v. Goldman, Case No. D2003-0044 (WIPO Apr. 15, 2003).

The complainant was a well-known provider of computer software and related goods that used the federally registered "Windows" mark. The respondent was the operator of the website located at the domain name windowscasino.com, from which respondent operated an online casino and offered software for prospective online casino operators. Although the domain name was confusingly similar to the complainant's mark, the panel found that the respondent's use of the term "windows" in its domain name was insufficient to demonstrate lack of legitimate interest in the website because "windows" is a generic term and respondent had used the term to market itself in other ways. The panel also found no evidence of bad faith, and held in favor of respondent.

Anuncios en Directorios SA v. Alvarez, Case No. D2002-0973 (WIPO Jan. 22, 2003).

The respondent registered the domain name seccionamarilla.com as part of a business plan to offer telephone directory services on the web. The complainant owned trademark rights in "seccion amarilla" (yellow pages), but the panel noted that many countries consider "yellow pages" a generic term, not protectable as a trademark. The panel found that the respondent had a legitimate interest in the domain name because the respondent had developed a business plan for creating an online directory with yellow pages, white pages and classified advertisements. The respondent proved that it had solicited business, signed contracts, initiated trademark protection for its logo and created a corporation prior to receiving notice of complainant's suit. The panel further found respondent had not acted with bad faith because there was no evidence that the respondent had acquired the domain names to sell them; the respondent had made an offer to sell but the sale included both the domain name and the business. Therefore, the panel refused to transfer the domain name to the complainant.

 Bayerische Motoren Werke AG v. Quality Services, Case No. D2003-0077 (WIPO Mar. 18, 2003).

The complainant registered the "BMW" trademark in many jurisdictions, including the United States. The respondent registered the domain name bmw-service.com, and stated that it intended to use the website to establish a gripe site because the respondent was unsatisfied with the service provided by the complainant. The panel agreed with the complainant that the domain name was confusingly similar to the complainant's mark, and that the addition of "service" to the mark heightened, rather than alleviated, the likelihood of consumer confusion. The panel rejected the respondent's free speech claims because respondent produced no evidence that it had taken steps to create a gripe website. The panel found that the respondent did not possess legitimate rights or interests in the domain name. The panel also found evidence of bad faith because the website included an offer to sell the domain name. The panel ordered the domain name transferred to the complainant.

 HBP Inc. v. Front and Center Tickets Inc., Case No. D2002-0802 (WIPO Feb. 11, 2003).

The complainant had an exclusive license to use the "Daytona 500" mark in the United States in connection with the well-known automobile race. The respondent registered the domain names daytona500tickets.net and daytona500tickets.com and set up websites from which he planned to sell tickets to a variety of car races, including events that compete with the Daytona 500. A divided panel held that both domain names must be transferred to the complainant. The panel found the domain names to be confusingly similar to the "Daytona 500" mark because the addition of the common noun "tickets" to the mark did not dispel potential consumer confusion. The respondent argued that it used the domain names for a bona fide offering of goods, but the panel rejected its argument because the respondent had had previous dealings with the complainant: the respondent had registered the domain name daytona500.net. After the complainant contacted him requesting transfer of the domain name, the respondent transferred the domain name to the complainant. The panel found that respondent could not have concluded in good faith that the complainant would not object to the domain names currently before it. The panel also found the respondent had registered the domain names in bad faith because the respondent prominently used the complainant's mark on its webpage promoting competing events.

Element 3: The Domain Name Was Registered and Is Being Used in Bad Faith

There is no uniform definition of what constitutes bad-faith registration or use. Among the important factors are the registrant's conduct and intention in securing the domain name. *See Hearst Magazines Prop., Inc. v. Spencer*, Case No. FA0093763 (NAF Feb. 13, 2000) (finding that although the registrant had registered esquire.com before cybersquatting became a public issue, the fact that it had registered other names confusingly similar to well-known marks was indicative of bad faith).

One panel found that, in a bad-faith analysis of whether a respondent had registered a domain name intentionally to attract users to a website, the panel must apply an objective standard to determine whether the conduct was "intentional." The panel determined that the proper test is whether the consequence or effect of respondent's conduct was to attract users away from a complainant's website, regardless of the subjective intent of the respondent in registering the domain name. *Paule Ka v. Paula Korenek*, Case No. D2003-0453 (WIPO July 24, 2003) (finding respondent, who had registered the domain name paulekacreations.com after she acquired the nickname Paule Ka, registered the domain name in bad faith by intentionally attempting to attract Internet users from complainant, French fashion accessory company Paule Ka, because the objective result of the registration was that the domain name attracted Paule Ka customers to respondent's website).

If a party does not respond to allegations of bad-faith registration or use, that silence will be taken as evidence of bad faith. *See Cigna Corp. v. JIT Consulting*, AF-00174 (eResolution June 6, 2000) (finding failure to dispute allegations supports a conclusion of bad-faith registration); *Alcoholics Anonymous World Services, Inc. v. Lauren Raymond*, Case No. D2000-0007 (WIPO March 6, 2000) (fact that the respondent did not contest the allegations of the complaint allows an inference that evidence would not have been favorable to the respondent, which, in turn, allows an inference of bad faith).

Failure to Use a Domain Name

Decisions are split regarding whether failure to use a domain name can be considered a bad-faith use. At least two UDRP decisions have found that passive holding of a domain name, in light of evidence of bad-faith registration, may constitute bad-faith use:

 Telstra Corp. Ltd. v. Nuclear Marshmallows, Case No. D2000-0003 (WIPO Feb. 18, 2000).

Telstra owns the trademark "Telstra" and is the registrant of various domain names that include that mark. The respondent, who could not be identified, registered telstra.org, which did not resolve to a website or any other online presence. The arbitration panel concluded that the passive holding of the domain name by the respondent amounted to bad faith because Telstra's trademark has a strong reputation and is widely known, the respondent provided no evidence of any actual or contemplated good-faith use of the domain name, and the respondent took steps to conceal its identity. Given these factors, the panel concluded that there could be no active use of the domain name by the registrant that would be legitimate.

 University of Iowa v. Juraj Vyletelka, Case No. D2002-0349 (WIPO May 31, 2002).

The complainant university had used the trademark "Virtual Hospital" for nearly ten years before it brought the action, and had owned a federal registration for the mark since 1997. The respondent registered virtualhospital.com, but the corresponding website remained "under construction." The respondent indicated that he planned to conduct business activities using the domain. In a letter to the complainant, he requested $10,000 in lost revenue from the planned business activities in exchange for transferring the domain name. The panel found that the respondent's passive holding of the website, coupled with his demand for $10,000, constituted bad faith and ordered the domain name transferred to the complainant.

However, some panels have concluded that passive holding alone does not constitute bad faith registration of a domain name. *See Ingram Micro, Inc. v. Ingredients Among Modern Microwaves*, Case No. D2002-0301 (WIPO May 15, 2002) (finding that the complainant failed to establish bad-faith registration where the registrant had not made an effort to sell the contested domain name, the registrant did not attempt to disrupt the mark owner's business and made no attempt to attract users to the site for commercial gain); *Mast-Jagermeister AG v. Jones*, Case No. D2002-1044 (WIPO Jan. 8, 2003) (finding that the complainant failed to establish bad faith in respondent's registration of a domain name incorporating the English translation of complainant's trademark because this translation was not widely known in the United States, a plausible good faith use of the website by respondent was conceivable, and there were numerous U.S. registrations that incorporated the mark's English translation).

Complainant Proved Bad Faith

The following decisions are examples of situations in which arbitration panels found evidence of bad-faith use.

 Twentieth Century Fox Film Corp. v. Risser, Case No. FA 0002000093761 (NAF May 18, 2000).

Respondent registered sixteen domain names that were variations on the "Fox" trademark, including foxnewsnetwork.com, foxvideos.com, and foxflicks.com. The panel found the domain names were obtained in bad faith because of registrant's intent to sell them to complainant Twentieth Century Fox.

 Sankyo Co., Ltd. v. Zhu Jia Jun, Case No. D2000-1791 (WIPO March 23, 2001).

The complainant owns the trademark "Sankyo," which is represented by a Chinese character identical to the character corresponding to the respondent's domain name. The panel concluded that the respondent registered its address in bad faith for the purpose of selling the domain name to the complainant. This is the first case finding that a multilingual domain name (MDN), which incorporates nonASCII characters, infringes an existing trademark. (ASCII stands for "American Standard Code for Information Interchange.")

 Dell Computer Corporation v. Parmi Phull, Case No. D2001-0285 (WIPO Apr. 11, 2001).

The respondent, a resident of Spain, registered the domain names dellonline.net and dellonline.org, which linked to his personal website where the domain names were listed for sale among other domain names he had acquired. In finding bad faith, the panel held that advertising to the public at large that the domain name is for sale is evidence of bad faith and is properly regarded as an offer to sell the domain name to the complainant or a competitor.

 America Online, Inc. v. John Deep Buddy USA, Inc., Case No. FA0103000096795 (NAF May 14, 2001).

The respondent operated a messaging and file-swapping site called "Aimster," located at aimster.com, which had functions similar to Napster and AIM (AOL Instant Messaging). The respondent registered misspelled variations of aimster.com that resolved to the Aimster site. A disclaimer on the Aimster site stated that "Aimster is in no way affiliated with America Online." A divided arbitration panel ordered the transfer of all the domain names to AOL, holding that the domain names infringed on AOL's AIM trademark. The dissenting panelist argued that the UDRP proceeding should be reserved for more egregious violations and that use of AIM was likely fair as it has developed a generic descriptive identity much as have the terms "kleenex" and "scotch" tape.

Reg Vardy PLC v. Wilkinson, Case No. D2001-0593 (WIPO July 3, 2001).

The complainant, Reg Vardy PLC, operates car dealerships in England and Scotland and operates a website at regvardy.com. The respondent, David Wilkinson, was involved in a dispute with Reg Vardy regarding the purchase of a van, and he registered the domain names reg-vardy.com, reg-vardy.net, and reg-vardy.org in order to associate them with a website containing disparaging remarks about Reg Vardy. The arbitrator found that Wilkinson's expressed intent to "disrupt [Reg Vardy's] business" was a valid basis for finding bad faith, even though Wilkinson was not a competitor of Reg Vardy.

Cable News Network, LLP v. Khouri, Claim No. FA0208000117876 (NAF Dec. 16, 2002).

The respondent registered over 300 domain names incorporating the complainant's trademark "CNN." The panel found that all the disputed domain names were confusingly similar to the complainant's mark, including domain names "cnn-country.com," "cnn-[geographic region].com," "cnn-[generic term].com," and "cnn-[additional letters].com." The panel stated that the complainant's CNN mark was widely known throughout the world, and that bad faith was evidenced by the respondent's primary purpose in registering so many domain names, that is, to exploit the inevitable consumer confusion. Accordingly, the panel ordered the transfer of all of the disputed domain names to the complainant.

Playboy Enterprises International, Inc. v. Domain Active Property, Ltd., Case No. D2002-1156 (WIPO Feb. 13, 2003).

The complainant owned several trademarks, including "Playboy" and "Playmate." In a three-week period, the respondent registered 74 domain names that incorporated the complainant's marks. The panel found ample evidence of respondent's bad faith in registering the domain names: the respondent's domain names were intended to attract Internet users interested in the complainant's products and services; the respondent had registered a large number of domain names that incorporated complainant's mark; and respondent directed the domain names to websites that offered goods and services of competitors of the complainant. The panel ordered the transfer of the domain names to the complainant.

See also, Bennett Coleman & Co. v. Lalwani; Bennett Coleman & Co. v. Long Distance Telephone Co., Case No. D2000-0014 and D2000-0015 (WIPO March 11, 2000) (finding bad faith in registering the domain names theeconomictimes.com and thetimesofindia.com because registrant was attempting to attract users seeking complainant's *Economic Times* and *Times of India* publications); *J. Crew International, Inc. v. crew.com*, Case No. D2000-0054 (WIPO Apr. 20, 2000) (concluding that respondent's crew.com domain name prevented J. Crew, the owner of the "Crew" mark, from registering a domain name corresponding to its mark); *Home Interiors & Gifts, Inc. v. Home Interiors*, Case No. D2000-0010 (WIPO March 7, 2000) (finding bad faith based on respondent's registration of the domain names homeinterioursandgifts.com and homeinteriors.net and posted advertisements for competitors of complainant and links to commercial websites hosted by competitors of the complainant); *Valspar Sourcing, Inc. v. TIGRE*, Case No. FA0204000112596 (NAF June 4, 2002) (finding respondent's registration of disputed domain name while on notice of complainant's rights in "paint.biz" was evidence of bad faith).

Complainants' Failure to Show Bad Faith

 Union des Associations Europeennes de Football v. Hallam, Case No. D2001-0717 (WIPO July 10, 2001).

The respondent's use of a domain name that was confusingly similar to a trademark of European soccer's governing body was not considered a bad-faith use because the uefa2004.com domain name was registered more than eight months before the complainant registered its UEFA EURO 2004 trademark, and the respondent had sufficient explanations for why his 2004 European soccer championship chat site was not yet constructed. The complainant also failed to show that the respondent had no rights or legitimate interests in the domain name.

 Gloria-Werke H. Schulte-Frankenfeld GmbH & Co. v. Internet Development Corp. and Gloria MacKenzie, Case No. D2002-0056 (WIPO Apr. 26, 2002).

The respondent registered gloria.com, which is identical to the complainant's registered mark. The panel declined to find bad-faith registration or use, however, because the complainant's mark was not well-known in the United States at the time of registration of the domain name. The panel also noted that the respondent was a dealer in domain names, which might ordinarily create an inference that the respondent was aware of Gloria-Werke's mark; however, this inference was unpersuasive because the name "Gloria" is also a common name for women, and as such "a commodity greatly to be desired by those dealing in domain names," even those having no desire to exploit the marks of others.

 Nike, Inc. v. Crystal International, Case No. D2002-0352 (WIPO July 4, 2002).

A WIPO panel refused to order the transfer of Nike-related domain names, including nikepark.com, nikeshops.com, nikegolf.net, and nikemen.com. Nike, Inc. owns numerous trademarks in its name and related names. Although the registrant of the domain names did not file a response to Nike's complaint, the panel found no evidence of bad faith on the part of the registrant, and no evidence that Nike made an effort to resolve the matter directly with the registrant prior to filing its complaint with WIPO. Accordingly, the panel denied Nike's request to order the names transferred.

 PwC Business Trust v. Ultimate Search, Case No. D2002-0087 (WIPO May 22, 2002).

The respondent's use of pwc.com was found not to be a bad-faith registration or use of PwC's trademark "PWC" (held in trust for PricewaterhouseCoopers) because the three letters are inherently indistinctive and are not uniquely associated with the complainant. The panel also considered the effect that the prior registration by a third party of the pwc.com domain name, which had previously lapsed, should have on its decision concerning bad faith. The panel determined that, while in certain cases such a lapsed registration may be evidence of a lack of bad faith, it should not be considered compelling as a matter of course.

 Besiktas Jimnastik Kulubu v. Avcioglu, Case No. D2003-0035 (WIPO Mar. 10, 2003).

The complainant was a Turkish sporting association that operated a soccer team under the mark "Besiktas." The respondent, a fan of the team, registered and operated a fan site at the domain name besiktas.com. When complainant decided to launch an official team website, it brought an action seeking transfer of the domain name. The complainant provided no evidence to refute respondent's claims that the website cost him time and money and that he made no profits from operating the website. Further, the complainant offered no evidence that Internet users confused the respondent's website with the team's official website. The panel found the site to be a genuine fan site that included multiple disclaimers that the site was not the official Besiktas team website. The panel found no evidence of bad faith. Although respondent used the "Besiktas" trademark to attract Internet users to the website, such use did not constitute bad faith, the panel held, when it was not for commercial gain. Respondent was not required to transfer the domain name. As a result of an apparent agreement between the two parties, Internet users who visit besiktas.com are directed to a web page that allows them to choose either complainant's official Besiktas website or respondent's unofficial website.

 Microsoft Corp. v. Goldman, Case No. D2003-0044 (WIPO Apr. 15, 2003).

The complainant was the well-known provider of computer software and related goods that uses the federally registered "Windows" mark. The respondent was the operator of a website located at the domain name windowscasino.com, from which respondent provided software for online casino operators. Complainant filed a UDRP complaint seeking transfer of the windowscasino.com domain name. Complainant argued that bad faith was evidenced by respondent's lack of contact information on the website, and respondent's failure to respond to complainant's attempts to contact respondent. The respondent stated that it purposely made it difficult to be contacted because the nature of its business often subjected it to harassment and violence, and that mail delivery to its foreign locations was often ineffective. The panel suggested that these explanations led it to question respondent's candor, but noted that the respondent provided unrefuted reasons for using "windows" in its domain name. The panel stated that despite the association of the "windows" trademark with complainant, it remains a generic term. The panel held that more than notoriety of a generic term incorporated in a domain name is required to demonstrate bad faith. Despite the confusing similarity between the "windows" mark and the domain name, the panel found in favor of the respondent.

 Urbani Tartufi v. Urbani U.S.A., Case No. D2003-0090 (WIPO Apr. 7, 2003).

Respondent registered the domain name urbani.com while operating under a distributorship agreement with the complainant, the owner of the "Urbani" trademark. The agreement allowed respondent to use complainant's "Urbani" trademark for purposes related to the agreement. Some years after respondent registered the urbani.com domain name, the complainant revoked the distributorship agreement and brought this action to compel respondent to transfer the domain name. The panel agreed with the complainant that the domain name was identical to complainant's trademark. However, the panel found that the respondent had a legitimate right to use the domain name because it had registered the domain name while the business agreement was in effect. The panel found no evidence of bad faith because respondent had registered the domain name with the complainant's consent, and respondent never tried to sell the domain name or disrupt complainant's business. The panel found that the end of a business relationship was not sufficient evidence of bad faith to warrant the transfer of the domain name to the complainant.

Domain Names Corresponding to Personal and Geographic Names

In addition to policing the misleading use of trademarks in domain names, UDRP arbitration panels have begun to expand protection to other intellectual property rights, such as trade and personal names and geographic regions.

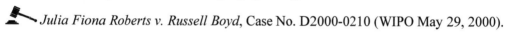*Julia Fiona Roberts v. Russell Boyd*, Case No. D2000-0210 (WIPO May 29, 2000).

The arbitration panel ruled that an accused cybersquatter who registered www.juliaroberts.com had no legitimate interest in the domain name and used it in bad faith. In finding bad-faith intent, the panel cited evidence that the defendant, Russell Boyd, had registered names of several famous movie and sports figures, and even tried to auction juliaroberts.com on eBay. *But see Gordon Sumner, p/k/a Sting v. Michael Urvan*, Case No. D2000-0596 (WIPO July 19, 2000) (finding inadequate evidence of bad faith and noting that, unlike "Julia Roberts," "sting" is a common word as well as a name); *Bruce Springsteen v. Jeff Burgar; Bruce Springsteen Club*, Case No. D2000-1532 (WIPO Jan. 25, 2001) (finding that the registrant has some legitimate right to the domain name and that Springsteen failed to establish bad faith).

Kur-und Verkehrsverein St. Moritz v. StMoritz.com, Case No. D2000-0617 (WIPO August 17, 2000).

The official organization representing the resort community of St. Moritz was unsuccessful in obtaining the rights to StMoritz.com from a company in the United Arab Emirates. The company runs a website at StMoritz.com about St. Moritz hotels and restaurants. The same company also owns rostock.com, malaga.com, majorca.com, et cetera, at which it runs websites providing similar information about those locations.

Kathleen Kennedy Townsend v. B. G. Birt, Case No. D2002-0030 (WIPO Apr. 11, 2002).

A WIPO panel issued a decision involving several domains using the name of Kathleen Kennedy Townsend, the former Lieutenant Governor of Maryland and the eldest daughter of the late Robert F. Kennedy. The panel declined to transfer the domains to Townsend, noting that the second WIPO report on the domain name process issued in the fall of 2001 indicated that the UDRP should be limited to personal names that had been commercially exploited. Townsend again failed to win transfer of the domain names from the same respondent in July 2002, when a group called Friends of Kathleen Kennedy Townsend brought the complaint instead of Townsend personally. This strategy sought to emphasize the commercial/political nature of Townsend's name. *Friends of Kathleen Kennedy Townsend v. B. G. Birt*, Case No. D2002-0451 (WIPO July 31, 2002).

Peter Frampton v. Frampton Enterprises, Inc., Case No. D2002-0141 (WIPO Apr. 17, 2002).

A WIPO panelist ordered the transfer of peterframpton.com from L. Peter Frampton to Peter Frampton, the singer. The panelist concluded that the use of the "Peter Frampton" trademark, in conjunction with the sale of goods and services similar to those offered by the singer, was an attempt by the registrant to benefit commercially from the inevitable confusion regarding ownership of the domain name.

Kevin Spacey v. Alberta Hot Rods, Claim No. FA0205000114437 (NAF Aug. 1, 2002).

After several failed attempts to compel the transfer of kevinspacey.com to him via the U.S. court system, the well-known actor succeeded in a UDRP action. The panel found that respondent's "persistent behavior" in registering celebrity names indicated his bad-faith intent in registering kevinspacey.com.

Martin v. Domains, Best Domains, Case No. D2003-0043 (WIPO March 12, 2003).

A WIPO panel ordered transfer of the domain name kelliemartin.com to actress Kellie Martin. The panel concluded that the complainant had common law trademark rights in her name because of her celebrity status. Also, the respondent used the domain name for a website that provided anti-abortion information, which the panel found did not constitute a legitimate interest because the domain name had no connection to the website's content. The panel also found the respondent had registered the domain name in bad faith because of the respondent's history and pattern of registering domain names incorporating famous surnames and other trademarks and directing the domain names to the same anti-abortion website.

The Hebrew University of Jerusalem v. Alberta Hot Rods, Case No. D2002-0616 (WIPO Oct. 7, 2002).

The complainant, Hebrew University, to which Albert Einstein had left his "literary property" rights, filed a UDRP complaint against the registrant of the domain name alberteinstein.com. The WIPO panel concluded that UDRP was not intended to apply to domain names consisting of personal names that were not used commercially and had not acquired secondary meaning as a source of goods or services. The panel found that the complainant failed to establish common law rights in the mark "Einstein." The panel recognized that although the respondent was a notorious cybersquatter, the complainant had failed to demonstrate in this action that the respondent was aware that the complainant had claimed any trademark rights in the name "Albert Einstein."

City of Potsdam v. Transglobal Networx, Inc., Case No. D2002-0856 (WIPO Nov. 5, 2002).

The city of Potsdam, Germany successfully obtained the rights to four domain names that incorporated the city's name: potsdam.com, potsdam.net, potsdam.org, and potsdam.info. These domain names corresponded to the website of a company providing IT services. The city contended that the city name trademark and the domain names are identical; that the registrant had no right or legitimate interest in the domain names; and that the registrant used the domain names in bad faith to mislead consumers. The respondent did not file a response to the complaint, and, the panel said, had no obvious connection to the domain names. Because an Internet user seeking information about the city of Potsdam would likely seek such information at the respondent's domain names and would find only the company in four major TLD's, the city had demonstrated sufficient bad faith on the part of the registrant to warrant transfer of the domain names.

 Empressa Municipal Promocion Madrid SA v. Easylink Services Corp., Case No. D2002-1110 (WIPO Feb. 26, 2003).

The complainant, a company owned by the Madrid City Council, filed a complaint requesting transfer of the domain name madrid.com from the respondent. The panel did not order the transfer of the domain name because it was not confusingly similar to any of complainant's trademarks, and the respondent had demonstrated that it had legitimate interests in the domain name. The complainant had no trademark rights in the word "Madrid," despite registering trademarks for phrases incorporating the word "Madrid." The panel stated that madrid.com was not identical to any of the complainant's registered marks that incorporated "Madrid." Further, the panel noted that geographical indicators are not *per se* protected under the UDRP. The panel also found that the respondent had legitimate interests in the domain name because it used the domain name in connection with an email service with thousands of subscribers.

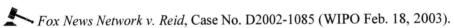 *Fox News Network v. Reid*, Case No. D2002-1085 (WIPO Feb. 18, 2003).

A WIPO panelist ordered the transfer of the domain name billoriley.com to the complainant, Fox News. The panel found that the domain name was confusingly similar to the name of the host of a Fox News program, "Bill O'Reilly," despite the different spelling. The panel found that the respondent had no legitimate interest in the domain name because it used the domain name to divert users to a search engine and to solicit advertising.

Puerto Rico Tourism Industry Co. v. Virtual Countries, Inc., Case No. D2003-1129 (WIPO Apr. 14, 2003).

The respondent operated a number of websites featuring "virtual countries" where Internet users could learn about various countries and regions. The respondent registered the domain name puertorico.com. The complainant was a tourism corporation in Puerto Rico. Prior to this proceeding, the parties were in negotiations for the sale of the domain name to the complainant, but the parties disagreed about which side made the initial offer to buy or sell the domain name. The panel refused to order transfer of the domain name, finding that the complainant did not demonstrate that it had any rights in the mark "Puerto Rico." While the complainant possessed trademark rights in phrases incorporating the words "Puerto Rico," "Puerto Rico" is a descriptive geographic term that has not acquired secondary meaning. The panel acknowledged that under UDRP standards and U.S. trademark law, one generally cannot own trademark rights in geographic names.

Amazon.com, Inc. v. Horner, Case No. D2003-0071 (WIPO Aug. 15, 2003)

Online retailer Amazon.com filed a UDRP complaint against the registrant of the domain names amazonbooks.net and amazonbooks.org. The respondent argued that Amazon.com cannot assert rights to the name of the River Amazon. Respondent claimed his sites provided information about the River Amazon to travelers. The panel found that the sites merely featured links to other sites with which Respondent had no affiliation, and the website was set up to look like the Amazon.com retail website. The panel ordered the domain names transferred to Amazon.com.

Typosquatting Cases Under the UDRP

 CompUSA Mgmt. Co. v. Khan, Claim No. FA0208000123921 (NAF Oct. 18, 2002).

The complainant, a vendor of software and computer-related products, registered the mark "CompUSA." The respondent registered the domain name copmusa.com, which resolved to a website containing links to Internet sellers of computers and video games. The UDRP panel agreed with the complainant that the domain name violated complainant's rights, and ordered the domain name transferred to the complainant. First, the panel found that transposing letters in a trademark satisfied the requirement that the domain name be confusingly similar to complainant's mark. Second, respondent's use of a typographical error to redirect Internet users was not a legitimate use. Finally, the panel found that diverting Internet users for personal commercial gain was evidence of bad faith, as was registering the domain name of a misspelled trademark.

 Societe Air France v. Collazo, Case No. D2003-0417 (WIPO July 22, 2003)

The French airline carrier Air France, which holds numerous trademark registrations for the mark "Air France" and has registered the domain name airfrance.com, brought a claim against the registrant of the domain name arifrance.com, which resolved to a website offering travel-related services. The panel found that the misspelling of the complainant's mark in the domain name was strong evidence of bad faith, and ordered the domain name transferred to Air France.

 National Association of Professional Baseball Leagues, Inc. v. Zuccarini, Case No. D2002-1011 (WIPO Jan. 21, 2003).

The complainant, the governing body of Minor League Baseball, registered the domain name minorleaguebaseball.com, and filed trademark applications for the phrase "Minor League Baseball." The respondent registered the domain name www.minorleaugebaseball.com (transposing two letters in "league"). The domain name resolved to a pornographic website. The League filed a UDRP complaint seeking transfer or cancellation of the domain name. Applying UDRP standards, the panel found that the domain name was confusingly similar to the League's mark, that the respondent did not have a legitimate interest in using the website to re-direct web users to a pornographic site, and that the intentional misspelling of a word in the trademark evidenced bad faith. Accordingly, the panel ordered the domain name transferred to the complainant.

Reverse Domain Name Hijacking

If a panel determines that a UDRP complaint was brought in bad faith and was an abuse of the administrative proceeding, the panel will make a declaratory finding of reverse domain name hijacking. A complainant need not "knowingly" file an insupportable claim but need only be reckless as to whether the complaint is supportable or not. One panel found that this recklessness standard was met by the initiation of a UDRP proceeding by the holder of a trademark in a generic name where the respondent was preparing to run a legitimate site. *See Smart Design LLC v. Carolyn Hughes*, Case No. D2000-0993 (WIPO Oct. 18, 2000).

A judgment in favor of the respondent is not sufficient, by itself, to support a finding of reverse domain name hijacking. The complainant must actually be found to have brought the complaint in bad faith. *EasyJet Airline Co. v. Holt*, Case No D2000-0465 (WIPO Aug. 24, 2000) (declining to make a finding of reverse domain name hijacking); *Windsor Fashions, Inc. v. Windsor Software Corp.*, Case No. D2002-0839 (WIPO Nov. 14, 2002) (finding reverse domain name hijacking because complainant had reason to know that the respondent was a legitimate business and because complainant delayed filing the complaint until after registering its mark with the United States Patent and Trademark Office, even though it was aware that the respondent had already registered the domain name); *Foundation Le Corbusier v. Weber*, Case No. D2003-0251 (WIPO July 4, 2003) (assessing complainant's bad faith with respect to each disputed domain name rather than as to the whole of the complaint, and finding bad faith in complainant's claims for 6 of the 32 disputed domain names, in which complainant should have recognized respondent had legitimate rights).

The reverse domain name hijacking concept also applies under the .biz Start-Up Trademark Opposition Policy (STOP), adopted by ICANN in May 2001. STOP is a policy exclusive to the .biz TLD to resolve disputes over domain names that were registered during the .biz start up period, from June 25 to September 21, 2001, under which the owner of intellectual property rights in a trademark was notified that an application for a domain name incorporating the mark had been submitted. The owner had an opportunity to dispute the application. All other .biz domain name disputes are required to go through the UDRP. *See Zuckerman v. Peeris*, Case No. DBIZ2002-00245 (WIPO Aug. 12, 2002) (finding that complainant had brought a STOP action in bad faith).

First Amendment Issues in Domain Name Registrations and Use

Parody and Criticism

Courts ordinarily will allow the use of a trademark in a domain name of a parody website or a "gripe site" so long as there is no confusion as to whether the site is conveying parody or criticism or as to the origin or sponsorship of the website itself.

Gripe Sites

Lucent Technologies, Inc. v. Lucentsucks.com, 95 F. Supp. 2d 528 (E.D. Va. 2000).

The court found that consumers would be unlikely to confuse lucentsucks.com with an official website of Lucent Technologies. The court also recognized that a so-called "cybergriping" or "sucks" site, if able to demonstrate genuine parody or critical commentary, could counter a trademark holder's claim of bad-faith intent in registration. Bad faith is a necessary element of a cybersquatting claim under the ACPA. Lucentsucks.com was allowed to retain its domain name based on Lucent Technologies' failure to comply with the jurisdictional requirements of an *in rem* action under the ACPA.

Ford Motor Co. v. 2600 Enterprises, 177 F. Supp. 2d 661 (E.D. Mich. 2001).

The defendant had registered the domain name fuckgeneralmotors.com and linked it to the Ford Motor Company website. Ford sought an injunction requiring the defendant to remove the link. On December 20, 2001, the U.S. District Court for the Eastern District of Michigan denied Ford's motion. The court ruled that the programmatic link was not a commercial use of "Ford" trademark or a use in connection with goods or services within the meaning of the Lanham Act. Therefore, there was no trademark infringement. The court distinguished and criticized two of the earlier cases on the Lanham Act's application to domain names used in connection with sites that disparage the mark's owners: *Jews for Jesus v. Brodsky*, 993 F. Supp. 282 (D.N.J. 1998) (enjoining defendant from using the domain names jewsforjesus.org and jews-for-jesus.com for a site criticizing the Jews For Jesus organization); *Planned Parenthood Fed'n of America, Inc. v. Bucci*, No. 97 Civ. 06 29 (KMW), 1997 U.S. Dist. LEXIS 3338 (S.D.N.Y. Mar. 27, 1997) (enjoining defendant's registration and use of plannedparenthood.com for an anti-abortion website).

The Taubman Co. v. Webfeats, 319 F.3d 770 (6th Cir. 2003).

The defendant registered the domain name shopatwillowbend.com after learning that the plaintiff planned to build a mall of that name near the defendant's home. The website included information about the mall, a disclosure that this was not the mall's official website, and a link to the mall's official website. The defendant described his website as a "fan site." The site also contained a link to the defendant's web design business. The plaintiff brought a claim for trademark infringement under the Lanham Act. In an apparent response to the suit, the defendant registered multiple domain names using the plaintiff's name and the mall's name ending in "sucks." The plaintiff amended its complaint to include claims for trademark infringement with respect to all of these domain names. The trial court entered a preliminary injunction, compelling the defendant to cease operation of all of the "(mall/plaintiff)sucks" websites and the original shopatwillowbend.com website. The defendant appealed. The U.S. Court of Appeals for the Sixth Circuit reversed. With regard to the initial shopatwillowbend.com website, the court found no likelihood of customer confusion because of the disclaimer and link to the official website. With regard to the "sucks" websites, the court found that defendant's use of the plaintiff's name and mall name followed by "sucks.com" constituted protected free speech. The Lanham Act could not be invoked to quiet the defendant's expression, the court reasoned, as long as his speech was not "commercially misleading."

Parody Sites

People for the Ethical Treatment of Animals v. Doughney, 113 F. Supp. 2d 915 (E.D. Va. 2000), *aff'd*, 263 F.3d 359 (4th Cir. Sept. 18, 2001).

The plaintiffs brought an action for trademark infringement, dilution, and cyber-squatting against the defendant, who used the domain name peta.org for his website "People Eating Tasty Animals." The plaintiff owns a service mark registration for PETA, People for the Ethical Treatment of Animals. The defendant claimed that the suit constituted an attempt to infringe his political speech and that his site was a parody. The trial court found the use of the identical mark prevented the defendant's site from protection as a parody because web users would not realize they were being taken to a parody of PETA until after they had used PETA's mark to access the website. The trial court granted summary judgment in favor of PETA, and the domain name was transferred. The Court of Appeals for the Fourth Circuit affirmed the district court's ruling, agreeing that the defendant was liable for trademark infringement, unfair competition, and violation of the ACPA.

OBH, Inc. v. Spotlight Magazine, Inc., 86 F. Supp. 2d 176 (W.D.N.Y. 2000).

The defendant operated a "parody" site criticizing The BUFFALO NEWS at www.thebuffalonews.com. The court found that confusion was likely because users would only realize they were visiting a parody site after they arrived. The defendant's use of a disclaimer on the site could not overcome this confusion. The court inferred from the circumstances that the defendant used the BUFFALO NEWS trademark knowingly and intentionally to trick some Internet users into receiving his message instead of the BUFFALO NEWS.

Gripe Sites and Parody Sites in UDRP Proceedings

Most of the proceedings brought under the UDRP involving [company name]sucks.com have led to a transfer of the domain name, particularly where they have involved a cybersquatter who acquired the domain name with the commercial purpose to sell the domain name to the trademark owner. *See, e.g., Wal-Mart Stores, Inc. v. Walsucks*, Case No. D2000-0477 (WIPO July 20, 2000); *Vivendi Universal v. Jay D. Sallen*, Case No. D2001-1121 (WIPO Nov. 7, 2001) (finding that many nonEnglish speakers may associate [trademark]sucks sites with the trademark owner, and that Sallen's free speech claim was concocted after receiving a cease-and-desist letter); *Bayer Aktiengesellschaft v. Dangos & Partners*, Case No. D2002-115 (WIPO Feb. 3, 2003) (ordering transfer of a "sucks" domain name because it was confusingly similar to the complainant's mark, the respondent offered to sell the domain name for a high price, and respondent registered the domain name for the primary purpose of selling it to the complainant or a competitor).

However, where the website operator has established a legitimate consumer gripe or parody site, the operator may be able to defend use of the domain name on the ground that it has a protectable First Amendment interest in criticizing the company. *See McLane Co. v. Craig*, Case No. D2000-1455 (WIPO January 11, 2001) (refusing to cancel or transfer mclanenortheast.com and mclanenortheastsucks.com).

Falwell v. Cohn, Case No. D2002-0184 (WIPO June 3, 2002).

A UDRP panel refused to transfer jerryfalwell.com and jerryfallwell.com to televangelist Jerry Falwell. The panel based its refusal to transfer on the ground that Falwell had failed to prove he had common law trademark rights in his name, but the panel also found that the respondent's use of the domain names to provide parody, satire, and criticism of Jerry Falwell was a legitimate noncommercial or fair use. In late June 2002, Falwell filed suit in a federal court in Virginia to force a transfer of the domain names. *See Falwell Files Suit Against Site Owner*, THE NEWS & ADVANCE (June 20, 2002). The federal trial court held that it lacked jurisdiction because the website was targeted to a national audience, rather than to Virginia residents specifically. *Falwell v. Cohn*, No CIV.A.6:02 CV 00040, 2003 WL 751130 (W.D. Va. Mar. 4, 2003). Following the trial court's decision, the defendant surrendered the domain names to Falwell. "Internet Win For Rev. Falwell," CBS News (June 20, 2003), *available at* www.cbsnews.com/stories/2003/06/20/tech/main559511.shtml.

⚖ *Legal and General Group PLC v. Image Plus*, Case No. D2002-1019 (WIPO Dec. 30, 2002).

The complainant registered the domain name legalandgeneral.com and owned the registration for the mark "Legal & General." The respondent registered the domain name legal-and-general.com and set up a website on which to post complaints about the complainant's company. The panel agreed with the complainant that the domain name was confusingly similar to the complainant's mark, despite the use of hyphens and the spelling out of the word "and." The panel split as to whether the respondent had legitimate rights and interests in the domain name. The panel noted that previous panels had used different approaches to decide whether a respondent's website was a "legitimate noncommercial or fair use of the domain name, without intent for commercial gain to misleadingly divert consumers or to tarnish the trademark or service mark at issue."

Some panels have found that a confusingly similar domain name is not fair use when the website's purpose is to criticize the trademark holder. Other panels have examined the content of the website to determine if it is a genuine criticism website, if it is a sham created after respondent tried to sell the domain name, or if it has links to competitors' websites. The majority of this panel used the second approach; it found no *per se* rule that a genuine complaint website is not a legitimate use of the domain name. A majority of the panel determined that the disputed website was a legitimate noncommercial site devoted to criticism of the complainant. The panel found that Internet users would recognize that the website was not affiliated with the complainant.

⚖ *The Royal Bank of Scotland Group plc, National Westminster Bank v. Lopez*, Case No. D2003-0166 (WIPO May 9, 2003).

The respondent registered multiple domain names that incorporated "National Westminster," the plaintiff's trademark. After the complainant initiated UDRP proceedings (which were heard and decided by another panel), the respondent registered the domain name natwestbanksucks.com. The complainant then filed a UDRP action seeking transfer of the natwestbanksucks.com domain name. The panel agreed with the complainant that the domain name was confusingly similar to the complainant's mark, despite the addition of "sucks" to the mark. The panel acknowledged that the respondent had First Amendment rights to comment publicly about the complainant, but these rights did not confer a legitimate interest in a domain name that includes the complainant's trademark. Respondent, the panel reasoned, could use other methods to express his views about complainant, such as registering domain names that are not confusingly similar to the complainant's mark. The panel ordered the domain name natwestbanksucks.com to be transferred to the complainant.

See also, Asda Group Ltd. v. Kilgour, Case No. D2002-0857 (WIPO Nov. 11, 2002) (permitting respondent to retain asdasucks.co.uk domain name despite respondent's use of the trademark "Asda" in the domain name because the inclusion of "sucks" after the mark eliminated any potential consumer confusion).

First Amendment Claims Brought against Domain Name Administrators

Suits have been brought against Network Solutions, Inc. (NSI) and the National Science Foundation (NSF) on First Amendment grounds based on NSI's policy of refusing to register second-level domain names that contain seven words widely regarded as indecent, and, based on NSI's policy of allowing trademark holders to contest domain-name registrations. *See Dluhos v. Strasberg*, No. 00-CV-03163 (D.N.J.), *aff'd*, 321 F.3d 365 (3rd Cir. 2003) (the plaintiff alleged that it was a violation of the First Amendment to "allow trademark law to trump free expression"); *National A-1 Advertising, Inc. v. Network Solutions, Inc.*, 121 F. Supp. 2d 156 (D.N.H. 2000); *Island Online, Inc. v. Network Solutions, Inc.*, 119 F. Supp. 2d 289 (E.D.N.Y. 2000). However, because NSI developed its policies independently of the NSF, the courts have held that NSI is not a state actor. Accordingly, they have rejected the assertion that there is a First Amendment right to domain names.

The courts have also noted that speech via domain names is not absolutely protected because NSF is not a public forum and that NSI's failure to register particular domain names does not serve as a prior restraint on speech because a domain name owner could still have any of the seven words in its URL by placing the desired words in a subdirectory. (The court explained that it saw no meaningful difference between www.photos.com/feelmytits and www.feelmytits.photos.com.). *Dluhos v. Strasberg*, No. 00-CV-03163 (D.N.J.), *aff'd*, 321 F.3d 365 (3rd Cir. 2003) (holding that NSI is not a state or federal actor capable of violating the First, Fourth, Fifth, or Fourteenth Amendments in its administration of domain-name registration and dispute resolution policy); *National A-1 Advertising, Inc.*, 121 F. Supp. 2d at 168 (holding that NSI is not a state actor capable of violating First Amendment free-speech rights in its denial of certain domain names); *Island Online, Inc.*, 119 F. Supp. 2d at 307 (holding that despite its Cooperative Agreement with NSF, NSI is not a state or federal actor under the close nexus, public function, and symbiotic relationship tests).

Domain-Name Slamming

Register.com v. Domain Registry of America, Inc., No. 02 Civ. 6915, 2002 U.S. Dist. LEXIS 24795 (S.D.N.Y. Dec. 26, 2002).

Domain-name registrar Register.com won a preliminary injunction against Domain Registry of America (DROA) for causing customers to change unwittingly their Internet domain service from Register.com to DROA. The defendant sent emails to the plaintiff's customers suggesting that they renew their domain-name registrations. Those who did had their registrations transferred from Register.com to DROA. The emails, the court said, misled customers by implying that DROA was somehow assisting Register.com. In issuing the preliminary injunction, the court dubbed the unlawful practice "domain name slamming" because of its similarities to the unlawful practice of automatically causing customers to switch long-distance telephone companies, commonly called "slamming."

Chapter 3: Domain Names
Summary of the Law

- A domain name is not always entitled to trademark protection. A domain name is protectable, under trademark law, only if it is used to brand the website to which the domain name resolves. If the domain name is only used as a web address, it is not protectable as a trademark.

- Registering a domain name that incorporates another's trademark can constitute trademark infringement, if the domain name creates a likelihood that consumers will confuse the domain name and the trademark.

- Courts analyze domain names disputes between trademark owners with competing claims to a domain name under the traditional principles of trademark law.

- "Cybersquatting" is registering a domain name that is associated with someone else's trademark in order to benefit from the association with that mark. "Typosquatting" is registering a domain name that is similar in spelling to another's domain name to capitalize on a user's typing error to lead the user to the squatter's sites instead of the site the user intended to visit. Prior to the 1999 enactment of the Anticybersquatting Consumer Protection Act (ACPA), cybersquatting and typosquatting cases were analyzed exclusively under traditional principles of trademark law.

- A federal law enacted in 1999, the ACPA, imposes liability for registering, trafficking in, or using a domain name that is identical or confusingly similar to another's trademark (or that dilutes a famous mark), with a bad-faith intent to profit from the domain name.

- Typically, courts have found violations of the ACPA where the registrant registered a domain name that was identical or confusingly similar to someone else's mark for the purpose of selling it or diverting consumers who are seeking the trademark owner's site, or where the registrant was a competitor of the trademark owner.

- Courts will ordinarily allow the use of a trademark in the domain name of a parody website or a "gripe site" on First Amendment grounds (described in Chapter 1), so long as neither the domain name nor the website is likely to cause consumer confusion as to the origin or sponsorship of the site.

- The Internet Corporation for Assigned Names and Numbers (ICANN) manages much of the domain name registration system. ICANN approves and accredits domain name registrars. ICANN-approved registrars administer domain name registrations for the top-level domains (TLDs) .aero, .biz, .com, .coop, .info, .museum, .name, .net, .org, and .pro. ICANN does not oversee the .edu, .gov, or .mil TLDs, which may be used only by qualified entities.

- ICANN adopted the Uniform Dispute Resolution Policy (UDRP), which governs disputes over all .com, .net, .org, .aero, .biz, .coop, .info, .museum, and .name domain names. Under the UDRP, a complainant (a person claiming to have rights in a domain name registered to another person) can bring a claim before one of three authorized dispute resolution providers: the World Intellectual Property Organization (WIPO), the National Arbitration Forum (NAF), or the CPR Institute for Dispute Resolution (CPR).

- A UDRP claim is an administrative procedure, separate and distinct from a claim brought in a federal court under the ACPA. The only remedy available in a UDRP claim is transfer or cancellation of the disputed domain name. To prevail in a UDRP proceeding, a complainant must establish: (1) that the domain name is identical or confusingly similar to a trademark in which the complainant has rights; (2) that the domain name registrant has no legitimate interests in the domain name; and (3) that the domain name was registered and is being used in bad faith.

- In addition to hearing disputes concerning domain names that include trademarks, UDRP service providers hear disputes over domain names that incorporate personal names or geographic identifiers.

COPYRIGHT

Copyright Basics

The need to protect the works of authors was considered so fundamental to the nation's well-being that the framers of the Constitution explicitly granted Congress the power to provide copyright protection in Article I, Section 8, Clause 8 of the United States Constitution. But copyright protection is not absolute; Congress and the courts must balance the rights of authors against the countervailing constitutional right of the public to engage in free speech under the First Amendment. Most fundamentally, copyright law does not protect ideas or facts, which are, by definition, in the public domain. Instead, copyright attaches to the unique manner in which ideas and facts are expressed. And while copyright law generally grants copyright owners the exclusive right to copy, display, reproduce, and distribute their works, it also limits the scope of these rights. For example, copyright law limits the duration of copyright protection, and permits certain unauthorized uses of copyright-protected material under statutory exemptions and the "fair use" doctrine.

Protected Works

The Copyright Act of 1976 affords copyright protection to "original works of authorship fixed in any tangible medium of expression." 17 U.S.C. § 102. Such works include, for example, literature, music, motion pictures, artistic works, photographs, essays, articles, computer programs, graphic designs, and sound recordings. They can also include collective works and other compilations. Copyright does not protect facts, ideas, procedures, or discoveries.

The Digital Millennium Copyright Act of 1998 (DMCA) expressly extends copyright protection to works created in digital media. 17 U.S.C. §§ 1201 *et seq.*, Pub. L. 105-304, 112 Stat. 2863, Oct. 18, 1998, § 512. Works created in digital media are considered "fixed" if they can be perceived, reproduced, or otherwise communicated for more than a transitory period, including fixation on a computer disc or in a computer's random access memory (RAM).

Scope of Protection

The owner of a copyright has the exclusive right to reproduce the copyright-protected work, prepare derivative works from it, distribute copies, and publicly display or perform it. 17 U.S.C. § 106. Since the passage of the Copyright Term Extension Act of 1998, copyright protection generally lasts for the life of the author plus 70 years, or, in the case of works for hire and anonymous works, the shorter of 95 years from the date of first publication or 120 years from the creation of the work. 17 U.S.C. § 302.

In the Sonny Bono Copyright Term Extension Act of 1998 (CTEA), Congress extended the term of existing copyrights by 20 years, from life of the author plus 50 years to life of the author plus 70 years. The Supreme Court rejected a constitutional challenge to the extension in *Eldred v. Ashcroft*, 537 U.S. 186 (2003), ruling that the extension did not exceed Congress's authority under the Copyright Clause of the Constitution. The ruling keeps works such as Disney's Mickey Mouse and the poems of Robert Frost out of the public domain for an additional 20 years. Justice Ginsberg wrote for the seven-member majority that the Constitution afforded broad powers to Congress to legislate with respect to intellectual property matters, authority that it exercised within appropriate limits when enacting the CTEA.

Registration

Copyright registration is not required to obtain copyright protection. Copyright springs into existence automatically when an original work of authorship is fixed in a tangible medium of expression. 17 U.S.C. § 102. However, copyright registration obtained before or within five years after a work's first publication is evidence of the validity of the copyright in the work and of the facts stated in the certificate of registration. 17 U.S.C. § 410(c). In addition, copyright registration is ordinarily a prerequisite to filing a copyright infringement lawsuit.

Available Remedies

The Copyright Act authorizes injunctive relief and damages. Available "actual" damages include not only the copyright owner's lost profits, but also any profits gained by the infringer as a result of the copyright violations. 17 U.S.C. §§ 502, 504(b). If the infringed works were registered at the time of the infringement, statutory damages of up to $30,000 per work for nonwillful infringement and up to $150,000 per work for willful infringement are available as an alternative to actual damages. 17 U.S.C. § 504(c). An award of attorney fees is also possible. 17 U.S.C. § 505.

Limits on Protection

The rights of the copyright holder are limited by the right of others to make "fair use" of copyright-protected material—that is, to use it in public discussion or for other permitted purposes. In determining whether a use of copyright-protected material is "fair," courts are directed by the Copyright Act to consider (1) the purpose for which the material was used, (2) the nature of the material, (3) the amount used, and (4) the effect of the use on the market for or value of the copyright-protected material. 17 U.S.C. § 107.

Other statutory exemptions permit unauthorized use of copyright-protected works by, for example, libraries or education institutions. The Digital Millennium Copyright Act grants Internet "service providers," as defined in the Act, a limited immunity from copyright infringement claims. This limited immunity is discussed at page 107, below.

Obtaining and Protecting Rights to Website Content

Methods of Obtaining Rights

A web publisher can make content available in three ways: (1) by developing original content, (2) by licensing content provided by others for display on its website, and (3) by linking to or framing material developed by others. Web publishers have encountered legal issues involving each of these methods.

Possession of Print Media Rights Does Not Necessarily Imply Online Rights

Ryan v. CARL Corp., 23 F. Supp. 2d 1146 (N.D. Cal. 1998).

Freelance journalists successfully sued an Internet service that had allowed subscribers to search an electronic database for articles, then select particular articles to be delivered by fax.

Greenberg v. National Geographic Society, 1998 U.S. Dist. LEXIS 18060 (S.D. Fla. 1998), *rev'd*, 244 F.3d 1267 (11th Cir. 2001), *cert. denied*, 122 S. Ct. 347 (Oct. 9, 2001).

The National Geographic Society produced a 30-CD-ROM set that included every issue of *National Geographic* published from 1888 through 1996. Some of plaintiff's photos were included in the work. National Geographic argued that its reproduction of Greenberg's work in the collection of CD-ROMs did not make the photos "new work." The trial court agreed, holding that the CD-ROM constituted a permissible revision of National Geographic's print compilations, but the U.S. Court of Appeals for the Eleventh Circuit reversed. The Eleventh Circuit assumed, without deciding, that to the extent the CD-ROM set merely reproduced digitally previously published issues of the magazine, it constituted a permissible revision, but found that the inclusion of a brief video sequence featuring various *National Geographic* covers and certain computer code that facilitated access to the images made the CD-ROM collection more than a mere revision. The court ruled that National Geographic's use amounted to an infringing use of Greenberg's photographs.

New York Times Co. v. Tasini, 533 U.S. 483 (2001).

The U.S. Supreme Court held that publishers that licensed articles by freelance writers for republication without obtaining the writers' permission or providing further compensation were violating copyright law.

The freelancer plaintiffs sued various periodicals, including *The New York Times*, *Newsday*, and *Sports Illustrated*, after the periodicals made available in searchable online electronic databases freelance articles they had previously published in print. The freelancers claimed that this practice infringed the copyrights they held in the individual articles. The Court of Appeals for the Second Circuit (*Tasini v. The New York Times Co.*, 206 F.3d 161 (2d Cir. 2000)) reversed a trial court ruling against the freelance journalists. The Second Circuit held that, in the absence of a contractual agreement with its freelance contributors, the publisher of a collective work (such as a magazine) may not grant an electronic database (such as Nexis) the right to republish in electronic form the individual freelance articles that make up the collective work. While a publisher's right of copyright in the collective work allows the publisher to create "revisions" of that work, the inclusion of individual freelance articles in electronic databases was more than mere revision under the Copyright Act and thus beyond the scope of the publishers' rights of copyright.

In affirming the court of appeals decision, the Supreme Court stated that in determining whether an electronic database would be deemed a permissible revision of the original collective work, a court should look to "whether the database itself perceptibly presents the author's contribution as part of a revision of the collective work."

Tasini at 504. The Court made it clear that a microfiche reproduction of issues of a magazine is a permissible revision of the original, because articles appear in microform "writ very small, in precisely the position in which the articles appeared in the [original print publication]." *Id.* at 501. Though the user of a microfilm version of a newspaper "can adjust the machine lens to focus only on the [a]rticle, to the exclusion of surrounding material," the user "first encounters the [a]rticle in context." *Id.* By contrast, the databases in which the plaintiff authors' works were reproduced "store[d] and retrieve[d] articles separately within a vast domain of diverse texts." *Id.* at 503. The articles, as reproduced in these databases, "appear[ed] disconnected from their original context."

⚖ *Marx v. Globe Newspaper Co., Inc.*, No. 00-2579-F, 2002 Mass. Super. LEXIS 455 (Mass. Super. Ct. Nov. 26, 2002).

In reaction to the Supreme Court's decision in *Tasini*, the *Boston Globe* required all freelancers to sign a license agreement granting the newspaper a nonexclusive license to use all of the freelancer's past and future works, including the right to reproduce the works, or derivatives of the works, in any medium, including electronic databases. Any freelancer who did not sign the new license would be ineligible for future freelance work from the *Globe*. Six of the freelancers sued the newspaper, contending that the license agreement was an unfair or deceptive act in violation of Massachusetts consumer protection and fair business dealing laws. The Massachusetts Superior Court granted the newspaper's motion for summary judgment. Because the plaintiffs were independent contractors, the court concluded, the newspaper had no duty to continue using their services. In the court's view, the *Globe* was free to comply with the *Tasini* ruling by requiring its freelancers, as a condition of continued assignments, to grant the newspaper the right to republish their prior works "even if one were to characterize this modification as 'extortion' obtained through the *Globe*'s strong bargaining position, the legitimate commercial reason for the *Globe* to have demanded this modification placed its demand within the rough and tumble, yet reasonable, commercial standards of fair dealing in the trade."

⚖ *Faulkner, et al. v. National Geographic Society*, No. 97 CV 9361, et al., 2003 U.S. Dist. LEXIS 22202 (S.D.N.Y., Dec. 11, 2003).

Plaintiff freelance photographers sued the National Geographic Society for copyright infringement for including their photographs in the magazine's CD-ROM collection (described in *Greenberg*, above). The trial court dismissed the plaintiff's claims. The court pointed out that its ruling was consistent with the Eleventh Circuit's decision in *Greenberg*, because the CD-ROM reproduced in digital form exact images of published issues of *National Geographic* magazine. Here, the plaintiffs' photographs did not appear in the brief video sequence created especially for the CD-ROM. Digitally reproducing exact images of the magazine covers featuring the plaintiffs' photographs constituted a permissible revision of the magazines, the court reasoned, and did not amount to infringement.

Using Content from Other Websites and the Doctrine of "Fair Use"

As noted above, one of the ways copyright law limits the exclusive rights of authors is through the doctrine of "fair use." Fair use, codified in the Copyright Act at 17 U.S.C. § 107, permits the use of copyright-protected works for limited purposes of comment, criticism, teaching, scholarship, and research without the permission of the copyright owner. Whether a use is a fair use is determined by considering at four factors: (1) the purpose and character of the use; (2) the nature of the original work; (3) the amount and substantiality of the portion of the original work used; and (4) the effect of the use on the potential market for or value of the copyright-protected work. The fourth factor is generally considered the most important. These four factors apply in the context of the Internet in essentially the same way they do in the context of traditional print use.

Kelly v. Arriba Soft Corp., 77 F. Supp. 2d 1116 (C.D. Cal. 1999), *aff'd in part and rev'd in part*, 280 F.3d 934 (9th Cir. 2002), *aff'd in part, rev'd in part, remanded on reh'g*, 336 F.3d 811, 67 U.S.P.Q.2d 1297 (BNA) (9th Cir. 2003).

The defendant operated an image search engine that would locate and display images based on search terms entered by users of the site. Each image could then be viewed without visiting the website on which the picture was located. The plaintiff was a photographer who objected to his work being copied and re-displayed via the defendant's search engine. The trial court acknowledged the copyright implications of the defendant's search engine, but found that the search engine's use of the works satisfied the requirements of the fair-use defense.

On appeal, the U.S. Court of Appeals for the Ninth Circuit held that Arriba Soft infringed Kelly's exclusive right to *display* his copyrighted works publicly by framing and "inline linking" to his photographs. The Ninth Circuit rejected Arriba Soft's fair-use defense with respect to Arriba Soft's inline linking to the full-sized images from Kelly's website because Arriba Soft displayed the entirety of Kelly's images for commercial gain and without any transformative purpose. But it held that Arriba Soft's use of "thumbnail" images did not violate Kelly's copyrights because it qualified as a protected "fair use." The thumbnails were low-quality reproductions whose purpose was to help the user select and access the full-sized image he wishes to view and not to act as substitutes for the original works.

On rehearing, in July 2003, the Ninth Circuit overturned its finding regarding inline linking and framing on procedural grounds, and it sent the case back to the trial court to determine whether these practices violated copyright law. The appellate court upheld its finding that the "thumbnails" qualified as a fair use.

For further discussion of this case in the context of framing, see page 104, below.

CNN v. GoSMS.com, Inc., 2000 U.S. Dist. LEXIS 16156 (S.D.N.Y. Oct. 30, 2000).

Several major news organizations, including Gannett, The New York Times Co., The Washington Post Co., and CNN, filed suit against GoSMS.com, Inc., a company whose technology would allow the transmission of headlines and news stories to wireless phones and other wireless devices. The lawsuit claimed direct and contributory copyright infringement, false advertising, trademark infringement, and dilution. This "short message service" technology allows for the transmission of data 160 characters at a time. The transmissions would reproduce the plaintiffs' news stories and strip their web content of its original advertising. After the court denied GoSMS.com's motion to dismiss, the case settled.

Los Angeles Times v. Free Republic, 2000 U.S. Dist. LEXIS 5669 (C.D. Cal. 2000), *stipulation for entry of final judgment*, 56 U.S.P.Q.2d (BNA) 1862, 2000 U.S. Dist. LEXIS 20484 (C.D. Cal. Nov. 14, 2000).

The U.S. District Court for the Central District of California ruled that posting entire articles from the *Los Angeles Times* and *The Washington Post* on an Internet bulletin board so that visitors could comment on and criticize them was not a fair use. In rejecting the fair-use defense, the court concluded that the use was not transformative, the Free Republic website profited from the exploitation of the copyright-protected material by attracting more users who made donations, the articles were posted verbatim rather than excerpted, and there was an adverse effect on the market for the newspapers, whose ability to sell or license the articles was diminished. In May 2002, the U.S. Court of Appeals for the Ninth Circuit dismissed the defendant's appeal. *Free Republic, et al. v. LA Times, et al.*, No. 00-57211, (9th Cir., May 15, 2002).

 Video Pipeline, Inc. v. Buena Vista Home Entertainment, Inc., 275 F. Supp. 2d 543 (D.N.J. 2003).

The plaintiff, Video Pipeline, provides previews of home videos to home-video wholesalers and retailers through its videopipeline.net network. The Buena Vista motion picture studio provided movie "trailers" to Video Pipeline pursuant to a license agreement, which Video Pipeline used to make its own video clips for its website. Video Pipeline originally filed suit against Buena Vista seeking a declaratory judgment that its use of movie "trailers" to make its own video clips does not constitute copyright infringement under the doctrine of fair use. The court disagreed, granting Buena Vista's motion for summary judgment because Video Pipeline's making of its own video-clip previews for transmission over the Internet is not protected from the copyright holder's claim of copyright infringement by the fair use defense or by the first-sale doctrine.

For a discussion of this case in the context of video streaming, see page 120 below.

Linking and Framing

Linking

Hypertext links lie at the heart of the Internet. As one commentator has noted, "if the Web's creators hadn't wanted linking, they would have called it the World Wide Straight Line." *See* "Linking, A Fundamental Premise of the Web, is Challenged," Siliconvalley.com (June 9, 2002), *available at* http://www.siliconvalley.com/mld/siliconvalley/news/editorial/3435606.htm.

Without more, a simple link to a website generally does not implicate the copyrights of the site being linked to. However, disputes have risen in cases of "deep-linking," where one website links to particular, internal pages of another site rather than the home page, enabling visitors to bypass certain site features, including advertising. Technology also exists for sites to prevent unauthorized deep-linking by only allowing deep-linking from specific sites. For a discussion of hyperlinks in the trademark context, see Chapter 2, pages 37 to 39.

Intellectual Reserve, Inc. v. Utah Lighthouse Ministry, Inc., 75 F. Supp. 2d 1290 (D. Utah 1999).

The plaintiff was the owner of the copyright in a church handbook. The defendant posted the contents of the handbook on its website without permission. In response to complaints from the plaintiff, the defendant removed the copyright-protected work from its website, but posted a notice that the work was available online at three other sites and provided hyperlinks to those websites. In addition, the defendant's website encouraged users to visit those sites, and one of the linked sites encouraged the copying and posting of the work. The court noted that "browsing" a website created a copy of the work on the user's computer, and found this copying sufficient to support a copyright infringement claim. 75 F. Supp. 2d at 1294. The court found that the defendant could be found contributorily liable for the actions of the users who displayed the copyright-protected work on their computers and granted a preliminary injunction against the website operator.

PCM, et. al. v. Kranten.com, (Netherlands 2000).

PCM and other major Dutch publishers sought an injunction against Kranten.com, a website that offers news headlines consolidated from the major newspapers. The injunction sought would have prevented Kranten.com from deep-linking to internal pages of the publishers' websites and by-passing the advertising on their homepages. The court in Rotterdam found that the links in fact directed extra traffic to the plaintiffs' sites and that the plaintiffs could easily place advertisements next to individual stories as well as on their home pages. The court denied the injunction. "Dutch Papers Fail in Internet Copyright Case," FINANCIAL TIMES, (Aug. 23, 2000).

Universal City Studios, Inc. v. Reimerdes, 111 F. Supp. 2d 294 (S.D.N.Y. 2000), *aff'd*, 273 F.3d 429 (2d Cir. 2001).

The trial court permanently enjoined a hacker website from, among other things, "knowingly linking" to any website containing any program, file, or device used to circumvent the encryption technology protecting DVDs. The court fashioned a test that would permit liability for linking to a website with knowledge that the site contains information on how to circumvent copyright protection with the purpose of disseminating information on the illegal circumvention methods.

On November 28, 2001, the U.S. Court of Appeals for the Second Circuit affirmed the decision of the trial court. For discussion of this case in the context of anti-circumvention under the Digital Millennium Copyright Act of 1998, see page 107, below.

Danish Newspaper Publishers Association v. Newsbooster.com (Bailiff's Court of Copenhagen, decided July 5, 2002).

The Danish Newspaper Publishers Association won an injunction against a web service called Newsbooster. Newsbooster provided users who signed up for membership the ability to use keyword searches to obtain links to news stories. Newsbooster claimed to "make news stories easier to find by presenting links to items with a keyword search." The Danish publishers objected to Newsbooster's practice of providing its members with deep-links to their content. This case is available at http://www.newsbooster.com/?pg=judge&lan=eng.

Ticketmaster Corp. v. Tickets.Com, Inc., No. CV99-7654-HLH(VBKx), 2003 WL 21406289 (C.D. Cal. Mar. 6, 2003).

Ticketmaster sued Tickets.Com for copyright infringement. Ticketmaster is the exclusive ticket distributor for a number of concert and sporting event venues across the United States. Its competitor, Tickets.Com, could not directly offer to sell tickets to events to which Ticketmaster had exclusive rights. So Tickets.Com used a "web crawler" to copy automatically information about events (date, time, location, etc.) from the Ticketmaster website to pages on Tickets.Com's own website. Then, Tickets.Com "deep-linked" from the page of the Tickets.com website that contained information about each event to the page on the Ticketmaster website on which Ticketmaster offered tickets to that event for sale, allowing its customers to purchase tickets directly from Ticketmaster. A federal court in California ruled that Tickets.Com's practice of "deep-linking" to the Ticketmaster website was not an unauthorized display of copyright-protected material.

For discussion of this case in the context of trespass, see Chapter 10, page 302.

 Verlagsgruppe Handelsblatt GmbH v. Paperboy, No. I ZR 259/00 (Bundesgerichtshof, July 17, 2003).

Germany's highest court ruled that deep-linking did not violate copyright law, stating that a copyright holder who makes copyright-protected material available on the Internet without protective measures accepts the risks that another user will exploit the work. The court characterized the deep-link as a short cut for accessing a page without typing the compete URL.

Framing

Framing technology allows a website to display the content of a third-party website without actually delivering the user to the third-party site. The framed content is displayed within the framing site, which may continue to display its branding and navigation to the user. To fit within the frame, the framed page may be reduced proportionally in size, content that appears "above the scroll" may be pushed down "below the scroll," or some of the framed content may be obscured by the frame. These modifications to the manner in which the framed site is displayed might arguably constitute the creation of derivative works, a right that is exclusive to the copyright holder.

 Washington Post, et al. v. Total News, No. 97 Civ. 1190 (PKL) (S.D.N.Y., filed Feb. 20, 1997).

Various news organizations sued Total News for displaying the news organizations' websites within a Total News frame and selling advertising in the frame. The case was settled in June 1997, with the defendants agreeing to stop framing the plaintiffs' content. For a discussion of this case in the context of trademark dilution, see Chapter 2, page 39.

Kelly v. Arriba Soft Corp., 77 F. Supp. 2d 1116 (C.D. Cal. 1999), *aff'd in part and rev'd in part*, 280 F.3d 934 (9th Cir. 2002), *aff'd in part on, rev'd in part, remanded on reh'g*, 67 U.S.P.Q.2D 1297 (BNA) (9th Cir. 2003).

The plaintiff, a professional photographer, sued Arriba Soft, the operator of an image search engine, over Arriba Soft's unauthorized display of copyright-protected photographs from Kelly's website.

Arriba Soft's website displayed each search result with a link to the identified website. When a user clicked on the link, the linked page was sometimes displayed in a frame generated by the Arriba Soft website. On other occasions, images from the linked-to pages were imported—linked-to directly—to be displayed as part of a web page generated by Arriba Soft. This practice is known as "inline" linking.

The U.S. Court of Appeals for the Ninth Circuit initially held that Arriba Soft's framing and inline linking infringed Kelly's exclusive right to *display* his copyright-protected works publicly. On rehearing, the court overturned this finding on procedural grounds and sent the case back to the trial court to determine whether this practice violated copyright law.

For further discussion of this case in the context of fair use, see page 100, above.

Protecting Electronic Databases of Factual Material

In *Feist Publications, Inc. v. Rural Tel. Service Co.*, 499 U.S. 340 (1991), the Supreme Court defined the scope of copyright protection afforded to compilations of factual information. The Court ruled that "if the selection and arrangement" of the compilation are "original," then the elements of the work that embody this originality can be protected under copyright law. The Court ruled that the "white pages" telephone listings at issue in *Feist* did not meet this standard of originality and were not subject to copyright protection. *But see Key Publications, Inc. v. Chinatown Today Publishing Enterprises., Inc.*, 945 F.2d 509 (2d Cir. 1991) (finding that a "yellow pages" telephone directory of Chinese businesses met the *Feist* test for original selection and arrangement and was eligible for copyright protection).

If material is not eligible for copyright protection, an electronic publisher may nevertheless attempt to place restrictions on its use by contract. See Chapter 7, pages 206 to 216 for a discussion of the enforceability of "shrinkwrap" or "click-through" licenses.

An electronic publisher may also attempt to restrict the use of its material through technological means. The Digital Millennium Copyright Act of 1998 (DMCA), discussed in more detail at pages 107 to 117 below, makes it unlawful to attempt to circumvent certain technological means of copy protection. 17 U.S.C. § 1201.

Mist-On Systems, Inc. v. Gilley's European Tan Spa, No. 02-C-0038-C, 2002 U.S. Dist. LEXIS 9846 (W.D. Wis. May 2, 2002).

The defendant tanning salon posted on its website a series of frequently asked questions (FAQs) about spray-on tanning that resembled the FAQs on the same subject on the plaintiff's website. The plaintiff, Mist-On Systems, sued for copyright infringement. Citing *Feist* for the proposition that the "stereotypical" Q&A format of an FAQ page is not copyrightable "as such," the court held that, even though the two pages contained some similarities, "these superficial similarities fall short of proving copying."

The court found that many of the similarities between the two pages were factual (*e.g.*, descriptions of processes and ingredients of the product described), and that the differences in layout, phrasing of questions, and arrangement of the two FAQ pages precluded a finding of copyright infringement.

⚖ *Telstra Corp. Ltd. v. Desktop Marketing Systems Pty Ltd.*, [2001] FCA 612 (May 25, 2001) appeal dismissed, [2002] FCAFC 112 (May 15, 2002).

The defendant challenged a trial court ruling that it had infringed Telstra's copyright in its white- and yellow-page listings by making CD-ROMs from the data. A trial judge in Australia held that the Australian Copyright Act of 1968 gave Telstra copyright rights in its telephone white pages, yellow pages, and lists of headings used in the yellow pages. In May 2002, the Australian Federal Court dismissed the defendant's appeal. The defendant's appeal to the High Court of Australia was dismissed in May 2002. The trial court's decision is available by searching the database located at http://www.fedcourt.gov.au/judgments/judgmts.html. The High Court's decision is available at http://www.austlii.edu.au/au/cases/cth/FCAFC/2002/112.html.

⚖ *Ticketmaster Corp. v. Tickets.Com, Inc.*, No. CV99-7654-HLH(VBKx), 2003 WL 21406289 (C.D. Cal. Mar. 6, 2003).

Ticketmaster sued Tickets.Com for copyright infringement. Ticketmaster is the exclusive ticket distributor for a number of concert and sporting event venues across the United States. Its competitor, Tickets.Com, could not directly offer to sell tickets to events to which Ticketmaster had exclusive rights. Tickets.Com used a "web crawler" to copy automatically information about events (*e.g.*, date, time, location, etc.) from the Ticketmaster website to pages on Tickets.Com's own website. Then, Tickets.Com "deep-linked" from the page of the Tickets.Com website that contained information about each event to the page on the Ticketmaster website on which Ticketmaster offered tickets to that event for sale, allowing its customers to purchase tickets directly from Ticketmaster.

On March 6, 2003, the U.S. District Court for the Central District of California ruled that Tickets.Com's use of a "web crawler" to obtain factual material about events from the Ticketmaster website did not violate copyright law. Because facts are not protected by copyright, the court held that reproducing this information does not infringe any Ticketmaster copyright right. In addition, the court decided that the momentary copy of each Ticketmaster event information page made by Tickets.Com as part of its crawling process was a protected fair use because the purpose of the copy was to obtain unprotected facts. The web crawler also copied the URLs on Ticketmaster's website, but the court ruled that URLs are uncopyrightable facts, analogous to a street address.

Liability of Electronic Publishers for Infringing Content Posted by Others

Web publishers often provide forums, chat rooms or bulletin boards, where website visitors can upload and display content. This can sometimes expose the website operator to copyright infringement claims—for instance, when the publisher (1) directly commits infringing acts, (2) knows of infringing activity and materially contributes to it (contributory infringement), or (3) has the capacity to control or police the infringer's activities and gets direct financial benefit from the infringing activities (vicarious infringement). These issues have been litigated in a number of cases.

Playboy Enterprises, Inc. v. Frena, 839 F. Supp. 1552 (M.D. Fla. 1993).

The defendant bulletin board operator insisted that (1) he had not known about the infringing photos being distributed through his bulletin board, and (2) he had taken the photos down as soon as he had learned of the infringement. The court nevertheless granted summary judgment for Playboy on its copyright claims, on the ground that because copyright infringement is a "strict liability" offense, the defendant's awareness or lack of awareness was irrelevant.

In *Sega Enterprises Ltd. v. MAPHIA*, 857 F. Supp. 679 (N.D. Cal. 1994).

The defendant was a bulletin board operator who had asked his fee-paying subscribers to upload certain types of files, including some subject to copyright protection, so that others could download them. The court issued a preliminary injunction, explaining that though the owner had not himself performed any of the specific infringing acts, it had enough knowledge of and involvement in such practices to establish a prima facie case of contributory copyright infringement.

Religious Technology Center v. Netcom, 907 F. Supp. 1361 (N.D. Cal. 1995).

The court set limits on Internet service provider liability. Netcom was the Internet access provider for a bulletin board operator at whose site an individual user had posted material copyright protected by the Church of Scientology. The church's Religious Technical Center (RTC) sued the user, the bulletin board operator, and Netcom. The court found no direct infringement by Netcom. Furthermore, it found no vicarious infringement, reasoning that Netcom had no policy of failing to enforce copyrights and had not benefited financially from the posting of RTC's copyright-protected material. However, the court refused to dismiss the case entirely, saying the access provider might be contributorily liable because RTC had given Netcom and the bulletin board operator notice of the violation, and the providers might not have acted reasonably upon receipt of this notice.

Playboy Enterprises, Inc. v. Webbworld, Inc., 968 F. Supp. 1171 (N.D. Tex. 1997).

A website owner had devised an automated electronic process that searched his website for photos, including copyright-protected *Playboy* photos, uploaded by users. The photos were then posted in a separate area of the website for paying subscribers. The court found the website owner liable for copyright infringement.

The Digital Millennium Copyright Act of 1998 (DMCA)

The Digital Millennium Copyright Act (DMCA), enacted in October 1998, amended U.S. copyright law to better protect digital works. Before enactment of the DMCA, protecting works in digital formats was particularly challenging because of the ease with which such works can be copied and shared over the Internet. The DMCA made it unlawful to circumvent any anti-access measure (such as encryption, coding, passwording, etc.) built in to software and other protected works. In other words, if a work in digital format is protected by an effective anti-piracy measure, it is unlawful to *access* the work without authorization, irrespective of what one does with the work once it has been accessed. The DMCA also includes safe-harbor provisions that protect ISPs from liability for the infringing acts of their users.

Safe-Harbor Provisions

Section 512 of the Digital Millennium Copyright Act, 17 U.S.C. § 512, limits the liability of service providers for their role in providing online material. The Act contains four limited exemptions from liability, known as the "safe-harbor" provisions. Each has its own requirements:

Section 512(a) protects service providers from liability for transmitting infringing material. A service provider is protected so long as it does not initiate the transmission, does not select or modify the material that is transmitted, does not select the recipients, and does not maintain a copy on its system that is ordinarily accessible to others or is retained for a period longer than is necessary to make the transmission.

Section 512(b) protects service providers from liability for system caching, the process some Internet service providers use to copy, store and re-post web pages to facilitate access to those pages by their subscribers. Among the many requirements to qualify for this immunity, service providers are not allowed to modify the cached content or to prevent the originating website from collecting information or receiving credit for traffic it would have received if the service provider's customer had accessed the page directly. The caching must also not interfere with any password or fee requirements on the originating website. The service provider must also comply with the originating website's rules concerning refreshing, reloading or updating the material so the original website's content is accurately represented when accessed from cache. The service provider must also take down any infringing material that the originating website has been asked to remove under Section 512(c)(3).

Section 512(c) protects service providers from liability for content that users post and store on their systems. The protection is provided only if the service provider can demonstrate: (1) that it does not have actual or constructive knowledge of the allegedly infringing material, or upon obtaining knowledge or awareness of infringing activity, it acted expeditiously to remove the material; (2) that it does not receive a direct financial benefit from the infringing material if it has the "right and ability to control" the material; and (3) that it promptly removed the allegedly infringing material upon receiving notification in the manner provided by Section 512(c)(3). To be eligible for protection under § 512(c), the service provider must designate with the Copyright Office an agent to receive such notices of copyright infringement.

Section 512(d) provides protection for service providers that link users to online locations that contain infringing material. The prerequisites to qualifying for protection under this section are similar to the prerequisites to protection under Section 512(c). Other copyright issues involving linking are discussed above.

ISP Lawsuits Under the DMCA

Hendrickson v. eBay, Inc., 165 F. Supp. 2d 1082 (C.D. Cal. 2001).

The U.S. District Court for the Central District of California ruled that the Internet auction company eBay was protected by one of the safe-harbor provisions of the DMCA. The plaintiff sued eBay when the auction company refused to remove allegedly pirated DVDs and videotapes of the plaintiff's documentary that were being offered for sale. The court held that eBay was entitled to safe-harbor protection under § 512(c) of the DMCA because it met all three prerequisites for safe-harbor protection. The court found that the evidence demonstrated that eBay did not have actual or constructive knowledge of the particular listings, nor did it have the "right and ability to control" the allegedly infringing activity. The court stated that the "right and ability to control" language of the DMCA "cannot simply mean the ability of a service provider to remove or block access to materials posted on its website or stored in its system [because] . . . [t]o hold otherwise would defeat the purpose of the DMCA and render the statute internally inconsistent." *Hendrickson*, at 1093. Finally, the court held that Hendrickson had failed to comply substantially with the notice requirements of § 512(c)(3). The court granted eBay's motion for summary judgment.

The same plaintiff, Hendrickson, later filed a similar suit against Amazon.com, alleging copyright infringement for Amazon.com's failure to monitor its site for the sale of pirated DVDs and videotapes of the plaintiff's documentary. In 2003, the U.S. District Court for the Central District of California again ruled in favor of the defendant, citing the plaintiff's failure to comply with the notice requirements of the DMCA § 512(c)(3). *See Hendrickson v. Amazon.com, et al.*, No. CV 02-08443 (C.D. Cal., Dec. 8, 2003).

ALS Scan, Inc. v. RemarQ Communities, Inc., 239 F.3d 619 (4th Cir. 2001).

Defendant, RemarQ, operated message boards and news groups to which third-party users posted over 10,000 photographs owned by ALS Scan. ALS Scan demanded that RemarQ disable two particular newsgroups where a majority of the infringing photographs was posted. RemarQ refused to comply, relying on DMCA safe harbor § 512(a) (17 U.S.C. § 512(a)), which shields a service provider from liability when it lacks knowledge of an infringement. RemarQ insisted it would only remove individual photographs that ALS Scan specifically identified, as required by the DMCA (§ 512(c)(3)(a)). ALS Scan argued that, by virtue of its letter informing RemarQ of the infringing postings, RemarQ had sufficient notice of infringement under the DMCA and was not, as it suggested, merely a passive conduit entitled to the DMCA's safe-harbor protections.

In February 2001, the U.S. Court of Appeals for the Fourth Circuit reversed the trial court's grant of summary judgment in favor of defendant RemarQ. The court determined that ALS Scan had substantially complied with the DMCA's notification requirements; therefore, defendant RemarQ could not rely on the DMCA's safe-harbor protections. The DMCA's notice provision requires the copyright holder to provide a service provider with a "representative list" of the infringing material appearing on its service. The court found that such a representative list need only be reasonably sufficient to allow the service provider to locate and remove the infringing material. Notification of every infringing use is not necessary to comply with the DMCA's notification procedures so long as the service provider is given notice sufficient to make it aware of infringing use. When ALS Scan directed RemarQ to the two offending newsgroups and advised RemarQ that each of its copyright-protected photographs contained the ALS Scan logo, it substantially complied with the DMCA notification requirements. Therefore, a trial court could reasonably rule that RemarQ must remove or disable access to all such copyright-protected material.

Ellison v. Robertson, et al., 189 F. Supp. 2d 1051 (C. D. Cal., 2002).

The plaintiff, novelist Harlan Ellison, alleged that the defendant, Steven Robertson, scanned large sections of the plaintiff's copyright-protected works and posted them to a

USENET newsgroup, alt.binaries.e-book. The U.S. District Court for the Central District of California held that the failure of Internet service provider America Online to track down and eliminate copyright infringers on USENET services did not negate AOL's safe-harbor protection under the DMCA.

 Rossi v. Motion Picture Association of America Inc., No. 02-00239BMK, 2003 U.S. Dist. LEXIS 12864 (D. Haw. Apr. 29, 2003) (decision also available at http://www.internetmovies.com/rossi-mpaa_sum_judge.pdf).

Under the DMCA, a copyright owner can request that an ISP remove or disable access to a website if the copyright owner has a good faith basis to suspect that the site distributes his copyright-protected material. In *Rossi*, the U.S. District Court for the District of Hawaii concluded that a copyright holder need not conduct a thorough investigation in order to demonstrate a good faith basis to suspect that a website is unlawfully distributing copyright-protected material. Michael Rossi, owner of internetmovies.com, filed suit against the Motion Picture Association of American (MPAA) after it demanded that Rossi's ISP remove the internetmovies.com website from its servers because of the allegedly infringing content on the site. The website did not contain any unauthorized copyright-protected material, so Rossi sued the MPAA for tortious interference with its contracts and business. The court held that statements on the website, such as "Full Downloadable Movies," which were placed immediately adjacent to screen shots taken from major motion pictures, led the motion picture industry to have a good faith basis to believe that the site illegally distributed copyright-protected material. The court ruled that the DMCA did not require the MPAA to conduct any further investigation into the allegedly infringing material, and granted the MPAA's motion for summary judgment.

ISP Liability

Despite the DMCA's general treatment of Internet service providers (ISPs) as "passive conduits" that are not held accountable for the online activities of customers, a few recent court cases have required ISPs to cooperate more fully with authorities.

 Graf v. Microsoft GmbH, OLGZ Cologne, No. 15 U 221/01 (May 28, 2002), available at http://www.terhaag.de/ra/bnawash-main.html.

In May 2002, a German court held ISP Microsoft Network responsible for content (pictures of tennis celebrity Steffi Graf's face pasted onto photos of naked bodies) placed on its server by private users. The court said that from the point of view of an objective user, the content of the online community where the pictures' were posted could be attributed to Microsoft because Microsoft provided the infrastructure, established the topic, permitted the posting on its web pages, framed the community page with advertisements, and stipulated basic rules for participation.

 Perfect 10 Inc. v. Cybernet Ventures Inc., 213 F. Supp. 2d 1146 (C.D. Cal. 2002).

The plaintiff, Perfect 10, operates a pornographic website. The defendant, Cybernet Ventures, operates an online age-verification service that is used by thousands of pornography websites. Visitors to pornographic websites that use Cybernet Ventures' service are automatically prompted by Cybernet Venture's Adult Check (AC) service to provide payment by a valid credit card in order to receive the passcodes required to access the adult content of the sites. The valid credit card requirement was intended to serve as a proxy for identifying site visitors who are at least 18 years of age. A number of websites that used Cybernet Ventures' age verification service displayed, without authorization, photographs that were identical to some of the copyright-protected photographs on Perfect 10's website.

In April 2002, Perfect 10 obtained a preliminary injunction against Cybernet Ventures, prohibiting Cybernet Ventures from providing services to sites that infringed Perfect 10's copyrights by posting Perfect 10's photographs on their sites. Perfect 10 successfully argued that Cybernet Ventures' AC service encouraged, and financially benefited from, unauthorized postings of Perfect 10's photos on websites operated by the Cybernet Ventures' clients, and was therefore contributorily and vicariously liable for the clients' infringing uses of the photographs. The court found that Perfect 10 was likely to prove that Cybernet Ventures benefited from the infringing uses because each client pornographic site paid an access fee directly to Cybernet Ventures' AC service based on the popularity of its site. The court found the DMCA safe-harbor provisions would not apply to Cybernet Ventures' AC service because of its failure to implement a policy terminating use of its service by repeat infringers. As a result of the injunction, Cybernet Ventures stopped providing its AC service to thousands of pornography websites. *See* "Dirty Sites Jittery After Ruling," WIRED (May 10, 2002), *available at* http://www.wired.com/news/business/0,1367,52429,00.html.

RIAA v. Verizon Internet Services (In re Verizon Internet Services., Inc.), 240 F. Supp. 2d 24 (D.D.C. 2003), *motion denied by, stay granted by, in part*, 258 F. Supp. 2d 6 (D.D.C. 2003), *stay denied by*, No. 03-7015, 2003 U.S. App. LEXIS 11250 (D.C. Cir. June. 4, 2003), *vacated and remanded by*, No. 03-7015, 2003 U.S. App. LEXIS 25735 (D.C. Cir., Dec. 19, 2003).

On behalf of the major recording labels, the Recording Industry Association of America (RIAA) filed suit against Verizon, an Internet service provider, seeking an order compelling Verizon to identify subscribers that RIAA had accused of illegally trading copyright-protected musical recordings using peer-to-peer file-sharing software. Verizon argued that because the infringing material was merely transmitted over its network, and not stored on it, the subpoena was beyond the scope of the DMCA. The court disagreed and ordered Verizon to identify the accused Verizon subscribers.

Verizon appealed to the U.S. Court of Appeals for the District of Columbia Circuit. In the meantime, the RIAA had served a second subpoena on Verizon seeking additional names. Verizon sought to quash the second subpoena, this time also arguing that the provision of the DMCA that authorizes the subpoenas was unconstitutional. The Constitution empowers the federal courts to adjudicate "cases" and "controversies." To the extent the DMCA authorized issuance of subpoenas without regard to whether a case or controversy was pending before the court, Verizon argued, it was unconstitutional. The trial court again rejected Verizon's arguments. *See RIAA v. Verizon Internet Servs. (In re Verizon Internet Servs., Inc.)*, No. 03-MS-0040 (JDB), 2003 U.S. Dist. LEXIS 6778 (D.D.C. Apr. 14, 2003). Verizon appealed again. Verizon also asked the Court of Appeals to stay the trial court's orders until the appellate court could decide its appeals. On June 4, 2003, the Court of Appeals denied Verizon's request for a stay, and, as a result, Verizon identified the Verizon subscribers that RIAA wished to pursue for copyright infringement. *See* Christopher Stern, *Verizon Identifies Download Suspects*, "Firm Says Fight Goes on to Guard Privacy," WASHINGTON POST (June 6, 2003), at E05.

On December 19, 2003, the D.C. Circuit ruled on the merits of Verizon's appeals. It agreed with Verizon that the DMCA's subpoena provision does not authorize the issuance of a subpoena to an ISP that *transmits* infringing material; only to an ISP that *stores* infringing material. Because the infringing music files are stored on individuals' computers and not on Verizon's servers, the court reasoned, the DMCA subpoena provision does not apply. The Court of Appeals vacated and remanded the trial court's decision with respect to the first subpoena, and granted Verizon's motion to quash the second subpoena.

Pacific Bell Internet Services v. RIAA, No. C 03 3560 (N.D. Cal., filed Jul. 30, 2003).

Pac Bell, an ISP, filed suit against the RIAA, seeking a declaration that the subpoenas it received demanding that it reveal to the RIAA the identities of its subscribers accused of unlawfully sharing digital music files, are not authorized by the DMCA. Pac Bell argues that it is acting as a conduit and does not store any of the allegedly infringing works on its servers. The DMCA subpoena provision, Pac Bell asserts, only applies to stored information.

Massachusetts Institute of Technology *v. RIAA*, No. 1:03-MC-10209-JLT (D. Mass., Aug. 7, 2003); *Boston College v. RIAA*, No. 1:03-MC-10210-JLT (D. Mass., Aug. 7, 2003).

Massachusetts colleges MIT and Boston College challenged subpoenas from the RIAA, arguing that the RIAA's requests for information about the colleges' students were not properly filed. All of the subpoenas RIAA had requested throughout the United States had been issued by a single federal court in the District of Columbia. MIT and BC argued successfully that they were not subject to subpoenas issued outside of Massachusetts. The court quashed the subpoenas, stating that federal rules require valid subpoenas to be issued in a local court.

A few weeks later, however, the RIAA had subpoenas issued by a federal court in Massachusetts. The universities agreed to comply with the subpoenas and to provide the names of students who used the universities' networks to share copyright-protected digital music recordings. *RIAA v. Massachusetts Institute for Technology*, No. 1:03-MC-10257 (D. Mass., filed Aug. 25, 2003); *RIAA v. Boston Coll.*, No. 1:03-MC-10255 (D. Mass., filed Aug. 22, 2003). Boston University, which had challenged the earlier subpoena in a letter to the RIAA, also agreed to comply with a subpoena issued by the local court. *RIAA v. Boston Univ.*, No. 1:03-MD-10256 (D. Mass., filed Aug. 25, 2003).

Online Policy Group, et al. v. Diebold, Inc., No. 03-4913 JF (N.D. Cal., filed Nov. 14, 2003).

Diebold, a manufacturer of electronic voting machines, discovered in March 2003 that an unknown hacker had obtained hundreds of internal emails from its computers. Some of the emails contained references to potential security flaws in the voting machines. Two students at Swarthmore College acquired these emails and posted them on their website, using the title "Diebold Internal Memos," to address concerns about voting technology in the democratic process. Because Diebold owns copyright rights in the emails, and the students' use arguably constituted copyright infringement, Diebold sent Swarthmore College (the students' ISP) notice of the infringement pursuant to the

DMCA. Swarthmore removed the infringing emails from its servers in compliance with the DMCA's statutory notification requirements.

The students, along with some organizations devoted to online privacy and free speech, sued Diebold, alleging that Diebold's DMCA "take down" notification constituted misuse of copyright interest. The plaintiffs sought an order barring Diebold from suing any students who posted the emails, or their ISPs, or threatening to sue them, for copyright infringement. The plaintiffs also waged a campaign against Diebold, soliciting college students nationwide to post the stolen emails as a gesture of solidarity and civil disobedience. In December 2003, Diebold withdrew its DMCA notifications, and announced it would not sue ISPs or their subscribers for copyright infringement for the noncommercial use of the posted emails. *See* Letter from Robert J. Urosevich, President, Diebold Election Systems, Inc., to Will Doherty, Online Privacy Group (Dec. 3, 2003), available at http://www.eff.org/Legal/ISP_liability/OPG_v_Diebold/diebold_wdrawal_letter.php. As of December 31, 2003, the plaintiffs were continuing to pursue a court order barring Diebold from filing suit. *See* Cynthia L. Webb, "Diebold Backs Down on Lawsuits," washingtonpost.com (Dec. 4, 2003), *available at* http://www.Washingtonpost.com/ac2/wp-dyn?pagename=article&node=&contentId=A355152003Dec4&notFound=true.

Fatwallet, Inc. v. Best Buy Enterprise Services, Inc., et al., No. 03 C 50508 (N.D. Ill., filed Nov. 25, 2003).

Fatwallet operates a website on which users share consumer retail information with other users. Some user postings on the website included sale and pricing information at various retail stores, including Best Buy, Kohl's, and Target. Some retail stores sent "take down" notifications to Fatwallet pursuant to the DMCA's notice requirements, demanding that Fatwallet remove from its website user postings containing pricing information on the ground that the postings infringed their copyright rights in the pricing information. Faced with multiple actions for copyright infringement, Fatwallet removed the postings from its website. In November 2003, Fatwallet filed suit against various retailers, seeking declarations that pricing information constitutes facts that are not copyright protected, and that the DMCA "take down" notices the retailers sent were a misuse of the DMCA and a violation of its First Amendment rights to free speech.

Liability for Circumventing Technological Copyright Protection Measures

While generally limiting the liability of online service providers, the DMCA also creates new liability with its anti-circumvention provision. Section 1201 of the DMCA outlaws conduct and devices primarily designed to circumvent technological measures put in place to control access to works and to protect the rights of copyright owners. *See* 17 U.S.C. § 1201. The DMCA provides both civil and criminal penalties for such conduct. *See id.* at §§ 1203-1204.

On May 3, 2002, the Electronic Frontier Foundation, a nonprofit organization devoted to protecting free speech in digital media, published a report on the "unintended consequences" of the DMCA over the past three years, including accounts of various researchers withholding electronic security research results for fear of prosecution under the DMCA's anti-circumvention provision. The report is available at http://www.eff.org/IP/DMCA/20020503_dmca_consequences.pdf.

RealNetworks Inc. v. Streambox, Inc., No. C99-2070P, 2000 U.S. Dist. LEXIS 1889 (W.D. Wash. Jan. 18, 2000).

RealNetworks Inc. filed suit against Streambox, Inc. in December 1999, alleging that three Streambox products violated the anti-circumvention provisions of the DMCA. The U.S. District Court for the Western District of Washington granted a preliminary injunction against Streambox, prohibiting it from distributing two of these products, the Streambox VCR and the Ferret. The Streambox VCR mimics a RealNetworks product, RealMedia, circumvents the authentication procedure created by RealNetworks (the "Secret Handshake"), and allows users to download RealMedia files that are streamed over the Internet. The court found that the Secret Handshake is a technological measure that effectively controlled access to copyright-protected works, and that the Streambox VCR is primarily, if not exclusively, designed to circumvent this protection. The court found that the Streambox VCR had no significant commercial purpose other than to enable users to access and to record protected content. The court also granted a preliminary injunction with respect to the Ferret (a plug-in that alters the RealPlayer). The court found a likelihood of success on the plaintiff's copyright infringement claim because the Ferret created an unauthorized derivative work based on the RealPlayer. The court denied a preliminary injunction as to another product, the Ripper (a file conversion tool that allows users to convert files from one format to another), because it did not circumvent any technological measure and had independently significant commercial purposes.

This case was settled in September 2000. In addition to a cash settlement, Streambox agreed to modify its Streambox VCR and Ripper software to prevent the unauthorized modification of RealMedia files. It also agreed to stop distributing the Ferret plug-in. Jim Hu, "RealNetworks Settles Lawsuit With Streambox," CNET News.com (Sept. 8, 2000), *available at* http://news.com/2100-1023-245482.html?legacy=cnet.

 Universal City Studios, Inc, et al.. v. Reimerdes, 111 F. Supp. 2d 294 (S.D.N.Y. 2000), *aff'd*, 273 F.3d 429 (2d Cir. 2001).

Members of the motion picture industry brought suit under the DMCA's anti-circumvention provisions against *2600 Magazine/The Hacker Quarterly* for posting and linking to "DeCSS" on its website. DeCSS is a utility designed to defeat the CSS encryption technology used to protect DVDs.

The U.S. District Court for the Southern District of New York permanently enjoined defendants from posting DeCSS on their own website and from linking to any other website containing DeCSS. The court ruled that the defendants' actions did not fall within any of the exceptions to the DMCA. The court also found that fair use was not a defense to the anti-circumvention provision of the DMCA. The court ruled that the defendants violated the anti-circumvention provision not only by posting DeCSS on their website, but also, under the particular facts of this case, by linking to other websites where DeCSS was available for download. The court also rejected the defendants' claims that the anti-circumvention provision of the DMCA is unconstitutional.

On November 28, 2001, the Court of Appeals for the Second Circuit affirmed the decision of the trial court.

DVD Copy Control Association v. Bunner, 93 Cal. App. 4th 648 (Cal. Ct. App. 2001), *rev'd*, 75 P.3d 1 (Cal. 2003).

A California Court of Appeal had reversed a trial court's injunction prohibiting the Internet publication of the source code for DeCSS. The appellate court stated that the DVD Copy Control Association's right to protect its trade secret does not outweigh the First Amendment right to freedom of speech. The California Supreme Court reversed the appellate court's ruling, finding that the injunction did not violate the publisher's First Amendment right to free speech because the injunction was content-neutral in that it prohibited a misappropriation of property, not speech. The injunction did not burden any more speech than was necessary to protect trade secrets and research and development benefits. The State Supreme Court sent the case back to the Court of Appeal to consider whether the trial court's factual findings establish that the injunction was warranted under California's trade secret law.

United States v. Elcom Ltd. a/k/a Elcomsoft Co., Ltd. & Dmitry Sklyarov, 203 F. Supp. 2d 1111 (N.D. Cal. 2002).

In the first indictment under the criminal provisions of the DMCA, Russian citizen Dmitry Sklyarov was charged with trafficking in a software product primarily designed or produced for the purpose of circumventing technological copyright protection. The DMCA provides criminal penalties for such conduct when it is perpetrated for purposes of commercial advantage or private financial gain. The indictment alleged that Sklyarov and his Russian employer, Elcomsoft, developed and marketed, for commercial advantage and financial gain, a program called the Advanced e-Book Processor (AEBP) for use in circumventing the Adobe Acrobat e-Book Reader. The Adobe Acrobat e-Book Reader allows reading of electronic books on personal computers, and it permits publishers and distributors to restrict or limit the purchaser's ability to copy, distribute, and print the text, or to have it read audibly by the computer. Sklyarov's AEBP program removes such limitations, allowing the purchaser freely to copy, distribute, and print the text or to have it read by the computer. The maximum statutory penalty for violation of the DMCA's anti-circumvention provisions is five years in prison and a fine of $500,000. Sklyarov, a Ph.D. student who studies cryptography, was arrested and jailed on July 17, 2001, in Las Vegas. He had come to Las Vegas to deliver a lecture on e-book security. In December 2001, the case against Sklyarov was dismissed in exchange for his testimony against his employer, Elcomsoft.

On May 8, 2002, a federal trial court denied motions to dismiss the lawsuit against Elcomsoft on grounds that the anti-circumvention provisions of the DMCA violate the First Amendment. The court stated that, while computer programs can legally qualify as speech, the DMCA is content-neutral because it controls the function of the programs it restricts, not their content. (For a discussion of content-based versus content-neutral speech restrictions, see Chapter 1, pages 1-2.) The court found that the DMCA does not prohibit more speech than necessary to promote the government's legitimate interests in preventing electronic piracy. The court also found that, while the DMCA may make it more difficult for an individual to exercise fair use rights (such as making back-up copies for personal use), the DMCA does not ban or eliminate fair use. On December 17, 2002, a jury acquitted Elcomsoft of all criminal charges. ("Not guilty" verdicts are not subject to appeal.)

321 Studios v. Metro-Goldwyn-Mayer Studios, Inc., No. C 02-1955 SI (N.D. Cal. filed Apr. 23, *2002*).

On April 23, 2002, 321 Studios filed suit against seven major motion picture studios seeking a declaratory judgment that its DVD X Copy and DVD Copy Plus software do not violate the anti-circumvention provisions of the DMCA. 321 Studios contended that its software is designed only to allow users to make back-up copies of their own DVDs; limitations built in to the software make it impractical to use for serial copying. Making back-up copies for personal use, 321 Studios argues, is a permissible "fair use" of the motion picture studios' films. The movie studios countersued 321 Studios, arguing that the DMCA prohibits all circumvention of any effective protective measure; the purpose of the copy is irrelevant because the DMCA does not include a fair-use exception for circumvention. As of December 31, 2003, the case remains pending before the trial court.

On September 5, 2003, the MPAA (Motion Picture Association of America) sued 321 Studios, which has a London office, in the United Kingdom, alleging that 321 Studio's DVD-copying software circumvents anti-copying protections in violation of the UK's Copyright, Designs and Patents Act. "DVD Boss Raring for Court Battle," BBC News (Sept. 8, 2003), *available at* http://news.bbc.co.uk/2/hi/entertainment/3090768.stm.

 Sunde v. Johansen, No. 02-507 M/94 (Norway Dist. Ct., Jan. 7, 2003), *available at* http://www.eff.org/IP/Video/DeCSS_prosecutions/Johansen_DeCSS_case/20030109_johansen_decision.html, *aff'd*, [Case No. unavailable] (Nor. App. Ct., Dec. 22, 2003).

On January 9, 2003, a court in Norway found Jon Johansen, the Norwegian teenager who developed DeCSS, the DVD decryption software, not guilty of copyright infringement. Because DeCSS has other legitimate uses, such as enabling DVD playback using the Linux operating system, developing and distributing the software is not a violation of Norwegian criminal copyright law. The prosecution appealed. On December 22, 2003, the Oslo Appeals Court upheld the trial court's judgment. Reuters, "Norwegian Cleared of DVD Piracy," CNET News.com (Dec. 22, 2003), *available at* http://rss.com.com/100-1030-5130503.html.

 Paramount Pictures Corp., et al. v. Tritton Technologies, Inc., et al., No. 03 CV 7316 (S.D.N.Y., filed Sept. 17, 2003).

Two motion picture studios sued makers of software that overrides CSS ("content scrambling system") technology intended to prevent unauthorized copying of DVDs for violating the DMCA's anti-circumvention provision. The plaintiff motion picture studios seek a permanent injunction, prohibiting the defendants from manufacturing or trafficking in software or other products that are used to copy copyright-protected works from DVDs. As of December 31, 2003, there have been no reported developments in the dispute.

Limiting the Scope of the DMCA

The DMCA's scheme for protecting digital materials has been criticized since the statute was enacted. Because the DMCA lacks a fair-use defense or other means to rationalize some legitimate uses of copyright-protected digital materials, efforts are under way to limit the scope and reach of the DMCA.

<u>Regulations and Proposed Legislation</u>

Exemption to Prohibition on Circumvention of Copyright Protection Systems for Access Control Technologies (37 CFR § 201 *et seq.*)

The Library of Congress, which oversees the U.S. Copyright Office, created four exemptions from liability under DMCA for circumventing digital protection measures. On October 28, 2003, the Library of Congress announced that protection can be circumvented to access (1) lists of Internet locations blocked by commercially marketed filtering software, not including spam filters or filters that operate to protect against damage; (2) computer programs that are protected by dongles (hardware locks) that are obsolete; (3) computer programs or video games that use obsolete hardware or formats; and (4) e-books with access controls that prevent enabling read-aloud functions and screen readers for visually impaired users.

Congress is considering several bills that would amend the DMCA.

Consumers, Schools, and Libraries Digital Rights Management Awareness Act of 2003 (S. 1621)

On September 16, 2003, Senator Sam Brownback (R-Kan.) introduced legislation that would limit subpoena power under the DMCA by requiring owners of digital media to file actual claims before obtaining identifying information about alleged infringers. The bill has been referred to the Committee on Commerce, Science, and Transportation.

On October 2, 2002, Rep. Zoe Lofgren (D-Cal.) introduced the Digital Choice and Freedom Act (H.R. 5522). The bill would provide protections for consumers who make backup copies or give away digital material they have purchased. Additionally, it would permit consumers to bypass technological protections on copyright-protected materials in order to use the copyright-protected work for a legal purpose.

On October 3, 2002, Rep. Richard Boucher (D-Va.) introduced the Digital Media Consumers' Rights Act of 2002 (H.R. 5544). The bill would amend the Federal Trade Commission Act to provide that the advertising or sale of a copy-protected music disc that is not clearly identified as copy-protected is an unfair method of competition and an unfair and deceptive act or practice. It would also amend the DMCA to include a fair-use defense for circumventing technological protections (for example, by passcode or other security measure) of copyright-protected digital works for noninfringing or otherwise defensible uses. When the 108th Congress convened in January 2003, Rep. Boucher (D-Va.) reintroduced the Digital Media Consumers' Rights Act of 2002 (H.R. 107), which is identical to the bill he introduced in November 2002 (H.R. 5544).

Video and Music on the Web

Webcasting

The proliferation of music on the Web has prompted the music industry to consider how best to regulate webcasting of copyright-protected musical works. Musical works are subject to two separate copyrights: the copyright in the musical composition (both music and lyrics) and the copyright in the musical performance (the recorded rendition of the musical composition). Typically, publishing companies own the copyrights to musical compositions, and record companies hold the rights to musical performances.

Radio stations pay royalties for blanket licenses for their rights to broadcast musical compositions. They have been statutorily exempt from paying royalties for the musical performances, because Congress believed that radio air-play promotes record sales. As many radio stations began making their broadcasts available on the Internet, copyright holders sought to be compensated for their work. Radio broadcasters argued that their existing blanket licenses should apply to webcasting the musical compositions, and that the promotional value of their webcasting should exempt them from paying performance royalties, as it exempted them from paying royalties with respect to their broadcasts. However, in December 2000, under the DMCA, the Copyright Office ruled that webcasting requires additional licenses for musical compositions, and that webcasters must pay royalties for the musical performances, as well.

Bonneville International Corp. v. Peters, 153 F. Supp. 2d 763 (E.D. Pa. 2001) *aff'd* 347 F.3d 485 (3d Cir. 2003).

In 2001, radio station operators filed suit in a federal court in Pennsylvania against the U.S. Copyright Office asking the court to review the Copyright Office ruling that imposed an obligation to pay royalties for musical performances on FCC-licensed broadcasters that webcast their signals over the Internet. The Recording Industry Association of America joined the Copyright Office as an intervenor-defendant. The court did not directly consider whether broadcast stations' webcasting activities should be exempt from royalties for musical performances in digital audio transmissions, but instead deferred to the Copyright Office's determination that they are not exempt. The court granted the motion for summary judgment filed by the Copyright Office and RIAA, which was affirmed on appeal.

The court's decision has serious implications for radio broadcasters who stream their own broadcast signals over the Internet: they must now (1) comply with the requirements of the DMCA to be eligible for a statutory license; (2) negotiate a separate license with the sound recording copyright owner; or (3) cease webcasting.

Royalty Fees for Internet Radio Broadcasts—History

The DMCA provides that the statutory license fees and terms for webcasts of musical performances are to be set by voluntary agreement as a result of industry negotiations, or by a Copyright Arbitration Royalty Panel (CARP) if the parties cannot agree. Because negotiations between webcasters and the recording industry did not result in an agreement, a CARP was convened. More than 15 webcasters and several broadcast groups proposed a royalty rate of $0.0015 per music webcast listener hour, while the Recording Industry Association of America proposed that webcasters pay $0.0004 per streamed performance, that is, per song per listener. Radio stations currently pay $0.0022 per listener hour for their terrestrial broadcasts to performance rights societies such as SESAC, BMI and ASCAP. On February 20, 2002, the CARP announced its recommended rates of $0.0007 for retransmissions of terrestrial broadcasts, and $0.0014 for all other Internet broadcasts.

On April 22, 2002, a bipartisan group of 20 lawmakers asked the Copyright Office to review the proposal in light of arguments that the fee structure would force small Internet broadcasters out of business.

On June 20, 2002, at the recommendation of the Registrar of Copyrights, the Librarian of Congress rejected the CARP's determination, stating that significant portions of it were arbitrary or contrary to law. The Librarian accepted the CARP's conclusion that an agreement negotiated between RIAA and Yahoo represented the best evidence of what rates would have been negotiated in the marketplace between a willing buyer and a willing seller, but rejected the CARP finding that Internet broadcasts have less promotional impact for the record companies than traditional broadcasts. The Librarian set a $0.0007 rate (a lower $0.0002 rate was established for noncommercial stations) for each song performance, regardless of whether the performance is a retransmission of a terrestrial broadcast or an Internet-only transmission. The rates applied retroactively to 1998, with initial payments due in October 2002. On April 3, 2003, a number of large webcasters, including Yahoo, America Online, Microsoft, and Real Networks, reached an agreement with SoundExchange, the royalty receiving agent designated by the recording industry. Under the agreement, which is effective through 2004, large webcasters have an option to pay the $0.0007 per performance rate established by the Librarian of Congress, less a 4% discount, or to pay $0.0117 per listener hour. Subscription services can opt to pay 10.9% of their subscription service revenues in lieu of any other royalty payment.

On December 4, 2002, President Bush signed into law the Small Webcaster Settlement Act of 2002 (SWSA) (17 U.S.C. § 114(8)(5)). The SWSA applies to "Noncommercial Webcasters" and to "Small Commercial Webcasters." The SWSA is intended to address Congressional concerns that noncommercial and small commercial webcasters were not adequately represented in the process that resulted in the Copyright Office's July 8, 2002 decision establishing royalty rates for webcasting digital sound recordings. The SWSA delayed until June 2003 the date by which noncommercial and small commercial webcasters must have made their initial royalty payments. The extra time was intended to allow noncommercial and small commercial webcasters to negotiate new royalty rate agreements with SoundExchange, the royalty receiving agent designated by the recording industry, with royalty fees to be based on a percentage of revenue rather than on a per performance basis.

On June 3, 2003, small webcasters announced they had reached an agreement, under which webcasters with fewer than 200 listeners per hour will pay a flat, yearly fee between $250 and $500. Stations exceeding the 200-listener limit must pay an additional fee per song per listener.

Retransmission of Television Broadcast Signals

With the increased use of broadband Internet connections in homes and businesses, entrepreneurs have sought to develop services that will allow users to view broadcast television signals on the web. In 1999, the Canadian Radio-television and Telecommunications Commission (CRTC) exempted Internet-based operations from the regulations of the country's Broadcasting Act. According to Canada's Copyright Act, a company whose operations are "comparable" to those of cable television providers may retransmit a live signal "in its entirety" if its operations are "lawful under the Broadcasting Act." Two companies, JumpTV and iCraveTV, argued that the exemption makes their operations automatically lawful under Canada's Broadcasting Act.

Twentieth Century Fox Film Corp., et al. v. iCraveTV, No. 2000 U.S. Dist. LEXIS 11670, 53 U.S.P.Q.2d (BNA) 1831 (W.D. Pa 2000).

A Canadian Internet publisher, iCraveTV.com, was capturing U.S. television programming by picking up the signals of television stations, converting the signals to digital form, and then streaming the broadcasts over its website. Several major U.S. motion picture studios, the National Football League, the National Basketball Association, and three major broadcasters filed suit to stop the webcasts, alleging copyright infringement and Lanham Act trademark violations. After a court-ordered preliminary injunction, iCraveTV.com announced in February 2000 that the parties had settled the lawsuit. iCraveTV.com halted its retransmission practices, and, in June 2000, announced its intention to relaunch using a software called "iWall" that would identify users by country and block users in the United States from receiving transmissions. Additionally, iCrave stated that it planned to pay copyright holders by charging a subscription fee, functioning much like a cable-television system. As of December 31, 2003, the domain name www.iCraveTV.com did not resolve to a functioning website.

Video Streaming

Video streaming refers to the process of providing users the ability to view (but not download) individual video files, such as feature-length films, over the Internet. Video streams are made available by the sender and are accessed by the recipient.

 Video Pipeline, Inc. v. Buena Vista Home Entertainment, Inc., 275 F. Supp. 2d 543 (D.N.J. 2003).

The plaintiff, Video Pipeline, provides previews of home videos to home-video wholesalers and retailers. It entered into a master clip license agreement with defendant Buena Vista, a motion picture studio. The license authorized Video Pipeline to exhibit certain video clips and promotional videos provided by Buena Vista through its videopipeline.net network. These previews could be viewed, but not downloaded, by Video Pipelines' retail clients. Video Pipeline originally filed suit against Buena Vista seeking a declaratory judgment that its use of the trailers to make its own video clips does not constitute copyright infringement. The court held that Video Pipeline's making of its own video-clip previews for transmission over the Internet is not protected from a copyright-infringement claim by the fair use defense or the first sale doctrine. The court denied Video Pipeline's motion for declaratory judgment, and granted Buena Vista's motion for summary judgment. Video Pipeline was ordered to return all the video clips Buena Vista had provided.

For a discussion of this case in the context of fair use, see page 102, above.

Taiwan-based Movie88.com sold unauthorized access to thousands of feature-length movies for $1 each. Taiwanese authorities shut down the site in February 2002 through cooperation with Movie88.com's Internet service provider under international provisions of the U.S. Digital Millennium Copyright Act. A replacement, Film88.com, appeared in June 2002. Although Film88 was headquartered in Iran, its servers were based in the Netherlands. The Motion Picture Association of America worked with Film88's Netherlands-based Internet service provider to shut down the site. The sites remain inactive. John Borland, "End of the Reel for $1 Movies," CNET News.com (Feb. 19, 2002), *available at* http://2dnet.com/2100-1106-840275.html.

Internet Music Technology

Music-file swapping has become widely popular in recent years. When MP3 file formatting entered the mainstream, Internet users downloaded programs such as Kazaa, Morpheus, Napster, and Gnutella, and, with relative ease, users transferred and downloaded many thousands of files a day over peer-to-peer networks. The recording industry and file-swapping supporters argue over whether Internet file sharing increases or decreases music sales. One 2002 study by Forrester Research showed that Internet piracy is not to blame for the 15% decline in record sales since 2000, but that the economy and competition from other media outlets are the source. Reuters, "Forrester Sees $2 Billion Digital Music Market By 2007" (Aug. 13, 2002), *available at* http://www.siliconvalley.com/mld/siliconvalley/news/editorial/3856253.htm.

Believing that file-swapping has had an extraordinary impact on the decline in record sales, the record industry has sued several file-swapping software distributors for copyright infringement, with mixed success, for their role in allowing users to share music files free of charge. Also, in an effort to compete with free music-sharing software and to provide legitimate alternatives to music file traders, members of the recording industry and software companies have developed and implemented online file delivery services that they hope will meet the demands of consumers and allow them to download files over the Internet without violating the copyright rights of content owners.

Distribution of Digital Audio "MP3" Files

UMG Recordings, Inc. v. MP3.com, Inc., No. 00 Civ 472 JSR, 2000 U.S. Dist. LEXIS 13293 (S.D.N.Y. Sept. 6, 2000).

The plaintiffs brought a copyright infringement action against MP3.com, Inc., which operated a commercial service (My.MP3.com) that allowed users to copy their own music CDs onto servers under MP3.com's control and then to access the music at any time from any place over the Internet. The defendant viewed its service as a "virtual CD player" and asserted a fair-use defense, stating that MP3.com provided a "transformative 'space shift' by which subscribers can enjoy the sound recordings . . . without lugging around the physical discs themselves." In April 2000, the court granted the plaintiffs' motion for partial summary judgment, rejecting the defendant's fair-use defense. The court concluded that the use was not transformative but rather repackaged the recordings to facilitate their transmission through another medium.

By mid-August 2000, MP3.com had settled with all of the plaintiff recording companies except UMG. MP3.com agreed to pay the recording companies between $75 and $100 million in one of the settlement agreements, in exchange for the right to offer music as part of its My.MP3.com service. Some of the settlements also involved a per-song or per-CD fee.

In September 2000, the court determined that MP3.com had willfully violated UMG's copyrights and awarded statutory damages of $25,000 per CD. While UMG's suit originally claimed 10,000 CDs were copied, in a November 2000 settlement, MP3.com admitted responsibility for 4,700 CDs and paid UMG $50 million in damages plus $3.4 million in legal fees.

Based on this decision, MP3.com subsequently was prohibited from arguing in a similar case brought against it that its My.MP3.com service did not willfully infringe copyrights. *See Teevee Toons v. MP3.com, Inc.*, 134 F. Supp. 2d 546 (S.D.N.Y. 2001).

MP3.com was eventually purchased by Vivendi Universal, one of its former major label legal opponents.

⚖ *Zomba Recording Corp., et al. v. Audiogalaxy, Inc.*, No. 02 Civ. 3999 (LTS) (S.D.N.Y., filed May 24, 2002).

In May 2002, RIAA members filed suit against the online music service Audiogalaxy, claiming the company willfully and intentionally encouraged millions of users to copy and distribute the copyright-protected works of its artists and facilitated that distribution and copying. The music search service allows users to download cover artwork and software in addition to songs. Audiogalaxy settled the suit in June 2002, agreeing to obtain appropriate permission or consent from songwriters, music publishers, and recording companies before using or sharing copyright-protected works. Additionally, the company was to pay the recording industry an undetermined amount of money to settle the lawsuit. *See* Gwendolyn Mariano, "Audiogalaxy to Ask First, Trade Later," CNET News.com (June 18, 2002), *available at* http://news.com.com/2100-1023-936932.html.

⚖ *A&M Records, Inc., et al. v. Napster, Inc.*, 284 F.3d 1091 (9th Cir. 2002).

The Recording Industry Association of America sued Napster, Inc., for contributory and vicarious copyright infringement. Napster operated a website and offered software enabling users to easily find and download MP3 music files stored on the hard drives of other users.

In May 2000, the U.S. District Court for the Northern District of California held that the Napster online music system is not a "service provider" entitled to the exemption from contributory and vicarious copyright infringement liability provided to service providers under § 512(a) of the Digital Millennium Copyright Act. The court found that Napster "enables or facilitates" connections between its users, but does not "transmit, route, or provide connections through its system," as required to qualify for the exemption. In July 2000, the trial court entered a preliminary injunction against Napster, rejecting its defenses that the Napster system was lawful because it was capable of being used for substantial noninfringing uses and that the file sharing Napster users engaged in constituted a protected fair use under copyright law.

In February 2001, the U.S. Court of Appeals for the Ninth Circuit ruled that Napster users infringed at least two of the copyright holders' exclusive rights: the rights of reproduction and distribution. The appeals court remanded the case to the trial court to modify the injunction in accordance with its ruling, allowing Napster to continue operating in the meantime. The trial court issued the modified injunction in March 2001, requiring the recording industry to provide Napster with a list of copyright-protected songs that it was required to remove from its servers. In July 2001, the trial court ruled that Napster had to remain offline until it could demonstrate that it could operate a music sharing service that effectively filtered musical works identified by the plaintiff record companies with 100% effectiveness. The U.S. Court of Appeals for the Ninth Circuit affirmed the trial court's injunction on March 25, 2002, effectively shutting off the Napster service.

Napster filed for bankruptcy in June 2002, putting the copyright infringement suit with the record labels on hold. Media conglomerate Bertelsmann initially agreed to purchase Napster, but the bankruptcy court blocked the sale, and the deal subsequently dissolved. On November 27, 2002, Roxio, creators of CD-burning technology, purchased Napster's assets without assuming Napster's legal liabilities. On May 19, 2003, Roxio acquired Pressplay from Universal Music Group and Sony Music Entertainment for approximately $39.5 million. In the fall of 2003, Roxio launched a subscription-based music downloading service under the Napster brand using Pressplay's content and infrastructure. The rebranded service is available at www.napster.com.

Arista Records, et al. v. MP3Board Inc., No. 00 Civ. 4660. 2002 U.S. Dist. LEXIS 16165 (S.D.N.Y. Aug. 28, 2002), *defendant's motion for partial final judgment granted by* 2003 U.S. Dist. LEXIS 11392 (S.D.N.Y. July 3, 2003).

The plaintiffs were several record companies that held copyrights in sound recordings. They alleged that the website mp3board.com enabled listeners to locate and download digital music files over the Internet without authorization, and sued the defendant for contributory and vicarious copyright infringement. The court rejected some of the plaintiffs' claims because they had not provided sufficient notice to the defendant under the DMCA. Of the three cease-and-desist letters that the plaintiffs had sent to the defendant, the court found that only one provided sufficient notice under the DMCA. The two that did not provide sufficient notice included only the names of the artists whose songs the plaintiffs claimed were made available on the site, and did not provide adequate notice for the defendant to locate and remove any infringing links. The letter that provided sufficient notice, on the other hand, included artist names and song titles, and was accompanied by printouts of pages from the MP3Board website, on which the plaintiffs indicated which links it believed were infringing its copyrights. The court indicated that for notice to be sufficient under the DMCA, the copyright holders had to provide, at a minimum, the names of the specific sound recordings they were seeking to protect.

Copyright.net Music Publishing Inc., et al. v. MP3.com Inc., 256 F. Supp. 2d 214 (S.D.N.Y. 2003).

More than 50 music publishers and songwriters, including Copyright.net Music Publishing, filed suit against MP3.com alleging copyright infringement based on MP3.com's distribution of digital audio files. The plaintiffs' complaint maintained that MP3.com willfully, contributorily, and vicariously infringed their copyrights by converting their works from compact discs to MP3 format, storing the allegedly infringing digital audio files on its servers, creating "on demand" access to the digital audio files by subscribers, and facilitating the "viral distribution" or rapid spread of the allegedly infringed works by allowing subscribers to download the files when it should have known that subscribers would distribute them to others in a "viral manner." The suit sought actual damages and profits of MP3.com, statutory damages in the amount of $25,000 for each musical composition copied, attorney fees and costs, and a permanent injunction against MP3.com.

In 2002, the court granted MP3.com's motion for partial summary judgment with respect to a retroactive license to copy musical compositions it entered into pursuant to a settlement agreement with one of the plaintiffs. *See Copyright.net Music Publishing, Inc., et al. v. MP3.com, Inc.*, No. 01-CV 7321, 2003 U.S. Dist. LEXIS 2988 (S.D.N.Y. Mar. 4, 2003) (memorializing the court's grant of partial summary judgment in 2002).

MP3.com asserted several affirmative defenses to the other claims against it, including fair use, innocent intent, express license, and advice of counsel, each of which was rejected by the court. Thereafter, the parties settled the dispute.

Metro-Goldwyn-Mayer Studios, Inc. v. Grokster, Ltd. and *Lieber v. Consumer Empowerment BV a/k/a/ Fasttrack,* Nos. CV 01-08541-SVW (PJWx) & CV 01-09923-SVW (PJWx), 269 F. Supp. 2d 1213 (C.D. Cal. 2003).

Twenty record companies and motion picture studios filed a copyright infringement claim against Grokster, StreamCast Networks, and Kazaa BV, distributors of peer-to-peer file-sharing software programs that gained popularity after Napster ceased operations in 2002. (Kazaa BV failed to defend and a default judgment was entered against it.) Neither Grokster nor StreamCast operates as a centralized file-sharing network like the network operated by Napster. Whereas Napster operated a server on which it indexed all files available for download anywhere on the network, users of Grokster and StreamCast's Morpheus search for downloadable files directly on the computers of other users running, respectively, the Grokster and Morpheus software.

On April 25, 2003, the U.S. District Court for the Central District of California ruled that, though users who download copyright-protected music using the Grokster or Morpheus software are engaging in direct copyright infringement, Grokster and StreamCast, as distributors of that software, are not liable for contributory or vicarious copyright infringement. The court held that to be liable for contributory copyright infringement, a party must have knowledge of the infringement at the time it occurs. Grokster and StreamCast only provide software for download. Once the software is downloaded, their role in file-sharing ceases. Even though Grokster and StreamCast are aware generally that users illegally copy music with their software, they do not materially contribute to copyright infringement because they provide no support to a user at the time illegal file-sharing occurs.

In addition, the court held that the distributors of the peer-to-peer programs are not liable for vicarious copyright infringement because they do not have the right or ability to supervise the infringing activity. In contrast, because Napster controlled the network over which the file-trading occurred, it had the ability to prevent users from trading copyright-protected material. Grokster and StreamCast, however, have no power to monitor or control how users employ their software. In fact, the court pointed out, if it were to order Grokster and StreamCast to shut down, it would have little effect on the use of the software. In August 2003, the plaintiffs appealed the ruling to the U.S. Court of Appeals for the Ninth Circuit. *Metro-Goldwyn-Mayer Studios, Inc. v. Grokster, Ltd.*, No. 03-55894 (9th Cir., filed Aug. 18, 2003). As of December 31, 2003, the Ninth Circuit had not heard the appeal.

 In re Aimster Copyright Litigation, 252 F. Supp. 2d 634 (N.D. Ill. 2002), *aff'd*, 334 F.3d 643 (7th Cir. 2003).

A federal trial court entered a preliminary injunction barring Aimster from continuing to operate its file-sharing service. On appeal, the U.S. Court of Appeals for the Seventh Circuit affirmed the trial court's ruling that Aimster was not entitled to a fair-use defense for the vicarious and contributory infringement claims against it. Aimster, now called "Madster," used instant-messaging technology to allow users to trade audio files. By facilitating infringement by end-users, the court concluded, Aimster vicariously and contributorily infringed the rights of the copyright holders. It could not defend its actions as "fair use." Aimster's reliance on the Supreme Court's decision in the "Betamax" case (*Sony Corp. v. Universal City Studios*, 464 U.S. 417 (1984)) was misplaced, the court said, because Aimster was in complete control of its ongoing service, and was not merely a manufacturer or seller of a potentially infringing device. Madster remained in operation, ignoring the preliminary injunction. On October 30, 2002, the trial court issued a preliminary injunction ordering Madster to shut down its website, but Madster remained in operation for an additional 34 days. In December 2002, the court found Madster in contempt and ordered that it disconnect its website and any computers it used to support the file-sharing service. As of December 31, 2003, the website located at the domain name www.madster.com was in operation, and file-trading software was available for download from the website.

⚖ *Buma/Stemra v. Kazaa*, *Dutch* Supreme Court (Dec. 19, 2003).

In December 2003, the Dutch Supreme Court ruled that the file-sharing software company Kazaa cannot be held liable for the copyright infringing activities of users of its software, affirming an appellate court's dismissal of the case.

On March 28, 2002, a Dutch appeals court ruled that Kazaa was not liable for any individual's abuse of its software, which is used around the world to locate copyright-protected games, music, pictures, and films. Kazaa had been sued by Dutch music rights organization Buma/Stemra. The ruling came too late to save Kazaa as an independent company; its principal assets were sold to an Australian company, Sharman Networks, after the initial ruling in favor of the music industry in 2001. The Dutch court found that the technology behind Kazaa did not require a Napster-like central server under control of the software developers. The court also found that it was important that the software was being used for noninfringing purposes. As of December 31, 2003, Sharman continued to offer the Kazaa software and to litigate and lobby vigorously in favor of the right to distribute the software. (The Dutch Court of Appeals decision is available at http://www.eff.org/IP/P2P/BUMA_v_Kazaa/20020328_kazaa_appeal_judgment.html.)

⚖ *RIAA v. Verizon Internet Services (In re Verizon Internet Services., Inc.)*, 240 F. Supp. 2d 24 (D.D.C. 2003), *motion denied by, stay granted in part by*, 258 F. Supp. 2d 6 (D.D.C. 2003), *stay denied by*, No. 03-7015, 2003 U.S. App. LEXIS 11250 (D.C. Cir. June. 4, 2003), *vacated and remanded by*, No. 03-7015, 2003 U.S. App. LEXIS 25735 (D.C. Cir. Dec. 19, 2003).

The Recording Industry of Association of America filed suit against Verizon, an Internet service provider, seeking an order compelling Verizon to identify subscribers the RIAA accused of illegally trading copyright-protected musical recordings in digital format using peer-to-peer software. Verizon argued that the copyright-protected music was merely transmitted over its network and not stored on it; therefore, the subpoena was beyond the scope of the DMCA. The court, however, rejected this argument based on the DMCA's definition of an ISP subject to subpoena and ordered Verizon to identify the accused Verizon subscribers.

Verizon appealed to the U.S. Court of Appeals for the District of Columbia Circuit. In the meantime, the RIAA served a second subpoena on Verizon, which Verizon sought to quash, this time also arguing that the DMCA subpoena provision is unconstitutional because it allows a federal court to issue a subpoena even if it does not have an actual "case or controversy" pending before it. (The Constitution empowers the federal courts to adjudicate "cases" and "controversies." To the extent the DMCA authorized issuance of subpoenas without regard to whether a case or controversy was pending before the court, Verizon argued, it was unconstitutional.) The trial court again rejected Verizon's arguments. *See RIAA v. Verizon Internet Servs. (In re Verizon Internet Servs., Inc.)*, No. 03-MS-0040 (JDB), 2003 U.S. Dist. LEXIS 6778 (D.D.C. Apr. 14, 2003). Verizon asked the U.S. Court of Appeals to stay the trial court's orders. On June 4, 2003, the appellate court denied Verizon's request, and, as a result, Verizon identified the Verizon subscribers that RIAA wished to pursue for copyright infringement. *See* Christopher Stern, "Verizon Identifies Download Suspects, Firm Says Fight Goes on to Guard Privacy," WASHINGTON POST (June 6, 2003), at E05.

On December 19, 2003, the D.C. Circuit ruled on the merits of Verizon's appeals. It agreed with Verizon that the DMCA's subpoena provision does not authorize the issuance of a subpoena to an ISP that *transmits* infringing material; only to an ISP that *stores* infringing material. Because the infringing music files are stored on individuals' computers and not on Verizon's servers, the court reasoned, the DMCA subpoena provision does not apply. The Court of Appeals vacated and remanded the trial court's decision with respect to the first subpoena, and granted Verizon's motion to quash the second subpoena.

Industry Action against Individual Users and Universities

Stymied in their efforts to shut down the peer-to-peer file-sharing networks, the recording and motion picture industries have begun to target individual file traders who are using file-sharing software to distribute copyright-protected works.

The RIAA has been using software that scours the Internet looking for hard drives on which copyright-protected digital files have been stored and made available for others to download. The RIAA then seeks to identify the owner of the computer on which the files are located by obtaining court-ordered subpoenas to the users' ISPs. The RIAA has sent messages to individuals it believes to have been trading copyright-protected music files using Kazaa and Grokster software stating: "When you break the law, you risk legal penalties. There is a simple way to avoid that risk: DON'T STEAL MUSIC."

Students using university-provided high-speed Internet connections are reportedly among the most active file traders. The recording industry has focused much of its attention on such university students. In July 2003, Loyola University of Chicago, after receiving a subpoena, released to the RIAA the names of two students who had allegedly offered copyright-protected material over the school's network. *See* Robert Becker and Angela Rozas, "Loyola Releases Two Student Names to RIAA," CHI. TRIBUNE (July 15, 2003) *available at* http://www.centredaily.com/mld/centredaily/news/6311463.htm. In March 2003, Penn State University, after receiving a complaint from the RIAA, denied Internet access to students it confirmed were illegally trading copyright-protected material over the University network. *See* Associated Press, "Students Lose Web Use in Copyright Case," SEATTLE POST-INTELLIGENCER (Apr. 21, 2003) *available at* http://seattlepi.nwsource.com. This followed similar disciplinary action by the U.S. Naval Academy for unlawful file-sharing by students. *See* John Borland, "Navy Disciplines Students for Downloading," CNET News.com (Apr. 15, 2003) *at* http://news.com.com/2100-1025-996990.html.

The University of Florida, in its efforts to curb students' unlawful file sharing, implemented a software program on its networks that identifies when a user is sharing files, and automatically sends a warning email and disconnects the user from the network. The software is called Integrated Computer Application for Recognizing User Services, or "Icarus." A first violation disables a user's connection for 30 minutes; a second violation results in suspended access for five days. A third offense subjects a student to the university's judicial process, and network access is cut off indefinitely. The university reported a 90% decrease in the number of students using peer-to-peer file-sharing software, and bandwidth use dropped 85%. "Florida Dorms Lock Out P2P Users," WIRED NEWS, Oct. 3, 2003, *available at* http://www.wired.com/news/digiwood/ 0,1412,60613,00.html.

In November 2003, Penn State University and Roxio announced they had reached an agreement to allow Penn State campus residents to use the legitimate, fee-based Napster file-sharing service as part of their student fee benefits. The agreement is intended to encourage college students to use licensed fee-based services instead of the free file-sharing software programs many college students have been using. *See* Chris Gaither, "Penn State, Roxio Link to Let Files Flow," THE BOSTON GLOBE (Nov. 7, 2003), at D1.

Actions against Peer-To-Peer Software Users

On June 25, 2003, the RIAA announced that it would begin gathering evidence and preparing lawsuits against individual computer users who unlawfully distribute copyright-protected music. *See* Press Release, "Recording Industry Association of America, Recording Industry to Begin Collecting Evidence and Preparing Lawsuits Against File 'Sharers' Who Illegally Offer Music Online" (June 25, 2003) *available at* http://www.riaa.com/news/newsletter/062503.asp. Between the summer of 2003 and late December 2003, the RIAA had filed suit against more than 380 individual file-sharers, and had settled disputes with more than 1,000 individuals who agreed to stop trading music files. *See* Vikas Bijaj and Crayton Harrison, "Ruling a Blow to Music Industry," THE BALTIMORE SUN (Dec. 20, 2003), at 1A; Bill Holland, "RIAA Serves More Suits," BILLBOARD (Dec. 13, 2003), at 12.

One study, from the NPD Group, Inc. (a market information research company in Port Washington, New York), reports that in August 2003, approximately 1.4 million U.S. households erased all digital music files from their computers. The study, based on the activities of 10,000 volunteer households, indicates that 4% of households that store digital music erased the files in August 2003. Ethan Smith, "Pace of Music-File Erasing Picks Up," WALL STREET JOURNAL ONLINE (WSJ.com) (Nov. 4, 2003), *available at* http://online.wsj.com/article/0,,SB106799426534737400,00.html.

Atlantic Recording Corp. v. Peng, No. 03-1441 (D.N.J. filed Apr. 3, 2003); *Atlantic Recording Corp. v. Sherman*, No. 03-CV-0416 (N.D.N.Y. filed Apr. 3, 2003); *Atlantic Recording Corp. v. Jordan*, 03-CV-0417 (N.D.N.Y. filed Apr. 3, 2003); *Atlantic Recording Corp. v. Nievelt*, No. 2:03CV0064 (W.D. Mich. filed Apr. 3, 2003).

On April 3, 2003, the RIAA, on behalf of 17 record companies, filed lawsuits against four students enrolled at Princeton University, Rensselaer Polytechnic Institute, and Michigan Technological University, marking the first lawsuits against users of peer-to-peer technology (as opposed to prior lawsuits against the distributors of peer-to-peer software). The complaints alleged that the students created and used programs that searched for files on their universities' local area networks and allowed users easily to trade copyright-protected material. On May 1, 2003, the RIAA announced that it had reached a settlement with the students who each agreed to pay the RIAA between

$12,000 and $17,000. Jefferson Graham, "Students Paying for Playing," USA TODAY (May 5, 2003), at 3D.

⚖ *Sony Music Entertainment (UK) Ltd., et al. v. Easyinternetcafe Ltd.*, No. HC 02 C01798 (Ch. Jan. 30, 2003), *available at* http://www.courtservice.gov.uk/judgmentsfiles/j1528/sony_v_easyinternetcafe.htm.

The British Phonographic Industry, along with recording labels Sony Music, EMI, and Universal Music, brought suit against an Internet café, Easyinternetcafe, claiming that it infringed copyright laws by charging customers a fee to allow them to download copyright-protected music recordings and record them onto CDs. The Internet café did not have the permission of the record labels, which are the copyright owners, to provide this service. A U.K. trial court rejected the Internet café's defense that it was not responsible for its customers' illegal copying. The parties settled the dispute, with Easyinternetcafe agreeing to pay the labels £80,000 in damages and £130,000 for legal costs. As part of the settlement, it agreed not to appeal the trial court's decision.

Fee-Based Internet Music Downloading Services

Record labels eventually realized that the digital online distribution model was catching on despite them, so they finally began to offer legitimate sources for online music. In October 2000, Napster and entertainment conglomerate Bertelsmann came together to launch an online music-downloading service with membership fees that would go toward compensating artists and record labels for use of their copyright-protected materials. The joint venture never got off the ground. MusicNet, a venture involving AOL Time Warner, Bertelsmann, and EMI Group, was launched in 2002, shortly followed by Pressplay, formed by Sony Corporation and Vivendi Universal.

Pressplay and MusicNet are subscription services. In the fall of 2002, Pressplay and MusicNet reached licensing agreements to offer songs from all five major recording labels. However, the services offered limited downloads that were not in the popular MP3 file format and usually could not be transferred to portable MP3 playing devices or burned to CDs. Most online music file-traders continued to download music files using the free peer-to-peer software rather than the labels' online music sources.

In 2003, legitimate online music services broke through, as record companies entered additional licensing agreements with a wide variety of online services. In April 2003, Apple launched its iTunes Music Store to Macintosh users (roughly 3% of computer users in the U.S.), and sold an average of 500,000 downloads per week during its first six months in operation. Apple launched its Windows-compatible iTunes program in October 2003, logging more than 1.5 million downloads in its first week. Apple's user-friendly, affordable source for music downloads is simple to navigate, offers a wide variety of music, and charges a flat fee of $0.99 per song and $9.99 per album. The iTunes site has helped Apple generate sales of its MP3 player, the iPod.

Other lawful services offering downloadable digital files include BuyMusic.com, launched in May 2003; MusicMatch, which Dell uses to generate sales of its portable MP3 players; Napster 2.0, which launched in October 2003; and RealNetworks, which reported a quarter of a million subscribers in October 2003.

According to Ipsos-Insight (an Internet research report), the number of American who have paid for music downloads doubled in 2003. *Keeping Pace With Digital Music Behavior,* Ipsos-Insight-TEMPO, Nov. 2003.

Industry Initiatives to Secure Digital Audio Files

Screening technologies, including encryption and watermarking systems, offer technical solutions to protecting copyright in digitally distributed works. The Secure Digital Music Initiative (SDMI), organized in 1999 by the RIAA, and involving major computer companies, consumer electronic companies, and record labels, was formed to develop and implement a multi-industry base to provide secure electronic music. The group agreed to go on hiatus in May 2001, having failed to reach a consensus to adopt any proposed technologies.

Other technologies, such as RealNetworks' extensible media commerce language (XMCL) and Microsoft's extensible rights markup language (XRML), that enable copyright-protection systems to work with one another, are also in development. These technologies would present entertainment content providers with the option of switching among various rights-management systems without having to reformat all of their content.

CD copy-protection methods are being implemented that prevent discs from being read by computer CD-ROM drives, some portable CD players, and some car stereo systems. These methods include CPMM (Content Protection for Pre-Recorded Media), which uses encrypted code embedded in a CD or DVD, or watermarking, which embeds digital watermarks into digital content, to verify the CD or DVD content's authenticity and protect against forgery.

Karen Delise, et al. v. Fahrenheit Entertainment, Inc., et al., Case No. CV 014297 (Cal. App. Dep't Super. Ct. 2001).

Plaintiffs asserted that Music City Records, Fahrenheit Entertainment, and Suncomm, a digital rights management firm, violated California's consumer-protection laws by failing to include an adequate disclaimer on the packaging for copy-protected CDs. Buyers complained that the copy protection prevented them from fully enjoying the CDs they purchased. The parties reached a settlement. As part of the settlement, distributors will include a warning on CD labels that the affected discs are not designed to work in DVD players or CD-ROM players, and that electronic copies of the songs made available for downloading by purchasers of the CDs are not compatible with MP3 players. They will also stop requiring consumers to enter their names and email addresses as a condition of downloading electronic copies of the songs. A copy of the settlement agreement is available at http://www.techfirm.com/sunnk.pdf.

Dickey v. Universal Music Group, et al, No. 02-0264 (Cal. Super. Ct., Mar. 27, 2002), *aff'd*, No. B164476 (Cal. Ct. App. Nov. 26, 2003).

Plaintiffs filed a class-action lawsuit against the five major record companies for producing and distributing copy-protected music CDs that plaintiffs are unable to play on some of their CD players and computers due to copy-protection measures the record companies embedded in the CDs. The complaint alleged that the record companies made false and misleading statements and distributed CDs that carry the "Compact Disc" logo but did not include warnings or labels informing consumers that the discs used copy-protection technology. The trial court denied the record labels' motion to dismiss and ordered the defendants to cease the manufacture, distribution, and sale of the copy-protected discs or to make them carry warning labels differentiating them from standard CDs. The appellate court affirmed the trial court's ruling.

Government Involvement in the Digital Audio Debate

In an effort to understand music on the web, the U.S. Senate held a fact-finding session in July 2000 on digital downloading and copyright law. The hearing, entitled "Music on the Internet: Is There an Upside to Downloading?" was chaired by Sen. Orrin Hatch (R-Utah), who is, incidentally, a country songwriter. Many vocal players from both the Internet and recording industries testified before the committee, including Metallica's Lars Ulrich, former Napster CEO Hank Barry, and Gene Kan, developer of Gnutella. Hatch stated that the Senate is not interested in interfering with the ongoing litigation surrounding digital downloading, but rather in pursuing a mutually beneficial relationship between music creators and the companies that make music available to distributors.

Congress considered several bills that would address the use of copy-protection technology. In March 2002, the Security Systems Standards and Certification Act, S. 2048, also known as the Consumer Broadband and Digital Television Promotion Act or the Hollings Amendment, proposed government-mandated copy-protection technology in consumer electronic devices. The Anticounterfeiting Amendments of 2002, S. 2395, would have expanded existing counterfeit laws to cover digital media. It would have made it a criminal violation to copy authentication devices such as holograms or watermarks, as well as create a civil cause of action for copyright owners to recover damages.

Artists' Rights and Theft Prevention Act of 2003 ("ART Act") (S. 1932)

On November 22, 2003, Senators John Cornyn (R-Tex.) and Dianne Feinstein (D-Cal.) introduced a bill that would facilitate prosecution for suspected digital music and motion picture pre-release piracy. Under current law, unauthorized peer-to-peer file sharing of music and movies before their release date constitutes a felony only when ten or more copies of a pre-release album or film, with retail value exceeding $2,500, are distributed. Under the ART Act, anyone making works available for distribution online before they are released would be subject to felony charges, regardless of the number of copies, the value, or whether any distribution actually occurred. The bill proposes imprisonment of up to three years and fines of up to $250,000 for violators.

Congressional International Anti-Piracy Caucus

Congressional representatives and Senators, joined by representatives from movie studios, record labels, and software industry associations, formed the Congressional International Anti-Piracy Caucus in October 2003. The Caucus will focus on international piracy concerns by briefing Congressional delegations traveling to countries with significant piracy problems, such as Brazil, China, Pakistan, Russia, Taiwan, and other countries on the 2003 international piracy "watch list"; hosting forums on international intellectual property protection and piracy; demonstrating new technologies and products designed to improve consumers' entertainment experiences and to reduce piracy; and working closely with House and Senate committees on related hearings and legislation.

The e-Books Debate

The issues surrounding digital music distribution—compensating authors and copyright owners and preventing piracy—are also at the center of the electronic book-publishing debate. Although online book distribution has not been as prevalent as digital music downloading, including explicit digital media rights provisions in contracts between freelance writers, artists, and their employers is becoming increasingly important.

Random House Inc. v. Rosetta Books, LLC, 283 F.3d 490 (2nd Cir. 2002).

Random House brought a copyright infringement action against electronic publishing start-up Rosetta Books, claiming that Rosetta Books had offered for online sale eight works to which Random House owned the exclusive publishing rights. Random House asserted that, in signing over the rights to publish their works in "book format," authors also licensed the rights to publish their works in electronic form, that is, e-book rights. A number of large traditional publishers jointly filed an amicus brief in support of Random House's position. Rosetta Books maintained that the authors in question still owned the e-book rights to their works and that they contracted with these authors for those rights. The authors simply chose to enter agreements with Rosetta rather than Random House. Rosetta argued that Random House's contracts with these authors preceded the advent of the Internet and thus could not have contemplated electronic publication.

On March 8, 2002, the U.S. Court of Appeals for the Second Circuit held that the trial court had not abused its discretion by denying Random House's motion for a preliminary injunction against the sale of Rosetta's e-books. Citing *Tele-Pac Inc. v. Grainger*, 570 N.Y.S.2d 521 (N.Y. App.. Div. 1991), the court found that Random House did not show a likelihood of success on the merits, a requirement for obtaining an injunction, because New York law, which controlled the dispute, narrowly construes the grant of rights when the contracting parties do not specify that the grant of rights extends to future media. The parties settled their dispute in December 2002, with Random House permitting Rosetta to publish the e-books in exchange for a share of the royalties. In April 2003, Rosetta announced it had reached an agreement with Random House to publish an additional 51 e-books. *See* Associated Press, "Random House and Online Publisher Agree on Deal to Release e-Books by John Updike and Others" (Apr. 9, 2003), *available at* http://www.siliconvalley.com/mld/siliconvalley/news/editorial/5595494.htm.

Licensing/Royalty Systems

In January 2001, BarnesandNoble.com created a new division that will pay authors royalties of 35% of the retail price of works sold in digital format.

In March 2001, National Writers Union and Brill's Contentville jointly launched a web-based licensing system, under which writers register their copyrights through a Publications Rights Clearinghouse and receive as royalties 30% of the fees paid by Contentville's customers. The clearinghouse operates in much the same way ASCAP does, collecting fees and distributing royalties for performances of musical compositions.

AOL Time Warner launched an e-book publishing division, iPublish, in July 2001. The Author's Guild has criticized iPublish because it perceives the terms it is offering to authors to be unfair. According to the Guild, iPublish would own the rights to any future digital format of the work, as well as audio book rights, but would insufficiently compensate authors by awarding them only 25% of its net sales as royalties. The Guild asserts that this amount is too low, considering the low cost involved in distributing e-books. AOL perceives the digital conversion of these works to be a major investment and feels authors should share some of the risk.

A new Internet clearinghouse called the Creative Commons has been launched at http://www.creativecommons.org. The site encourages copyright holders to donate their material for royalty-free, noncommercial use.

Digital Video Recording

Digital Video Recorders (DVR) are the digital version of VCRs. Using computer hard drives instead of video tape, DVRs allow users seemingly to pause and rewind live television while the DVR continues to record. Some DVRs have the ability to skip forward at preprogrammed intervals, effectively skipping commercials, or to send recorded programs to other DVR machines.

In an interview in the April 29, 2002 issue of *CableWorld*, Turner Broadcasting CEO Jamie Kellner said that skipping commercials amounts to theft of the programming, but that there is "a certain amount of tolerance for going to the bathroom."

Paramount Pictures Corp. v. ReplayTV Inc., Case No. 01CV-9358 (C.D. Cal., filed Oct. 31, 2001); *Time Warner Enter. Co. v. ReplayTV Inc.*, No. 01CV-9693 (C.D. Cal., filed Nov. 9, 2001); *Metro-Goldwyn-Mayer v. ReplayTV Inc.*, No. 01CV-9801 (C.D. Cal., filed Nov. 15, 2001); *Columbia Pictures v. ReplayTV Inc.*, No. 01CV-10221 (C.D. Cal., filed Nov. 28, 2001).

Paramount and a number of other media companies have brought suit against ReplayTV for contributory and vicarious copyright infringement. The lawsuit challenges features of ReplayTV's 4000 series DVR. The plaintiffs specifically oppose the "send show" feature, which allows users to distribute recorded programs to other ReplayTV users, and the "autoskip" feature, which automatically deletes commercials during the playback of a recorded program.

In early May 2002, a federal magistrate ordered ReplayTV's owner, SonicBlue, to develop software that would allow it to monitor the viewing habits of its ReplayTV set-top box owners and to turn the information over to the plaintiffs. Without addressing the possible privacy implications, on May 31, 2002, the District Court for the Central District of California overturned the ruling, saying it impermissibly required SonicBlue to create new data that is not currently in existence.

In August 2002, these suits were consolidated pursuant to a Court Order Denying Motion To Dismiss; Order Denying Motion to Stay; Order Granting Motion To Consolidate, *Newmark, et al. v. Turner Broad. Network, et al.*, No. CV 02-0445 FMC (C.D. Cal. Aug. 15, 2002), discussed below.

Newmark, et al. v. Turner Broadcasting System Inc., No. CV 01-9358 (C.D. Cal., filed June 6, 2002).

A group of ReplayTV 4000 DVR owners filed suit against entertainment-industry companies, seeking a declaratory judgment that use of a DVR to record and time-shift programs, skip commercials, and distribute copies of programs to other ReplayTV owners does not violate copyright law. The complaint named ReplayTV, Inc. and

SonicBlue Inc., manufacturers and distributors of the ReplayTV DVR, as defendants. (Subsequent to the filing of the suit, SonicBlue filed for bankruptcy, and the court stayed the action. In November 2003, plaintiffs stipulated to a voluntary dismissal of claims against SonicBlue.) DVR owners are worried that the outcome of Replay's lawsuit with Paramount may force Replay to disable some DVR features. As of December 31, 2003, the suit remains pending.

Copyright Law versus Contract Law

Courts have addressed whether copyright law trumps contract provisions that limit or otherwise alter legitimate uses, and defenses to unauthorized uses, of copyright-protected works.

Softman Products Co. v. Adobe Systems, Inc., 171 F. Supp. 2d 1075 (C.D. Cal. 2001).

To encourage customers to buy multiple Adobe programs at the same time, Adobe bundled its software into various boxed collections, which it sold for less than the included programs would have cost if purchased separately. Each copy of each program contained a license agreement that popped up on installation, purporting to prohibit a buyer from breaking up the collections and selling the individual programs separately. When Softman Products Co., a Los Angeles-based software distributor, did just that, Adobe sought an injunction prohibiting sale of the "unbundled" software. By re-selling the individual programs, Adobe argued, Softman was breaching the license agreement under which Adobe had distributed the boxed collection.

Softman countered that the license agreement could not prohibit the company from selling the unbundled programs because it had bought copies of the software collections, not licensed them. And as the owner of the copies, Softman argued that it had a right under copyright law to sell those copies regardless of any restriction Adobe sought to impose under the license agreement. The court agreed.

Though Adobe characterized each transaction in the chain of commerce—from Adobe to its distributors to Softman, and eventually to the consumer—as a license, the court looked to the "economic realities" of these exchanges to conclude that Adobe had actually sold, not licensed, the copies of its software Softman had obtained: "Adobe transfers . . . merchandise to distributors. Distributors pay full value for the merchandise and assume the risk that the software may be damaged or lost. The distributors also assume the risk that they will be unable to sell the product. The distributors then resell the product to other distributors in the secondary market. The secondary market and the ultimate consumer also pay full value for the product and accept the risk that the product may be damaged or lost." And the rights are transferred in perpetuity; the buyer does not have to return the software to the seller upon expiration of some specified period of time. All in all, the court concluded, the transactions looked more like sales of copies of the software than like licenses to use the software.

One of the exclusive rights that copyright law grants to the owner of copyright in a work is the right to distribute copies of that work. But copyright law has long provided that the owner of a copy of a work has a right to sell that copy without any permission from the copyright owner. In other words, the owner of the copyright in a work has the exclusive right to sell each copy of the work the first time it is sold, but once a copy is sold, the buyer has the right to dispose of that copy as he sees fit. Adobe could not use its license agreement to compel Softman to relinquish rights granted to Softman by copyright law under this "first sale doctrine." *See* J. Hart and S. Blumenthal, "Software Is Often Sold, Not Licensed, Despite What License Agreements Say," WSJ.com (June 27, 2002), *available at* http://online.wsj.com/public/resources/documents/SB1024436103624547920.htm.

◣ *Adobe Sys., Inc. v. Stargate Software, Inc.*, 216 F. Supp. 2d 1051 (N.D. Cal. 2002).

Adobe sued Stargate alleging that the defendant was selling its software without authorization. The U.S. District Court for the Northern District of California held that the agreement between Adobe and Stargate, which characterized each software transaction as a license rather than a sale, was valid. The court rejected the conclusion of the *Softman* court that such a license was a sale.

◣ *Bowers v. Baystate Technologies*, Nos. 01-1108, 01-1109 (Fed. Cir. Aug, 20, 2002), *modified by Bowers v. Baystate Technologies*, Nos. 01-1108, 01-1109 (Fed. Cir. Jan. 29, 2003) (dissenting opinion added).

Bowers, a software designer, and Baystate entered into a license agreement, which included a provision that prohibited Baystate from reverse-engineering[1] Bowers' software. Baystate reverse-engineered the software, and Bowers sued, claiming damages for both breach of contract and violation of the Copyright Act. The federal trial court awarded only the contract claim damages, refusing to award copyright claim damages because, the trial court said, such damages would be duplicative of the contract damages.

The U.S. Court of Appeals affirmed the trial court's ruling that Baystate had breached its contract with Bowers, and held that the trial court did not abuse its discretion in omitting copyright damages as duplicative. This holding suggests that state contract law authorizing shrinkwrap licenses that prohibit reverse-engineering is not preempted by federal copyright law.

---

[1] "Reverse-engineering" is the process of taking apart an object to see how it works in order to duplicate or enhance the object. Software reverse-engineering involves reversing a program's compiled, machine-readable code back into source code readable by humans in order: (1) to retrieve the source code of a program because it was lost; (2) to study how the program performs certain operations; (3) to improve the performance of a program; (4) to fix a bug; (5) to identify malicious content in a program, such as a virus; or (6) to adapt a program written for use with one type of microprocessor for use with a different type of microprocessor. Reverse-engineering for the sole purpose of copying or duplicating programs constitutes a copyright violation and is illegal. In some cases, the licensed use of software specifically prohibits reverse-engineering. From whatis.com on the TechTarget Network at http://whatis.techtarget.com/definition/0,,sid9_gci507015,00.html.

Chapter 4: Copyright
Summary of the Law

- The Copyright Act of 1976 affords copyright protection to "original works of authorship fixed in any tangible medium of expression." Copyright law does not protect ideas, facts, procedures, or discoveries; copyright protection instead attaches to the unique manner in which ideas or facts are expressed.

- Registration with the U.S. Copyright Office is not required to achieve copyright protection. Rather, copyright attaches automatically at the moment a work is fixed in a tangible form.

- Examples of works subject to copyright protection include literature, music, motion pictures, artistic works, photographs, essays, articles, computer programs, graphic designs and sound recordings. Under the Digital Millennium Copyright Act of 1998 (DMCA), works created in digital media are also protected, provided such works can be perceived, reproduced, or otherwise communicated for more than a transitory period.

- The duration of a copyright is usually the life of the author of the work plus 70 years. For corporate-authored works or works made for hire, the term of copyright protection is 95 years from the date of publication, or 120 years from the date of creation, whichever is shorter.

- A copyright owner has certain exclusive rights with respect to a protected work. A copyright owner has the right, or the right to authorize others: (1) to reproduce the work; (2) to prepare derivative works; (3) to distribute copies of the work; (4) to display the work publicly; (5) to perform the work; and (6) in the case of sound recordings, to transmit the work in digital format. Using a copyright-protected work in any of these manners without permission ordinarily constitutes copyright infringement.

- The doctrine of "fair use" provides a limited defense to otherwise infringing uses of a copyright-protected work. Fair use permits the use of a copyright-protected work, for such purposes as commentary, criticism, teaching, scholarship and research, without permission of the copyright owner. Whether a use is fair under this doctrine requires a fact-based analysis, and is decided on a case-by-case basis. Courts will consider four factors in determining whether an infringing use may be excused as "fair": (1) the purpose and character of the use; (2) the nature of the original work; (3) the amount and substantiality of the portion of the original work that is used; and (4) the effect of the use on the potential market for or value of the original work. Courts have applied these factors to web publishers in essentially the same way they have applied them to traditional print media.

- There are several statutory exemptions to copyright infringement. In certain situations, entities including libraries, schools, broadcast stations, and cable systems may use copyrighted works, or parts of such works, without authorization from the copyright owner.

- Linking from one website to another generally does not constitute copyright infringement. Providing a "deep-link" to a page that is not the home page of the linked site may have copyright implications, although a number of courts have held that such practice does not infringe copyrights.

- Several courts have found that framing another's site without permission—that is, displaying the site within a frame that makes the framed content appear to be incorporated within the framing site—violates the framed site's copyrights.

- The owners of a website can be found liable for infringing content posted to the site by others. Website operators can be found liable for direct, contributory, or vicarious copyright infringement, depending on the website operator's knowledge of and control over the activities of the infringer.

- Under the DMCA, it is unlawful to access a work in digital format that is protected by an effective anti-piracy measure, such as encryption, coding, or password protection. The DMCA includes a "safe harbor" that shields Internet service providers from liability for the copyright-infringing activities of their subscribers.

- Copying and distributing copyright-protected content, such as movies and music, without authorization from the copyright owner, may constitute a violation of copyright law.

- The ease with which content in digital format can be reproduced and shared over the Internet has led to growing concern about copyright protection in the music and motion picture industries. In their efforts to combat Internet music file-sharing, record labels first sought relief from the distributors of file-sharing software. In 2002, the U.S. Court of Appeals for the Ninth Circuit found that Napster, which provided software that enabled Internet users to download digital files, typically music files, from other users, was not entitled to immunity from copyright infringement liability under the DMCA. The court found Napster vicariously and contributorily liable for infringing the copyrights of various record companies. In contrast, in 2003 a federal trial court in California found that the Grokster music service, which, like Napster, provided software that allowed users to share music files, was not liable for vicarious and contributory infringement. The court distinguished Napster, noting that while Napster had indexed files available for download on a central server controlled by Napster, users running the Grokster software conducted searches directly on other users' computers.

- The Record Industry Association of America has also taken steps to curb infringing file-sharing by bringing widely publicized suits against individual Internet users who allegedly share copyright-protected music over the Internet without compensating the copyright owners. While millions of Internet users reportedly continue to download and share music over the Internet freely, and in apparent violation of copyright law, several legitimate music file-sharing services are now available on the Internet.

DEFAMATION

Libel Basics

A defamatory statement is one that injures the reputation of another. The common-law torts of libel and slander punish the publication of statements that are both defamatory and false. A libelous statement was traditionally a false and defamatory statement published in writing. A slanderous statement is a false and defamatory statement expressed orally. False and defamatory oral statements broadcast over radio or television are now widely considered libel, rather than slander. Money damages may be awarded to compensate the victim of libel or slander for the reputational injury caused by publication of the false and defamatory statement.

There is an unavoidable tension between the common-law protections of reputation and the mandate of the First Amendment to the Constitution that "Congress shall make no law. . . abridging the freedom of speech, or of the press . . ." To ensure that debate on public issues remains "uninhibited, robust and wide-open," *New York Times v. Sullivan*, 376 U.S. 254, 270 (1964), the Supreme Court has found that the First Amendment limits the circumstances under which a speaker or publisher may be punished for making false and defamatory statements: "Neither lies nor false communications serve the ends of the First Amendment. . . [b]ut to insure the ascertainment and publication of the truth about public affairs, it is essential that the First Amendment protect some erroneous publications as well as true ones." *St. Amant v. Thompson*, 390 U.S. 727, 732 (1968).

Accordingly, to recover for libel or slander, the plaintiff must establish not only (1) that the defendant published a defamatory statement, (2) that the statement was made about the plaintiff, and (3) that the statement was demonstrably false, but the plaintiff must also prove that the statement was made with "fault." The degree of fault the plaintiff must establish depends, as a matter of federal constitutional law, on whether the plaintiff is a public official or public figure, on the one hand, or a private figure, on the other. A public official or public figure must establish constitutional "actual malice" (publication with knowledge of falsity or subjective awareness of probably falsity), while a private figure need only demonstrate that the defendant was "at fault" in publishing the false statement at issue (a showing of negligence is sufficient in most states). *See New York Times Co. v. Sullivan*, 376 U.S. 254 (1964); *St. Amant v. Thompson*, 390 U.S. 727, 732 (1968); *Gertz v. Robert Welch*, 418 U.S. 323, 347 (1974); *Philadelphia Newspapers v. Hepps*, 475 U.S. 767, 768 (1986); and *Milkovich v. Lorain Journal Co.*, 497 U.S. 1 (1990).

The Constitutionalization of Defamation Law

In *New York Times Co. v. Sullivan*, 376 U.S. 254 (1964), the Supreme Court ruled that the First Amendment limits common-law defamation claims brought by public officials. The Court held that to recover for publication of a defamatory falsehood, a public official must prove that the challenged statement was "of and concerning" the public official plaintiff, that the statement was false, and that the defendant acted with "actual malice." The Court defined "actual malice" as publication with knowledge that the statement was false or with reckless disregard of whether the statement was false or not.

Later, the Supreme Court extended the standard announced in *New York Times Co. v. Sullivan* to defamation cases brought by "public figures." Public figures include individuals who voluntarily inject themselves into public controversy, as well as those who are involuntarily thrust into the limelight, even if only with respect to a particular activity or incident.

A private-figure defamation plaintiff can recover damages based on the defendant's negligence (or a more speech-protective standard, under the law of some states). In no instance, however, can a private-figure plaintiff recover damages for defamation without a showing of fault amounting, at least, to negligence. Any lesser standard, the Supreme Court concluded, would unduly burden free speech. *Gertz v. Robert Welch, Inc.*, 418 U.S. 323, 347 (1974). And, at least when the speech relates to an issue of public concern, a private-figure plaintiff must bear the burden of proving falsity; the defendant speaker is not obligated to prove the truth of the challenged statements. *Philadelphia Newspapers, Inc. v. Hepps*, 475 U.S. 767, 768 (1986).

Public Persons

Public Officials

Public officials are, at the very least, "those among the hierarchy of government employees who have, or appear to the public to have, substantial responsibility for or control over the conduct of government affairs." *Rosenblatt v. Baer*, 383 U.S. 75, 85 (1966). In general, public figures include elected officials, candidates for elected office, most law enforcement officers, and other public servants with discretionary authority, as opposed to those who perform purely ministerial functions.

Public Figures

Pervasive Public Figure. A pervasive or all-purpose public figure is a person or entity that has achieved such pervasive fame or notoriety that he/she/it becomes a public figure for all purposes and in all contexts. *Gertz v. Robert Welch, Inc.*, 418 U.S. 323, 351 (1974).

Limited Purpose Public Figure. A limited purpose public figure is a person or entity that voluntarily injects himself/herself/itself into a particular public controversy and thereby becomes a public figure for a limited range of issues related to that controversy. *Gertz* at 351.

Involuntary Public Figure. An involuntary public figure is a person or entity involuntarily drawn into public events. *Gertz* at 345.

The Supreme Court has identified two factors for courts to evaluate in determining whether a plaintiff is a public figure. First, public figures are those who "invite attention and comment" through their actions and thus have "voluntarily exposed themselves to increased risk of injury from defamatory falsehood concerning them." Second, public figures "usually enjoy significantly greater access to the channels of effective communication and hence have a more realistic opportunity to counteract false statements than private individuals normally enjoy." *Gertz*, 418 U.S. at 344-45.

Applying the Public Figure Doctrine in Cyberspace

A plaintiff who claims to have been libeled on an electronic bulletin board or in another online forum may more readily be deemed a limited-purpose public figure than a plaintiff claiming to have been libeled through a more traditional means of communication.

Inviting Attention and Comment

The Internet has developed a reputation as a free-wheeling environment in which the unrestrained comments of one speaker may well be met with vigorous rebuttal. Arguably, anyone who regularly posts electronic messages, whether on a bulletin board or in a chat room or other online forum, may be deemed to have "invite[d] attention and comment" about himself or herself and thus to have voluntarily assumed an increased risk of being defamed.

For example, in *Ellis v. Time, Inc.*, 26 Media L. Rep. 1225 (S.D.N.Y. 1997), Richard Ellis, a photographer for Reuters, posted a series of messages in the National Press Photographers Association discussion group on CompuServe accusing a photographer at *Time* magazine of staging several pictures depicting child prostitution. Ellis also met with the head of the prostitution ring and allegedly offered to pay him to admit that the photos were faked. *Time* later published a letter to its readers admitting that some of the photos were, in fact, staged. Ellis claimed, among other things, that he was defamed by certain internal and external publications by *Time* questioning the manner in which Ellis attempted to prove that the photos were staged.

The court granted *Time's* motion for summary judgment on the libel claim. The court found that Ellis was a limited-purpose public figure because he had thrust himself into the forefront of a particular public controversy, that is, whether *Time* had staged photographs, in order to influence the resolution of the issues involved. *Id.* at 1228. The court found that Ellis voluntarily injected himself into this debate by posting messages for discussion among his press colleagues and by meeting with the head of the prostitution ring. *Id.* at 1228-29. The court, however, was careful to note that a person who posts messages on an electronic bulletin board is not by definition a limited-purpose public figure. *Id.* at 1229.

Greater Access to Channels of Effective Communication

The Internet also provides a readily accessible forum for a person or other entity that has allegedly been defamed to respond to the defamation widely and effectively. Indeed, where the allegedly defamatory statements were made on a particular bulletin board or in a particular chat room, the defamed individual may be able to respond almost instantly to the very audience that received the defamatory statement.

The community with respect to which a plaintiff's private or public status is determined is the audience to which the alleged defamation was actually published. *See, e.g., Harris v. Tomczak*, 94 F.R.D. 687, 701 (E.D. Cal. 1982) ("The relevant population in considering the breadth of name recognition is to be measured by the audience reached by the alleged defamation."); *Reliance Ins. Co. v. Barron's*, 442 F. Supp. 1341, 1349 (S.D.N.Y. 1977) (finding the plaintiff a public figure with regard to an article published in *Barron's* magazine based on court's conclusion that "[p]robably [he] is well known among *Barron's* readership"). Thus, a plaintiff who frequents the particular chat room or posts messages to the electronic bulletin board where the allegedly defamatory statements appear may be deemed a public figure with respect to that particular virtual community even if he or she is not well known outside that community. *See also Norris v. Bangor Publ'g Co.*, 53 F. Supp. 2d 495, 499, 505 (D. Me. 1999) (finding that one of the reasons that the plaintiff, a political consultant, was a limited-purpose public figure was his access to traditional and electronic media).

Public Forum

 Bidbay.com, Inc. v. Spry, No. B160126, 2003 WL 723297 (Cal. Ct. App. Mar. 4, 2003) (unpublished opinion).

Plaintiff Bidbay claimed that the defendants made defamatory comments about Bidbay in an Internet chat room. The defendants allegedly stated that Bidbay sells child pornography and that the CEO of Bidbay did not pay his income taxes. The defendants moved to dismiss Bidbay's suit under California Code of Civil Procedure § 425.16 (California's anti-Strategic Litigation Against Public Participation (anti-SLAPP) statute), arguing that Bidbay violated their rights to free speech in a public forum.

The court held that the chat room was a public forum under the meaning of the anti-SLAPP statute. To qualify as a public forum, a forum, such as a chat room, must be available to the public or a large segment of the community. Nevertheless, the court determined that Bidbay had shown a sufficient likelihood that it would prevail in its defamation claim to warrant denial of the defendants' motion to dismiss. *See also Barrett v. Rosenthal*, 112 Cal. App. 4th 749, 759 (2003) ("Considering that the Internet provides 'the most participatory form of mass speech yet developed,' it is not surprising that courts have uniformly held or, deeming the proposition obvious, simply assumed that conventional Internet venues constitute a 'public forum' or a place 'open to the public' within the meaning of section 425.16.").

Online Service Provider Liability

General Background

At common law, one who repeats the statements of another is as responsible for the defamatory content of those statements as the original speaker. *See, e.g., Cianci v. New Times Publ'g Co.*, 639 F.2d 54, 60-61 (2d Cir. 1980). This common-law rule, however, is subject to the federal constitutional limitation against imposing liability without fault. *See Gertz v. Robert Welch, Inc.*, 418 U.S. 323, 347 (1974). One cannot be held liable in a defamation action unless he or she has "'tak[en] a [r]esponsible part in the publication.'" *Lewis v. Time, Inc.*, 83 F.R.D. 455, 463 (E.D. Cal. 1979), *aff'd*, 710 F.2d 549 (9th Cir. 1983) (citation omitted).

Publishers, Distributors, and Common Carriers

Courts have long recognized a distinction among those who publish or republish a defamatory statement, those who deliver or transmit material published by a third party, and those who merely provide facilities used by a third party to publish defamatory material. *See, e.g., Lerman v. Chuckleberry Publishing, Inc.*, 521 F. Supp. 228, 235 (S.D.N.Y. 1981), *rev'd on other grounds*, 745 F.2d 123 (2d Cir. 1984), *cert. denied*, 471 U.S. 1054 (1985); *Anderson v. New York Telephone Co.*, 361 N.Y.S.2d 913 (N.Y. 1974). "Publishers," such as newspapers, magazines, and broadcasters, control the content of their publications and are, accordingly, held legally responsible for any libelous material they publish. *Restatement (Second) of Torts* § 578 (1977). "Distributors," such as bookstores, libraries, and newsstands, cannot be held liable for a statement contained in the materials they distribute unless "[they knew] or had reason to know of the defamatory [statement at issue]." *See, e.g., Auvil v. CBS "60 Minutes,"* 800 F. Supp. 928, 931-32 (E.D. Wa. 1992). Distributors are under no duty to examine the publications that they offer for sale to ascertain whether they contain defamatory statements. *See Lewis*, 83 F.R.D. at 463. Common carriers, such as telephone companies, which do no more than provide facilities by which third parties may communicate, cannot be held liable for defamatory statements communicated through those facilities unless they have participated in preparing the defamatory material. *See Anderson*, 361 N.Y.S.2d at 913 (adopting dissenting opinion in *Anderson v. New York Telephone Co.*, 345 N.Y.S.2d 740, 750-752 (N.Y. App. Div. 1973)).

Development of the Law

Whether an online service provider is properly classified as a publisher or distributor was one of the first major issues to arise in Internet libel jurisprudence. Initially, two courts in New York addressed this issue, with contrary results. Then, in the Communications Decency Act of 1996, Congress immunized providers and users of "interactive computer services" from liability for statements made by other information content providers. 47 U.S.C. § 230(c)(1).

Liability of Interactive Service Providers Prior to the Enactment of the Communications Decency Act of 1996

Cubby, Inc. v. CompuServe Inc., 776 F. Supp. 135 (S.D.N.Y. 1991).

CompuServe operated a bulletin board that contained a daily newsletter called "Rumorville." When the plaintiff, Cubby, began a competing electronic publication called "Skuttlebutt," Rumorville published various unflattering statements about Skuttlebutt, including an allegation that Skuttlebutt was a "start-up scam." 776 F. Supp. at 141. Cubby sued the creators of Rumorville for libel and sued CompuServe on the grounds that it had republished the statements.

The court found that CompuServe was properly deemed a distributor, rather than a publisher. *Id.* at 141. In reaching this conclusion, the court focused on the fact that CompuServe did not exercise control over the bulletin board, but instead had contracted with an independent entity to "manage, review, create, delete, edit and otherwise control the contents" of the bulletin board. *Id.* at 143. The court further noted that CompuServe had "no opportunity to review" content before it was uploaded and made available to subscribers, and thus had "no more editorial control . . . than does a public library, bookstore, or newsstand." *Id.* at 140. Based on these findings, the court granted CompuServe's motion for summary judgment. *Id.* at 144.

Stratton Oakmont, Inc. v. Prodigy Services Co., 23 Media L. Rep. (BNA) 1794 (N.Y. Sup. Ct. 1995).

An anonymous user of Prodigy's "Money Talk" bulletin board posted statements claiming that Stratton Oakmont, a securities firm, had committed criminal and fraudulent acts and was a "cult of brokers who either lie for a living or get fired." 23 Media L. Rep. at 1795. Stratton Oakmont sued Prodigy and, anticipating the "distributor" defense that had been successful for CompuServe, moved for summary judgment on the limited issue of whether Prodigy had exercised sufficient editorial control over its online services to be deemed a publisher.

The court, in ruling for Stratton Oakmont, found that Prodigy exercised substantial control over the bulletin board and thus should be classified as a publisher rather than a distributor. *Id.* at 1795. Specifically, the court stated that Prodigy "held itself out to the public and its members as controlling the content of its computer bulletin boards" and controlled the content of its bulletin boards through the use of screening software and by engaging bulletin-board leaders charged with monitoring content for compliance with specific guidelines. *Id.* at 1797. The court added that Prodigy had made a "conscious choice" to regulate the content of its bulletin boards and thereby exposed itself to greater potential liability than other computer networks that undertook a less active role. *Id.* at 1798.

⚖ *Lunney v. Prodigy Services Co.*, 250 A.D.2d 230 (N.Y. App. Div. 1998), *aff'd*, 723 N.E.2d 539 (N.Y. 1999), *cert. denied*, 529 U.S. 1098 (2000).

A Boy Scout sued Prodigy after an allegedly defamatory email message was sent in his name (but not by him) to his Scoutmaster. The trial court ruled that the ISP could not be held liable simply because it provided the facilities used by a third party to communicate a defamatory message. Thus, the court treated the ISP not as a publisher or distributor, but rather as a common carrier, such as a telephone company, for purposes of defamation suits. The court declined to decide whether an ISP is immune under the Communications Decency Act of 1996, presumably because the suit had been filed prior to the enactment of that statute. The New York Court of Appeals affirmed the ruling, noting that "an ISP, like a telephone company, is merely a conduit." 723 N.E.2d. at 542. Accordingly, "Prodigy was not a publisher of the electronic. . . messages." *Id.*

The United Kingdom has not adopted this approach. *See Godfrey v. Demon Internet Ltd.*, 3 W.L.R. 1020 (Q.B. 1999) (holding that ISPs sued over defamatory messages posted by a third party are protected by the innocent-dissemination defense up to a point; however, once the provider is notified about the defamatory message, it becomes responsible for it, and thus can be sued for defamation as the publisher of the statement), available at http://www.haledorr.com/pdf/Godfrey _v_Demon.pdf.

Communications Decency Act of 1996 (CDA)

<u>*Section 230*</u>. Following the *Stratton Oakmont* decision, discussed above, Congress recognized the increased potential for liability for speech published online. In an attempt to encourage continued private investment in, and free discussion on, the Internet, Congress enacted sweeping and far-reaching protections from liability for Internet service providers and those operating websites in § 230 of the Communications Decency Act of 1996, 47 U.S.C. § 230, which provides, in relevant part, as follows:

"No provider or user of an interactive computer service shall be treated as the publisher or speaker of any information provided by another information content provider." 47 U.S.C. § 230(c)(1).

Section 230 also prohibits any imposition of liability under state law that would be inconsistent with the protection afforded under § 230: "No cause of action may be brought and no liability may be imposed under any state or local law that is inconsistent with this section." 47 U.S.C. § 230(e)(3).

Legislative History. The Conference Committee Report states that the legislation was intended to overrule the *Stratton Oakmont* holding that online service providers can be held liable as publishers of third-party comments. *See* Joint Explanatory Statement of the Congressional Conference Committee, H.R. Conf. Rep. No. 104-458 (1996), published in 142 Cong. Rec. H1078, 1130 (Jan. 31, 1996).

Liability of Interactive Service Providers and Users After the Enactment of the Communications Decency Act of 1996

Most courts have applied the protection of § 230 broadly, ruling that ISPs and those operating websites generally enjoy immunity from liability. As long as the material complained of was written by a third party, rather than an agent or employee of the ISP or website, the ISP or website is immune from liability. At the same time, the operator of a website may choose to exercise control over the content of its site by removing or editing content provided by third parties without becoming liable as the "publisher" of the third-party statements. Local governments, however, do not enjoy the same level of immunity under the statute as private providers. In 1998, the United States Court of Appeals for the Fourth Circuit held that even if a publisher or website is put on notice that it is distributing a libelous statement posted by a third party, it cannot be held liable for failure to remove the statement. *Zeran v. America Online, Inc.*, 129 F.3d 327 (4th Cir. 1997), *cert. denied*, 118 S. Ct. 2341 (1998). Though most courts have followed *Zeran*'s reading of § 230, recent decisions from the California Court of Appeal and from the U.S. Court of Appeals for the Seventh Circuit have suggested a more constrained view of § 230 immunity.

Zeran v. America Online, Inc., 129 F.3d 327 (4th Cir. 1997), *cert. denied*, 118 S. Ct. 2341 (1998).

An unidentified person posted messages on an America Online bulletin board offering t-shirts featuring tasteless slogans relating to the bombing of the federal building in Oklahoma City. Those interested in purchasing the shirts were instructed to call the plaintiff's home phone number in Seattle. The plaintiff requested that AOL remove the postings, and AOL agreed to do so. AOL declined, however, to print a retraction as a matter of policy. The parties disputed the date that AOL actually removed the postings from its bulletin board. The plaintiff filed suit against AOL for negligence, alleging that it had unreasonably delayed removing the defamatory messages, refused to post retractions, and failed subsequently to screen for similar postings.

The district court granted judgment for AOL on grounds that § 230 of the Communications Decency Act barred the plaintiff's claims. On appeal, the plaintiff argued that § 230 left intact distributor liability for interactive computer service providers who possess notice of defamatory material posted through their services and fail to remove such material.

The Court of Appeals for the Fourth Circuit affirmed the judgment for AOL: "By its plain language, § 230 creates a federal immunity to any cause of action that would make service providers liable for information originating with a third-party user of the service. . . . Thus, lawsuits seeking to hold a service provider liable for its exercise of a publisher's traditional editorial functions—such as deciding whether to publish, withdraw, postpone or alter content—are barred." *Id.* at 330. The court noted, among other things, that holding AOL liable under the circumstances before the court would directly contradict one of the important purposes of § 230—namely, "to encourage service providers to self-regulate the dissemination of offensive material over their services." *Id.* at 331. *See also Doe v. America Online, Inc.*, 25 Media L. Rep. (BNA) 2112 (Fla. Cir. Ct. 1997) (holding that § 230 immunizes AOL from liability for statements made by subscribers in chat rooms), *aff'd*, 718 So. 2d 385 (Fla. Dist. Ct. App. 1998).

Cases Reading § 230 Broadly

Aquino v. Electriciti, Inc., 26 Media L. Rep. (BNA) 1032 (Cal. Super. Ct. 1997).

In a California state case pre-dating the Zeran decision, the plaintiffs sued Electriciti, Inc., an ISP, and one of its employees for negligence and intentional infliction of emotional distress. The plaintiffs alleged that the defendants disseminated statements, posted by an anonymous individual, that the plaintiffs were "ring leaders" of an "international conspiracy" to further "Satanic Ritual Abuse" of children and that the plaintiffs engaged in kidnapping, cannibalism, and murder. Plaintiffs' First Amended Complaint ¶ 10 (filed June 23, 1997). After the court dismissed the plaintiffs' claims on grounds that the plaintiffs' action was barred by § 230 of the Communications Decency Act, the plaintiffs amended their complaint to claim breach of contract and civil rights violations. Specifically, the plaintiffs asserted that the defendants breached a purported contract with them by failing to disclose to the plaintiffs the name of the third party who posted the defamatory statements and violated the plaintiffs' civil rights by aiding and abetting the third party in an effort to discriminate against the plaintiffs based on their religious beliefs. In a brief order, the court again dismissed the plaintiffs' claims, apparently adopting the defendants' broad interpretation of § 230 as immunizing online service providers. 26 Media L. Rep. at 1032.

Blumenthal v. Drudge, 992 F. Supp. 44 (D.D.C. 1998).

The plaintiffs, Sidney Blumenthal, a former White House aide, and his wife, sued Matt Drudge, publisher of an electronic publication known as the *Drudge Report*, and AOL for libel, invasion of privacy, and intentional infliction of emotional distress. The plaintiffs alleged that Drudge libeled them by reporting that "top GOP operatives" believed that "Blumenthal ha[d] a spousal abuse past." *Blumenthal*, 992 F. Supp. at 46. The plaintiffs asserted that AOL, which had entered into a license agreement with Drudge by which it paid him a monthly royalty in exchange for the right to make the *Drudge Report* available to AOL users, jointly published the allegedly defamatory statements with Drudge and thus was not immune from liability under § 230. The plaintiffs also alleged that AOL could be held liable on the ground that Drudge was an employee or agent of AOL.

AOL filed a motion for summary judgment, and Drudge filed a separate motion to dismiss or transfer for lack of personal jurisdiction (jurisdictional issues are discussed in Chapter 9). AOL, which based its motion entirely on § 230, asserted that, as an interactive computer service, it was immune from liability for any cause of action arising from material prepared by a third party. In granting AOL's motion, the court held that the fact that AOL had the right to make changes in the *Drudge Report* was not sufficient to make it a joint publisher of the report. Rather, the plaintiffs were required to present evidence that AOL had some role in creating or developing the information in the *Drudge Report*. They failed to do so. "Indeed, plaintiffs affirmatively state that 'no person, other than Drudge himself, edited, checked, verified, or supervised the information that Drudge published in the Drudge Report.'" *Id.* at 50. The court also found that "there is no evidence to support the view originally taken by plaintiffs that Drudge is or was an employee or agent of AOL." *Id.* Judge Friedman made it clear that he would have preferred a different result but that he felt compelled to dismiss plaintiff's claims in light of § 230: "If it were writing on a clean slate, this Court would agree with plaintiffs. . . [b]ut Congress has made a different policy choice. . . In some sort of tacit *quid pro quo* arrangement with the service provider community, Congress has conferred immunity from tort liability as an incentive to Internet service providers to self-police the Internet for obscenity and other offensive material, even where the self-policing is unsuccessful or not even attempted." *Id.* at 51-52.

Mainstream Loudoun v. Board of Trustees of the Loudoun County Library, 2 F. Supp. 2d 783 (E.D. Va. 1998), *reh'g denied*, 24 F. Supp. 2d 552 (E.D. Va. 1998).

Citizens of Mainstream Loudoun sued their public library because the library installed filtering software on its computers as part of the Library Board's "Policy on Internet Sexual Harassment." *Mainstream Loudoun*, 2 F. Supp. 2d at 787. The plaintiffs claimed the policy impermissibly blocked their access to protected speech, and sought declaratory and injunctive relief. The library moved for summary judgment, claiming it was immune from suit under § 230.

In denying the motion, the court held that the public library was not immune from suit because § 230(c)(2), providing immunity from suit for providers who restrict access to certain content, should apply only to private Internet content providers. *Id.* at 790. The purpose of the CDA was to protect ISPs from government regulation, not to insulate government regulation from judicial review. *Id.* Therefore, § 230 does not protect government entities.

The court also noted that even if § 230 were construed to apply to public libraries, the "tort-based" immunity from "civil liability" would not bar an action for declaratory and injunctive relief. *Id.* at 790. The court emphasized this line of reasoning in denying the library's motion for reconsideration. *See Mainstream Loudoun v. Board of Trustees of the Loudoun County Library*, 24 F. Supp. 2d 552, 561 (E.D. Va. 1998) (holding that § 230 provides immunity for actions for damages, but does not immunize a defendant from an action for declaratory and injunctive relief). For discussion of this case in the context of First Amendment issues, see Chapter 1, page 13.

Ben Ezra, Weinstein, and Co. v. America Online, Inc., 206 F.3d 980 (10th Cir. 2000), *cert. denied*, 531 U.S. 824 (2000).

The plaintiff, a publicly traded company, sued AOL for libel, among other things, on the grounds that AOL repeatedly published inaccurate information regarding the value of the plaintiff's stock. AOL moved for summary judgment pursuant to § 230. The trial court found that the allegedly libelous statements were created by third-party content providers, not by AOL. Accordingly, the court found that § 230 provided AOL with immunity from the plaintiff's claims and entered summary judgment for AOL.

The U.S. Court of Appeals for the Tenth Circuit affirmed the ruling: "Plaintiff presents no evidence to contradict Defendant's evidence that [the third-party content providers] alone created the stock information at issue." 206 F.3d at 986. The court added that there also was no evidence that AOL was "'responsible, in whole or in part, for . . .

the creation and development of information' published on its Quotes & Portfolios area." *Id.* (quoting 47 U.S.C. § 230(f)(3)). For discussion of this case in the context of requests to stay discovery, see pages 150–151, below.

Sabbato v. Hardy, 29 Media L. Rep. 1860, No. 2000CA00136, 2000 Ohio App. LEXIS 6154 (Ohio Ct. App. December 18, 2000).

In *Sabbato*, a website manager who designed and operated a site where opinions could be read and posted by users was sued for both distribution of, and participation in, libelous remarks. Citing § 230 of the Communications Decency Act, the trial court dismissed the entire action.

The Ohio Court of Appeals reversed in part, holding that the applicability of the good-faith immunity protection afforded by the Communications Decency Act could not be determined without converting the motion into one for summary judgment, in which a decision can be reached only if there are no material facts in dispute. *Id.* at 1862. The court reasoned that, because there was a question of fact concerning the website manager's participation in the creation of the libelous remarks, some evidence had to be presented concerning good faith in order to secure immunity from suit. *Id.* The decision of the trial court to dismiss a claim regarding the *distribution* of defamatory material by the manager was upheld.

Doe v. America Online, Inc., 718 So. 2d 385 (Fla. Dist. Ct. App. 1998), *aff'd*, 783 So. 2d 1010 (Fla. 2001), *cert. denied*, 122 S. Ct. 208 (2001).

A mother sued AOL and Richard Lee Russell, an AOL user, for emotional injuries caused by Russell's marketing through AOL of videotapes depicting the mother's 11-year-old son engaged in sexual activities. The plaintiff claimed that AOL had notice that Russell was using AOL to distribute obscene photographs, and yet did not warn or advise Russell to stop, nor did it suspend or terminate his service. The trial court found that "making AOL liable for Russell's chat room communications would treat AOL as the publisher or speaker of those communications," and that therefore AOL was immune from suit under § 230. *Id.* at 387.

Relying on *Zeran*, the court of appeals rejected the plaintiff's attempt to hold AOL liable as a distributor (rather than as a publisher or speaker) to avoid § 230 immunity. Because of the sheer number of message postings, subjecting an interactive computer service to distributor liability would create an impossible burden to investigate each time a potentially actionable statement is brought to the attention of the service. *Id.* at 389. The court also held that § 230 applies retroactively, meaning that complaints instituted after the effective date of § 230 are subject to its provisions, regardless of when the conduct giving rise to the claim occurred. *Id.* at 383. The court of appeals dismissed the suit, but certified questions to the Florida Supreme Court for clarification about whether Florida law was preempted by § 230 and whether § 230 applies retroactively. The Florida Supreme Court concluded that Florida law was preempted and that § 230 applies retroactively, and summarily affirmed the appeals court's dismissal of the case.

Schneider v. Amazon.com Inc., 31 P.3d 37 (Wash. Ct. App. 2001).

The plaintiff, Jerome Schneider, author of several books, filed suit against the defendant, Amazon.com, an online bookseller, alleging defamation and tortious interference with business expectancy based on negative comments about the author that appeared on the Amazon.com website. The Amazon.com website allows visitors to post comments about the books made available on the site; at least ten anonymous comments were posted that were critical of the plaintiff and his books.

The court held that Amazon.com was immune from suit under § 230 because it qualified as an "interactive service provider" within the meaning of § 230(c). The court relied heavily on *Zeran v. America Online Inc.*, 129 F.3d 327 (4th Cir. 1997), discussed above at pages 143–144, which held that AOL was immune from liability for material posted on its online bulletin boards. Comparing the two cases, the court noted that reader postings on Amazon.com "appear indistinguishable from AOL's message board for § 230 purposes." 31 P.3d 37, 40. The fact that Amazon.com was not providing access to the Internet was irrelevant to the court because "[u]nder the statutory definition [in § 230(f)], access providers are only a subclass of the broader definition of interactive service providers entitled to immunity." *Id.* The court also rejected the plaintiff's arguments that § 230 immunity only applies to tort claims and that Amazon.com, by reserving the right to edit visitors' postings and claiming license rights in the content of these postings, became the content provider. Instead, the court concluded that the requirements of § 230 were met, and that, accordingly, Amazon.com was immune from suit.

Smith v. Intercosmos Media Group d/b/a Directnic.com, 2002 WL 31844907 (E.D. La. 2002).

The plaintiffs, Greg Smith and Kestel Trade Corp., sued an Internet service provider, Intercosmos, under Louisiana state law for maintaining allegedly libelous content on its servers. Intercosmos argued that it was immune from liability under § 230. The federal trial court agreed and granted summary judgment for Intercosmos. The court relied on the reasoning of *Zeran v. America Online, Inc.*, 129 F.3d 327 (4th Cir. 1997), discussed above at pages 143–144.

Batzel v. Smith, 333 F.3d 1018 (9th Cir. 2003), *reh'g en banc denied*, 2003 U.S. App. LEXIS 24304 (9th Cir. Dec. 3, 2003).

Defendant Ton Cremers, director of security at Amsterdam's Rijksmuseum, operated a website and a listserv devoted to museum security and stolen art. Cremers received an email from a man named Bob Smith, who identified himself as a building contractor in North Carolina. Smith told Cremers that he understood that one of his clients was Heinrich Himmler's granddaughter and that she had numerous works of art Smith believed had been looted in World War II. Smith identified his client as "Ellen J. Batzel." Cremers posted Smith's email, "with some minor wording changes," to the Museum Security Network website and distributed it through the Network listserv. Batzel sued.

The Court of Appeals for the Ninth Circuit found that § 230 potentially immunized Cremers from liability, both for republishing Smith's email on the Network website and for distributing the email through the Network listserv. Neither the minor wording changes Cremers made before disseminating Smith's email, nor his decision to disseminate the email, made Cremers a creator or developer of the email so as to permit liability despite § 230. The court also held, however, that the immunity afforded under § 230 "applies only with regard to third-party information provided *for use on the Internet* or another interactive computer service." *Id.* at 1033. The court remanded the case to the trial court to determine "whether, under all the circumstances, a reasonable person in Cremers' position would conclude that the information [in Smith's email] was sent for internet publication." *Id.* at 1035.

 Carafano v. Metrosplash.com, 339 F.3d 1119 (9th Cir. 2003).

The plaintiff, Christianne Carafano a/k/a Chase Masterson, a professional actor who appeared in the television show "Star Trek: Deep Space Nine," sued the operator of a matchmaking website for publishing a false dating profile that included her real telephone number and address. The site, "Matchmaker.com," asked users to complete an extensive questionnaire, including an essay and as many as 62 multiple-choice questions, that was used to gather information from which the matchmaking profile was created. The site also screened all photographs submitted by users for posting, but did not screen the text of the profiles. Carafano alleged that the website's publication of the false profile constituted invasion of privacy, libel, misappropriation, and negligence on the part of the matchmaking service.

The trial court held that the operator of the matchmaker website was not eligible for immunity under § 230. The Court of Appeals reversed. The trial court based its decision on a finding that the extensive work Metrosplash did in constructing the questionnaire used to create the profiles made the website a "content provider" with respect to the profile of Carafano, even though the questionnaire was completed by an anonymous third party. The Court of Appeals disagreed, noting that its recent decision in *Batzel v. Smith* provided for a broader interpretation of the CDA than the trial court recognized. The court noted that the "content" provided by Metrosplash through the questionnaire was only placed there to facilitate matching similar user-entered profiles to each other. This constituted, in the court's view, the same kind of minor editing upheld in *Batzel*.

 Green v. America Online, 318 F.3d 465 (3d Cir., Jan. 16, 2003), *cert. denied*, 124 S. Ct. 200 (2003).

The plaintiff, John Green, sued AOL for failing to prevent two other AOL subscribers from posting allegedly libelous messages in a chat room and from transmitting a "punter" program that caused his computer to freeze. Green alleged that as a result of having his computer shut down, he lost five hours of work, causing him damages of about $400. The U.S Court of Appeals for the Third Circuit found that AOL was immune to Green's libel claim under § 230. In addition, relying on the reasoning of *Zeran v. America Online, Inc.*, 129 F.3d 327 (4th Cir. 1997), discussed above at pages 143–144 and 147, the court held that § 230 immunizes AOL from liability based on a user's transmission of a "punter" program to Green, through AOL, because such programs are forms of "information" that are covered by § 230.

 Noah v. AOL Time Warner Inc., 318 F.3d 465 (E.D. Va. 2003).

The plaintiff, Saad Noah, sued AOL for refusing to prevent chat room participants from posting harassing comments. The comments, appearing in chat rooms dedicated to Islam, insulted and allegedly defamed Muslims and their religion. Noah brought suit under Title II of the Civil Rights Act of 1964, 42 U.S.C. § 2000a *et seq.* The federal trial court found that § 230 immunized AOL against Noah's Title II claim. In addition, the court found that even if AOL were not immune under § 230, it would still not be liable on the Title II claims because AOL chat rooms are not places of "public accommodation," unlike inns, restaurants, or theaters (physical places that are included in Title II as examples of places of public accommodation). The court dismissed Noah's suit. (For more discussion of whether websites qualify as places of public accommodation, see Chapter 10, pages 318–320.)

Grace v. Neeley, No. BC288836 (Cal. Super. Ct., Apr. 28, 2003)

A California Superior Court dismissed a libel claim against eBay by a buyer who received negative feedback from a seller. eBay posts evaluations that buyers and sellers submit about one another after they complete transactions. In this case, the seller wrote that the buyer "should be banned from eBay" and was "dishonest all the way." The court held that eBay was immune to the claim under § 230 because eBay qualified as an "interactive service provider" under the statute.

Barrett v. Fonorow, 2003 WL 22455494 (Ill. App. 2 Dist., 2003).

Plaintiff Stephen Barrett filed suit against the operator of a website that published unedited articles authored by a third party which were allegedly libelous. Barrett argued that the construction of § 230 gave immunity to publishers of content, but not to distributors who know or have reason to know that the statements are libelous. The Appellate Court for the Second District of Illinois disagreed, citing the *Zeran* court's interpretation of the CDA, and rejecting Barrett's narrow construction of § 230. Note that in another case brought by the same plaintiff against different defendants, a California appeals court came to the opposite conclusion. (See immediately below.)

Cases Suggesting a Narrower View of § 230 Immunity

Barrett v. Rosenthal, 5 Cal.Rptr.3d 416 (Cal. App. 2003), *certified for partial publication; prev. pub. at* 112 Cal.App.4th 749 (Cal. App. 2003).

Over a period of months, defendant Ilena Rosenthal posted to Usenet newsgroups email messages sharply criticizing plaintiffs Stephen Barrett and Terry Polevoy, physicians who opposed the promotion and use of alternative healthcare products and practices. Though the trial court found the vast majority of the messages were statements of opinion that could not support a libel claim, it found that one message, received by Rosenthal from codefendant Timothy Bolen and posted by Rosenthal to a newsgroup, could reasonably be interpreted to state defamatory facts about Polevoy. Though the plaintiffs "informed Rosenthal [that Bolen's message] was false and defamatory, asked that it be withdrawn, and threatened suit if it was not," Rosenthal refused to withdraw the message and, in fact, reposted it on numerous occasions. 112 Cal. App. 4th at 420. Nevertheless, the trial court dismissed Polevoy's libel claim because Rosenthal did not originate, but merely republished, the defamatory statement and thus was immune from suit under § 230.

The California Court of Appeal reversed in a lengthy opinion that rejected the reasoning and the holding of *Zeran*. The court noted that under the common law, one who disseminates a libelous statement made by another may be treated as a publisher, a distributor, or a conduit, depending on the circumstances. (For a discussion of publisher, distributor, and conduit liability, see pages 140–141, above.) Though the U.S. Court of Appeals for the Fourth Circuit had held in *Zeran* that § 230 barred all lawsuits seeking to hold the provider or user of an interactive computer service liable for any "exercise of a publisher's traditional editorial functions—such as deciding whether to publish, withdraw, postpone, or alter content," 129 F.3d at 330, the California Court of Appeal held that § 230 only barred holding an Internet republisher liable as a *publisher* of a defamatory statement originally made by another; it did not immunize an Internet republisher against *distributor* liability. In other words, the court held that Rosenthal could be found liable as a distributor of the defamatory statement originally made by Bolen if she knew or had reason to know of the defamatory nature of the statement she republished.

The court recognized that "[s]ince the decision in *Zeran*, no court has subjected a provider or user of an interactive computer service to notice liability for disseminating third-party defamatory statements over the Internet." 112 Cal. App. 4th at 765. The court based its ruling on a narrow reading of § 230, its view of the importance of protecting the individual's interest in protecting his/her reputation, the principle that a statute should not be read to abrogate common law unless it does so directly and unequivocally, a review of the legislative history of the Communications Decency Act, and its conclusion that *Zeran* had exaggerated the danger that Internet publishers would engage in excessive self-censorship if subjected to distributor liability.

For a discussion of the court's finding that "conventional Internet venues constitute a 'public forum'" within the meaning of the California anti-SLAPP statute, see page 140, above.

Doe v. GTE Corp., 347 F.3d 655 (7th Cir. 2003).

Various college athletes brought suit over videotapes sold over the Internet that had been made, without their knowledge or consent, by someone who had hidden video cameras in locker room, bathrooms, and showers at various universities. The athletes sued not only those who had produced and marketed the videotapes, but also the universities that had failed to detect the cameras and the corporations that operated the services that hosted the websites over which the tapes were marketed (which the court referred to as "informational intermediaries").

The trial court dismissed the claims against the hosting services under § 230. Though the U.S. Court of Appeals for the Seventh Circuit ultimately affirmed the dismissal on the ground that none of the states in which the defendant colleges and universities were located "requires suppliers of web hosting services to investigate their clients activities and cut off those who are selling hurtful materials," it did so only after questioning, at some length, the reading of § 230 that has been adopted by the Courts of Appeals for the Fourth, Tenth, Third, and Ninth Circuits. See *Zeran v. AOL*, discussed at page 143–144, above; *Ben Ezra Weinstein v. AOL*, discussed at pages 145–146, above, *Green v. AOL*, discussed at page 140, above, and *Batzel v. Smith*, discussed at pages 147–148, above. The Seventh Circuit suggested, without deciding, that even though § 230 prohibits the states from imposing liability on any provider of interactive computer services acting as a *publisher*, the law might nevertheless allow states to impose liability against such providers when acting as mere *informational intermediaries*.

Congressional Support for Broad Interpretation of § 230 Immunity

Congress has expressly endorsed a broad interpretation of § 230 immunity consistent with *Zeran v. American Online* and the subsequent holdings that rely on the analysis of the *Zeran* court. When the House of Representatives passed the "dot Kids Implementatin and Efficiency act of 2002" (discussed at pages 13 and 64), it specifically invoked the immunity provisions of § 230 in the text of the "Dot Kids" Act. See 47 U.S.C. §

941(e)(1). The legislative history of the Dot Kids Act indicates that Congress's intention in including the imunity provision was to apply the same broad protection under the Dot Kids Act as courts had recognized under the *Zeran* line of cases. "The courts have correctly interpreted section 230(c), which was aimed at protecting against liability for such claims as negligence (*See, e.g., Doe v. America Online*, 783 So. 2d 1010 (Fla. 2001)) and defamation (*Ben Ezra, Weinstein, and Co. v. America Online*, 206 F.3d 980 (2000); *Zeran v. America Online*, 129 F.3d (1997)). The Committee intends these interpretation of section 230(c) to be equally applicable to those entities covered by [the Dot Kids Act]." H.R. Rep. No. 107-449, at 13 (2002).

Requests to Stay Discovery Under § 230 Pending Ruling on Dispositive Motion

Ben Ezra, Weinstein, and Co. v. America Online, Inc., 27 Media L. Rep. (BNA) 1794 (D.N.M. 1999), *aff'd*, 206 F.3d 980 (10th Cir. 2000), *cert. denied*, 531 U.S. 824 (2000).

In this case, described in more detail above at pages 145–146, AOL moved to delay discovery until after the trial court decided AOL's motion for summary judgment under § 230. The court granted AOL's motion, holding that the immunity afforded to ISPs under § 230 should also relieve ISPs from the burdens of litigation, which include discovery. *Id.* at 2213. However, the court noted that the discovery bar is not absolute. A plaintiff is free to file an affidavit under Rule 56(f) of the Federal Rules of Civil Procedure, showing what discovery they wish to take and how that discovery would assist in defeating the defendant's invocation of § 230. *Id.*

On appeal, the plaintiff argued that it had been improperly denied an opportunity to take discovery. The U.S. Court of Appeals for the Tenth Circuit rejected this argument, stating that the plaintiff failed to "demonstrate precisely how additional discovery [would] lead to a genuine issue of material fact." 206 F.3d at 987.

Other Defamation Issues Peculiar to the Internet

Discovery of the Identities of Anonymous Defendants

Anonymity and the freedom to speak one's mind that comes from that anonymity are attractive to many Internet users. Increasingly, those who are the subjects of unflattering anonymous speech are turning to the courts to try to identify their detractors. They bring libel suits against "John Doe" defendants and subpoena the message-board hosts in an effort to obtain identifying information about the authors of the allegedly libelous remarks. The courts must balance the plaintiff's interest in having a forum for grievances with the defendant's right to anonymous speech. These cases are discussed in Chapter 1, pages 20 to 24.

Libel Suits by Anonymous Plaintiffs

America Online, Inc. v. Anonymous Publicly Traded Company, 542 S.E.2d 377, 385 (Va. 2001).

A Virginia appeals court held that a company suing AOL in an attempt to discover the identity of John Does allegedly posting defamatory material on AOL message boards must reveal its own identity. Mere possibility of economic harm, without more, does not permit plaintiff to proceed anonymously. (Overruling *In re Subpoena Duces Tecum to America Online, Inc.*, 52 Va. Cir. 26 (Va. Cir. Ct. 2000)).

Sovereign Immunity as Applied to a Government Website

John Doe v. United States, 83 F. Supp. 2d 833 (S.D. Tex. 2000).

The plaintiffs, individuals associated with various temporary employment companies, initiated a suit seeking money damages from the United States pursuant to the Federal Tort Claims Act, alleging invasion of privacy and intentional infliction of emotional distress. The claims alleged that the U.S. Attorney's Office for the Southern District of Texas had posted a "News Release" on its website indicating that the plaintiffs had been charged with mail fraud and/or money laundering, when, in fact, no such charges had been filed.

The court held that the plaintiffs' allegations "arose out of" libel or slander claims regardless of how the plaintiffs had labeled their allegations. As a result, 28 U.S.C. § 2680(h), which precludes suits against the United States for libel and slander, applied, and the government's motion to dismiss for lack of subject matter jurisdiction was granted.

Republication of Defamatory Statements Contained in Official Documents and Pleadings

Amway Corp. v. Procter & Gamble Co., No. 01-2561 (6th Cir. Oct. 8, 2003).

Rival companies Amway Corp. and Procter & Gamble (P&G) have been engaged in litigation with each other for decades, each accusing the other of myriad wrongs spanning so many years and cases that the Sixth Circuit remarked that a full recital of the history of litigation between the two would be "as long as both the Old and New Testaments and involve at least one of the Good Book's more prominent players." In one such lawsuit, P&G sued Amway for defamation in spreading a persistent urban legend that P&G's upper management were Satanists and that the profits from P&G sales went to support Satanic churches. In gathering evidence for this case, P&G retained as a consultant one Sidney Schwartz, an admitted long-time critic of Amway, who agreed to furnish P&G's attorneys with information and guidance helpful to their case. Schwartz requested copies of P&G's pleadings in the litigation, but P&G refused. Afterward, Schwartz obtained the pleadings by his own efforts, charged P&G for the photocopying fee, and proceeded to post the documents on his website.

This led to the next round of litigation, settled by the U.S. Court of Appeals for the Sixth Circuit, as Amway objected to the posting of the pleadings on Schwartz's site and sued both Schwartz and P&G for libel. According to Amway's complaint, the libelous statements were contained in the pleadings themselves. The Sixth Circuit upheld the trial court's finding that Michigan's "fair reporting" privilege protected the publication of the pleadings on the Internet. The "fair reporting" privilege immunizes speakers who publish or broadcast a "fair and true report of matters of public record," including "report[s] or record[s] generally available to the public." MCLA § 600.2911(3).

Motions to Dismiss

 Global Telemedia International, Inc. v. Doe, 132 F. Supp. 2d 1261 (C.D. Cal. 2001).

Two users posted allegedly libelous statements about Global Telemedia in a chat room. *Id.* at 1264. Global Telemedia sued the two participants over these messages. The defendants moved to dismiss the suit pursuant to California Civil Procedure § 425.16, which was designed to discourage Strategic Litigation Against Public Participation (SLAPP) lawsuits. *Id.* at 1264-65.

The anti-SLAPP procedure allows the defendant to obtain dismissal of the suit if the alleged bad acts arose from the exercise of free speech in connection with a public issue and if the plaintiff cannot show a probability of success on the claims. *Id.* at 1265. Though the court noted that competitors may not be protected by the anti-SLAPP provisions, the defendants, as small individual investors not in the same business as the plaintiffs, could properly invoke the protection of the statute. *Id.* at 1266. The court also held that, given the offhand nature of the comments and the context of the bulletin board itself, a reasonable reader would recognize the statements to be expressions of opinion, not actionable as business libel. *Id.* at 1267.

ComputerXPress v. Lee Jackson, 93 Cal. App. 4th 993, 113 (Cal. Ct. App. 2001).

On November 15, 2001, the California Court of Appeals, Fourth District, ruled that criticism of public companies on an Internet message board is protected from frivolous litigation by California's anti-SLAPP statute, which encourages early dismissal of, and can impose sanctions for, frivolous libel suits. In this case, the court decided that while the defendant may have made disparaging comments, they were of public interest and couched more in the tone of opinion than fact.

Donato v. Moldow, Docket No. BER-L-6214-01 (Sup. Ct. N.J., Bergen Cty. Div., Dec. 21, 2001).

A New Jersey Superior Court dismissed a libel suit against the operator of a website that let visitors anonymously criticize their town's public officials. The court also quashed a subpoena issued by four politicians who had sought the identity of 60 anonymous posters on the site. The unknown people who posted statements that included allegations that public officials were involved in extramarital affairs and questionable business practices, remained "John and Jane Doe" defendants.

MacDonald v. Paton, 782 N.E.2d 1089 (Mass. App. Ct. 2003).

Mark MacDonald sued Elsa Paton for publishing statements on her website suggesting that MacDonald is a Nazi. MacDonald was a town official in Athol, Massachusetts, and Paton considered her website to be a forum for speech about public issues in Athol. Although Paton sometimes contributed to the content on the website, the statement about MacDonald appeared in an e-mail posted on the website by a website visitor. Paton moved to dismiss the lawsuit under the Massachusetts anti-SLAPP statute, G.L. c. 231 § 59H. A Massachusetts appeals court found that MacDonald's suit constituted a SLAPP suit, intended to chill Paton's right to free speech. The court dismissed the suit under the anti-SLAPP statute.

International Forum Shopping

The Global Nature of Cyberspace

While many U.S. media companies may distribute their print publications only in the United States and in a few select foreign countries, those same publications, if available online, may be accessed around the world. Thus, the likelihood that a statement will be deemed published in a distant country, subjecting the publisher to foreign defamation laws, is substantially heightened. U.S. media companies are likely to face a growing number of defamation lawsuits abroad.

The Appeal of International Forum Shopping

In the United States, publishers enjoy unparalleled protection against libel suits. The First Amendment requires, among other things, that a public figure or public-official plaintiff prove by clear and convincing evidence that a defendant published the challenged statements with "actual malice," that is, with knowledge of falsity or serious subjective doubt as to truth. *See St. Amant v. Thompson*, 390 U.S. 727, 729 (1968); *New York Times Co. v. Sullivan*, 376 U.S. 254, 279-80 (1964). Defendants in libel actions also enjoy numerous protections afforded by state constitutions, state statutory and common law, and, since enactment of § 230 of the Communications Decency Act, federal statutory law.

British Commonwealth

Outside the United States, libel laws are not so forgiving. Both British and Canadian law, for example, apply a strict liability standard, meaning that libel plaintiffs need not prove negligence or some other degree of fault on the part of the publisher to prevail on a libel claim. Mere publication of a false and defamatory statement is sufficient. British and Canadian courts also do not distinguish between public and private figures; even libel plaintiffs who are in the public eye are not required to prove negligence. The law presumes that a statement capable of conveying defamatory meaning is false unless the defendant proves the statement is true. And, Internet service providers do not have the protection of the Communications Decency Act. *Compare Godfrey v. Demon Internet Ltd.*, 3 W.L.R. 1020 (Q.B. 1999), *available at* http://www.haledorr.com/pdf/Godfrey_v_Demon.pdf (holding that in the United Kingdom, ISPs that exercise no editorial control over messages posted by third parties are protected by the common-law innocent dissemination defense, but if the provider receives notice of the posting, then it acquires the responsibility of a publisher and can be held liable if the posting is not promptly removed) *with Zeran v. America Online, Inc.*, 129 F.3d 327 (4th Cir. 1997) (holding ISPs immune from suit even where they exercise editorial power over third-party-produced content), *cert. denied*, 118 S. Ct. 2341 (1998).

In the United Kingdom, the impact of the *Godfrey* rule has spurred a movement to limit ISP liability. The *Godfrey* rule, coupled with the European Union's E-Commerce Directive requiring member states (including the U.K.) to adopt laws prohibiting ISP liability for transmitting tortious or illegal information, led the U.K.'s Internet Service Providers Association (ISPA) to sponsor a forum to address ISP liability. Conference participants proposed alternatives to the *Godfrey* rule. For example, they proposed that an ISP would only be liable for failure to remove materials after a court has ruled the materials to be illegal or defamatory. This would create a doctrine by which only a court's decision would provide "notice" to the ISP triggering a removal obligation.

Patrick J. Carome & C. Colin Rushing, "Online Defamation Law Abroad: Developments in the United Kingdom," *Libel Defense Resource Center Libel Letter*, April 2001, at 23. In early 2003, a British governmental advisory committee advocated an official review of defamation law as it applies to the Internet given continued concerns about free speech and the burdens placed on ISPs, but no action has yet been taken. *See* "E-Business: Lawyers Call for Internet Law Review," BIRMINGHAM POST (Jan. 14, 2003), at 22.

Dow Jones & Co. v. Harrods, Ltd., 237 F. Supp.2d 394 (S.D.N.Y. 2002), *aff'd*, 346 F.3d 357 (2nd Cir. 2003).

Harrods department store of the United Kingdom issued a fake press release as an April Fool's joke stating it was offering shares in a new venture to create a mobile Harrods store on a ship. When Dow Jones' *Wall Street Journal* discovered that the story was a joke, it countered with a story warning readers to question Harrods' future disclosures. Dow Jones sued Harrods in the U.S. District Court for the Southern District of New York, seeking declaratory judgment to preclude Harrods from pursuing a defamation claim against Dow Jones that Harrods had already filed in the United Kingdom. The court granted Harrods' motion to dismiss, and the Court of Appeals for the Second Circuit affirmed. Dow Jones is vulnerable to a suit outside the United States for its publication by virtue of the story's availability on the Internet, at wsj.com. On May 22, 2003, a trial court in the United Kingdom refused to dismiss Harrods' libel action against Dow Jones, stating that Harrods is entitled to demonstrate that the imputations in the claim were unjustified. "Harrods and WSJ in April Fool Libel Battle," THE GUARDIAN (May 22, 2003), *available at* http://media.guardian.co.uk/presspublishing/story/0,7495,961625,00.html.

In a case reaching across the Pacific, an Australian court took the unusual step of finding an American man guilty of defamation and assessed a fine against him for US$61,000. The defendant, Bill White, allegedly created numerous websites accusing various people of child molestation. One of White's targets, a university professor in Perth, Australia, sued in the Australian courts and won. *See* Steve Hymon, "Australian Judge Finds L.A. Webmaster Liable," L.A. TIMES (Sept. 4, 2003), *available at* http://www.latimes.com/technology/la-me-cyber4sep04,1,6659398.story.

Other Nations

On July 15, 2002, A Zimbabwe court aquitted Andrew Meldrum, a journalist for *The Guardian*, a London-based newspaper, of "publishing falsehoods." Under Zimbabwe law, a person can be convicted for "abusing journalistic privilege," which is punishable by up to two years in prison and loss of the mandatory license required of reporters and editors in Zimbabwe. The prosecution argued that the law allows for strict liability over reporters, meaning if an article is proved to have been false, the reporter is criminally liable no matter what lengths the reporter went to ensure the accuracy of his report. *See* Geoffrey Robertson, "Mugabe Versus the Internet," THE GUARDIAN (June 17, 2002), *available at* http://www.guardian.co.uk/internetnews/story/0,7369,739026,00.html. Only hours after the court acquitted Meldrum, Zimbabwean immigrations officials informed him that his residency permit was being revoked. Meldrum managed to stay in the country for almost a year after his aquittal before he was forcibly deported to the United Kingdom. *See* Andrew Meldrum, "From Hope to Corruption, Tyranny and Poverty," MANCHESTER GUARDIAN WEEKLY, May 28, 2003, at 7.

In Thailand, a man has been found guilty of posting defamatory messages on the Internet. Thanet Songkran was given a two-year suspended sentence and was ordered to pay fines and perform community service for violating Thailand's cyber-defamation criminal statute. He was convicted of posting a note on a web bulletin board listing contact information for a young woman and claiming she was a prostitute. This case marks the first time a Thai court has ruled on online defamation. *See* "Man Found Guilty in Thailand's First Case of Cyber-defamation." ABC News (Australia) Online (Aug. 7, 2002), *available at* http://abc.net.au/news/newsitems/s642477.htm.

The German high court recently ruled that ISPs could not be held liable for illegal content absent a showing that the ISP was notified of both the presence of the offensive material and the exact location of that material. The court cited to German telecommunications law which exempts ISPs from liability unless it can be proven that the ISP was aware of the illegal content and did nothing to eliminate it. *Bundesgerichtshof,* Case No. VI ZR 335/02 (Sept. 23, 2003).

Potential Limitations on International Forum Shopping

The United Kingdom and Canada, as English-speaking countries lacking the speech protections afforded under the U.S. Constitution, are attractive forums for defamation suits brought against U.S. publishers. For a discussion of the limits of international jurisdiction in such cases, see Chapter 9, page 293..

Choice of Law

Choice of Law in Libel Cases

Even if a libel plaintiff can obtain jurisdiction over a nonresident defendant, that does not necessarily mean that the law of the state in which the court sits will be applicable. Although the First Amendment provides certain rights to libel defendants in all U.S. jurisdictions, many aspects of libel law vary from state to state. Accordingly, a court's decision as to which state's law to apply in an online libel action will often be significant.

Basic Choice of Law Principles Applied in Traditional Libel Cases

States employ a variety of choice-of-law principles. Most states, however, have adopted the approach set forth in the *Restatement (Second) of the Conflict of Laws*, which provides that the law of the jurisdiction with the most significant relationship to the occurrence and the parties applies. *Restatement (Second) of the Conflict of Laws* § 145 (1971).

The *Restatement* sets forth several factors designed to inform a court's analysis of the "most significant relationship" test, including, among other things, the place where the injury occurred, the place where the conduct causing the injury occurred, and the place where the relationship between the parties is centered. *Restatement (Second) of the Conflict of Laws* § 145.

The *Restatement* approach in multistate libel cases often results in applying the law of the state where the plaintiff lives if the defamatory statement was published in that state. *Restatement (Second) of the Conflict of Laws* § 150.

Application of Choice of Law Principles in International Libel Cases

In addition to the principles outlined above, U.S. courts may consider U.S. public policy as a factor when choosing between a foreign country's law and U.S. law. For example, in *Ellis v. Time, Inc.*, 26 Media L. Rep. (BNA) 1225 (S.D.N.Y. 1997), the court refused to apply English libel law, although the plaintiff claimed that the defendant defamed him in England through a message transmitter on the Internet, because applying English libel standards would violate the First Amendment's protection of free speech. *Id.* at 1234. The court reasoned that U.S. courts must apply rules of law consistent with the Constitution, regardless of where the alleged wrong occurs. Although principles of international comity give the United States the choice of whether to acknowledge the laws of another nation, they do not impose a duty to do so. *Id.* at 1235. For further discussion of international choice of law principles, see Chapter 9, pages 293–294.

Application of Traditional Choice of Law Principles in the Context of Internet Libel

So far, courts have applied traditional choice-of-law principles to the cyberspace context without analyzing the complexities created by cyberspace defamation. *See Dahl v. Muller*, No. 99L6585 (Ill. Ct. Cl., Jan. 19, 2001) (existence of a licensing agreement with an Illinois business provided sufficient notice to the defendants that Illinois could exercise proper jurisdiction over nonresident radio stations webcasting a syndicated program in which allegedly defamatory statements were made about the plaintiff's minor son); *Wells v. Liddy*, 186 F.3d 505 (4th Cir. 1999) (publication on website is another example of a multistate defamation and thus under traditional choice-of-law doctrine, the law of the plaintiff's domicile should apply because that is where the harm occurred), *cert. denied*, 528 U.S. 1118, 120 S. Ct. 939 (Jan. 18, 2000). *See also Isuzu Motors Ltd. v. Consumers Union*, 12 F. Supp. 2d 1035 (C.D. Cal. 1998), and *Hitchcock v. Woodside Literary Agency*, 15 F. Supp. 2d 246 (E.D.N.Y. 1998) (finding that under traditional choice-of-law doctrine, the law of the plaintiff's residence should apply because that is where the injury occurred; neither *Hitchcock* nor *Isuzu Motors* discussed the fact that the defamation occurred on the Internet).

However, the *Restatement*'s emphasis on geographical borders may not work well in the cyberspace context. For instance, given that speech on the Internet may be received anywhere in the world, libel plaintiffs will argue that the injury that results from the distribution of a libelous statement may be deemed to have occurred in every jurisdiction in which the speech is received. Moreover, it is not obvious whether the site of the conduct causing injury is the jurisdiction where the libel was written or, instead, is the jurisdiction where the server housing the libelous content is located.

These, and other similar questions, have yet to be answered definitively by the courts. Where a publisher once was able to control its area of distribution, online publication potentially subjects a publisher to the laws of every jurisdiction in which the Internet is available. An inadequate choice-of-law regime may lead to diminished predictability for online publishers, forum shopping by libel plaintiffs, and, ultimately, a chilling effect on speech.

Banco Nacional de Mexico, S.A. v. Mario Renato Menendez, No. 603429/00 (N.Y. Sup. Ct., Dec. 5, 2001).

Banco Nacional brought libel claims in New York against defendant Mario Menendez-Rodriguez, a Mexican resident and journalist, Marco News, a website whose purpose is to educate users about the drug trade, and Al Giordana, publisher of the Marco News website, over articles accusing Roberto Hernandez-Ramirez, the bank's largest shareholder, general director, and chairman of the board of directors, of involvement in illegal drug trafficking and money laundering, and contending that the bank was funded with the proceeds of drug trafficking. The bank claimed these assertions were false. In the court's view, the First Amendment demanded that the court apply New York libel law and not Mexican criminal or tort law. Claims against Menendez-Rodriguez were dismissed because the court lacked personal jurisdiction. Although the defendant, Giordana, lived in Mexico, the court found he had sufficient business interests in New York for the court to have jurisdiction. The court determined that the bank was not a public figure, but that the defendants were media defendants, which under New York law required the plaintiffs to prove "actual malice," knowledge of falsity, or reckless disregard for the truth in order to prevail in a libel case. The allegations published by the defendant had all been previously published in a Mexican newspaper. The court found that the defendants were entitled to rely on those published reports and therefore dismissed the libel claims for failure to state a claim.

 Young v. New Haven Advocate, 315 F.3d 256 (4th Cir. 2002).

Two Connecticut newspapers, the New Haven *Advocate* and the Hartford *Courant*, reported on the harsh conditions in a Virginia prison and posted articles on their websites about the prison and its warden. The warden of the prison sued the Connecticut newspapers in Virginia. The newspapers moved to dismiss the case on the grounds that Virginia courts lacked personal jurisdiction over the newspapers.

A federal appellate court agreed with the newspapers and dismissed the case. Combined, the two newspapers had only eight subscribers in Virginia. In addition, the newspapers neither solicited subscriptions from Virginia residents nor gained any substantial revenue from business there. Based on these facts, the court found that the newspapers did not post material on the Internet with the intent of targeting Virginia readers. The newspapers could not have reasonably anticipated being sued in Virginia, and the Virginia court could not exercise personal jurisdiction over the newspapers. For a discussion of this case in the context of personal jurisdiction, see Chapter 9, page 290. *See also Griffis v. Luban*, 646 N.W.2d 527 (Minn. 2003), *cert. denied*, 123 S. Ct. 1483 (2003) (holding that a Minnesota resident's posting of defamatory comments about an Alabama resident on a website did not subject the Minnesota resident to the jurisdiction of Alabama courts).

 Dow Jones & Co. v. Gutnick, [2002] HCA 56 (Dec. 10, 2002).

On December 10, 2002, Australia's highest court rejected the efforts of Dow Jones & Company to have a libel suit against it transferred from Australia to a U.S. court. The case involved an allegedly libelous article about Australian mining magnate Joseph Gutnick, who lives and works in Victoria, Australia. Gutnick claimed to have been libeled by a February 2000 *Barron's* article that appeared on WSJ.com, the online edition of *The Wall Street Journal*. The court found that Australian courts have jurisdiction to hear a libel claim based on the article, even though few print copies of the article circulated in Australia and the online version of the article was likely accessed by a few hundred readers, at most, in Australia. Dow Jones sought to have the case transferred to a U.S. court, arguing that the online version of the article was "published" in New Jersey where Dow Jones' web servers are located, and, therefore, a U.S. court, not an Australian court, should hear any challenge to the article. Dow Jones contended that subjecting a web publisher to suit in every nation in the world from which its website could be accessed would severely curtail freedom of speech on the web. The High Court of Australia, however, disagreed, finding that "the spectre which Dow Jones sought to conjure up in the present appeal, of a publisher forced to consider every article it publishes on the World Wide Web against the defamation laws of every country from Afghanistan to Zimbabwe is seen to be unreal when it is recalled that in all except the most unusual of cases, identifying the person about whom material is published will readily identify the defamation law to which that person may resort." This case is available at http://www.austlii.edu.au/cgi-bin/disp.pl/au/cases/cth/high%5fct/2002/56.html?query=%22dow%22+and+%22jone%22+and+%22gutnick%22.

The reporter who wrote the article responded by filing a writ with the United Nations Human Rights Commission. The reporter claimed that he has been denied his right to free speech in violation of Article 19 of the United Nations' International Covenant on Civil and Political Rights. He also claimed that because Australia has submitted to the jurisdiction of the United Nations Human Rights Commission, Australia would be obligated to modify its libel laws if the United Nations finds a violation. *Australian Laws Challenged at UN* (Apr. 18, 2003), *at* http://www.smh.com.au/articles/2003/04/18/1050172745955.html. The trial in Victoria is scheduled to take place in early 2004. For a discussion of this case in the context of personal jurisdiction, see Chapter 9, page 292.

Retraction Statutes

General Background

Most states have a retraction statute of some kind. These statutes generally protect writers and publishers by requiring that notice be given to potential defendants before a libel action may be filed so that a timely correction, apology, or retraction can be published, if warranted. Depending on the nature of the alleged libel, the jurisdiction in which the suit is brought, and the plaintiff's compliance or noncompliance with the requirements of the relevant statute, application of a retraction statute may enable a defendant to reduce the range of recoverable damages, or avoid suit entirely. For example, retraction statutes in many states provide that the plaintiff may recover only for actual injury (and may not recover punitive damages intended to punish the defendant) unless a retraction is demanded and not published.

Application of Retraction Statutes in the Context of Online Libel

A threshold question may arise as to whether online services are covered by a particular retraction statute. A number of retraction statutes designate only newspapers or other traditional printed matter as falling within their protections. Other statutes refer only to newspapers, radio stations, and television stations. Still others apply to defamatory statements published in any medium.

Arguably, online newspapers sharing mastheads and content with traditional print counterparts should be covered by statutes specifically applicable to "newspapers." While in theory retraction statutes should equally protect publications that exist only online, it is less clear that such publications are covered. However, determination of whether a particular online offering is covered by a retraction statute logically should be governed by the underlying purpose intended to be served by the statute.

For instance, the Florida retraction statute is based on a legislative desire to accommodate the "public interest in the 'free dissemination of news,' and the reasonable likelihood of occasional error as a result of the tremendous pressure to deliver the information quickly." *Davies v. Bossert*, 449 So. 2d 418, 420 (Fla. Dist. Ct. App. 1984) (citation omitted). Although online news sites might fit comfortably within this underlying purpose, libelous statements made in other online contexts—a chat room, for example—might arguably not be subject to the protection of the retraction statute.

Montana's retraction statute, by contrast, is intended to apply to those members of the media capable of publishing a quick and effective retraction. Its purposes are almost surely served by offering protection to a broad array of online content. *See Fifield v. American Auto Ass'n*, 262 F. Supp. 253, 257-58 (D. Mont. 1967) (a book publisher not covered by Montana statute intended to cover situations where "a retraction would have an almost instant countering effect").

Case Law Dealing with Retraction Statutes

It's In The Cards, Inc. v. Fuschetto, 535 N.W.2d 11 (Wis. Ct. App. 1995).

The Wisconsin Court of Appeals found the state retraction statute did not apply to an online bulletin board that contained allegedly libelous statements. At issue were statements posted by the defendant on a sports-memorabilia-trading website. The trial court had held that the bulletin board qualified as a "periodical" under the statute, which applies to "any libelous publication in any newspaper, magazine or periodical." Because the plaintiff failed to comply with the requirements of the retraction statute, the trial court granted summary judgment for the defendant.

The appellate court reversed, holding the retraction statute did not apply to bulletin-board postings because: (1) the plain meaning of the word "periodical" encompasses only "'publication[s] of which the issues appear at stated or regular intervals'"; (2) a prior judicial interpretation of the statute held it applicable only to the "print" media, a designation the Court of Appeals held inapplicable to online bulletin-board postings; and (3) the Wisconsin retraction statute was enacted before the Internet existed and "it is for the legislature to address the increasingly common phenomenon of libel and defamation on the information superhighway." *Fuschetto*, 535 N.W.2d at 14 (citation omitted).

The decision in *Fuschetto* does not address the arguments that might be raised where an online publication serves many of the same functions and carries much of the same content as a traditional newspaper or magazine. Indeed, the typical online newspaper or magazine would probably qualify under the definition of a "periodical" applied by the Wisconsin Court of Appeals.

Zelinka v. Americare Healthscan, Inc., 763 So. 2d 1173 (Fla. Dist. Ct. App. 2000).

The plaintiffs brought suit in Florida alleging libel based on the publication of statements made by the defendant on an Internet message board. Section 770.01 of the Florida Statutes requires that, in certain circumstances, notice must be given to a potential defendant before a libel action can be filed. The statute is meant to allow potential defendants to avoid punitive damages by the timely publication of a correction, apology, or retraction. The defendant filed a motion to dismiss, claiming that the plaintiffs had failed to provide the proper written notice before bringing their libel suit.

Florida courts have interpreted § 770.01 as applying only to "media defendants," and not to private individuals. The court held that notice was not required because the defendant was simply "a private individual who merely made statements on a website owned and maintained by someone else." 763 So. 2d at 1174. The court stated that "[i]t may well be that someone who maintains a website and regularly publishes internet 'magazines' on that site may be considered a 'media defendant' who would be entitled to notice," but this defendant was not such a person. *Id.*

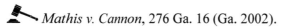 *Mathis v. Cannon*, 276 Ga. 16 (Ga. 2002).

The plaintiff, Thomas Cannon, brought suit in Georgia against the defendant, Bruce Mathis, for statements made in an Internet chat room. The trial court awarded Cannon punitive damages. The Georgia Court of Appeals found that Georgia's retraction statute, which states that plaintiffs cannot collect punitive damages if the publisher of the libelous item prints (or broadcasts) a retraction in as conspicuous and public a manner as the original libelous statement, do not apply to statements made in an Internet chat room. Cannon's failure to request a retraction therefore did not preclude Cannon's claim for punitive damages. The Georgia Supreme Court reversed, finding that there was no distinction in the statute between media and nonmedia defendants. Thus, the retraction statute applied to Mathis's statements in an Internet chat room. Accordingly, the court found that Cannon's failure to request a retraction precluded his claim for punitive damages.

Responding to Retraction Demands

Demands for Retraction of Third-Party Content

Under § 230 of the Communications Decency Act, no provider of an interactive computer service may be treated as the publisher of information provided by another information content provider. 47 U.S.C. § 230(c)(1). Treating a website operator as the publisher of allegedly libelous statements by a third party therefore violates the Act. *Zeran v. America Online, Inc.*, 129 F.3d 327 (4th Cir. 1997), *cert. denied*, 524 U.S. 937, 118 S. Ct. 2341 (1998). *See* pages 143–144, above. Accordingly, the *Zeran* holding suggests that where an online service receives a retraction demand relating to statements it did not compose, the demanding party should be redirected to the third-party originator.

Publishing Retractions Online

Even in jurisdictions where the applicable statute does not explicitly cover all media, publishing retractions or corrections still serves the traditional functions of mitigating damages and evidencing good faith.

Traditional Publication Requirements

Retraction statutes commonly call for a correction or retraction to be published in as conspicuous a manner as the statement claimed to be libelous. *See, e.g.*, Cal. Civ. Code § 48a(2). With regard to traditional print publications, statutes often call for publication of a retraction/correction in the same editions and/or in the same position and/or in the same type size as the alleged libel originally appeared. *See, e.g.*, Fla. Stat. Ann. § 770.02(1).

Online Publication of Corrections and Retractions

What is necessary to fulfill the conspicuousness requirement depends on the specific provisions of the applicable statute. However, the underlying question is whether the correction is likely to reach substantially the same audience as did the article being corrected. Section 6(b)(1) of the Uniform Correction or Clarification of Defamation Act (1993), for instance, requires publication "with a prominence and in a manner and medium reasonably likely to reach substantially the same audience as the publication complained of."

Correction Demands on Print Publications with Online Counterparts

Even where a correction demand served on a newspaper references only the print publication, a plaintiff may argue that failure to publish a correction in the online counterpart renders the correction ineffective, if the story being corrected was published in the online edition. Generally, a demand for a correction or retraction is deemed sufficient if it informs the publisher of the statements claimed to be defamatory. *See, e.g., Mahnke v. Northwest Publications, Inc.*, 124 N.W.2d 411 (Minn. 1963) (demand is sufficient if it gives notice of the exact words complained of); Ky. Rev. Stat. Ann. § 411.051(2) (1996) (sufficient demand "specifies the statement or statements claimed to be false and defamatory, states wherein they are false, and sets forth the facts"). Newspapers and magazines that have online counterparts might consider whether a correction published in a print edition should also appear in their online publications.

Archived Materials

Problems Raised by Continued Archival Publication after Learning of Falsity

Maintaining an online archive raises the possibility that information that was believed to be accurate when originally published will remain available to users even though the publisher has received a correction demand and perhaps even published a correction. Once the publisher has received a retraction demand coupled with documentation demonstrating falsity, or has discovered an error through other means, the availability of the original in online archives may attract defamation claims. Plaintiffs may argue that defenses applicable at the time of initial publication do not apply to archival "republication."

Demands to "Correct" Defamatory Matter in Archival Versions

Though libel plaintiffs ordinarily recognize that a print product cannot be changed once it hits the newsstand, they may demand that an article available in an online archives be edited to remove allegedly libelous matter or that the entire offending publication be removed permanently from the archive. Plaintiffs' attorneys may argue that an online publication's refusal to "correct" an archived online article as soon as an error is brought to the publisher's attention should be punished as an additional affront to the plaintiff. *Cf. Southern Bell Tel. & Tel. Co. v. Coastal Transmission Serv., Inc.*, 307 S.E.2d 83, 88 (Ga. Ct. App. 1983) (continued distribution of yellow pages after learning of libelous matter contained therein held sufficient to support imposition of punitive damages).

Archived Copies as Part of the Initial "Single Publication"

A compelling argument against liability for alleged libel contained in archived material is that archiving online does not constitute republication. The "single publication" rule allows only one action for damages as to any single publication. *See Restatement (Second) of Torts* § 577A(4) (1977). Republication usually will not be found in the traditional newspaper or book publishing context unless a new edition of the same work containing the libelous statements is released. *See Cox Enters., Inc. v. Gilreath*, 235 S.E.2d 633, 634 (Ga. Ct. App. 1977) (publication of different editions of a daily newspaper not deemed single publication); *Rinaldi v. Viking Penguin, Inc.*, 5 Media L. Rep. (BNA) 1295, 1297 (N.Y. Sup. Ct. 1979) (paperback edition of book deemed separate publication from hardcover edition), *modified*, 425 N.Y.S.2d 101 (N.Y. App. Div. 1980), *aff'd*, 438 N.Y.S.2d 496 (N.Y. 1981).

An archived hard copy of a newspaper is considered part of the initial publication. Similarly, producing microfilm or microfiche copies of the original editions of a newspaper on a regular basis following publication should fall within the initial publication. *Cf. Restatement (Second) of Torts* § 577A, cmt. d (1977) ("The printing and distribution of extra copies . . . of a book may properly be treated as mere continued circulation of the first edition and hence as still part of the single publication, if it is done not long after the original publication as soon as the supply is exhausted. If it occurs ten years later, it is indistinguishable from a second edition and there is a new cause of action").

Print Original

Firth v. State of New York, 706 N.Y.S.2d 835 (N.Y. Ct. Cl. 2000), *aff'd*, 731 N.Y.S. 2d 244 (N.Y. App. Div. 2001).

The plaintiff, a former director of the division of law enforcement in New York's Department of Environmental Conservation, was criticized in an Inspector General's report for allegedly improper disposition of surplus handguns. He sued the State of New York for defamation. Though he filed a notice of intention to file a claim for defamation within 90 days of release of the report, he failed to file his defamation complaint within one year of the initial publication of the report.

The defendant moved to dismiss the lawsuit as time barred pursuant to CPLR § 215(3), which requires that a cause of action for libel or slander be commenced within one year of accrual. The plaintiff asserted that his lawsuit should not be dismissed because, after releasing the report at a press conference, the Inspector General made the report available on the Internet (where it remained available). The plaintiff argued that the continuing availability of the report on the Internet constituted a continuing wrong. His claim, he argued, accrued anew each and every day. The Court of Claims rejected this argument, instead holding that the "single publication rule applies to defamatory publications upon the Internet." 706 N.Y.S.2d at 841.

The Court stated: "This Court sees no rational basis upon which to distinguish publication of a book or report through traditional printed media and publication through electronic means by making a copy of the text of the Report available via the Internet. While the act of making the document available constitutes a publication, in the absence of some alteration or change in form its continued availability on the Internet does not constitute a republication acting to begin the Statute of Limitations anew each day." *Id.* at 843. Accordingly, the Court of Claims dismissed plaintiff's claim.

The plaintiff filed an appeal contending that the statute of limitations started running anew each time that the report was accessed by an Internet user. The appellate court was not persuaded, ruling that the Court of Claims properly dismissed the complaint. Future accesses of the report by Internet users would not constitute new and actionable publications.

At least two federal courts recently have applied *Firth*'s single publication rule to statements posted on the Internet. *See Van Buskirk v. New York Times Co.*, 325 F.3d 87 (2d Cir. 2003) (finding that the online posting of a letter is a single publication for purposes of determining commencement of statute of limitations); *Mitan v. Davis*, 243 F. Supp. 2d 719 (W.D. Ky. 2003) (finding that under Kentucky common law, the online posting of allegedly defamatory statements on a privately owned website is a single publication for purposes of determining commencement of statute of limitations).

See also Miles Simon v. Arizona Bd. of Regents, 28 Media L. Rep. 1240 (Ariz. Super. Ct. 1999) (treating online publication of allegedly defamatory article and subsequent print edition of article as a single publication for purposes of determining commencement of statute of limitations).

Another court that has addressed this issue (in the context of a breach of contract action) found that Internet archiving of past editions does not constitute republication of articles, because an online archive, though readily available to anyone with capacity to search the Internet, is no different from other forms of archiving, such as microfiche. *Bartel v. Capital Newspapers*, 664 N.Y.S.2d 398, 25 Media L. Rep. 1959 (Small Claims Court, July 3, 1997), *aff'd*, 26 Media L. Rep. 2500 (New York County Court, July 22, 1998).

Electronic Original.

The act of making an article originally published online accessible through an archive index, rather than through the index with which it was associated on the first day of publication, should not be deemed republication. Rather, it is solely a matter of making the original publication available at a different location. Just as physically moving the hard copy of a newspaper into a library does not constitute republication, changing the manner in which an online article may be accessed should not be considered a separate act of publication.

Labeling

Publishers might reduce any risk that reasonable users could misconstrue archival material as current by ensuring that their online archives are clearly labeled. Similarly, if a current story includes a link to an earlier story, dating the earlier story should reduce the risk that the earlier story will be perceived as current. A more elaborate disclaimer might specifically inform users that material in the online archive is presented in its original form, has not been updated since the original date of publication, and does not reflect information subsequently obtained by the publisher.

Mechanisms might also be employed to ensure that when errors are identified, any published correction will be electronically linked to the archived report.

Chapter 5: Defamation
Summary of the Law

- A defamatory statement is one that injures the reputation of another. The common-law torts of libel and slander punish the publication of statements that are both defamatory and false. Money damages may be awarded to compensate the victim of libel or slander for the reputational injury caused by publication of the false and defamatory statement.

- A libelous statement was traditionally a false and defamatory statement published in writing. A slanderous statement is a false and defamatory statement expressed orally. False and defamatory oral statements broadcast over radio or television are now widely considered libel, rather than slander.

- To reconcile the tension between libel law, which punishes speech, and the First Amendment guarantee of freedom of speech, the Supreme Court has limited the circumstances under which a publisher may be punished for making false and defamatory statements.

- A libel plaintiff must prove that the challenged statement is false; the publisher does not have the burden of proving truth.

- A plaintiff that is a public official or a public figure can only recover for libel if he/she/it can prove that the defendant published the defamatory statement either with knowledge that the statement was false or with serious subjective doubt about the truth of the statement.

- A private figure plaintiff must prove, at a minimum, that the defendant was negligent in publishing the allegedly defamatory falsehood.

- Courts have long distinguished among those who publish or republish a defamatory statement, those who deliver or transmit material published by a third party, and those who merely provide facilities used by a third party to publish defamatory material.

- "Publishers," such as newspapers, magazines, and broadcasters, control the content of their publications and are, accordingly, held legally responsible for any libelous material they publish.

- "Distributors," such as bookstores, libraries, and newsstands, cannot be held liable for a statement contained in the materials they distribute unless they knew or had reason to know of the defamatory statement at issue. Distributors are under no duty to examine the publications that they offer for sale or distribution to ascertain whether they contain defamatory statements.

- Common carriers, such as telephone companies and Internet service providers, which do no more than provide facilities by which third parties may communicate, cannot be held liable for defamatory statements communicated through those facilities unless they have participated in preparing the defamatory material.

- Section 230 of the Communications Decency Act immunizes the provider of an "interactive computer service" from being held liable as the publisher or speaker of any information provided by "another information content provider." With only a few exceptions, courts have interpreted § 230 broadly, immunizing publishers from liability for freelance content, bulletin board postings, and other third-party content.

- In *Zeran v. AOL*, the leading case interpreting § 230, the Court of Appeals for the Fourth Circuit held that "§ 230 creates a federal immunity to any cause of action that would make service providers liable for information originating with a third-party user of the service. . . . Thus, lawsuits seeking to hold a service provider liable for its exercise of a publisher's traditional editorial functions—such as deciding whether to publish, withdraw, postpone or alter content—are barred."

- No other country enjoys defamation laws that are as speech-protective as those of the United States. A number of U.S. publishers have been sued for libel in foreign jurisdictions based on statements published on their websites, which are accessible worldwide.

- Many states have retraction statutes that protect writers and publishers by requiring that a potential libel plaintiff give notice before filing suit to allow the publisher and/or the writer to issue a clarification, correction, or retraction, if warranted. Depending on the state, publishing a retraction that conforms to the statutory requirements can reduce the damages available to the plaintiff or even bar a libel claim completely.

- It is not clear that all categories of online "publication" fit within the definitions of such statutes. However, courts have indicated that the closer an online publication is in form and content to a protected "traditional" printed publication, the more likely the online publisher will be protected under the retraction statute. Similarly, the more broadly the statute is written, the more likely "new" media publishers will be able to argue successfully that the statute applies to them.

- Courts have ruled that an electronic version of a print original does not constitute "republication." Archived copies of original publications are likewise part of the original publication (and not separate "republications").

DATA COLLECTION AND PRIVACY

General

Although businesses have long collected data about consumers, the rapid growth of the Internet has sparked a new debate about the collection of personal information and the consumer's right to privacy. In the online world, information often can be gathered and processed more quickly than in the offline world. As in the offline world, the mechanisms by which this is accomplished may not be immediately apparent to consumers.

On the one hand, web publishers—like other businesses online and off—want to gather information about their customers that will allow them to serve those customers (and their advertisers) better. On the other hand, some consumers care passionately about restricting the information businesses gather, and controlling how it is used.

Types of Data Collected

An online publisher may find itself collecting a variety of personal data from visitors to its website. This data most likely will take one of five forms: (1) registration information; (2) data provided by users who choose to interact with the website, for example by participating in an online promotional contest; (3) data collected through the use of cookies; (4) clickstream data; and (5) data collected through the use of pixel tags, sometimes called "clear gifs" or "web bugs."

Registration Information

As the web matures, an increasing number of websites are requiring users to register if they wish to obtain full website access. The information requested upon registration may be useful for product design, marketing, advertising sales, and other purposes. *The New York Times'* website, for example, requires users to register and asks for information such as gender, household income and zip code. Many websites also ask for an e-mail address, a mailing address and personal interests.

Customer Information

Visitors often provide information to websites when they enter online promotional contests, participate in online surveys, make purchases, request information, or sign up for services.

Cookies

A cookie is a brief string of computer code placed by a website on the hard drive of a user's computer. Cookies allow websites to personalize the pages displayed to particular users by keeping track of user names and passwords, preferences, and even the items users have placed in their "shopping carts." Websites can use cookies to keep track of the pages being accessed by users and can aggregate this data to gauge the popularity and effectiveness of various website features.

The default settings on Netscape Navigator and Microsoft Explorer allow cookies to be placed on the user's computer. However, both browsers permit the user to change the default settings to alert the user when a cookie is sent or to reject cookies entirely.

Cookies come in two flavors: "session cookies," which expire when the user terminates his or her browser session (*e.g.*, by closing the browser); and "persistent cookies," which persist until a specified expiration date, which may be days, weeks, or even months after they are placed.

Clickstream Data

While a user visits various sites on the Internet, each website visited and each page viewed within a site can be tracked by the user's Internet service provider. The ISP can maintain a record of a user's online activities, including websites visited, ads viewed, purchases made, and more. Website operators can also record more limited usage data through the deployment of cookies and can identify the visitor's ISP, the website through which the user linked to the site, and the site for which it left, as well as which pages on the operator's website were visited and the amount of time spent on each page.

Pixel Tags

Pixel tags, sometimes called "clear gifs," "web bugs," or "single pixel gifs," are visually unnoticeable graphic files that allow websites and advertisers to identify when a visitor has accessed a web page containing the tag. A pixel tag is loaded as part of the web page and therefore, unlike a cookie, cannot be blocked by changing the default browser settings. As the web page that contains the pixel tag is loaded, the entity that placed the tag can track visitors and read cookies it has previously set. Pixel tags can also be inserted into html e-mail messages, allowing an advertiser to correlate a user's email address with a cookie it has previously set.

Federal Regulations

General

With the exception of the Children's Online Privacy Protection Act (COPPA), discussed below at pages 175 to 178, there are no federal laws specifically and exclusively addressing the collection and use of information from websites. However, various federal laws, including the Health and Human Services Privacy Rule and the Gramm-Leach-Bliley Act, regulate certain online activities. In addition, other federal laws, including the Federal Trade Commission Act, the Electronic Communications Privacy Act, and the Computer Fraud and Abuse Act, have also been construed to apply online. With more than 100 privacy bills proposed in the 107th (2002-03) and 108th (2003-04) sessions of Congress, it is possible that more comprehensive privacy legislation will be passed before long.

Enforcement authority over most existing federal privacy laws has been granted to the Federal Trade Commission. As discussed in more detail below, the FTC's position on privacy laws has evolved over the past few years, especially as the value and efficacy of enforcing current laws have been called into question.

Several states have also passed privacy legislation, resulting in a concern that, absent federal legislation, web publishers could have to comply with 50 different privacy regimes in the U.S. alone. *See, e.g.*, California Online Privacy Protection Act of 2003, CAL. BUS. & PROF. CODE § 22575 et seq. (requiring website operators to post conspicuous privacy policies and to comply with those policies); NEB. REV. STAT .§ 87-302(a)(14) (prohibiting website operators from knowingly making false or misleading statements regarding use of personal information submitted by members of the public).

The FTC's Five Core Principles of Privacy Protection

The FTC's involvement with online privacy issues stems largely from its broad mandate to enforce the Federal Trade Commission Act, which prohibits "deceptive acts or practices in or affecting commerce." 15 U.S.C. § 45(a). This allows the FTC to punish, as an unfair and deceptive practice, data collection, use, or distribution practices that violate a website's own privacy policy. In June 1998, the Federal Trade Commission articulated the five core principles of privacy protection that it believes must be part of any attempt at either government regulation or industry self-regulation:

1. *Notice* to consumers about when, how, and for what purposes their personal information will be collected.

2. *Choice* for consumers as to how any personal information collected from them may be used.

3. *Access* for consumers to data collected about them and an opportunity to contest the accuracy and completeness of the data.

4. *Security* of personal information.

5. *Enforcement* mechanisms to enforce these core principles.

See "Privacy Online: A Report to Congress," FTC REPORT (June 1998), *available at* http://www.ftc.gov/reports/privacy3/priv-23.pdf.

In December 1999, the FTC established the Advisory Committee on Online Access and Security to provide recommendations on practices to meet these access and security principles. This committee also coordinated the FTC's 2000 Online Privacy Survey to review the nature and substance of U.S. commercial websites' privacy policies.

Surveys

In February and March 2000, the FTC conducted a survey of commercial sites' information practices. Two groups of sites were studied: (1) a random sample of 335 websites; and (2) 91 of the 100 busiest sites. Almost all sites (97% in the random sample, and 99% in the most popular group) collected an e-mail address or some other type of personal identifying information from users. The survey analyzed the nature and substance of privacy policy statements in light of the fair-information practice principles previously articulated by the FTC. While the survey results show that there had been a steady increase in the percentage of websites that posted some form of privacy policy statement, the survey also found that only 20% of websites in the random sample that collected personal identifying information implemented, at least in part, all of the FTC's "fair information practice principles," and that only 41% of sites in the random sample and 60% of sites in the most popular group met the basic "notice" and "choice" standards. The survey also revealed that 8% of sites in the random sample and 45% of sites in the most popular group displayed the "privacy seal" of one of the self-regulatory bodies (such as TRUSTe and BBBOnline).

More recently, a March 2002 survey conducted by Ernst & Young on behalf of the Progress & Freedom Foundation reported that website operators had become more attentive to online privacy issues. *See* "Privacy Online: A Report on the Information Practices and Policies of Commercial Websites" (March 2002), *available at* http://www.pff.org/publications/ privacyonlinefinalael.pdf. The study found broader use of privacy policy statements by online companies, and found that the privacy policy statements surveyed were more prominent and provided greater detail of how companies use consumer information. The Ernst & Young study was the first major examination of online privacy practices since the FTC survey of early 2000.

In June 2003, Professor Joseph Turow of the University of Pennsylvania conducted telephone interviews of 1,200 adults who use the Internet. He found that, despite the detailed privacy policy statements posted on many major websites, many Internet users do not understand how website operators collect and use information and make little effort to educate themselves. For example, more than half of the adults surveyed mistakenly believed that if a website has posted a privacy policy statement, it will not share personal information collected from users with other websites or companies. *See* Joseph Turow, *Americans and Online Privacy: The System is Broken*, Annenberg Public Policy Center of the University of Pennsylvania (June 2003).

Relationship Between Online Privacy Policies and Offline Data Collection Practices

Speaking at a Q&A session at the Promotion Marketing Association's annual meeting in December 2001, Howard Beales, the FTC's consumer protection chief, stated that, if a company posts a privacy policy statement on its website, the FTC will assume that the statement governs all data collection and use by the company, online and offline, unless the statement clearly states that it applies only to data collected online. This could have significant repercussions for many businesses, which may have collected and used customer information offline for generations without ever articulating (or even thinking about) a privacy policy.

FTC Enforcement

FTC privacy-related enforcement actions include:

GeoCities

In August 1998, in the FTC's first Internet privacy-related enforcement proceeding, GeoCities agreed to settle FTC charges of deceptively collecting personal information. The FTC charged that GeoCities had misrepresented how personal registration information collected on its site would be used. Rather than only using the information to provide members with the particular advertising or product information they had requested (as had been promised in GeoCities' posted privacy policy statement), GeoCities disclosed this information to third parties who used it to target promotional messages to GeoCities members. The FTC also charged that GeoCities had misrepresented that GeoCities itself maintained information collected from children participating in the "GeoKidz Club." In fact, third parties ran the Club and maintained the collected information.

Under the terms of the settlement, GeoCities must post a clear and prominent "privacy notice" consistent with the FTC's core principles of privacy protection. The notice must tell consumers what information is being collected and for what purpose, to whom it would be disclosed, and how consumers can access and remove information from GeoCities' databases. GeoCities also agreed to institute procedures to obtain parental consent before collecting personal data from children under age 13. GeoCities must also provide its members with an opportunity to have their personal data deleted from GeoCities' and any third parties' databases. GeoCities was also required to provide, at least until August 2003, a hyperlink within its privacy notice to the FTC's website on consumer privacy. *See Geocities*, FTC No. 982-3051, Agreement Containing Consent Order (Aug. 13, 1998), *available at* http://www.ftc.gov/os/1998/08/geo-ord.htm.

DoubleClick

On February 10, 2000, the FTC commenced an inquiry into whether DoubleClick, Inc. had engaged in unfair and deceptive trade practices by tracking the online activities of Internet users and combining the tracking data with detailed personal profiles contained in a national marketing database. The Electronic Privacy Information Center had alleged that this was done without the knowledge of users and in violation of DoubleClick's assurances (included in versions of its privacy policy) that such tracking information would remain anonymous. The FTC announced in January 2001 that it would close its investigation (without citing any specific reasons for the closure, but maintaining its right to reopen the matter if necessary) after obtaining DoubleClick's voluntary, but not binding, assurance that it would not link users' browsing activities to their buying habits. As part of the settlement, DoubleClick modified its privacy policy to disclose its use of pixel tags, and agreed to create an opt-out for cookies and to clarify its Internet address finder email practices. *See* Stefanie Olsen, "FTC Drops Probe into DoubleClick Privacy Practices," CNET News.com (Jan. 22, 2001), *at* http://news.com.com/2100-1023_3-251325.html.

On August 26, 2002, DoubleClick announced that it had agreed to pay a $450,000 fine, and to amend its policies as part of a settlement of a multi-state investigation into its use of personal data. A copy of the Settlement Agreement is available at http://news.findlaw.com/wp/docs/cyberlaw/agsdclick82602agr.pdf.

Toysmart

On July 10, 2000, the FTC filed suit against Toysmart, Inc., an Internet firm that had ceased operations in May 2000, for allegedly trying to sell confidential, personal information collected from its customers in violation of its articulated privacy policy. *FTC v. Toysmart.com, LLC*, No. 00-11341-RGS (D. Mass. July 12, 2000). Toysmart's privacy policy statement stated that "personal information . . . such as name, address, billing information and shopping practices, is never shared with a third party." But in June 2000, the company placed an ad in *The Wall Street Journal* offering its customer lists and databases for sale as part of bankruptcy proceedings.

At the end of July 2000, Toysmart settled the suit. The settlement allowed Toysmart to sell its customer information as part of a sale of the whole website to a "qualified buyer." The qualified buyer was required to agree to adhere to the terms of the Toysmart privacy policy. Any changes to the policy would have required providing notice to customers and giving them an opportunity to decide whether to opt in to the change. *See FTC v. Toysmart.com, LLC*, No. 00-11341-RGS, Stipulated Consent Agreement and Final Order, July 21, 2002, *available at* http://www.ftc.gov/os/2000/07/toysmartconsent.htm. Toysmart finally sold the customer list to Disney's Buena Vista Internet Group for $50,000, and the list and database were immediately destroyed.

Microsoft

In August 2002, Microsoft entered into a consent agreement with the FTC, under which it agreed to make substantial changes to its Passport system. The Passport system stores a computer user's login names and passwords so the user can visit various password-protected websites without having to log in each time. Microsoft uses Passport to control access to its own sites, and markets it to other websites. The FTC alleged that Microsoft collected too much information, used unfair or deceptive practices, and failed to protect adequately its users' privacy and the security of the personal information it collected. Microsoft agreed (1) not to misrepresent its information practices in any way; (2) to establish and maintain a comprehensive information security program; (3) to obtain, from an objective third party, biannual reports assessing its security program; and (4) to allow the FTC to inspect its representations to consumers about its information collecting practices, as well as plans, reports, and reviews related to its compliance with the FTC's order. Microsoft is required to comply with these inspection requests through August 2007. *See Microsoft Corp.*, FTC No. 012-3240, Agreement Containing Consent Order (Aug. 8, 2002), *available at* http://www.ftc.gov/os/2002/08/microsoftagree.pdf.

The FTC's Position Regarding the Enactment of New Privacy Laws

The FTC's position regarding the enactment of new privacy laws has changed over the past few years. In June 2000, the FTC called for the passage of new, comprehensive privacy laws after it concluded that self-regulation was not working. However, since the appointment of Chairman Timothy J. Muris in 2001, the FTC has instead advocated the enforcement and strengthening of existing privacy rules, rather than the passage of new laws.

The FTC's change in position appears to have been based on several factors. Experience with COPPA and the Gramm-Leach-Bliley Act, discussed below, showed that certain types of privacy laws cannot only be costly to businesses, but may do very little to benefit consumers. The FTC also expressed concern that new online privacy laws would be of little value if the offline world is not regulated as well. On June 11, 2002, Chairman Muris reiterated these concerns in a speech at the Networked Economy Summit and emphasized that the online industry has made significant improvements in providing privacy protection to consumers without any legislative mandates. Timothy Muris, *Protecting Consumers' Privacy: Goals and Accomplishments* (Remarks on June 11, 2002 at the Networked Economy Summit), *available at* http://www.ftc.gov/speeches/muris/gmason.htm.

The FTC's position does not preclude Congress or the states from adopting privacy rules, but it does affect congressional debate on the issue. *See* Daniel Sieberg, "FTC Sidelines the Call for New Privacy Laws" (Oct. 4, 2001), *available at* http://www.cnn.com/2001/US/10/04/inv.online.privacy/.

Proposed Federal Legislation

Notwithstanding the FTC's current position on new online privacy laws, more than 100 privacy bills have been proposed in the 107th (2002-03) and 108th (2003-04) sessions of Congress. Most reiterate common themes, requiring that consumers be notified of companies' data-collection policies and requiring that companies give consumers the ability to opt in or opt out of such collection. A summary of some recent bills is provided below. More information can also be found at http://thomas.loc.gov.

Consumer Privacy Protection Act of 2003

The Consumer Privacy Protection Act (H.R. 1636), introduced in April 2003, would allow businesses in both the online and offline world to share information about customers who have not opted out of such data sharing. The bill would override state laws that place more restrictions on any commercial use of personal information. It would grant the FTC enforcement powers but would not give individuals the right to sue for privacy violations. In April 2003, the bill was referred to the House subcommittee on Commerce, Trade, and Consumer Protection, and no other action has been reported as of December 31, 2003.

Online Privacy Protection Act of 2003

The Online Privacy Protection Act (H.R. 69), introduced in January 2003, would require the FTC to prescribe regulations to protect the privacy of personal information collected from and about individuals who use the Internet and who are not covered by COPPA. The bill would provide greater individual control over the collection and use of personally identifying information. The bill was referred to the House subcommittee on Commerce, Trade and Consumer Protection in February 2003, with no further action reported.

Social Security On-line Privacy Protection Act

The Social Security On-line Privacy Protection Act (H.R. 70), which was introduced in January 2003, would prohibit Internet service providers from disclosing, without an individual's prior informed consent, an individual's Social Security number or other personally identifying information that can be acquired by use of a Social Security number. In February 2003 the bill was referred to the House subcommittee on Commerce, Trade and Consumer Protection. No further action had been taken on the bill as of December 31, 2003.

Defense of Privacy Act

The Defense of Privacy Act (H.R. 338) was introduced on January 27, 2003. The bill would require federal agencies to consider individual privacy issues when promulgating rules and regulations. The House subcommittee on Commercial and Administrative Law held hearings on the bill in July 2003, with no further action reported.

Social Security Number Misuse Prevention Act

In response to the public's growing concerns about identity theft, Senator Dianne Feinstein (D. Cal.) introduced the Social Security Number Misuse Prevention Act (S. 228; identical bill H.R. 637) on January 28, 2003. The bill would require the removal of Social Security numbers from Internet records, government checks, and driver's licenses. In addition, the bill would prohibit the sale of Social Security numbers to the general public. As of December 31, 2003, the bill was awaiting action in the Senate.

Constitutionality of Privacy Laws

Case law suggests that any newly enacted privacy laws may face substantial constitutional challenges.

U.S. West v. Federal Communications Commission, 182 F.3d 1224 (10th Cir. 1999).

The U.S. Court of Appeals for the Tenth Circuit vacated an FCC order prohibiting phone companies from using customer proprietary network information (CPNI) for marketing purposes without the affirmative approval of their customers. CPNI includes such sensitive information as when, where, and to whom a customer places calls. The court found that the regulations authorized by the order were not narrowly tailored to serve the government's purpose because the FCC required that telephone customers affirmatively opt-in (grant the carrier express approval through written, oral, or electronic means before the carrier may use the customer's CPNI data) without considering whether an "opt-out" approach (in which approval would be inferred from the customer-carrier relationship unless the customer specifically requested that his CPNI be restricted) would have been sufficient. While the ruling was relatively narrow, the court's reasoning suggests that broad privacy legislation may be unconstitutional:

> Although we agree that privacy may rise to the level of a substantial state interest, the government cannot satisfy the second prong of the [applicable] test by merely asserting a broad interest in privacy. . . . [P]rivacy may only constitute a substantial state interest if the government specifically articulates and properly justifies it. . . . [With regard to a speech restriction imposed to protect privacy by keeping certain information confidential, the] government must show that the dissemination of the information desired to be kept private would inflict specific and significant harm on individuals, such as undue embarrassment or ridicule, intimidation or harassment, or misappropriation of sensitive personal information for the purposes of assuming another's identity. . . . Although we may feel uncomfortable knowing that our personal information is circulating in the world, we live in an open society where information may usually pass freely. A general level of discomfort from knowing that people can readily access information about us does not necessarily rise to the level of a substantial state interest . . . for it is not based on an identified harm. *Id.* at 15.

 Verizon N.W. Inc, et al.. v. Showalter, 282 F. Supp. 2d 1187 (W.D. Wash. 2003).

The State of Washington promulgated regulations on the use of CPNI that were broader than the FCC's regulations. On November 21, 2002, Verizon Northwest, Inc. and other telecommunications companies sued the State of Washington claiming that the State's CPNI regulations were unconstitutional. In August 2003, the U.S. District Court for the Western District of Washington ruled that the state regulatory scheme, which required that telecommunications companies get opt-in consent from consumers before making certain uses of their CPNI, unconstitutionally restricted the companies' commercial speech rights. The court found that although there was a substantial state interest in allowing customers to have approval rights over use of CPNI, the regulation did not materially advance that interest, was not narrowly tailored to further that interest, and unacceptably burdened the plaintiffs' free speech rights. Accordingly, the court permanently enjoined Washington from enforcing the privacy regulations.

ACLU, et al. v. Ashcroft, 322 F.3d 240 (3d Cir. 2003), *cert. granted* 124 S. Ct. 399 (2003).

Also challenged on First Amendment grounds was the Child Online Protection Act, which prohibits companies from using the Internet to engage in "any communication for commercial purposes . . . available to any minor . . . that is harmful to minors." Because of the statute's vague wording as to the types of speech it regulates, the plaintiffs argued that COPA violates the First Amendment, as a content-based restriction on speech. As such, it has to satisfy a "strict scrutiny" analysis, *i.e.*, that the regulation is narrowly tailored to meet a compelling government interest. A three-judge panel of the U.S. Court of Appeals for the Third Circuit agreed with the plaintiffs and declared the Act unconstitutional. The court held that the Act was not sufficiently narrowly tailored because the terms "minor" and "harmful" were overly broad such that the Act would deter adults from accessing speech that was constitutionally protected. *ACLU v. Ashcroft*, 322 F.3d 240 (3d Cir. 2003). On October 14, 2003, the Supreme Court agreed to review the case. Oral arguments were scheduled for March 2, 2004. For further discussion of this case as it relates to freedom of speech on the Internet, see Chapter 1, page 7.

Protection of Children's Personal Information

To protect against the collection of information from children who may not be sufficiently sophisticated to appreciate the significance of their information disclosures, Congress passed the Children's Online Privacy Protection Act of 1998 (COPPA).

Children's Online Privacy Protection Act of 1998

COPPA required the FTC to establish notice, parental consent, and access requirements regarding the collection of information from children. 15 U.S.C. §§ 6501, *et seq*. The rules took effect on April 21, 2000 and are available at http://www.ftc.gov/privacy/index.html. They apply to commercial websites that are directed to, or that knowingly collect information from, children under 13. Operators of those websites must:

1. Provide a clear and prominent link to a statement detailing their information practices, including names and contact information for all operators who collect or maintain personal information, the types of personal information collected from children, how such personal information is used, whether personal information is disclosed to third parties, and, if information is disclosed to third parties, a description of the businesses in which these third parties are engaged. The link must be on the home page of the site or on the home page of a separate children's area, if one exists. The link must also be displayed in each area where personal information is collected. The statement must be updated if the operator's practices materially change.

2. Obtain prior, verifiable parental consent for the collection, use, and/or disclosure of personal information from children. Discussion of the method of verifying consent occupied much of the FTC's debate leading up to the new rules. Ultimately, the FTC decided to phase in the requirements according to a "sliding scale approach." This approach allowed the use of emailed consent from the parent for the first two years after the effective date of the rules (April 21, 2000), unless the website used personal information in ways that posed greater risks to children (such as, disclosing such information to a third party, or revealing it in a

message board or chat room). The FTC has extended this sliding scale rule through 2005. The emailed consent must be confirmed by a follow-up email, letter, or telephone call to the parent confirming the consent. For those activities that pose what the FTC views as greater risk to children, and for all information collected after the extension period expires, methods deemed more reliable by the FTC must be used to verify consent. These methods might include requiring parents to print and mail or fax a consent form, use of a credit card, setting up a toll-free number where trained staff can receive calls, email with password or PIN, or some other technological measure that is "reasonably calculated . . . to ensure that the person providing consent is the child's parent."

3. Give parents the option to consent to the collection and use of the child's personal information without consenting to disclosure of his or her personal information to third parties.

4. Allow parents a chance to review the personal information about a child that is collected and to have the information deleted if they choose. The website operator may not condition a child's participation in an activity or promotional contest on disclosure of more personal information than is reasonably necessary for participation in the activity or contest.

5. Establish and maintain reasonable procedures to protect the confidentiality, security, and integrity of the personal information collected.

Nonprofits and COPPA

Nonprofit organizations, whose activities are outside the scope of 5 of the FTC Act, are not subject to COPPA. The FTC has cautioned, however, that some nonprofits operating for the profit of their for-profit members, such as industry associations, would be subject to COPPA. *See California Dental Assn. v. FTC*, 526 U.S. 756 (1999).

COPPA Safe Harbor

The FTC's rules include a safe-harbor provision allowing for industry self-regulation in lieu of FTC regulation. Website operators that participate in industry "seal" programs (such as TRUSTe) that are approved by the FTC would be subject to the review and disciplinary procedures of the industry programs instead of the FTC's procedures. The FTC announced on May 23, 2001 that TRUSTe has been approved as a safe-harbor program under the terms of COPPA. Programs submitted by the Children's Advertising Review Unit of the Council of Better Business Bureaus, an arm of the advertising industry's self-regulation program, and the Entertainment Software Rating Board have also been approved as COPPA safe harbors.

Five-Year Review

Within five years of the effective date of the rules, the FTC will conduct a review to evaluate the effect of the rules, children's ability to obtain access to information of their choice online, and the availability of websites directed to children. The FTC will report its conclusions to Congress.

The Cost of Compliance

There is significant concern over the costs of complying with COPPA. Many websites have simply stopped providing content aimed at children under age 13, citing the hassle and expense of complying with the new rules. *See* Lynn Burke, "Kids' Sites Cite COPPA Woes," WIRED NEWS (September 14, 2000), *available at* http://www.wired.com/ news/politics/0,1283,38666,00.html.

Prosecution Under COPPA

On April 19, 2001, the FTC announced settlements with three website operators for violations of COPPA. The FTC charged Monarch Services, Inc. and Girls Life, Inc., operators of www.girlslife.com; Bigmailbox.com, Inc. and Nolan Quan, operators of www.bigmailbox.com; and Looksmart Ltd., operator of www.insidetheweb.com, with illegally collecting personal information from children under age 13 without parental consent. The companies agreed to pay an aggregate total of $100,000 in civil penalties and to comply with COPPA in the future. The settlements also required the operators to delete all personal information they had collected from children online at any time since COPPA's effective date. These three cases mark the first civil penalties levied by the FTC under COPPA. More information can be found on the FTC's website, http://www.ftc.gov/opa/2001/04/girlslife.htm.

In April 2002, Ohio Art, noted for its product Etch-A-Sketch, was fined $35,000 by the FTC over a COPPA infraction on the Etch-A-Sketch site. According to the consent decree, the site was collecting information from children before obtaining parental consent. The consent decree and settlement can be found at http://www.ftc.gov/os/2002/04/ohioartconsent.htm. Similar actions by the FTC against Lisa Frank Inc., a maker of toys for girls, and American Pop Corn Company, which runs the website www.jollytime.com, were also settled.

On February 27, 2003, the FTC exacted its largest civil penalties to date for COPPA violations. The penalties were paid in connection with consent decrees that the FCC entered into with Mrs. Fields Cookies and with Hershey Foods. The FTC had determined that both companies' websites were targeted to children. Although Mrs. Fields Cookies did not disseminate any of the personal information that it collected via its website, it settled with the FTC by agreeing to pay a $100,000 fine for collecting personal information from children through its websites without obtaining prior parental consent. *See United States v. Mrs. Fields Famous Brands, Inc.*, No. 2:03 CV205 JTG (D. Utah 2003) (Consent Decree and Order for Civil Penalties, Injunctive, and Other Relief).

The FTC levied an $85,000 fine against Hershey Foods for failing to ensure that its method of obtaining prior parental consent was sufficiently effective. The civil penalty against Hershey Foods was the first levied against a website for implementing a parental consent process that the FTC found inadequate. Hershey's parental consent form was designed to be completed and submitted online, but it lacked an effective mechanism to ensure that the form had been actually completed by the parent. Further, the FTC alleged that Hershey collected personally identifying information from children regardless of whether the parental consent form had been completed. *See United States v. Hershey Foods Corp.*, No. 4:CV03-350 (M.D. Pa. 2003) (Consent Decree and Order for Civil Penalties, Injunctive, and Other Relief).

In addition to the civil penalties imposed under the consent decrees, Mrs. Fields Cookies and Hershey Foods were ordered not to violate COPPA in the future, to delete any information that they had obtained while violating COPPA, and to allow the FTC to monitor their future compliance with COPPA.

At least 50 other operators of children's websites have received letters from the FTC warning of COPPA noncompliance.

On April 22, 2003, the Electronic Privacy Information Center (EPIC) filed a complaint with the FTC, alleging that online retailer Amazon.com violated COPPA by knowingly posting children's names, email addresses, ages, genders, and mailing addresses on product review websites without obtaining parental consent as required by COPPA. Amazon.com claimed that its website was not directed toward children. But EPIC noted that several posted product reviews explicitly referenced the reviewer's age. EPIC contended that if Amazon.com reviewed submissions before posting them, as it claimed it did, it would have known that the reviewers were under the age of 13. The day after EPIC filed its complaint, Amazon.com removed the children's personally identifying information from its site. *See* Complaint of Electronic Privacy Information Center, FCC (filed Apr. 22, 2003), available at: http://www.epic.org/privacy/amazon/coppacomplaint.html; Ira Teinowitz, *Amazon.com Pulls Children's ID Features* (Apr. 23, 2003), *at* http://www.adage.com/news.cms?newsID=37684.

Prosecution beyond COPPA

Of course, in addition to the rules announced to implement COPPA, the FTC maintains its general authority to prohibit unfair and deceptive practices with respect to the collection of information from children.

In May 1999, Liberty Financial Companies, Inc., operator of the Young Investor site (http://www.younginvestor.com), settled with the FTC over charges that the site falsely collected personal information from children. The FTC alleged that the site falsely represented that personal information collected from children in a survey would be maintained anonymously, whereas information about the child and the family's finances was maintained in an identifiable manner. The consent agreement requires the site to post a privacy notice and obtain verifiable parental consent before collecting a child's personal information. *In re Liberty Financial Companies, Inc.*, FTC File No. 982 3522 (1999), available at http://www.ftc.gov/os/caselist/9823522.htm.

Privacy of Medical Information

In November 1999, the U.S. Department of Health and Human Services (HHS) published its Proposed Rule implementing the privacy requirements of the Health Insurance Portability Accountability Act of 1996 (HIPAA). In December 2000, HHS issued the Final Rule, which included significant changes received during the comment period. The Rule took effect on April 14, 2001, and required covered entities to comply with the Final Rule's provisions as of April 13, 2003. See 45 C.F.R. Pts. 160, 164.

Defining protected health information as individually identifiable health information transmitted in electronic form, the Rule provides that covered entities can use or disclose protected information for purposes of treatment, payment, and health-care operations, or for other specified purposes (such as public health, research, or law enforcement). Covered entities may continue to use or disclose protected information for any purpose if individual authorization is obtained. Additionally, the Rule establishes three rights: (1) to obtain access to, inspect, and obtain a copy of information about oneself; (2) to be afforded a good-faith effort by health-care providers to provide written notice of their information-sharing practices; and (3) to request amendment or correction of incomplete or inaccurate information about oneself. While the Rule does not grant individuals the right to sue over violations of these rights, it does provide monetary penalties and criminal penalties, including imprisonment for up to ten years, for obtaining protected information under false pretenses, disclosure of protected information with intent to sell, or disclosure of protected information for malicious harm.

In 2002, HHS issued further amendments to patient privacy practices as part of HIPPA. The new rules abandon the requirement that doctors, hospitals, and other health-care providers obtain written acknowledgment from patients that they have received notice of the potential uses of the information they provide, and written consent from patients before disclosing personal medical information for purposes of treatment or paying claims. Instead, health-care providers are required to make a "good faith effort" to obtain written acknowledgment from their patients of the notice. The new rules limit the types of information that can be disclosed, and guarantee patients access to their medical records. HHS officials and other supporters of the new HIPAA rules explain that the new rules are intended to strike a balance between protecting patients' privacy on one hand, and maintaining quality health care on the other.

Privacy in the Financial Services Industry

The Gramm-Leach-Bliley Act (codified in relevant part at 15 U.S.C. §§ 6801-6809) (Title V, subtitle A, Pub. L. No. 106-102, §§ 501-510, 113 Stat. 1338, 1436-45 (Nov. 12, 1999)) was signed into law on November 12, 1999. The Act is intended to enhance competition in the financial services industry. The Act includes privacy provisions that require financial institutions to provide notice to consumers of their privacy policies regarding personal information, and to allow consumers the opportunity to opt out of disclosures of personal information. Although the law does not directly address online privacy, it could affect certain online services because the definition of "financial institution" is quite broad.

On May 12, 2000, the FTC issued its Final Rule implementing the Gramm-Leach-Bliley Act (full text available at http://www.ftc.gov/os/2000/05/glb000512.pdf). The Final Rule mandates that "financial institutions" notify customers about the collection of personal information and offer some choice as to how such data are shared. This Rule applies to a wide range of entities (because the definition of "financial institutions" is broad), including companies that perform activities "closely related" to banking, such as financial-data processing, sales of financial software, and property-appraising services. The Rule applies to data collected as part of the sale or provision of a financial product or service. Companies covered by the Rule are required to give notice to consumers of what personal, nonpublic information they collect, and with whom they share such information. This notice may not simply be posted on a website. Instead, the company must verify that consumers have seen it. Additionally, the Rule states that consumers must be given the right to prohibit sharing of their personal information with unaffiliated third parties. The Rule became effective November 13, 2000, and full compliance was required by July 1, 2001.

The Final Rule was challenged in the U.S. District Court for the District of Columbia as being unlawful and unconstitutional. *Individual Reference Services Group, Inc. v. FTC*, 145 F. Supp. 2d 6 (D.D.C. 2001). In upholding the Rule, the court stated that the Rule does not contravene the plain meaning of the Gramm-Leach-Bliley Act and that it is a permissible construction of the statute. In addition, the FTC's actions in promulgating the Rule were not arbitrary and capricious. The Rule was held not to violate the plaintiff's right to free speech under the First Amendment or to violate the plaintiff consumer-reporting agency's right either to due process or equal protection under the Fifth Amendment.

The Gramm-Leach-Bliley Act has come under fire from industry representatives and privacy advocates. Industry representatives claim that compliance with the law, which entails mailing thousands of privacy notices, is too expensive. Privacy advocates, on the other hand, claim that the Act fails to provide enough protections for consumer privacy. *See* http://www.epic.org/privacy/financial/glb_comments.pdf. The FTC held a public workshop in December 2001 in response to concerns about the clarity and effectiveness of privacy policies. *See* http://www.ftc.gov/bcp/workshops/glb/index.html.

A number of federal agencies recently issued a Notice of Proposed Rulemaking in which they solicited comments on whether Gramm-Leach-Bliley should be amended to allow financial institutions to provide alternative privacy notices that would be easier for consumers to understand. The agencies asked that submissions address issues such as the goals, elements, language and format of privacy notices, and the costs and benefits of short privacy notices, as well as such things as whether a short notice should be mandatory for all financial institutions, and comments about the costs and benefits of a short notice. *See* Interagency Proposal to Consider Alternative Forms of Privacy Notices Under the Gramm-Leach-Bliley Act, 68. Fed. Reg. 75,164 (proposed Dec. 30, 2003).

Several bills have been introduced in the 108th (2003-04) Congress that would change the way the Gramm-Leach-Bliley Act protects customer data. The Privacy Protection Clarification Act (H.R. 781) excludes attorneys from Gramm-Leach-Bliley's definition of "financial institution," thereby exempting attorneys from disclosure requirements. The Identity Theft Consumer Notification Act (H.R. 818) requires that financial institutions inform consumers when their nonpublic personal information has been compromised. It also requires that the financial institution reimburse the consumer for any losses that are incurred as a result of such disclosure. The National Uniform Privacy Standards Act (H.R. 1766) would preempt all state laws that would regulate subject matter that is otherwise covered by the Gramm-Leach-Bliley Act.

California has also enacted sweeping financial privacy legislation. The law, signed by Governor Gray Davis in August 2003 and set to take effect July 1, 2004, gives consumers an opt-in right of consent for the sale or sharing of financial information with unaffiliated third parties, and an opt-out right for sharing such information among company affiliates. It also permits consumers to bar companies from sharing information with an affiliated company if that company is in a different line of business. *See* Cal. Fin. Code § 4050 *et seq.* The statute may face legal challenges, however, given that similar provisions enacted by several California localities were recently found to have been preempted by federal law. *See Bank of America, N.A., et al. v. City of Daly City, et al.*, Nos. C-02-4343-CW, C-02-4943-CW (N.D. Cal. 2003). The law may also ultimately be preempted by new federal legislation. In November 2003, the U.S. Senate defeated an amendment to the Fair Credit Reporting Act proposed by California senators that would have made the new California standard the national standard. Instead, the Senate passed a less restrictive bill, which may supersede the California law. *See* Ryan Singel, "Setback for Financial Privacy," WIRED NEWS (Nov. 5, 2003), *available at* http://www.wired.com/news/print/0,1294,61080,00.html.

Suits over Privacy Issues Relating to Financial Information

Only a few cases have been brought alleging violations of consumer privacy with respect to financial information.

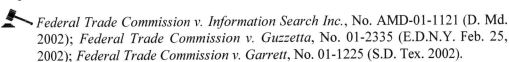 *Federal Trade Commission v. Information Search Inc.*, No. AMD-01-1121 (D. Md. 2002); *Federal Trade Commission v. Guzzetta*, No. 01-2335 (E.D.N.Y. Feb. 25, 2002); *Federal Trade Commission v. Garrett*, No. 01-1225 (S.D. Tex. 2002).

Under settlements reached with the FTC on February 25, 2002, several information brokers who allegedly used deception to obtain consumers' confidential financial information will be required to refrain from these practices and forgo their earnings.

Smith, et al. v. Chase Manhattan Bank, USA, N.A., et al., 741 N.Y.S.2d 100 (N.Y. App. Div. 2002).

The New York Appellate Division upheld the dismissal of a suit under New York consumer-protection laws complaining of the sale of personal financial information by a bank to third-party telemarketers. The plaintiffs, a group of Chase Manhattan credit card and mortgage holders, alleged that the bank violated its Customer Information Principles by selling their information to nonaffiliated vendors, who, in turn, used the information to make unwanted telephone solicitations and send junk mail. Even though consumers were not given an opportunity to opt out, the court found that receipt of junk mail and unwanted telephone solicitations did not constitute actual harm, as required for recovery under the state statute: "the harm at the heart of this purported class action, is that two class members were merely offered products and services which they were free to decline. This does not qualify as actual harm." 741 N.Y.S.2d at 102. For discussion of this case in the context of spam, *see* Chapter 8, page 221–222.

Federal Trade Commission v. 30 Minute Mortgage, Inc., No. 03-60021 (S.D. Fla., filed Jan. 8, 2003).

The FTC filed a complaint in the U.S. District Court for the Southern District of Florida, alleging that 30 Minute Mortgage had violated the Gramm-Leach-Bliley Act by deceiving customers into revealing personal information through its website, which offered low interest rates for mortgages. Specifically, the FTC alleged that 30 Minute Mortgage had falsely held itself out to be a "national mortgage lender" and that it advertised low mortgage loans that did not necessarily exist. The FTC also alleged that after collecting personal information using deceptive practices, 30 Minute Mortgage then sold the personal information to third parties without the consumers' consent. 30 Minute Mortgage agreed to halt these allegedly deceptive practices until the court issues a final ruling on the FTC's allegations. On November 26, 2003, the principals of 30 Minute Mortgage settled the case with the FTC by agreeing to post $1 million bonds before sending commercial email solicitations advertising the company's services. *See FTC v. 30 Minute Mortgage, Inc.*, Stipulated Final Judgments, No. 03-60021-CIV (S.D. Fla., Nov. 26, 2003), *available at* http://www.ftc.gov/opa/2003/12/30mm2.htm.

Privacy of Government Workers

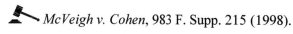 *Florida v. City of Clearwater*, No. SC02-1694 (Fla. Sept. 11, 2003), *available at* http://www.flcourts.org/sct/sctdocs/ops/sc02-1694.pdf.

The Florida Supreme Court ruled that public employees did not have to turn over private email messages for public inspection. *The St. Petersburg Times* had sued the city of Clearwater, Florida, seeking disclosure of private emails of two state officials under a state statute giving citizens the right to inspect any public record made or received in connection with the "official business" of the state. The trial court denied *The Times* access to the emails on the ground that private emails did not fall within the definition of public records under the statute. The court said that the private emails were no different than personal letters delivered to government workers via a government post office box and stored in a government-owned desk. Recognizing the importance of the issue, the appellate court certified the question to the Florida Supreme Court, which affirmed the trial court. The Supreme Court held that the nature of the record controls whether it is public or private; private documents do not become public records solely by being placed on an agency computer.

The Electronic Communications Privacy Act and Computer Fraud and Abuse Act

Two federal statutes, the Electronic Communications Privacy Act (ECPA) (18 U.S.C. § 2511 (2000)) and the Computer Fraud and Abuse Act (CFAA) (18 U.S.C. § 1030 (2000)), have been invoked as bases for asserting privacy claims. Neither of these laws was enacted with the goal of providing comprehensive privacy rights, but they have been broadly construed to permit recovery for certain narrowly defined invasions of privacy.

The ECPA, a federal criminal statute, forbids the use of wiretaps without a court order and prohibits the unauthorized use or interception of the contents of any wire, oral, or electronic communication. 18 U.S.C. § 2511(1) (2000). The ECPA also prohibits unauthorized access to stored electronic communications. *Id.* at § 2701.

The CFAA, also a federal criminal statute, generally prohibits unauthorized access to a "protected computer" with the intent to obtain information, defraud, obtain anything of value, or cause damage to the computer. 18 U.S.C. § 1030(a). A "protected computer" is defined broadly as a computer that is used by or for a financial institution or the United States Government or is used in interstate or foreign commerce or communication.

Suits under the ECPA and CFAA

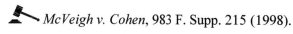 *McVeigh v. Cohen*, 983 F. Supp. 215 (1998).

The plaintiff, an allegedly homosexual member of the armed forces, contended that the Navy violated his rights under the ECPA in an effort to discharge him in contravention of the statutory policy known as "Don't Ask, Don't Tell, Don't Pursue." The Navy contacted America Online under false pretenses for information that could connect the screen name "boysrch" and the accompanying user profile to McVeigh. The court found that there was a likelihood of success on the merits with regard to the issue of whether the Navy had violated, or solicited a violation of, the ECPA. The court said the government can obtain information concerning the identity of an online subscriber from an online service provider, but only if it (1) obtains a warrant or (2) gives prior notice to the online subscriber and then issues a subpoena or receives a court order authorizing disclosure of the requested information. The Department of Defense and the Navy were therefore enjoined from discharging or taking any adverse action against McVeigh.

Crowley, et al. v. Cybersource Corp., 166 F. Supp. 2d 1263 (N.D. Cal. 2001).

The plaintiffs brought a class-action suit against Amazon.com and Cybersource, a company that verifies the identities of those making online purchases. The plaintiffs claimed that when they gave Amazon their names, e-mail addresses, mailing addresses, telephone numbers, and credit-card information, Amazon transmitted this information to Cybersource. Cybersource then unlawfully stored this information and used it to create a personal profile of each plaintiff. The court found that Amazon is not a provider of electronic communications services and, therefore, could not have violated provisions of the ECPA prohibiting disclosure of information by electronic information service providers. It also found that Amazon did not violate the provisions of the ECPA prohibiting unauthorized access to the facilities through which an electronic communication service is provided because Amazon received voluntary email transmissions from its customers. The court noted Amazon did not access the information on customers' computer systems, nor could it have unlawfully accessed its own computer systems.

In re Intuit Privacy Litigation, 138 F. Supp. 2d 1272 (C.D. Cal. 2001).

A federal court in California issued a split decision in a class-action privacy suit in which the plaintiffs alleged that the placement of cookies on the computers of visitors to the quicken.com website violated the ECPA and the CFAA. The court held that the plaintiffs could proceed with their suit based on their claim of unauthorized access to electronic communications, but dismissed claims based on the interception of electronic communications and fraudulent computer activity. The parties settled the case in June 2003.

Specht v. Netscape Communications Corp., 150 F. Supp. 2d 585 (S.D.N.Y. 2001), *aff'd*, 306 F.3d 17 (2d Cir. 2002).

In July 2000, a New Jersey-based website operator filed a class-action lawsuit charging that AOL/Netscape's "SmartDownload" software violated the ECPA and the CFAA. The suit alleged that AOL/Netscape secretly monitored file transfers between websites and Internet users when users utilized the "SmartDownload" feature in the Netscape Communicator web browser. The SmartDownload software enables Netscape to track the name, type, and source of executable files a user downloads, along with cookie information that uniquely identifies the user. Netscape and AOL sought to compel arbitration and stay the proceedings, arguing that the dispute is subject to binding arbitration under a clause in the Netscape license agreement. The court held that the users of SmartDownload were not bound by the arbitration clause in the license agreement because they were not necessarily aware that they were entering a contract at the time of the download. (For discussion of this case in the context of enforceability of electronic agreements, *see* Chapter 7 at page 209). Although the case was sent back to the trial court to continue the proceedings, following the Second Circuit's decision, AOL announced that it was dropping the consumer tracking feature from future versions of SmartDownload. As of December 31, 2003, the case was pending in the U.S. District Court for the Southern District of New York.

In a related matter, on June 13, 2003, Netscape agreed to a settlement with the State of New York regarding its SmartDownload software. Under the terms of the settlement, Netscape admitted to no wrongdoing but agreed to pay $100,000, delete data collected through the software, and submit to privacy audits. Assurance of Discontinuance at 9-13, *In re Netscape Comms. Corp.* (June 13, 2003).

EF Cultural Travel v. Explorica, Inc., 274 F.3d 577 (1st Cir. 2001).

The plaintiff and the defendant competed in providing global tours for high-school students. The Court of Appeals for the First Circuit upheld a trial court injunction against the defendant's use of an electronic agent, which combed through the database of its competitor, the plaintiff, for pricing information. The court found that the plaintiff would likely succeed on the merits of its CFAA claim.

In re DoubleClick Inc. Privacy Litigation, 154 F. Supp. 2d 497 (S.D.N.Y. 2001).

In March 2001, a New York District Court dismissed a class-action suit against DoubleClick, an online advertising company. The plaintiffs had challenged DoubleClick's practice of placing cookies, claiming violations of the ECPA, the Wiretap Act, and the CFAA. The court dismissed all of these claims.

Chance, et al. v. Avenue A Inc., 165 F. Supp. 2d 1153 (W.D. Wash. 2001).

The plaintiffs brought a class-action suit against Avenue A, a provider of Web advertising services, claiming that Avenue A had used cookies and pixel tags (also known as "web bugs" or "clear gifs") to monitor their electronic communications without their consent in violation of the ECPA, the CFAA, and state law. The court granted Avenue A summary judgment on the CFAA claims on the ground that no single act of placing or accessing a cookie on a user's computer caused that user damages in excess of the CFAA's $5,000 threshold, and that damages caused by multiple acts cannot be aggregated under the CFAA to reach the threshold. "[T]he transmission of internet cookies," the court found, "is virtually without economic harm." The court also found that Avenue A had not violated the wiretap provision of the ECPA, which prohibits interception of a wire, oral, or electronic communication without the consent of at least one party to the communication. Even if the users did not consent to transmit cookie data to Avenue A, the websites they were visiting had consented to the interception of such cookie data.

United States v. McGuire, 307 F.3d 1192 (9th Cir. 2002).

In the first reported case addressing law-enforcement interception of fax transmissions, the issue before the court was whether federal law-enforcement agents were required to "minimize" the number of fax documents that they intercepted and stored that were unrelated to criminal activity, much as they are required to minimize phone tapping. The U.S. Court of Appeals for the Ninth Circuit ruled that the police did not violate federal wiretap laws when they collected faxes while spying on a group convicted of bank fraud. To eavesdrop on the "Montana Freeman," the FBI obtained a court order permitting interception of voice conversations and faxes. The agents did not take steps to minimize the number of faxes they intercepted or the time during which they monitored fax transmissions.

Konop v. Hawaiian Airlines, Inc., 302 F.3d 868 (9th Cir. 2002), *cert. denied*, 537 U.S. 1193 (2003).

The U.S. Court of Appeals for the Ninth Circuit found that a defendant-employer did not violate the ECPA when it accessed the plaintiff-employee's secure, password-protected website, which criticized the employer. The court found, however, that the ECPA only prohibits unlawful "interceptions" of communications. Although the employer had used the names and passwords of other employees to access the website, the court found that no interception had taken place because the information was in storage, not in transit. According to the court, accessing stored data does not amount to "intercepting" communications under the Wiretap Act; for there to be an "interception," the data must be acquired during transmission. On February 24, 2003, the Supreme Court declined to review the Ninth Circuit's decision.

The U.S. District Court for the District of Massachusetts used the same reasoning to dismiss charges against the defendant in *United States v. Councilman*. See No. 01-CR-10245-MAP (D. Mass. 2003).

See also Fraser v. Nationwide Muual Insurance Co., et al., No. 01-2921 (3d Cir. Dec. 10 2003) (holding that employer's search of employee's email stored on company's servers was not a violation of the ECPA because the employer did not "intercept" the transmission of emails, and also finding that employer was a "communications service provider" and, as such, could search any files on its servers without violating ECPA).

In re Guess?, Inc., Consent Order FTC File No. 022 3260 (June 18, 2003).

On June 18, 2003, Guess, Inc. entered into a consent order with the FTC to amend the information security claims it made on its website. Guess had represented that its website employed security measures that protected customers' private information, such as credit card numbers. In fact, according to the FTC, Guess had not successfully deployed such security measures; in February 2002, a visitor to Guess's website was able to hack into Guess's database and read credit card numbers in clear text.

As part of the consent order, Guess agreed to refrain from making statements about its security protections until it has a comprehensive security system in place that meets standards specified in the consent decree. In addition, Guess agreed to submit to an audit by an independent auditor within one year and every other year thereafter until 2023, and to submit documentation related to its compliance with the consent decree to the FTC.

In re Pharmatrak, Inc. Privacy Litigation, 329 F.3d 9 (1st Cir. 2003), *on remand*, 292 F. Supp. 2d 263 (D. Mass. 2003).

Seven individual plaintiffs, seeking to represent a larger class of similarly situated individuals, sued Pfizer, Inc, Pharmacia Corp., SmithKline Beecham Corp., Glaxo Welcome, Inc., and American Home Products Corp., as well as a Pharmatrak, Inc., which the drug companies had hired to monitor their corporate websites and analyze their website traffic. The plaintiffs claimed that the defendants intercepted their electronic communications and accessed their hard drives in order to collect private information without their consent, all in violation of the ECPA and the CFAA. The plaintiffs complained about the defendants' use of "web bugs" and "cookies." The court dismissed the ECPA claims on technical legal grounds. It decided the CFAA claims based on the statutory requirements of the CFAA.

The CFAA permits recovery for "any impairment to the integrity or availability of data, a program, a system, or information" causing damages of at least $5,000. Without addressing the merits of the plaintiffs' CFAA claims, the trial court found that the plaintiffs had failed to offer any evidence sufficient to establish damages that would meet the $5,000 threshold. Accordingly, the trial court granted the defendants' motion for summary judgment and dismissed the plaintiffs' claims under the CFAA.

The U.S. Court of Appeals for the First Circuit reversed the trial court and found that the Pharmatrak's practices violated the ECPA by intercepting and collecting personally identifying information without the pharmaceutical companies' consent. The court found that Pharmatrak had repeatedly assured its pharmaceutical clients that it was unable to collect such data and that these clients had based their decision to purchase Pharmatrak's services on these assurances. Although some courts had limited the ECPA's interception requirement to include only communications contemporaneous with transmission, the First Circuit was reluctant to give such a narrow reading to a statute that was enacted before use of the Internet was so widespread. But the court reversed the judgment and sent the case back to the trial court to determine whether the interception had been "intentional," as required under the Act, a question the parties had not briefed in the trial court. On remand, the trial court determined that the defendants had not intended to intercept the data, and thus, on November 6, 2003, granted their motion for summary judgment.

▚ *Four Seasons Hotels and Resorts B.V. v. Consorcio Barr, S.A.*, 267 F. Supp. 2d 1268 (S.D. Fla. 2003).

Plaintiff, the operator of the Four Seasons hotel chain, contracted with defendant to build the Four Seasons Hotel in Caracas, Venezuela. Under the agreement, defendant was to retain ownership of the physical premises of the hotel, but plaintiff was to be responsible for its operations. Defendant was not supposed to have access to the plaintiff's computer network, which, among other things, contained extensive proprietary information, including customer data. Nonetheless, after the hotel began operations, Defendant's employees used several means to attempt to gain access to Plaintiff's computer network, including "spoofing" of the hotel's server's IP addresses and sending employees into Four Seasons employees' offices to steal information. The court found the spoofing "impaired the integrity" of plaintiff's computers, causing damage within the scope of the CFAA. It also found that the costs plaintiff incurred in investigating defendant's actions were compensable. The court awarded more than $2.1 million in damages on the CFAA claim. On plaintiff's ECPA claim, the court found that, because the evidence demonstrated that defendant had intercepted electronic communications, it was liable under the statute. The court was only able to award plaintiff its attorneys fees and expenses on that claim, however, because the specific data that had been intercepted were not available for the court to inspect and evaluate.

▚ *Theofel, et al. v. Farey-Jones*, 341 F.3d 978 (9th Cir. 2003).

Plaintiffs were involved in commercial litigation against defendants. In the course of that litigation, defendants served a subpoena on plaintiffs' Internet service provider to produce copies of all emails sent or received by plaintiffs. The ISP, citing the substantial number of emails to which the subpoena applied, agreed to post a sampling of the email messages on one of its websites. When plaintiffs discovered that their emails had been posted pursuant to the subpoena, they sued defendants for violating the Stored

Communications Act (SCA), the ECPA, the CFAA, and various state laws. The U.S. District Court for the Northern District of California dismissed the claims, finding that the federal statutes did not apply.

The Court of Appeals for the Ninth Circuit affirmed the denial of the ECPA claim under the reasoning in *Konop*, discussed above, finding that the ECPA does not apply to *stored* electronic communications. The court, however, reversed the dismissal of the SCA and CFAA claims. On the CFAA claims, the trial court had concluded that the CFAA did not apply to unauthorized accessing of a third party's computer (the emails that were accessed were stored on computers owned by plaintiffs' employer). The Ninth Circuit found that nothing in the language of the statute supported this finding, and that individuals other than the computer's owner may be harmed by unauthorized access to it.

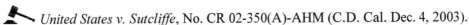 *United States v. Sutcliffe*, No. CR 02-350(A)-AHM (C.D. Cal. Dec. 4, 2003).

Federal prosecutors obtained their first conviction under a federal statute that makes it a crime to post Social Security numbers online. The statute, 18 U.S.C. § 1028, though distinct from the CFAA, is similar in that it regulates fraud in online activity. Specifically, it prohibits the placing of "means of identification" (which includes Social Security numbers, driver's license numbers, alien registration numbers, passport numbers and tax ID numbers) in online locations where such information is available to others, if the intent in posting the information is to aid and abet another felony. In this case, the defendant, William Sutcliffe, was fired by his employer, Global Crossing. After his termination, he accessed the company's personnel files and posted the Social Security numbers, phone numbers, home addresses and dates of birth of some 8,000 of the company's employees. Sutcliffe faces a maximum possible penalty of 30 years in prison.

State Laws and Proposals

Many states are considering proposals that address online privacy, and a few states have already passed such measures. For example, on December 19, 2001, New York Governor George Pataki signed into law a bill that requires state agencies to develop privacy policies. Minnesota has also passed a significant new piece of privacy legislation. The Minnesota law, effective March 1, 2003, requires Internet service providers either to obtain consent from consumers or to provide them with "conspicuous" notice and an opportunity to opt out before disclosing personally identifying information to third parties. By its terms, the law applies only to ISPs that provide consumers authenticated access to, or presence on, the Internet, and does not apply to online businesses in general. Virginia enacted legislation in April 2003 that prohibits court clerks from posting on the Internet documents that contain Social Security numbers, birthdates, or signatures. Va. Code Ann. § 2.2-3802.2 (2003).

California has gone one step further by enacting a law that requires state agencies and businesses that hold or license computer data that contain personal information to disclose any breach of the security of such data to any California resident whose unencrypted personal information is reasonably believed to have been acquired by an unauthorized person. Cal. Civ. Code § 1798.82 (2003). In October 2003, California became the first U.S. jurisdiction to require all websites that collect personally identifiable information about California residents to post a privacy policy statement. The Online Privacy Protection Act of 2003, Cal. Bus. & Prof. Code § 22575 *et seq.*, requires that every website conspicuously post a privacy policy statement, and that it comply with that policy statement. Among other things, the statute requires that the privacy policy statement identify the categories of personally identifying information the site collects, as well as the third parties with whom the website might share information. The statute becomes effective July 1, 2004.

At the local level, San Francisco adopted the Financial Information Privacy Ordinance that requires financial institutions doing business in the city to give paper or electronic notice to, and to obtain prior consent from, consumers before disclosing consumers' confidential information to third parties. Negligent or willful disclosures can result in financial penalties of $2,500 per violation, and entities that disclose for their own financial gain are subject to higher penalties.

Several states also are considering legislation specifically directed at preventing Internet companies from selling personal information obtained by tracking users' online movement. In addition, more than 20 states are considering legislation to address the privacy of health records stored in computer databases.

Online merchants have complained loudly, however, over the prospect of 50 different sets of rules governing the collection and use of information, arguing instead for uniformity. Proposed federal legislation would address the problem by expressly preempting state privacy laws.

Some privacy cases have already been brought under existing state consumer-protection laws and the common law of trespass.

 In re RealNetworks, Inc. Privacy Litigation, 2000 U.S. Dist. LEXIS 6584 (N.D. Ill. May 11, 2000).

In November 1999, two class-action lawsuits were filed against RealNetworks, Inc. alleging that the company's software (which allows users to download compressed music files) also collected information, without disclosure, about user listening habits. Both lawsuits alleged violations of, among other things, state consumer-protection laws, because the RealNetworks privacy statement indicated that information was not being collected. In response to public criticism of its privacy practices, RealNetworks disclosed the use of identification numbers in its privacy statement and offered a patch to replace the identification codes in its products. The company also stated that it did not associate the identification code with user listening habits or personal information. The cases were consolidated in the federal court for the Northern District of Illinois. The court held that the plaintiffs were bound by the arbitration clause in the licensing agreement, because it was a written agreement and was not unconscionable. For a discussion of the enforceability of licensing agreements generally, *see* Chapter 7.

The State of Texas brought suit against Living.com, an online furniture retailer that went out of business in August 2000, to enjoin the company from selling personal information it had obtained through its website. The case was settled. As part of the agreement, Living.com agreed to destroy any records of customer credit-card numbers, bank accounts, and Social Security numbers gathered through its website. Living.com may sell the names and email addresses of its customers, but only after the customers have been given the opportunity to opt out of the sale of their information. *See* Greg Sandoval, "Texas Officials, Living.com Reach Settlement on Privacy," CNET News.com, Sept. 20, 2000, *at* http://news.com.com/2100-1017-246198.html?legacy=cnet.

In re Toys R Us, Inc. Privacy Litigation, No. M-00-1381 MMC, 2001 U.S. Dist. LEXIS 16947 (N.D. Cal. Oct. 9, 2001).

In July 2000, a class-action suit was filed in California alleging that Toys 'R' Us violated California citizens' constitutional right of privacy, California's consumer-protection laws, and the common law of trespass by engaging a third-party marketing company to collect data from users of the toysrus.com and babiesrus.com websites without users' knowledge. According to the complaint, the third-party marketer used "web bugs," data tags, and cookies to track consumer habits. After widespread consumer backlash, Toysrus.com announced that it would no longer use the services of the third-party marketing company to collect data.

On January 2, 2003, Toysrus.com formally entered into a settlement agreement with the plaintiffs pursuant to which it agreed to improve its privacy practices and to pay the plaintiffs' attorneys fees up to $900,000. Toysrus.com agreed to provide clear links on its website to its privacy policy, to provide notice and obtain consent from its customers before disclosing their personal information, and to destroy any information that was previously obtained in violation of its stated privacy policy.

Toysrus.com also entered into a consent decree with the New Jersey Division of Consumer Affairs. On December 26, 2001, Toysrus agreed to pay a fine of $50,000, covering costs and the development of programs to inform the public about issues related to Internet privacy. Toysrus will also maintain improvements to its privacy policy and ensure that any third parties who received personally identifying information on New Jersey customers who used the Toysrus website will destroy or return the information. *See* Release From New Jersey Department of Law & Public Safety, Division of Consumer Affairs, *Toys R Us.com Enters Into Agreement With State*, Jan. 3, 2003.

Supnick v. Amazon.com, et al., No. C00-0221P (W.D. Wash. July 21, 2001) (settlement).

In February 2000, two complaints seeking class-action certification were filed in the U.S. District Court for the Western District of Washington against Amazon.com and Alexa Internet, charging that Alexa's software (which was distributed by Amazon) obtained information from users without disclosing the collection. The plaintiffs alleged that Alexa's program violated the ECPA, state deceptive-practices statutes, and the common law of trespass and invaded the privacy of users. Alexa settled the suit and agreed to make numerous changes to its data-collection practices, including requiring customers to opt in to having their data collected before they can download the company's software. The FTC stated that it will not take action against Alexa now that it has changed its stated privacy policy. The terms of the settlement can be found at http://www.alexa.com/settlement/.

In January 2001, e-Games, an online vendor of family oriented game software, settled a suit brought by the attorney general of Michigan. e-Games agreed to revise its software and to provide full disclosure of its data collection and use practices. The company also offered software online that removes the existing clear-gif collection software from installations of the games. *See* Catherine Par, "Attorney General Settles with eGame," NEWSFACTOR NETWORK (Jan. 12, 2001), *at* http://www.newsfactor.com/story.xhtml?story_id=6630.

Steelman, et al. v. Doubleclick, Inc., G.D. No. 03-12899 (Pa. Ct. Com. Pleas, filed July 10, 2003).

Plaintiffs brought a class action lawsuit against Doubleclick, Inc., alleging that Doubleclick's practice of disguising banner advertisements as standard Microsoft Windows systems alerts constituted a deceptive business practice, fraud, nuisance, trespass, and invasion of privacy under Pennsylvania law. The advertisements appear in the form of "message alerts," which, the complaint alleges, confuses users into believing that the messages are important alerts about the user's Windows operating system. In fact, clicking on the messages takes the user directly to the advertiser's website. The complaint claimed that the ads invade the privacy of users by wrongfully intruding upon the class members' solitude and seclusion. Plaintiffs seek injunctive relief, and compensatory and punitive damages. As of December 31, 2003, the suit remains pending.

Retailer Victoria's Secret agreed to settle claims brought by the New York attorney general alleging that the company had left security holes in its website that allowed visitors to see the contents of other customers' orders. New York had accused the company of violating state deceptive business practice laws, engaging in false advertising, and conducting fraudulent business activities. The information the company had left open did not include credit card numbers, but the attorney general claimed that some information, such as information on items purchased from a store selling lingerie and other similar products, can be as sensitive as financial data. Under the settlement, reached in October 2003, Victoria's Secret agreed to pay $50,000 to the state. Press Release, Office of New York State Attorney General, "Victoria's Secret Settles Privacy Case" (Oct. 21, 2003), *available at* http://www.oag.state.ny.us/press/2003/oct/oct21b_03.html.

Industry Self-Regulation

The FTC's Support for Self-Regulation

On July 27, 2000, the FTC announced its support of the self-regulation principles created by the Network Advertising Initiative (NAI). According to its website, NAI represents over 90 percent of companies that help provide online advertising based on consumer information gathered from the Internet, referred to by NAI as "Online Preference Marketing." The member companies include 24/7 Real Media, Atlas DMT, DoubleClick, and ValueClick, Inc..

As stated on the NAI website (http://www.networkadvertising.org), participants in the NAI program agree:

1. Not to use personally identifying information about sensitive medical or financial matters, information of a sexual nature, or Social Security numbers for purposes of targeting online ads.

2. To post a privacy policy that clearly and conspicuously discloses (a) the customer's use of the advertiser's services, (b) the type of information that may be collected by the advertiser, and (c) the customer's ability to opt out, including a link to an opt-out page.

3. Not to merge personally identifying information with previously collected information that is not personally identifying without the consumer's prior consent.

4. To provide robust notice and choice about the collection of personally identifying information that will be merged with information that is not personally identifying before such collection is undertaken on a going-forward basis.

Other Self-Regulation Efforts

- The Online Privacy Alliance, a coalition of industry groups, promulgated its Online Privacy Guidelines for members to follow when collecting personally identifying information from online consumers. Members must indicate what information is being collected, how it is used, and what security measures are installed. Members must also provide consumers with adequate choices regarding data collection. The Guidelines are available at http://www.privacyalliance.org/resources/ppguidelines.shtml.

- TRUSTe is a nonprofit privacy organization that websites can join if they commit to TRUSTe's announced privacy principles and agree to comply with TRUSTe's oversight and dispute-resolution processes. TRUSTe's core principles—notice, choice, access, and security—correspond to those of the FTC. In addition, TRUSTe has articulated three primary principles for collecting personal information. These principles are: (1) mandatory third-party oversight of customer information; (2) consumer opt-in on the sharing of personally identifying information; and (3) corporate pledges to honor privacy agreements even after bankruptcy filings.

    Members may display the TRUSTe logo or seal on their websites. Information about the TRUSTe program can be found at http://www.truste.org. TRUSTe also offers an EU Safe Harbor seal indicating a site's compliance with the safe-harbor agreement between the United States and the European Union effective November 1, 2000. *See* pages 195–196, below, for a discussion of the EU Directive.

    On October 25, 2000, TRUSTe filed a trademark infringement claim against American-Politics.com in the U.S. District Court for the District of Columbia. The suit claimed that American-Politics.com displayed the TRUSTe "seal of approval" without actually having received approval, and sought at least $1 million in damages. On March 31, 2001, the court dismissed the case on procedural grounds, and as of December 31, 2003 it had not been re-filed.

- BBBOnline, operated by the Better Business Bureau, offers a privacy program that awards seals to websites that meet BBB's guidelines. Its core principles also mirror those endorsed by the FTC: notice, choice, access, and security. Information on BBBOnline can be found at http://www.bbbonline.com.

- The McGraw-Hill Companies introduced a Customer Privacy Policy that the FTC hailed as an industry model. That policy conforms to the FTC's core principles of privacy protection. The McGraw-Hill privacy policy can be found at http://www.mcgraw-hill.com.

- Health on the Net (HON) is an international nonprofit organization focused on the use of the Internet for health and medicine. HON has issued a code of conduct to help provide some consistency in the quality of medical and health information available on the Internet and offers a seal to demonstrate that a member website follows the HON code principles. The code of conduct includes a confidentiality principle pledging that confidentiality of personal data is respected, and that the website operators will follow or exceed applicable privacy laws, and also extends to matters beyond privacy.

- In the fall of 2002, it was reported that some Internet merchants had been testing a new feature designed to enhance privacy options for Internet customers wary of providing credit-card numbers or other sensitive financial information over the Internet. I4 Commerce has developed a "bill me later" option, which works much like a credit card online in that a user enters information when making a purchase, but instead of the charge number, the user provides a date of birth, or some part of a Social Security number. I4 Commerce will then pay the merchant directly, and send a bill to the customer. Consumers will receive bills monthly, which, like credit card bills, are subject to finance charges if not paid on time. *See* Troy Wolverton, "Web Shoppers' New Option: Bill Me Later," CNET News.com (Oct. 1, 2002), *available at* http://news.com.com/2100-1017-960380.html?tag=lh.

Self-Protection

- The Anonymizer (http://www.anonymizer.com) allows individuals to surf the web anonymously.

- Cookie Central (http://www.cookiecentral.com) teaches individuals how to delete cookies from their computers. It also provides a comprehensive FAQ on cookies.

- Users can visit http://www.privacy.net/Analyze/ to obtain a free privacy analysis. The site automatically reports information they disclose to the sites they visit. This includes the user's IP address, the user's computer name, any cookies placed by the site on the user's system, the site from which the user linked, the user's operating system and browser type, the user's e-mail address, and the owner of the user's network.

- The World Wide Web Consortium has created the "platform for privacy preferences" or "P3P," an automated mechanism that allows users to specify how much personal information they will allow their computers to transmit to websites they visit. If the operator of a website expresses its privacy policy in a language that can be read by a P3P-enabled browser, the browser can compare the privacy preferences set by users with a "snapshot" of the website's privacy policy to see if the website meets the user's privacy requirements. Microsoft's Internet Explorer 6 browser implemented the P3P standard. Its introduction sparked a debate as to the feasibility of P3P technology. A machine-readable privacy policy cannot convey the nuances that often characterize website privacy policies. This raises concerns about unfair trade practices liability for misleading P3P programming, and loss of website traffic due to a poorly translated privacy policy. For more information on P3P visit the World Wide Web Consortium's P3P website at http://www.w3.org/P3P/.

- Microsoft has created "cookie alert" software that enables users to detect whether cookies have been placed on their computers and to indicate whether they wish to accept or reject them.

- Some private companies also play a role in monitoring the Internet for security breaches that could result in disclosure of private information. In December 2003 security analysts at Symantec discovered that a sensitive database run by LocatePlus.com had been left open to public Internet access. The database, which is frequently used by law enforcement, credit agencies and private investigators, contained millions of names, social security numbers, phone records and other personal information. Symantec discovered the breach and reported it to the FBI, which in turn informed LocatePlus. As a result, the vulnerability lasted only a few hours. *See* Robert Lemos, "Slip-up Exposes Database to Prying Eyes," CNET News.com (Dec. 9, 2003), *at* http://news.com.com/2100-1029-5118138.htm.

- Users can simply opt not to disclose personal information when requested.

USA PATRIOT Act

On October 26, 2001, President Bush signed the USA PATRIOT Act into law. The Act (Uniting and Strengthening America by Providing Appropriate Tools Required to Intercept and Obstruct Terrorism) provides law enforcement with a variety of new tools and procedures to allow the monitoring of information that is transmitted by communications service providers. These changes mostly affect the way that law-enforcement officials interact with the judiciary and the way that telecommunications carriers and ISPs assist with investigations by providing information. Service providers can most likely expect that, because the government now has easier access to warrants and other authority to intercept communications of all kinds, new demands may be placed on their systems and their information processing and retrieval capabilities with respect to customer information. Generally, the Act:

- Details a variety of new procedures available to law-enforcement authorities to allow better monitoring of international terrorist activities;

- Expands the definition of terrorist activities, expands government access to surveillance techniques, and amends banking procedures to better track financial resources that may support terrorist activities; and

- Amends several existing laws concerning government surveillance and privacy and, to a certain extent, seeks to harmonize disparate obligations among different types of communications service providers.

The Act is of particular interest to Internet companies, Internet service providers, and telecommunications carriers, which have expanded obligations and immunities under the Act.

- The definition of a "trap and trace device" for purposes of the trap-and-trace statute (which governs the collection of noncontent traffic information associated with communications, such as the phone numbers dialed from a particular telephone) has been significantly expanded to allow for access to routing and address information in any electronic communication, including Internet communications and email.

- There is an obligation to respond to nationwide service of process so that a single court having jurisdiction over an offense can issue a nationwide search warrant for stored data, such as email.

- Nothing in the Act creates any new requirements for technical assistance, such as design mandates.

- In several important areas, the Act expands service-provider protections (include-ing immunities and good-faith defenses) for complying with new or existing surveillance authority.

- The Act expands the government's authority to conduct, at the request of service providers, wiretaps of hackers and other "trespassers" on service-provider networks.

- The Act amends and limits the Cable Act to make it clear that companies offering cable-based Internet or telephone service will be subject to the provisions of the Cable Act requiring notice to subscribers of government-surveillance requests only where detailed cable-viewing information is being sought; in all other instances, cable operators offering these services can respond to a government-surveillance request under ECPA, which does not require service providers to notify subscribers of requests for information.

Legislation was recently introduced in the Senate which would amend the USA PATRIOT Act to limit some of its applications. The Protecting the Rights of Individuals Act (S. 1552), introduced July 31, 2003, by Sen. Lisa Murkowski (R-Ala.), would impose limitations on law enforcement agencies in conducting electronic surveillance. Among other things, the amendments would require a law enforcement agency seeking to review a person's medical, library or Internet records to have probable cause to believe that such person is a foreign power or an agent of a foreign power.

In addition to privacy protections sacrificed by the USA PATRIOT Act, the U.S. Department of State announced that it would open its visa database to law enforcement officials across the country. This will allow law enforcement officials to access a visa applicant's photograph, home address, date of birth, passport number, and names of relatives to further its goal of preventing future terrorist acts. Expanded access to the visa database is a central feature of a new inter-agency computer system that will also allow the Department of State, the CIA, the FBI, and other agencies to share information via encrypted email. *See* Jennifer Lee, "State Department Link Will Open Visa Database to Police Officers," N.Y. TIMES (Jan. 31, 2003), at A12.

Opposition to the USA PATRIOT Act

The USA PATRIOT Act has been criticized by advocates of civil liberties. For example, in addition to the more than 25 lawsuits for civil liberties violations it has initiated since the September 11, 2001 attacks, the ACLU initiated a national campaign to challenge the government's anti-terror policies and the USA PATRIOT Act's provisions that expand government's authority to monitor citizens' activities. On July 30, 2003, the ACLU filed the first law suit challenging the constitutionality of Section 215 of the USA PATRIOT Act. The complaint, brought by the ACLU on behalf of six Arab-American and Islamic community groups, alleges that § 215 violates the First, Fourth and Fifth Amendments to the Constitution because it allows the FBI to require that particular entities, including Internet service providers, turn over individuals' belongings as part of intelligence or terrorism investigations with no notification to the targeted person or group. *See Muslim Community Association of Ann Arbor, et al. v. Ashcroft*, Civ. A. No.

03-72913 (E.D. Mich. filed July 30, 2003), *available at* http://news.findlaw.com/cnn/ docs/aclu/mcaa2ash73003cmp.pdf.

On August 21, 2002, the ACLU filed Freedom of Information Act requests with the Department of Justice for information concerning the government's increased surveillance activities since the September 11 attacks. In its request, the ACLU sought aggregate statistics and policy directives from the FBI and the DOJ in their implementation of the USA PATRIOT Act. *See* Ryan Singel, "Privacy Groups Turn Screws on DOJ" (Nov. 15, 2002), *available at* http://www.wired.com/news/politics/ 0,1283,56423,00.html. In response, the DOJ released certain documents to the ACLU and agreed to prepare a list of documents it would not disclose for national security reasons. *See* "U.S. to Release Documents to ACLU" (Nov. 26, 2002), *at* http://www.wired.com/ news/business/0,1367,56601,00.html.

Opposition to the USA PATRIOT Act has also occurred at the local level. The city of Oakland, California, enacted a resolution that prohibits municipal employees from cooperating with federal officials investigating its residents. In addition, some librarians in Oakland are reportedly attempting to avoid the effects of the USA PATRIOT Act by purging borrowing records and Internet caches so that federal officials cannot access them as part of their investigations. Some Oakland libraries have also posted signs that advise library users to adjust their actions accordingly because of the potential for increased federal surveillance. For example, one sign that is reportedly posted in an Oakland library states, "We're sorry! Due to national security concerns, we are unable to tell you if your Internet surfing habits, passwords and email content are being monitored by federal agents; please act appropriately." *See* Julia Scheeres, "Cities Say No to Federal Snooping" (Dec. 19, 2002), *at* http://www.wired.com/news/politics/ 0,1283,56922,00.html.

Homeland Security Act of 2002

President Bush signed the Homeland Security Act of 2002 into law in 2002 (6 U.S.C. §§ 101, *et seq.*). The Act establishes new mechanisms for law enforcement officials to prevent future terrorist activities. Among other things, the Act makes it easier for law enforcement officials to track and identify suspected individuals by shielding Internet service providers from liability when they share private subscriber information with law enforcement officials. ISPs had been reluctant to release such private information for fear that their subscribers would bring claims against them. The Homeland Security Act also encourages companies to share information with the government about their electronic security vulnerabilities by providing that such information is exempt from release to the public under the Freedom of Information Act.

International Response to Privacy Concerns

The EU Directive

The European Union's Directive on Data Protection (95/46/EC) became effective on October 24, 1998. The Directive requires member states to adopt national legislation meeting specified requirements for the collection and use of personal information.

The Directive requires, subject to limited exceptions, that personal data be processed only if the data subject has unambiguously given his or her consent. Article 25 of the

Directive prohibits the transfer of personally identifying data to countries that do not provide an "adequate" level of privacy protection.

Safe Harbor

Because of the Directive's potential to lead to disputes that could seriously hamper U.S.-EU trade, the two sides have worked for years to devise a way for U.S. companies to comply with the EU Directive without unnecessarily harming online commerce. The United States and European Union reached agreement on May 31, 2000 (the "Safe Harbor Agreement"), with the EU member states unanimously approving the U.S. "safe-harbor" proposal. The European Commission approved the Safe Harbor Agreement on July 26, 2000. The agreement took effect on November 1, 2000. The agreement is a compromise between the two culturally divergent approaches to privacy, and is an attempt to accommodate both the U.S. self-regulatory framework and the EU's strict standards. As of December 31, 2003, more than 450 companies had taken advantage of the safe harbor by registering with the Department of Commerce. A list of registered companies is available at www.export.gov/safeharbor.

The decision to enter into the safe harbor is voluntary; companies may qualify for the safe harbor in different ways. For example, a company can join a self-regulatory privacy program that adheres to the safe-harbor principles, or it can develop its own self-regulatory privacy policies that conform to the principles. U.S. companies adhering to the agreement's principles will be viewed as providing adequate privacy protection, and would gain "safe harbor" from prosecution or lawsuits by EU governments. While European citizens do not lose their rights to sue U.S. companies directly, they are encouraged to follow a process whereby they first raise any complaints with the potential defendant and go through dispute resolution before proceeding with any suit.

To take advantage of the safe harbor, companies self-certify by providing an annual letter to the Department of Commerce or its designee, signed by a corporate officer, containing the information required by the Safe Harbor Agreement. The Department of Commerce or its designee maintains a list of all organizations that file such letters. Both the list and the self-certification letters submitted by the organizations are publicly available. All companies that self-certify for the safe harbor must also state in their relevant published privacy policy statements that they adhere to the safe-harbor principles. Companies do not need to subject all personal information that they retain to the safe-harbor principles; rather, they need to make sure that personal information received from the EU after they have joined the safe harbor is handled according to the principles. The Safe Harbor Agreement does not cover the financial services sector.

The Safe Harbor Agreement sets forth the following safe-harbor principles:

1. *Notice*. A company must notify consumers of the reasons for which it collects and uses personal information; how to contact the company with inquiries; the types of third parties with which it shares personal information; and the options consumers have to limit the use and disclosure of personal information. The notice must be clear and conspicuous and must be made when consumers are asked to provide information, or reasonably soon afterwards. Notice must be given before the company uses the information for something other than the original purpose for which it was collected, or before the company discloses the information to a third party for the first time.

2. *Choice*. For most information, a company must allow consumers to choose to opt out of the use and disclosure of personal information. In most cases where sensitive personal information (defined to include information about medical conditions, race, and political opinions) is involved, consumers must opt in to disclosures to third parties or uses other than those for which the information was originally collected.

3. *Onward Transfer*. A company may disclose personal information to a third party only if it determines that the third party adheres to the safe-harbor principles.

4. *Security*. A company must take reasonable precautions to protect collected personal information.

5. *Data Integrity*. A company must not use personal information for purposes inconsistent with the original purpose for which the information was collected absent authorization from the consumer from whom the information was collected.

6. *Access*. Consumers must have reasonable access to personal information that has been collected about them so they can review and correct the information.

7. *Enforcement*. A company must agree to submit to enforcement mechanisms to address consumer complaints and investigate company practices, and must obligate itself to correct failures to adhere to safe-harbor principles. An enforcement mechanism will be deemed acceptable only if it includes "sufficiently rigorous" sanctions for failure to comply.

The Safe Harbor Agreement also contains a series of frequently asked questions that provide greater detail about the obligations of companies that choose to participate in the safe harbors. All documents can be accessed through http://www.ita.doc.gov/td/ecom/menu.html.

The safe-harbor guidelines can be found in the *Federal Register* at 65 Fed. Reg. 45,666 (July 24, 2000).

Sanctions

Sanctions for noncompliance with the Safe Harbor Agreement range in severity from publicity for findings of noncompliance to a requirement to delete data; from suspension and removal of a seal to compensation to individuals for losses incurred as a result of noncompliance. Injunctive orders are also available. noncompliance with the safe-harbor principles could also be subject to action under § 5 of the Federal Trade Commission Act prohibiting unfair and deceptive acts. Article 2 of the agreement provides that member state authorities may exercise their powers to suspend data flows to an organization if they have determined that there is a "substantial likelihood" that the safe-harbor principles are being violated; that there is a reason to believe that the enforcement mechanism in place is not taking or will not take adequate and timely steps to settle the case; that the continuing transfer would create an "imminent risk of grave harm to data subjects"; or that the competent authorities in the member state have made reasonable efforts to provide the organization with a notice and opportunity to respond. The suspension of data flows would cease as soon as compliance with the principles is assured and the proper EU authorities are notified.

Other International Privacy Laws

Canada

Canada has taken a comprehensive approach to online privacy similar to that of the EU, passing the Personal Information Protection and Electronic Documents Act (PIPEDA), which took effect January 1, 2004. The law requires organizations to obtain an individual's consent before collecting, using or disclosing his or her personal information, and such personal information may only be used for the purpose for which it was collected. The law also requires that businesses appoint the equivalent of an internal privacy compliance officer. The law does not specify the type of consent that must be obtained—i.e., opt-in or opt-out—but leaves to the organization soliciting the information the discretion to decide on a mechanism, based on the "sensitivity of the information" and the "reasonable expectations of the individual." The law also requires that companies that have collected personal information prior to the law's enactment notify the individuals from whom the information was collected about the new law and their privacy policies. A copy of the law is available at http://www.parl.gc.ca/36/2/parlbus/chambus/house/bills/government/C-6/C-6_4/C-6TOCE.html.

On December 30, 2003, two days before the PIPEDA was to take effect, the attorney general of Quebec was given clearance to file a lawsuit challenging the validity of the statute under the Canadian Constitution. The suit would take the position that the law "interferes with Quebec's constitutional competence in matters of civil rights" and that the government exceeded its jurisdiction by enacting the statute. *See* Tyler Hamilton, "Privacy Law Faces Legal Challenge," TORONTO STAR (Dec. 30, 2003).

Japan

On May 23, 2003, Japan enacted the Personal Information Protection Law, which applies to the national government, independent public corporations, municipal governments, and other related bodies. Effective 2005, it will also apply to private companies that use personal information. Under the law, entities that collect and use personal information must notify the owner of the information, refrain from providing such information to third parties without owner consent, correct errors promptly and provide the owner of information, upon request, with the name of the collecting entity, and purposes for using the information to the owner upon request. Personal Information Protection Law, Law No. 57 of Heisei 15 nen.

South Africa

In December 2002, South Africa passed the Regulation of Interception of Communications Act, which subjects private companies to fines for monitoring employees' email, mail, and telephone calls without the employees' consent. Individuals who violate the Act may also be subject to jail sentences. *See* Penny Sukhraj, "New Law Stops Bosses Spying on E-Mail," SUNDAY TIMES (Johannesburg) (Feb. 2, 2003), *available at* http://allafrica.com/stories/printable/200302010167.html.

China

In contrast to the European Union and South Africa, which passed legislation to protect further the privacy of its citizens, a Chinese province instituted a requirement that Internet café users buy access cards so that police can monitor their Internet activities. This allows authorities to block certain sites, track users' attempts to access barred websites, and filter email for forbidden content. "Chinese Net Café Users Must Get ID Cards," SAN JOSE MERCURY NEWS (Nov. 5, 2002), at 2C.

Ireland

In Ireland, the Department of Justice drafted a bill in November 2002 that would allow the government to retain detailed personal data from telephone calls, faxes, email, and Internet usage for up to four years. Previously, such data could only be stored for shorter periods—three to six months—before being destroyed. Civil liberties groups have criticized this new bill as an invitation to government abuse. As of December 31, 2003, the bill remains pending. *See* "Department to Store Data on Citizens for Four Years" (Nov. 28, 2002), *available at* http://www.ireland.com/newspaper/front/2002/1128/pf901350883HM1TECH.html; Karlin Lillington, "Don't Believe State on Data Retention," NEW IRISH TIMES (Mar. 14, 2003).

Chapter 6: Data Collection and Privacy
Summary of the Law

- The only federal law that requires a website to post a privacy policy statement is the Children's Online Privacy Protection Act (COPPA). COPPA prohibits collection of personally identifying information from anyone under 13 without prior, verifiable parental consent. And it requires any website that is targeted at children under 13, or that knowingly collects information from children under 13, to post a privacy policy statement that clearly identifies all data that the site collects, and clearly discloses how the site uses that data and with whom the site shares the data.

- No other federal law requires a website to post a privacy policy statement.

- A California law, effective July 1, 2004, requires every website that collects personally identifying information about California residents to post a privacy policy statement and to adhere to the articulated policy.

- If a website chooses to post a privacy policy, it must adhere to that policy. The Federal Trade Commission (FTC) considers a website's failure to adhere to its own articulated privacy policy to be punishable under the FTC's broad mandate to police "unfair and deceptive acts and practices." Consumers that have provided information pursuant to a website's posted privacy policy may also be able to sue the website for breach of contract if it violates its articulated policy.

- The FTC recommends that anyone maintaining a commercial website follow its five core privacy protection principles: (1) provide *notice* to consumers about how the website uses personal information; (2) offer *choice* as to how such information is used; (3) give consumers *access* to the information that is compiled on them; (4) ensure that the information is *secure*; and (5) provide a mechanism by which users can *enforce* these core principles.

- Medical information is protected from disclosure under the Health Insurance Portability Accountability Act (HIPAA). The law establishes patient rights with respect to personal health-related information, including the right to access the information, the right to be told how the information may be shared, and the right to request correction of erroneous information.

- The Gramm Leach Bliley Act (GLB) regulates the privacy practices of "financial institutions." GLB requires that financial institutions provide notice to consumers of their policies regarding the collection and use of personal information, and that they allow consumers to opt out of the disclosure of personal information.

- The Electronic Communications Privacy Act (ECPA) and the Computer Fraud and Abuse Act (CFAA) have both been invoked to protect privacy online. The ECPA prohibits the unauthorized "interception" of electronic communications. Courts have found that, to be actionable, conduct must involve the interception of an electronic communication during its transmission; accessing stored communication does not violate the ECPA. The CFAA prohibits unauthorized access to certain computers with the intent to cause damage. A suit can be maintained under the CFAA only if the party injured has suffered monetary damages of at least $5,000.

- Some online privacy protections have been displaced by the USA PATRIOT Act. The Act provides law enforcement agencies with the ability to monitor some information that is transmitted by communications service providers, thereby reducing the level of anonymity that once existed for online communications. One section of the statute has recently been challenged on constitutional grounds. The suit alleges that the statute permits law enforcement agencies to require ISPs to turn over customers' personal information without first providing notice to those customers, in violation of the First, Fourth and Fifth Amendments to the Constitution.

- Many nations have enacted legislation that deals directly with the issue of online privacy. The European Union adopted a Directive in 1998 that, among other things, requires websites that collect personal information from their customers to obtain unambiguous consent from such customers. The Directive provides a safe harbor for U.S. companies doing business abroad to allow them to comply in some respects with the Directive in order to insulate themselves from lawsuits for failure to comply with its requirements. More recently, Canada adopted an online privacy statute that requires businesses collecting personal information to obtain consent of customers, and also to name a privacy compliance officer to ensure compliance with the statute.

ELECTRONIC CONTRACTS

Electronic Contract Basics

The term "electronic contracts" refers to agreements that are similar to traditional contracts, except that they are made online or using electronic media rather than on paper. An electronic contract involves the formation of an agreement between two or more people, just like a traditional contract, written on paper and signed in ink. Not surprisingly, courts have applied familiar principles of traditional contract law when deciding disputes involving electronic contracts.

Website Disclaimers and User Agreements. Web publishers often seek to reduce exposure to liability and to protect the integrity and proprietary value of their content by posting "visitor agreements" on their websites. Such agreements contain various disclaimers of liability and notices concerning rights to content, restrictions on site use, and the like. Similarly, computer manufacturers and software publishers often include license agreements that are either printed on or included within a product's packaging materials. Case law indicates that these disclaimers and user agreements, which are often referred to as "click-wrap," or "browse-wrap" agreements, may constitute enforceable contracts.

Electronic Signatures (E-Signatures). An electronic signature has the same function as a traditional signature: to affirm the signer's intent to abide by the terms of the contract to which he or she affixes the signature. In the case of e-signatures, this affirmation takes place digitally instead of by the use of ink on paper. The federal government has passed legislation mandating that electronic signatures be given the same validity as ink signatures. 15 U.S.C. § 7001. All state-level governments in the United States have passed legislation to the same effect.

Visitor Agreements

Web publishers often use visitor agreements (also referred to as "user agreements," "terms of use," "terms of service," and the like) to establish the ground rules for access to their websites and use of the contents provided within. Users who violate the visitor agreement may be denied access to the site in the future. They may also be liable for breach of contract. Visitor agreements also often include language intended to limit the publisher's liability and reduce the publisher's exposure to lawsuits.

Intellectual Property Statements

Use of Publisher's Content

Visitor agreements typically notify users that the publisher and those who license content to the publisher hold copyright in the content that appears on the site. The publisher often includes language alerting users that, though they are free to use material on the website for personal, noncommercial purposes, they may not reproduce or distribute content found on the website without permission from the copyright holder. Such a provision puts users on notice of the terms on which they are being granted access to the content on the site. The visitor agreement may also advise users how they can contact the site if they want permission to publish content appearing on the site.

Publisher's Use of User-Supplied Content

If a site features bulletin boards or other forums in which users can post messages or other content, the visitor agreement may include a grant of rights from users to the publisher, allowing the publisher to use, reproduce, transmit, store, and display any user-supplied content for any purpose. Such a grant of rights is designed to protect the web publisher against any claim by a user that the publisher's use of the material exceeded the rights granted by the user, and it protects the publisher's right to archive the material or republish it in a different format. Visitor agreements often state that by posting material to the site, the user is representing that it either owns copyright in the material or has a license that allows it to post the material.

Restrictions on Framing and Linking

Publishers often include in their visitor agreements an explicit prohibition against framing their sites. Such a provision may give the publisher a breach of contract claim against a website that frames the publisher's site in violation of the visitor agreement. Some web publishers also include language in their visitor agreements addressing linking to their sites. These clauses typically state that linking to the site is permitted, but only in a manner that is not likely to cause confusion or imply an affiliation or endorsement of the site by the site that links to it. However, there are some sites that object to linking without permission or that try to prohibit linking to interior pages (as opposed to the home page) of the site.

Disclaimers

Responsibility Statements

Websites often advise users that the site and all material that may be found on the site are provided "as is," that the publisher does not guarantee that site or any service provided on the site will function as intended or will always be available to users. Websites often link to other websites. Sites sometimes include explicit disclaimers making clear that the website is not responsible for the content of the sites to which it links.

Liability Statements

Websites often disclaim liability for any injury resulting from actions taken in reliance on site content or from use of any feature of the site. Such disclaimers are particularly common on sites that include medical information, legal information, product reviews, or consumer recommendations. Sites often disclaim categories of damages, such as consequential damages or punitive damages, and may limit the publisher's total liability to users to some modest amount. The visitor agreement may also disclaim liability for any harm to the user's computer that may result from any virus or other harmful code to which the user may be exposed while visiting the site.

Terms Relating to User-Supplied Content

User-Supplied Content: Controversial Content

Web publishers often note that chat rooms, bulletin boards, and similar areas within their sites contain user-supplied content that may not be regularly monitored, and could be considered controversial or offensive. Visitor agreements typically contain a disclaimer of responsibility for such content.

User-Supplied Content: User Responsibility

Visitor agreements often warn users not to post material that is defamatory, infringing, obscene, or otherwise unlawful. The visitor agreement may also prohibit harassment of other users and other actions that interfere with enjoyment of the site by other users. The visitor agreement may stipulate that if the user posts unlawful content or otherwise violates the visitor agreement, the user's access to the site may be terminated.

Indemnification

Some sites provide that by accessing the site users agree to indemnify the operator of the site against claims resulting from user-supplied content or from the user's conduct while on the site.

Other Common Provisions

Reservation of Rights

Visitor agreements often include reservation of rights language, allowing the publisher to remove any material posted by a user, to deny the user access to the site, or to discontinue any service provided on the site for any reason. Prompt removal of material that becomes the subject of a complaint may help the publisher avoid liability for copyright infringement or libel.

Prohibitions against Data Scraping and Harvesting of Email Addresses

Increasingly, visitor agreements prohibit the use of automated "bots" to collect data, such as classified listings, from the publisher's website. Many sites now also explicitly prohibit visitors from harvesting email addresses (such as the email addresses of other users that may appear in connection with bulletin board postings) for purposes of sending spam to those addresses.

Dispute Resolution

Websites often seek, in various ways, to reduce the cost of resolving disputes with users. For example, a visitor agreement may stipulate that any disputes between users and the publisher will be resolved by arbitration or some other alternative mechanism for dispute resolution. Or the agreement may specify that by accessing the website the user is agreeing to resolve any suit under the law of the publisher's home state and in the state and federal courts located in that state.

Privacy Policy

The visitor agreement may include a link the website's privacy policy statement, and admonition that the user read the statement, and an assertion that by accessing the website, the user is agreeing that any privacy-related dispute the user may have with the website will be resolved according to the dispute resolution mechanism specified in the visitor agreement.

DMCA Notice

To take advantage of protections that may be available to website operators under the Digital Millennium Copyright Act, many websites include information on how a copyright holder that believes its intellectual property has been improperly posted on the site can bring the problem to the site's attention.

Enforceability of Electronic Contracts

A contract is formed when two or more parties, with notice of the terms of the contract, manifest their assent to those terms. Case law suggests that a reasonable contract of which a website user had notice may be enforceable even if the user never "signs" the agreement.

"Effective Notice": Was User Aware of Contract?

Whether an electronic contract is enforceable will likely depend in large part on whether the agreement is effectively brought to the attention of the user. Courts generally seek to determine if the user had effective notice of the terms of the contract before any analysis of the validity of the terms themselves takes place. For publishers, three methods of bringing visitor agreements to the attention of users are most common:

1. Requiring users who wish to enter a website or an area of a website to click on a button to manifest assent to the agreement.

2. Including a link to the visitor agreement in a reasonably noticeable location, such as a footer at the bottom of the home page, or, perhaps, each page of the site, often in proximity to copyright notices. The text accompanying the link may advise users that by using the website, they agree to be bound by the terms of the visitor agreement.

3. Posting a less obtrusive link to the visitor agreement, often in an area of the website that includes other information about the site. This alternative, however, may be more likely to subject the agreement to challenge by users claiming insufficient notice of its terms.

General Enforceability of Electronic Contract Upheld

ProCD, Inc. v. Zeidenberg, 86 F.3d 1447 (7th Cir. 1996).

A "shrinkwrap" license was enforced against the purchaser of a CD-ROM product who uploaded data from the CD-ROM to a website in violation of the license. A shrinkwrap license is an unsigned license agreement included in the packaging of a product that states that the user accepts the terms of the license if he or she opens the packaging and proceeds to use or install the product. Although the terms of the license agreement were not printed on the outside of the package, the agreement permitted a buyer who was dissatisfied with terms of the agreement found inside to return the product for a full refund. By using the software, rather than returning it after reviewing the license agreement, the defendant manifested his consent to the terms of the license: "ProCD proposed a contract that a buyer would accept by using the software after having an opportunity to read the license at leisure. This Zeidenberg did. He had no choice, because the software splashed the license on the screen and would not let him proceed without indicating acceptance." 86 F.3d at 1452.

See also Moore v. Microsoft Corp., No. 2001-05569 (N.Y. Super. Ct. Apr. 15, 2002) (holding a clickwrap agreement valid, noting that users were subjected to "prominent[ ] display" of contract terms and had to click on an "I Agree" button before downloading the software); *Hill v. Gateway 2000, Inc.*, 105 F.3d 1147 (7th Cir. 1997), *cert. denied*, 118 S. Ct. 47 (1997) (enforcing an arbitration clause included in the "Terms & Conditions" shipped with a computer); *Brower v. Gateway 2000, Inc.*, 676 N.Y.S.2d 569

(N.Y. App. Div. 1998); *M.A. Mortensen Co. v. Timberline Software Corp., Inc.*, 998 P.2d 305 (Wash. 2000) (holding that a license agreement, which was printed on the outside of sealed envelopes containing the diskettes of the defendant's software and the inside cover of the user manual for that software, and referred to on the introductory screen to the software, was enforceable despite the fact that its terms were not mentioned during negotiations).

Hotmail Corp. v. Van$ Money Pie, Inc., 47 U.S.P.Q.2d 1020 (N.D. Cal. 1998).

A federal trial court granted a preliminary injunction, finding, among other things, a likelihood that Hotmail would prevail on its breach of contract claim. The defendant had signed up for several accounts with Hotmail Corp., whose terms of service prohibited using the accounts to send spam and/or pornography. Although the court did not analyze the formation of the contract in any detail, the court noted that Hotmail had complied with all applicable conditions of the contract. The defendant, however, had breached the terms of service by facilitating the sending of spam and/or pornography.

Pollstar v. Gigmania Ltd., 170 F. Supp. 2d 974 (E.D. Cal. 2000).

The court held that a "browse-wrap" license agreement may be enforceable. The plaintiff's website provided time-sensitive concert information. The plaintiff placed a link to a license agreement on its home page, but the site could be accessed without the user specifically clicking, otherwise indicating acceptance of, or even viewing the actual text of the license agreement. The agreement limited use of the concert information to noncommercial purposes. The defendant used the information to create its own commercial concert-information site. The court allowed the plaintiff to proceed with its claims for misappropriation, unfair competition, and breach of contract, holding that browse-wrap licenses are not invalid as a matter of law.

i.LAN Sys., Inc. v. NetScoutServ.Level Corp., 183 F. Supp. 2d 328 (D. Mass. 2002).

The United States District Court for the District of Massachusetts found a clickwrap license agreement enforceable under Article 2 of the Uniform Commercial Code. The plaintiff, i.LAN, helped companies monitor their computer networks. The defendant, NetScout (formerly NextPoint Networks), sold sophisticated software that monitors networks. In 1998, the parties signed a Value Added Reseller agreement under which i.LAN agreed to resell NextPoint's software to customers. The dispute involved the interpretation of that agreement, the purchase order associated with the transaction, and the clickwrap agreement to which i.LAN agreed upon receipt of the NetScout software. The court relied on the fact that i.LAN specifically agreed to a limitation of liability provision when it clicked on the "I Agree" button to install the software. The court determined the clickwrap contract was a "counteroffer," which i.LAN expressly accepted by clicking on the "I Agree" button. The court acknowledged that "Article 2 technically does not, and certainly will not, in the future, govern software licenses [alluding to the Uniform Computer Information Transactions Act ('UCITA'), which specifically addresses software licenses], but for the time being, the Court will assume it does." 183 F. Supp. 2d at 332. (For discussion of UCITA generally, *see* Chapter 10, pages 306 to 308.)

Mathias v. America Online, Inc., 2002 WL 377159 (Ohio App. Ct., Feb. 28, 2002), appeal denied, 775 N.E.2d 859 (Ohio 2002).

The Ohio Court of Appeals affirmed summary judgment in favor of America Online, ruling that AOL did not breach its agreement with plaintiff users when users experienced access and connection problems. When it first began offering users unlimited Internet access for a flat monthly rate, AOL posted several notices advising subscribers to read AOL's "Terms of Service" and "Rules of the Road" if they were interested in the new service. The plaintiffs all admitted to clicking on the terms, which included a notice of possible access problems and how to unsubscribe from the unlimited access rate. The plaintiffs subscribed to the new flat-rate service. The court found that by clicking on AOL's terms, and subsequently not canceling their service, the plaintiffs were deemed to have acknowledged that the services would be provided on an as-available basis and that traffic congestion might occur.

 Mudd-Lyman Sales v. United Parcel Service, Inc., 236 F. Supp. 2d 907 (N.D. Ill. 2002).

The U.S. District Court for the Northern District of Illinois ruled that a limitation of liability contained in a clickwrap license that accompanied shipping software distributed by UPS to its customers was enforceable against the customers. To open the package in which the software was distributed, a customer had to break a seal that included the statement "By breaking this seal, you indicate your agreement to the terms and conditions of the software license. . . ." To install the software, the user also had to click on "Yes" when the same license agreement appeared on his computer screen. The court found that these two actions, breaking the seal and clicking "Yes," constituted agreement to the limitation of liability in the license agreement, and held that the customer was bound by its terms.

 DeJohn v. .TV Corp., et al., 245 F. Supp. 2d 913 (C.D. Ill. 2003).

Plaintiff DeJohn attempted to register several domain names in the .tv domain administered by .TV Corporation. Register.com, a domain name registrar, incorrectly listed on its website the registration fee for each domain name as $50. DeJohn submitted registration applications through the Register.com website and tendered payment of $50 per registration based on the fee listed on the website. Register.com sent DeJohn emails confirming registration of the requested domain names. But .TV Corporation rejected the applications because the registration fees for the names sought by DeJohn were actually considerably higher than the fees listed on the Register.com website. DeJohn sued both Register.com and .TV Corporation. He argued that the confirming email he got from Register.com created an implied contract between him, as buyer, and Register.com, as seller, and that this implied contract imposed on Register.com a duty of good faith and fair dealing. The court rejected this argument and concluded that DeJohn was bound by the terms of a clickwrap agreement to which he had assented as part of the application process. The clickwrap agreement stated that the contract could only be modified in a written document signed by both parties; the alleged implied contract could not override the terms of the clickwrap agreement. The court also rejected DeJohn's argument that the clickwrap agreement was an unfair "contract of adhesion." Even though the terms of the contract were dictated solely by Register.com, "DeJohn expressly indicated that he read, understood, and agreed to those terms when he clicked the box on Register.com's website." DeJohn was bound by the terms of the clickwrap agreement and .TV Corporation was free to reject his application because the Register.com clickwrap agreement expressly reserved the right to refuse to process an application in the event of an error, including an error based on price.

State ex rel. Stovall v. DVM Enterprises, et al., 62 P.3d 653 (Kan. 2003).

The Kansas attorney general filed suit against defendants alleging that they had violated the state's Consumer Protection Act by engaging in unconscionable and deceptive practices when they sold prescription drugs over the Internet. Purchasers were required to consent to an online waiver of liability before defendant would process their orders. The Supreme Court of Kansas affirmed the trial court's decision that defendants did not violate Kansas' Consumer Protection Act because selling controlled substances over the Internet was not unconscionable, and defendants did not "deceive, oppress or misuse superior bargaining power" in providing medication over the Internet. The court concluded that defendants' clickwrap waiver did not attempt to disclaim or waive any warranty of merchantability or warranty of fitness for a particular purpose; such waivers would have been void under Kansas law. The court also rejected the attorney general's contention that defendants acted unfairly, because the consumers received exactly what they understood they were purchasing.

Baker v. Microsoft Corp., No. CV 030612 (Cal. Super. Ct. filed Feb. 7, 2003).

Plaintiff filed a class action law suit against various software producers and retailers alleging that shrinkwrap licenses for software are inherently unfair and deceptive. The complaint alleges that users who decline to accept license terms they first see upon installing software they have already purchased are barred from using the software and cannot return it to the store from which they purchased it. Baker also alleged that shrinkwrap licenses impose unfair and illegal contract terms that relieve software producer Microsoft from any liability for damage to a user's computer system. As of December, 31 2003, this case remained pending before the court.

General Enforceability of Electronic Contract Denied

Specht v. Netscape Communications Corp., 150 F. Supp. 2d 585 (S.D.N.Y. 2001), *aff'd*, 306 F.3d 17 (2d Cir. 2002).

The U.S. Court of Appeals for the Second Circuit found that users of Netscape's "SmartDownload" Internet software download feature were not bound by an arbitration clause in the software-license agreement because they were not necessarily aware that they were entering a contract at the time they downloaded the SmartDownload software. The trial court noted that the user was not required to assent to or even to *view* the terms of the license agreement before downloading the software. Though the site contained the admonition: "Please review and agree to the terms of the Netscape SmartDownload license agreement before downloading and using the software," the trial court found that this admonition did not indicate "that a user *must* agree to the license terms before downloading and using the software." Rather, "this language reads as a mere invitation, not as a condition." *Specht*, 150 F. Supp. 2d at 596. The court of appeals agreed that users were not placed on sufficient notice of the agreement to be bound by the arbitration clause. The court of appeals emphasized that though the button that users clicked to download the software was above the scroll on users' computer screens, users would have had to scroll down below the fold to find any reference to the license agreement: "In circumstances such as these," the court of appeals wrote, "where consumers are urged to download free software at the immediate clicking of a button, a reference to the existence of license terms on a submerged screen is not sufficient to place consumers on inquiry or constructive notice of those terms." 306 F.3d at 32.

Wei Zhu v. Merrill Lynch HSBC, 2002 BCPC 0535 (Dec. 18, 2002).

The Provincial Court of British Columbia concluded that Wei Zhu, a user of Merrill Lynch's Net Trader system, was not bound by either of two Merrill Lynch disclaimers because there was no evidence Zhu had ever received either of them. Zhu submitted an order to sell shares of stock through Merrill Lynch's NetTrader system, but then immediately canceled the request. He received a message on his screen that read "Below is a confirmation that your cancellation request has been sent . . . . Your trade was cancelled at [time of cancellation]." After waiting five minutes, Zhu sold the shares. The cancellation had not been completed; as a result, Zhu sold his shares twice, leaving him in a short position. Merrill Lynch demanded he pay nearly $10,000 to make up the short position. Zhu claimed that the cancellation message was a valid and sufficient confirmation of cancellation, while Merrill claimed that a cancellation is not confirmed until a user calls a Merrill representative for verification. The court rejected this reasoning and concluded that the common sense understanding of "cancellation" would lead Zhu to believe that the online message meant he had successfully cancelled the transaction, without any need to follow up with a call to a Merrill Lynch representative. Moreover, the court concluded that the disclaimers were unconscionable and unenforceable, as they relieved Merrill Lynch of all liability for errors and inaccuracies in its trading system. The court reasoned that no user would voluntarily agree to terms that permitted a company to commit grossly negligent errors without any liability.

People v. Network Assoc., Inc., 758 N.Y.S. 2d 466 (N.Y. Sup. Ct. Jan. 6, 2003).

The attorney general of New York brought suit against Network Associates, creator of anti-virus and firewall software, for unfair restrictive clauses in its license agreement. The license agreement included a clause forbidding users from writing reviews of Network Associates' software without prior consent from Network Associates. The language, and the location of this clause in the license agreement, rendered the clause unlawfully deceptive, the court ruled, because it misled software users into believing that the restrictions were not imposed by Network Associates, but by some other legal entity. The court issued an order prohibiting Network Associates from distributing, advertising, or selling any software containing the deceptive language.

Other courts have also found shrinkwrap licenses unenforceable under particular circumstances. *See Vault Corp. v. Quaid Software Ltd.*, 655 F. Supp. 750 (E.D. La. 1987), *aff'd*, 847 F.2d 255 (5th Cir. 1988); *Step-Saver Data Systems, Inc. v. Wyse Technology*, 939 F.2d 91 (3d Cir. 1991); *Arizona Retail Sys. v. Software Link*, 831 F. Supp. 759 (D. Ariz. 1993); *Novell, Inc. v. Network Trade Center, Inc.*, 25 F. Supp. 2d 1218 (D. Utah 1997); *Klocek v. Gateway, Inc.*, 104 F. Supp. 2d 1332 (D. Kan. 2000).

Enforceability of Particular Provisions: Forum Selection and Arbitration Clauses

Not surprisingly, if a provision is usually found enforceable in a traditional paper contract, a court will ordinarily find it enforceable in an electronic contract.

Forum Selection and Arbitration Clauses Enforceable

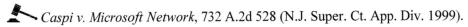 *Caspi v. Microsoft Network*, 732 A.2d 528 (N.J. Super. Ct. App. Div. 1999).

A forum-selection clause contained in a click-through online subscriber agreement was held enforceable. The plaintiffs sued Microsoft in a New Jersey court on various contract and fraud theories relating to membership fee practices. Microsoft moved to dismiss on the grounds that the Microsoft Network membership agreement dictated that all disputes would be adjudicated in the courts of King County, Washington.

Before signing up for the Microsoft Network, users were given an opportunity to review the membership agreement online. To subscribe, they had to click on an "I Agree" button. The court found that the plaintiff subscribers must have known that they were entering a contract when they did so. The court also found that the plaintiffs had proper notice of the forum-selection clause, which was the first item in the last paragraph of the membership agreement. *See also Barnett v. Network Solutions, Inc.*, 38 S.W.3d 200 (Tex. Ct. App. 2001) (holding forum-selection clause requiring adjudication in Virginia to be valid); *Hughes v. America Online*, Civil Action No. 2001-10981-RBC (D. Mass. May 28, 2002) (upholding a forum-selection clause; it was undisputed that the plaintiff had agreed to AOL's terms of service when he became an AOL customer).

Lieschke v. RealNetworks Inc., No. 99-C-7274 (N.D. Ill. Feb. 10, 2000), and *Simon v. RealNetworks Inc.*, No. 99-C-7380 (N.D. Ill. Feb. 10, 2000) (both cases combined and available at 2000 WL 198424).

A federal trial court found enforceable an arbitration clause in a clickwrap agreement that had to be accepted before installation of a software package. *See also Stan McClain Inc. v. Smith-Gardner*, B149630 (Cal. Ct. App., 2d App. Dist April 22, 2002) (holding that where both disputants were sophisticated commercial entities, a forum selection clause in a contract to provide software was valid despite the fact the plaintiff alleged a tort claim rather than a breach-of-contract claim).

Forrest v. Verizon Communications, Inc., 805 A.2d 1007 (D.C. 2002).

A District of Columbia court found the forum-selection clause in a clickwrap agreement for DSL service to be reasonable and enforceable against a subscriber. The court rejected the plaintiff's arguments that the provision should not be enforced because it was buried in a lengthy online agreement, it was viewable only in a small scroll box, and the agreement required consumers to waive their rights to bring class-action suits. The court found that the plaintiff had failed to demonstrate that the forum-selection clause was fraudulent or overreaching, that it would "deprive the plaintiff of a remedy or of its day in court," or that its enforcement would be against public policy.

Net2Phone v. Superior Court of Los Angeles County, 109 Cal. App. 4th 583 (2003).

Consumer Cause, acting as a "private attorney general," sued Net2Phone in California for deceptive and fraudulent business practices. Consumer Cause contended that Net2Phone failed to disclose its practice of "rounding up" to the next minute its charges for telecommunications services. Net2Phone moved to dismiss the case based on the forum selection clause in its End User License Agreement, which said that any claim against the company had to be brought in New Jersey. Consumer Cause protested that its suit would be thrown out by a New Jersey court because New Jersey law prohibits an entity from bringing suit unless it has itself suffered harm. The California Court of Appeal dismissed the California suit against Net2Phone, pursuant to the End User License Agreement, and told Consumer Cause it would have to litigate its claim in New Jersey.

SmartText Corp. v. Interland, Inc. et al., Case No. 03-2393-JWL (D. Kan. Dec. 19, 2003).

A federal judge allowed a jury to decide whether an electronic arbitration clause and an electronic forum selection clause were enforceable. The plaintiff, SmartText, hired the defendant, Interland, to host the plaintiff's website on the defendant's servers. Before "migrating" the website to the defendant's servers, the defendant created a "mirrored" image of the plaintiff's existing website and asked the plaintiff to review the mirrored site for errors and click either "Accept" or "Decline" to approve or reject the mirrored site. When the plaintiff did not review the mirrored website after the first notification, the defendant sent the plaintiff an email which stated, in part, "If we still have not heard from you within five more days, we will assume that the mirrored site is correct and redirect your domain to point to your site hosted at Interland." *Id.* at 3. In addition, if the plaintiff did not review the site and click either "Accept" or "Decline," the email stated that the plaintiff would be bound by the defendant's terms of service, which included a mandatory arbitration clause and a mandatory forum selection clause. After the plaintiff initially rejected the mirrored website for alleged malfunctions, the defendants modified the website and sent another email asking the plaintiff to either accept or decline the revised site. The plaintiff did not respond, and the defendants migrated the site after five days.

After the migration was completed, the plaintiffs alleged the migrated site did not work and that the defendant had breached the contract. The plaintiff sued for breach of contract in a federal court in Kansas, and the defendants asked the court to dismiss the claim, arguing that the suit violated the arbitration and forum selection clauses contained in the terms of service. Applying the Restatement (Second) of Contracts, the court found the plaintiff could only have accepted the terms of the contract by inaction if the plaintiff took the benefits of the defendant's services with a reasonable opportunity to reject them. The court said this presented an issue for a jury to decide, and allowed the case to proceed.

 Freedman v. America Online, Inc., No. 3:03cv1048 (D. Conn. Dec. 8, 2003).

A federal court upheld a forum selection clause in AOL's terms of service against an AOL subscriber who filed a privacy-related lawsuit in his home state. The plaintiff, Clifton Freedman, allegedly harassed two members of a Fairfield, Connecticut, political campaign by sending them an email message stating "The End is Near." Fairfield police sent a warrant application, which was not approved by any judge, to AOL requesting Freedman's address and AOL complied.

Freedman sued AOL in a federal court in Connecticut, alleging a privacy violation. AOL asked the court to dismiss the claim because the AOL member agreement required all disputes be decided by Virginia courts. The court found that Freedman was bound by AOL's terms of service and agreed with AOL's argument that the case should have been brought in Virginia, since Freedman had not shown enough evidence that requiring him to sue in Virginia was "unreasonable."

Arbitration and Forum Selection Clause Unenforceable

Forum-selection clauses have not always been enforced:

Williams v. America Online, Inc., 2001 WL 135825 (Mass. Dist. Ct. Feb. 8, 2001).

A Massachusetts judge ruled that the forum-selection clause in America Online's membership agreement, which requires all disputes to be resolved in Virginia, was not enforceable against the plaintiffs because they were already AOL members at the time that the forum-selection clause was added to the membership agreement and therefore had insufficient notice of the addition of the forum selection clause to the agreement. (*See* "Effective Notice," at page 206, above.)

America Online, Inc. v. Superior Court of Alameda County, 2001 Cal. App. LEXIS 473 (Cal. Super. Ct. June 21, 2001), *petition for review denied*, 2002 Cal. LEXIS 6519 (Cal. Oct. 2, 2002).

An Alameda County, California judge found the forum-selection clause in AOL's user agreement to be unenforceable on two independent policy grounds. First, the court held that the clause's prohibition against class-action relief, though valid under Virginia law, violated California public policy recognizing the importance of the class action remedy, and thus made the law that would apply in Virginia materially different from applicable California law. Second, the court held that the forum-selection clause was unenforceable under the anti-waiver provision of the California Consumers Legal Remedies Act. Under this Act, waivers of such consumer protections are void, rendering the forum-selection and the choice of law clauses in AOL's user agreement unenforceable in California. *See also Thompson v. Handa-Lopez, Inc.*, 998 F. Supp. 738 (W.D. Tex. Mar. 25, 1998) (finding unenforceable a provision in an online agreement governing use of the defendant's Internet casino that called for all disputes to be settled by arbitration in San Jose, California).

Comb v. PayPal, 218 F. Supp. 2d 1165 (N.D. Cal. 2002).

A federal trial court denied defendant PayPal's motion to compel individual arbitration proceedings for each person who had joined a class-action suit against it. The court refused to uphold an arbitration clause in PayPal's clickwrap agreement, citing its unconscionability and questioning the notice provided to the plaintiffs. The court also indicated that the forum-selection provision in the clickwrap agreement was unreasonable.

Evans v. Matlock, 2002 WL 31863294 (Tenn. Ct. App. Dec. 23, 2002).

Evans bid on an antique Dr. Pepper dispenser that Matlock offered for sale on eBay. When Matlock sold the dispenser to another bidder, Evans sued Matlock for breach of contract, claiming that Matlock had accepted his bid before he sold the dispenser to the other bidder. Matlock sought to terminate the suit on the ground that the eBay user agreement required arbitration of all disputes. The court of appeals affirmed the trial court's finding that the user agreement only applied to disputes that arose between eBay and an eBay user, not to disputes between two eBay users.

Electronic and Digital Signatures

General

Online publishers, in their capacities as purchasers and vendors, may depend on the ability to make their e-commerce transactions secure by authenticating the signatures that enable such transactions. Signature authentication has been the subject of extensive state, federal, and international legislative efforts, as well as activity by private organizations.

In the early days of e-commerce regulation, e-signatures were hailed as a new way to streamline the contracting process and the filing of government documents. The promises of new technology have not yet been fulfilled, as the combination of consumers' concerns over security and competing technological standards among companies marketing e-signature software have slowed the transition from ink to electrons. *See* Troy Wolverton, "Despite Law, Few People Use E-Signatures," CNET News.com (Apr. 17, 2002), *available at* http://news.com.com/2100-1017-884544.html.

Definitions

A signature is a mark made with the intent to authenticate a document, and an *electronic signature* is simply a signature transmitted electronically. An electronic signature is an electronic sound, symbol, or process attached to or logically associated with a contract or other record and executed or adopted by a person with the intent to sign the record. Electronic signatures can include typed signature notations; other typed notations, such as email headers; and ink-on-paper signatures scanned electronically.

The term *digital signature* is more narrowly defined. A digital signature is the result of encoding and decoding information through an encryption method, often a method known as public-key cryptography. Despite this distinction, many documents and even statutes use the term "digital signature" as a synonym for the broader, less-specialized "electronic signature."

Legislative Efforts

State Legislation

All 50 states and the District of Columbia have enacted legislation to require or encourage acceptance of some type of electronic signature. Most of these statutes apply to electronic signatures broadly defined. Many of these laws limit themselves to mandating acceptance of electronic or digital signatures by public agencies or require acceptance only in specific areas, such as medical records.

The National Conference of Commissioners on Uniform State Laws voted to approve the Uniform Electronic Transactions Act (UETA) on July 29, 1999. This model state legislation provides for acceptance of electronic signatures but does not require any specific type of electronic signature or method of authentication. As of December 31, 2003, 43 states, the District of Columbia, and the U.S. Virgin Islands had adopted UETA, and two other states had introduced UETA in their legislatures.

Federal Legislation

On June 30, 2000, President Clinton signed into law the Electronic Signatures in Global and National Commerce Act (E-SIGN). 15 U.S.C. § 7001. E-SIGN was enacted at the federal level to avoid wide variations in state law and to bolster the public's confidence in the legal validity of electronic contracts. E-SIGN makes electronic signatures legally binding, like "wet," or ink signatures, by prohibiting a rule of law from denying the legal effect of certain instruments of electronic commerce on the ground (1) that they are not in writing, if they are electronic records; or (2) that they are not signed or affirmed by a signature, if they have been signed or affirmed by electronic signature.

The law further states that "[i]f a statute, regulation or other rule of law requires that a contract or other record relating to a transaction in or affecting interstate or foreign commerce be retained, that requirement is met by retaining an electronic record of the information in the contract." 15 U.S.C. § 7001(d)(1). Under this provision, a record that accurately reflects the information set forth in the electronic contract and that remains accessible to the parties for the period required by statute, law, or regulation will suffice as a record of the transaction under such statute, law, or regulation. *See id.*; *see also In re Real Networks, Inc.*, 2000 U.S. Dist. LEXIS 6584 (N.D. Ill. May 11, 2000) (decided before E-SIGN was enacted, this case involved an electronic agreement that was held to be an enforceable "writing" under the Federal Arbitration Act because it was easily printable and storable).

E-SIGN also preempts any state law addressing electronic signatures that gives greater legal status or effect to a particular technology. This technology-neutral approach allows merchants to decide which technology will best facilitate electronic commerce in their products. However, E-SIGN specifically provides that qualifying state versions of UETA are allowed to preempt E-SIGN.

International Efforts

In November 1999, the European Commission approved a directive to be incorporated into member states' laws. The directive provides that all member states should accept electronic signatures considered valid by member states. The directive is technology-neutral and addresses acceptance of electronic signatures by countries outside the European Union. An October 2003 report, issued by the Interdisciplinary Centre for Law and Information Technology at the request of the European Commission, reviewed the implementation of the directive and found that most European member states have adopted legislation regarding electronic contracts. However, the report noted several problems with implementation of the directive, including a lack of uniformity of treatment of electronic signatures across national boundaries. The report also suggested that member states revise their policies as necessary to adjust to new technological advancements. *See* Jos Dumortier, *et al.*, "The Legal and Market Aspects of Electronic Signatures," Study for the European Commission (Oct. 19, 2003), *available at* http://www.secorvo.de/publikationen/electronic-sig-report.pdf.

On September 29, 2000, the electronic commerce working group for the United Nations Commission on International Trade Law (UNCITRAL) adopted a model law on electronic signatures. The model law was presented to UNCITRAL in the summer of 2001. The draft is available at: http://www.uncitral.org/english/sessions/wg_ec/wp-84.pdf. The Working Group released a report on March 21, 2002 summarizing the Group's findings and recommendation that the United Nations prepare an international treaty dealing with electronic contracting issues. This report can be found at http://www.uncitral.org/english/sessions/unc/unc-35/509e.pdf.

Case Law Developments: E-SIGN and E-Signatures

Although electronic signature technology and the E-SIGN legislation are relatively new, a few cases have considered the validity of electronic signatures.

In *Sea-Land Service, Inc. v. Lozen International, LLC*, 285 F.3d 808 (9th Cir. 2002).

The Court of Appeals for the Ninth Circuit found the presence of an electronic signature on a document sufficient proof that the document was authored by a party opponent and admissible as evidence under the applicable rules of evidence. 285 F.3d at 821.

On the state level, courts at opposite ends of the country have come to conflicting conclusions as to the validity of electronic signatures under the statute of frauds. (Though contracts do not ordinarily have to be in writing to be valid, the statute of frauds provides that certain categories of contracts—such as contracts for the sale of real estate and contracts that cannot be fully performed within a year of execution—are not enforceable unless memorialized in a signed written agreement.) A Massachusetts superior court held that typewritten names of the authors at the end of email messages were equivalent to written signatures and thus fulfilled the requirements of the state's statute of frauds. *See Shattuck v. Klotzbach*, Civil Action No. 01-1109A (Mass. Super. Ct. Dec. 11, 2001). This view was also supported by the U.S. Court of Appeals for the Seventh Circuit, which ruled that the sender's name on an email satisfied the statute of frauds. *Cloud Corp. v. Hasbro, Inc.*, 314 F.3d 289 (7th Cir. 2002) (applying Illinois Uniform Commercial Code), *reh'g denied*, 2003 U.S. App. LEXIS 1112. *See also Roger Edwards, LLC v. Fiddes & Son, Ltd.*, 245 F. Supp. 2d 251 (D. Me. Feb. 14, 2003) (finding email correspondence could satisfy the Maine statute of frauds, as long as the parties intended the correspondence to be binding).

However, the Washington State Court of Appeals rejected the validity of some email communications under that state's statute of frauds because the emails were written prior to acceptance of the offer. The court concluded that the emails were merely part of "continuing negotiations," and that even if the signatures were otherwise valid, the email exchanges did not meet the writing requirement of Washington's statute of frauds. *See Hansen v. Transworld Wireless TV-Spokane, Inc., et al.*, 44 P.3d 929 (Wash. Ct. App. 2002), *appeal denied*, 60 P.3d 1211 (Wash. 2003).

Chapter 7: Electronic Contracts
Summary of the Law

- Electronic contracts are the functional equivalent of traditional, paper contracts, except that they are made online or using electronic media rather than on paper.

- A contract is formed when two people or entities, with knowledge of the terms of the contract, manifest their assent to those terms. Though some contracts (such as contracts for the sale of real estate, contracts to transfer copyright ownership, and contracts that can't be fulfilled within a year from the date of formation) typically must be memorialized in writing to be enforceable, most contracts can be formed without a written document.

- An electronic contract, like a traditional paper contract, is formed when two people or entities manifest their assent to the material terms of a relationship memorialized in a written form. That assent may be express (for example, where a computer user types his name in the signature block of a contract presented electronically or clicks the "I agree" button on an online brokerage agreement) or it may be implied from conduct (for example, where a user continues to access a website with the knowledge that by using the site he is accepting the terms of the site's visitor agreement).

- Websites often post visitor agreements (also referred to as "terms of use," "terms of service," "terms and conditions," and the like) to establish the ground rules for accessing the site and using the content and services provided within. Visitor agreements often include language intended to reduce the website operator's exposure to liability, to advise users of the intellectual property rights claimed by the site operator, and to prohibit data scraping, harvesting of email addresses, framing of the site's content, and the like.

- Much of the litigation over the enforceability of electronic contracts has been over contract formation. Did the party seeking to enforce the contract properly notify the other party of the terms of the proposed agreement, and did the party against which the contract is to be enforced understand that it was entering into a contract?

- A signature is a mark made to indicate assent. An electronic signature is an electronic indication of intent to sign a document. A digital signature is a signature executed through an encryption method that authenticates the signer's signature.

- All 50 states and the District of Columbia have enacted legislation to require or encourage acceptance of electronic or digital signatures.

- The Uniform Electronic Transactions Act (UETA), which provides for acceptance of electronic signatures, but does not require any particular type of electronic signature or method of authentication, has been adopted by 43 states, the District of Columbia, and the U.S. Virgin Islands.

- The federal Electronic Signatures in Global and National Commerce Act (E-SIGN) was enacted to avoid wide variations in state law and to bolster public confidence in the legal validity of electronic contracts. E-SIGN makes electronic signatures legally binding, by prohibiting any rule of law that would deny legal effect to certain electronic contract on the ground that they are not in writing (if they are electronic records) or that they are not signed (if they have been signed electronically). E-SIGN preempts any state law addressing electronic signatures that gives greater legal effect to a particular technology.

ADVERTISING AND MARKETING

Unsolicited Commercial Email ("Spam")

"Spam" is common parlance for unsolicited (usually commercial) email. From the marketers' perspective, spam can be an economical means of reaching variously targeted, mass audiences. From the recipient's point of view, it is often considered the Internet equivalent of junk mail.

Estimates on the pervasiveness of spam vary. According to a study by Brightmail, a San Francisco-based, anti-spam software maker, unsolicited messages accounted for 58% of all email in December 2003. *See* http://www.brightmail.com/spamstats.html. The Spam Filter Review, which rates the effectiveness of various spam filters, estimates that 40% of all email traffic in 2003 was spam. *See* http://www.spamfilterreview.com/spam-statistics.html. A U.K. company, Message Labs, found that in December 2003, 62.7% of all email messages were spam. *See* Message Labs Intelligence Report, Dec. 2003, *at* http://www.messagelabs.com/viruseye/research/default.asp. According to Message Labs, May 2003 marked the first time that more than half of all messages that people received at work were spam. Stefanie Olsen, "Corporate In-Boxes Choke on Spam" (June 2, 2003), *at* http://news.com.com/2100-1024-1012418.html. The majority of all spam is generated by 150 to 200 spammers. Saul Hansell, "Finding Solution to Secret World of Spam," N.Y. TIMES (May 5, 2003), at C8.

As the amount of spam grows, so do efforts to combat it. Until recently, the most comprehensive response had come from state legislatures: 36 states have passed anti-spam laws. The impact of these statutes will be reduced substantially by the recent enactment of the first federal anti-spam measure, the CAN SPAM Act of 2003, which (with some limitations) preempts state laws regulating spam. In addition, the FTC has also stepped up efforts to stop commercial emails that are fraudulent or deceptive.

CAN SPAM Act of 2003

In December 2003, Congress passed, and President Bush signed, the Controlling the Assault of Non-Solicited Pornography and Marketing Act of 2003, or "CAN SPAM Act," the first federal statute regulating the sending of unsolicited commercial email messages. The Act prohibits many of the most egregious spamming practices. Most important, at least from the perspective of legitimate email marketers, the Act preempts all state anti-spam laws, except to the extent those laws prohibit falsity or deception in any portion of an email message. Among other things, the Act:

- Prohibits the transmission of commercial email messages that contain false or misleading header information (that is, the source, destination and routing information in the email message);

- Prohibits the use of deceptive subject headings;

- Requires that all commercial email messages include a functioning return email address or another Internet-based reply mechanism (such as a hyperlink to a web page) that allows any recipient to submit a request not to receive future messages from the sender, and prohibits the sender, or anyone acting on the sender's behalf, from continuing to send messages to such a user after receiving such a request;

- Requires that every commercial email message contain a clear and conspicuous notice that the message is an advertisement, and offers the recipient a clear means to opt out of receiving future emails. If a recipient chooses to opt out, that request must be honored within 10 business days of the receipt of the request by the sender;

- Requires that every commercial email include a valid physical postal address of the sender;

- Prohibits the sending of emails to illegally harvested email addresses, and/or employing dictionary attacks to generate email addresses. (A "dictionary attack" uses software to open a connection to an email server and rapidly submits millions of random possible email addresses to the server. The software records the "live," active email addresses to add to the spammer's list); and

- Requires the use of warning labels in the subject line of commercial emails containing sexually oriented material. Although the statute does not require that other types of commercial emails contain labels in the subject line (such as the "ADV" indicator called for by many state statutes), it does require that the FTC prepare a report to Congress setting forth a plan to require subject line labeling in the future.

Generally, the statute does not prohibit sending commercial email to any recipient who has given the sender his or her affirmative consent to receive email messages. Affirmative consent means that the user has expressly consented to receive the message and, if the message is from a party other than the party to whom consent was given, that the recipient was given notice that his or her email address could be transferred to that other party.

The Act also criminalizes fraudulent conduct with respect to commercial emails. It prohibits the unauthorized transmission of multiple commercial emails from or through a protected computer, the falsification of header information in multiple commercial emails, and the use of a false identity to register for five or more email accounts with the intent to transmit multiple commercial emails. For purposes of the Act, a "protected computer" is one that is used by the U.S. government, by a financial institution, or for interstate or foreign commerce. Criminal penalties for violations include fines and imprisonment. The severity of the applicable penalty depends on such factors as whether the offense was committed in the furtherance of a felony, and the number of prohibited emails that the violator sent.

Criminal enforcement power under the Act is primarily vested in the FTC (a violation of the Act is considered the equivalent of an unfair or deceptive trade practice under the FTC Act) along with the Department of Justice. Other federal agencies also have some limited enforcement power. On the civil side, state attorneys general will be the ultimate enforcing agents; they are empowered to seek injunctive relief, actual damages or statutory damages on behalf of the residents of their respective states for violation of the Act. The authorized statutory damages are $250 per email sent in violation of the Act, with recovery not to exceed $2 million; the damages may be trebled if a court determines that the violations were committed knowingly and willfully, or if they involved practices such as illegal harvesting or dictionary attacks. Internet service providers that have been affected by the actions of spammers also are entitled to bring suit to enjoin future spamming activity or to seek actual damages. In actions brought either by a state attorney general or by an ISP, the statute provides that costs of bringing the enforcement action, as well as attorneys fees, may be recovered from spammers.

CAN SPAM also authorizes, but does not require, the FTC to create a national "Do-Not-Email" registry. The FTC is to provide a report to Congress detailing a plan, and timetable, for establishing such a registry by late May of 2004. CAN SPAM also authorizes the FCC to create rules to protect consumers from unwanted messages that may be sent to their mobile telephones.

The CAN SPAM Act took effect January 1, 2004.

State Law

As of December 31, 2003, 36 states had passed laws designed to regulate spam. These state statutes were all enacted prior to the passage of the CAN SPAM Act, which borrowed liberally from the approaches of various states. The CAN SPAM Act supercedes all state statutes that expressly regulate the use of commercial email, although the state statutes retain viability to the extent that they prohibit false or deceptive content in email messages.

Some commentators have criticized the CAN SPAM Act, arguing that it gives too much latitude to spammers. A more restrictive approach was reflected in a California anti-spam law enacted in September 2003. The California statute took effect January 1, 2004, but like other state anti-spam laws, is largely preempted by the federal CAN SPAM Act. It prohibits sending commercial email to any recipient that does not have a pre-existing business relationship with the advertiser, unless the advertiser (not just the sender of the email) has received prior opt-in consent from the recipient.

The California statute was designed to have a national reach; it prohibits sending unsolicited commercial messages from or to any California email address, with the burden on the sender to determine if the recipient has a California email address. "California email address" is broadly defined, and includes not only an email address registered to a California resident, but also an email address that is "regularly accessed" in California, as well as any address registered to a California resident, even if not accessed in the state. The law gives individuals a private right of action against spammers, permitting recovery of up to $1,000 for each message received and up to $1 million per campaign. *See* Cal. Bus. & Prof. Code § 17529, *et seq.*

The California law is extreme; no other state has attempted to reach as much out-of-state conduct and no other state requires consent from the recipient to receive email not only from the sender but from each advertiser featured in an email message. Indeed, it appears that one of Congress's primary motivations in hastily passing the CAN SPAM Act just before recessing for 2003 was to preempt the California statute before it took effect. *See* Tim Lenke, *Can Spam Act Leaves Little Time to Comply*, WASHINGTON TIMES, Jan. 10, 2004, at C10.

Most states have been less aggressive in their efforts to control spam. Although there is no model state statute, states have followed some common approaches to anti-spam laws. The statutes generally provide a private right of action against the senders of unsolicited commercial email. In most states, both the recipient of the email and Internet service providers that suffer actual damages managing the email may bring the claim. The plaintiffs often have the choice of recovering actual damages or a per email statutory dollar amount, capped at a certain amount per day. However, a New York state court has held that the bother of receiving junk mail and unwanted telephone solicitations did not constitute actual harm and therefore dismissed a class-action suit against a bank that had allegedly sold marketers information about its customers. For more discussion of this case, *Smith v. Chase Manhattan Bank*, 741 N.Y.S.2d 100 (N.Y. App. Div. 2002), *see* Chapter 6, page 181.

Prohibition of Fraud. Some states have sought to combat senders of bulk unsolicited email who hide their identity or fraudulently disguise themselves. Typically, states have prohibited falsifying the header information that accompanies an email. Such states provide a cause of action not only for the recipient of forged email, but also for any third party who may be fraudulently identified as the email's sender.

Self-Identifying Disclosures. Other states require those who want to send unsolicited bulk commercial email to supply self-identifying information, such as name and postal address, as well as a way for recipients to opt out of receiving future emails. Some states require spammers to create a toll-free telephone number that recipients may call to stop receiving the emails.

Labels. Another method some states have adopted to combat spam is to require unsolicited emails to include in the subject line a label such as "ADV" for commercial emails, or "ADV:ADLT" for commercial emails promoting adult content.

Technical Prohibitions. By prohibiting "trespass" on a third-party computer server, some states prohibit a technique spammers use to bounce emails off a third-party server in order to hide the actual sender's identity. States have also prohibited the intentional distribution of software that could be used to falsify email header or routing information when that software has little use beyond such falsification.

Do Not Email Lists. Modeling their proposals on "do not call" lists used to combat telemarketing, a number of states have proposed legislation to institute "do not email lists." Each state's list would operate slightly differently, but all would prohibit sending unsolicited commercial email to individuals who register their email addresses with the state. In Michigan, Missouri, and Colorado, individuals who continue to receive unsolicited email after placing their email addresses on the list would have the right to file a claim against the violating marketers. Under a proposed Oregon law, offenders would be fined, but individuals would not have a private right of action. Although the "do not email" lists would be freely accessible to companies in Missouri and Oregon, Colorado would require that companies that wish to access the list pay a fee.

As of December 31, 2003, the following states had enacted laws regulating spam:

- Alaska. Alaska Stat. § 45.50.479 (2003).

- Arizona. Ariz. Rev. Stat. §§ 44-1372, *et seq.* (2003).

- Arkansas. Ark. Code §§ 5-41-201, *et seq.* (2003).

- California. Cal. Bus. & Prof. Code §§ 17529, *et seq.* and Cal. Penal Code § 502 (West 2004).

- Colorado. Colo. Rev. Stat. §§ 6-2.5-101, *et seq.* (2003).

- Connecticut. Conn. Genn. Stat. § 53-451 (2003).

- Delaware. Del. Code. Ann. tit. 11, §§ 931, *et seq.* (2003).

- Idaho. Idaho Code § 48-603E (2003).

- Illinois. 815 Ill. Comp. Stat. 511/1-10 (West 2003).

- Indiana. Ind. Code §§ 24-5-22, *et seq.* (2003).

- Iowa. Iowa Code Ann. § 714.E (West 2003).

- Kansas. Kan. Stat. Ann. § 50-6,107 (2003).

- Louisiana. La. Rev. Stat. Ann. § 73.1-6 (West 2003).

- Maine. Me. Rev. Stat. Ann. tit. 10, § 1497 (2003).

- Maryland. Md. Laws 323 and 324 (2003).

- Michigan. 2003 Mich. Pub. Acts 42.

- Minnesota. Minn. Laws 325 F.694 (2003).

- Missouri. Mo. Rev. Stat §§ 407.020, *et seq.* (2003).

- Nevada. Nev. Rev. Stat. §§ 41.705, *et seq.* (2003).

- New Mexico. N.M. Stat. Ann. §§ 57-12-23 to -24 (2003).

- North Carolina. N.C. Gen. Stat. §§ 14-453, 14-458 (2003).

- North Dakota. N.D. Cent. Code §§ 51-27-01 to -09 (2003).

- Ohio. Ohio Rev. Code Ann. § 2307.64 (West 2003).

- Oklahoma. Okla. Stat. tit. 15, § 776 (2003).

- Oregon, Or. Rev. Stat. § 646.607 (2004)

- Pennsylvania. Pa. Cons. Stat. § 5903 (2000), Pa. Stat. Ann. tit. 73, §§ 2250.1 to 2250.8 (2002).

- Rhode Island. R.I. Gen. Laws §§ 6-47-1, *et seq.* and §§ 11-52-1, *et seq.* (2003).

- South Dakota. S.D. Codified Laws § 37-24-6, and §§ 37-24-36, *et seq.* (2003).

- Tennessee. Tenn. Code Ann. §§ 47-18-2501, *et seq.* (2003).

- Texas. Tex. Bus. & Com. Code Ann. § 46.001, *et seq.* (2003).

- Utah. Utah Code §§ 13-34-101, *et seq.* (2003).

- Virginia. Va. Code Ann. §§ 18.2-152.2, *et seq.* (2003).

- Washington. Wash. Rev. Code § 19.190 (1999), Wash. Rev. Code §§ 3.66.020, 3.66.040 (2003).

- West Virginia. W. Va. Code § 46A-6G (2003).

- Wisconsin. Wis. Stat. § 944.25 (2003).

- Wyoming. Wyo. Stat. Ann. §§ 40-12-401 to -404 (2003).

State Approaches to Spam Regulation

The following chart outlines the provisions of the current state statutes relating to unsolicited commercial email and lists the states that have enacted each such restriction:

Typical Provisions in State Unsolicited Commercial Email Statutes	Statutes Containing Such Provisions
DEFINITION OF "SPAM"	
Does not include commercial email sent by a party who has a prior business or personal relationship with the recipient.	Arizona, California, Colorado, Delaware, Illinois, Indiana, Kansas, Michigan, Minnesota, Nevada, North Carolina, North Dakota, Ohio, Rhode Island, Utah, Washington, West Virginia.
Prohibits any commercial email sent without express consent or request from the recipient.	California, Colorado, Delaware, Illinois, Michigan, Nevada, Rhode Island, Tennessee, Washington, West Virginia.
Exempts Internet service providers who merely transfer the unsolicited commercial email via their networks.	Arkansas, California, Delaware, Idaho, Iowa, Maryland, Michigan, Missouri, Nevada, Ohio, Rhode Island, Tennessee, Virginia, Washington, West Virginia.
Exempts organizations that send unsolicited commercial email to their members.	Colorado, Connecticut, Delaware, Idaho, Indiana, Iowa, Louisiana, Minnesota, North Carolina, North Dakota, Rhode Island, Virginia.
Exempts free email service providers (such as Hotmail or Yahoo!) that require their members to consent to receiving unsolicited advertisements from certain authorized third parties as a condition of signing up a free email account.	Arizona, Idaho, Indiana, Iowa, Maryland, North Dakota, Wyoming.
Exempts an employer sending emails to employees.	Arizona, Colorado, Indiana, Minnesota, North Dakota, Oregon.

Typical Provisions in State Unsolicited Commercial Email Statutes	Statutes Containing Such Provisions
Exempts electronic mail advertisements voluntarily accessed by the recipient from an electronic bulletin board or other source.	Idaho, Iowa, Michigan, Nevada, North Dakota.
REQUIRED DISCLOSURE	
Requires mailer to use specific language in an email's subject line to disclose its commercial nature (*e.g.*, "ADV:," "ADV:ADLT," "ADVERTISEMENT," "COMMERCIAL EMAIL," etc.).	Arizona, Colorado, Indiana, Kansas, Michigan, Minnesota, New Mexico, North Dakota, Pennsylvania, South Dakota, Tennessee, Utah, Wisconsin.
Requires mailer to disclose the actual point of origin of the email, so that the transmission information cannot be falsified or misrepresented.	Colorado, Idaho, Illinois, Indiana, Iowa, Kansas, Michigan, Oklahoma, Rhode Island, South Dakota, Utah, Virginia, West Virginia.
UNSUBSCRIBE PROVISIONS	
Requires mailer to provide a cost-free method for recipient to notify mailer not to send further email. (Possible methods include a toll-free phone number, sender-operated email, etc.).	Arizona, Colorado, Idaho, Indiana, Iowa, Kansas, Michigan, Minnesota, Missouri, Nevada, New Mexico, North Dakota, Ohio, Rhode Island, Tennessee, Utah.
Requires mailer to inform recipients in a conspicuous manner of how to notify mailer not to send further email.	Kansas, Michigan, Minnesota, New Mexico, North Dakota, Ohio, Rhode Island, Tennessee, Utah.
Requires that the mailer stop sending email to any recipient who so requests.	Colorado, Idaho, Indiana, Iowa, Kansas, Michigan, New Mexico, Ohio, Rhode Island, Tennessee, Utah.
ACCURATE SENDER, ROUTING, AND SUBJECT LINE INFORMATION	
Prohibits false or misleading information in the subject line.	California, Indiana, Kansas, Maryland, North Dakota, Wyoming.

Typical Provisions in State Unsolicited Commercial Email Statutes	Statutes Containing Such Provisions
Prohibits falsification of transmission information or any other routing information.	Arizona, Arkansas, California, Colorado, Connecticut, Delaware, Idaho, Illinois, Indiana, Iowa, Kansas, Louisiana, Maryland, Michigan, Minnesota, North Carolina, North Dakota, Ohio, Oklahoma, Pennsylvania, Rhode Island, Virginia, Washington, West Virginia, Wyoming.
Prohibits using a third party's name as the name of the sender without that third party's permission.	Arkansas, California, Colorado, Idaho, Illinois, Iowa, Kansas, Maryland, Michigan, Minnesota, North Dakota, Rhode Island, Washington, West Virginia, Wyoming.
Requires email to contain sender information (name, address, etc.).	Michigan, Nevada, Ohio, Rhode Island, Utah, Washington, West Virginia.
Prohibits distribution of software that would enable falsification of email transmission information.	Kansas, Michigan, Oklahoma, Rhode Island, Tennessee, Virginia.
CONTENT RESTRICTION	
Prohibits sending of sexually explicit materials via unsolicited commercial email.	Pennsylvania, Utah, West Virginia.
REMEDIES	
Classifies the first offense as a misdemeanor.	California, Connecticut, Delaware, Illinois, Louisiana, Michigan, North Carolina, Pennsylvania, Utah, Virginia.
Escalates the offense to a felony under certain circumstances (such as recklessness, malice, actual damages above a certain monetary limit, multiple offenses).	Arkansas, California, Connecticut, Illinois, Louisiana, Michigan, North Carolina, Pennsylvania, Rhode Island, Virginia.

Typical Provisions in State Unsolicited Commercial Email Statutes	Statutes Containing Such Provisions
Permits a recipient of unsolicited commercial email to recover actual damages.	Arizona, California, Colorado, Connecticut, Idaho, Illinois, Indiana, Iowa, Kansas, Maryland, Michigan, Minnesota, Missouri, Nevada, New Mexico, North Carolina, North Dakota, Oklahoma, Rhode Island, Tennessee, Virginia, Washington, West Virginia.
Permits a recipient of unsolicited commercial email to recover, in lieu of actual damages, the lesser of either a fixed amount per email (generally, $10) or per day (generally, $25,000).	Arizona, Colorado, Connecticut, Illinois, Michigan, Minnesota, Nevada, New Mexico, North Carolina, Oklahoma, Rhode Island, South Dakota, Tennessee, Utah, Virginia.
Permits a recipient of unsolicited commercial email to recover, in lieu of actual damages, the greater of either a fixed amount per email (generally, $10) or per day (generally, $1,000).	Idaho, Iowa, Missouri, Washington, West Virginia.
Permits an email service provider to recover, in lieu of actual damages, the greater of either a fixed amount per email (generally, $10) or per day (generally, $25,000).	Colorado, Connecticut, Illinois, Iowa, Maryland, Minnesota, Missouri, New Mexico, North Carolina, Ohio, Oklahoma, Rhode Island, Tennessee, Virginia, Washington, West Virginia.
Permits a recipient of unsolicited commercial email to recover a fixed amount for each violation ($100), not to exceed a maximum amount ($50,000).	Ohio.
Permits a recipient of unsolicited commercial email, an electronic mail service provider, or the attorney general to recover liquidated damages of $1,000 for each email sent in violation of the law, not to exceed a maximum amount ($1,000,000).	California.

Additionally, some states have enacted legislation to prohibit unsolicited text messages to mobile telephones. Former California Governor Gray Davis signed such a bill in September 2002, which became effective January 2003. *See* Cal. Bus. & Prof. Code § 17538.41. Pennsylvania has adopted a similar bill. *See* Pa. Stat. Ann. tit. 73, § 2250. As noted above, the federal CAN SPAM Act also contains a provision allowing the FCC to enact regulations to address wireless telephone spam.

Constitutionality of Spam Laws

Courts have addressed the constitutionality of a number of laws regulating unsolicited communications:

The Telephone Consumer Protection Act of 1991

Before addressing unsolicited email, Congress targeted a different type of unsolicited communication: "junk faxes." With the passage of the Telephone Consumer Protection Act of 1991 (the "TCPA"), 47 U.S.C. 227, Congress made its first foray into the regulation of unsolicited advertising messages. The TCPA, among other things, makes it unlawful "to use any telephone facsimile machine, computer, or other device to send an unsolicited advertisement to a telephone facsimile machine." This statute allows anyone who receives such an unsolicited advertisement to sue for an injunction and/or for actual damages or $500 in statutory damages, whichever is greater. A court may award treble damages for willful violation of the statute.

First Amendment challenges to the TCPA have generally been unsuccessful. The Court of Appeals for the Ninth Circuit rejected one such challenge on the basis that unsolicited fax advertisements shift significant costs to consumers. *See Destination Ventures, Ltd. v. FCC*, 46 F.3d 54 (9th Cir. 1995). The Ninth Circuit noted that "regulation of commercial speech must directly advance a substantial government interest in a manner that forms a 'reasonable fit' with the interest," and that "the burden is on the government to demonstrate the reasonable fit." *Id.* at 55. The plaintiff argued that although the government had a substantial interest in preventing the shifting of advertising costs to consumers, the government had not demonstrated the "reasonable fit" element because faxes containing advertising are no more costly to consumers than other types of unsolicited faxes. The court disagreed, finding that Congress' goal was to prohibit the shifting of *advertising* cost shifting, not *all* cost shifting. *Id.* at 56 (emphasis added).

Similarly, the U.S. Court of Appeals for the Eighth Circuit held that the TCPA does not violate the First Amendment. The court recognized the costs that companies would have to incur to combat unwanted faxed solicitations, including the costs of buying filters, installing bigger computer networks, and consuming more paper. The court also noted that unwanted faxed solicitations would prevent legitimate faxes from reaching their destinations. Finding that the TCPA directly advanced the government's interest in preventing these costs from being passed to consumers and that the TCPA was sufficiently narrow to address this interest, the appellate court found the TCPA to be constitutionally valid. *Missouri v. American Blast Fax, Inc.*, 323 F.3d 649 (8th Cir. 2003).

The Superior Court of Pennsylvania has rejected an effort to use the TCPA to combat spam. In *Aronson v. Bright-Teeth Now, LLC*, the court declined to apply the TCPA to unsolicited email communications because the statute only prohibits sending unsolicited advertisements to a "telephone facsimile machine." Because a computer is not a fax machine, the court reasoned, the TCPA was inapplicable to spam. See *Aronson v. Bright-Teeth Now, LLC*, 2003 PA Super. 187, 2003 WL 21027145 (Pa. Super. Ct. 2003).

Constitutional Challenges to Spam Laws

Like the TCPA, state anti-spam laws have been challenged on constitutional grounds:

State v. Heckel, 24 P.3d 404 (Wash. 2001); *cert. denied* 534 U.S. 997 (2001).

On October 29, 2001, the U.S. Supreme Court declined to hear an appeal of a challenge to Washington State's anti-spam law. The Washington Supreme Court had upheld the law on appeal from a ruling by a trial court that the law was unconstitutional. The trial court had held that the State of Washington could not successfully sue Jason Heckel of Salem, Oregon, under Washington's anti-spam law because the Commerce Clause of the U.S. Constitution gives Congress the power to regulate interstate commerce and implies that states are limited in the ways that they can regulate businesses located in other states. The trial court noted that if the Washington statute were enforceable against a resident of Oregon a person could be subject to 50 standards of conduct under 50 different state laws. The trial court saw this inconsistency as problematic under the Commerce Clause. The State of Washington appealed directly to the state supreme court, which reversed the trial court's ruling and held that Washington's anti-spam law does not unduly burden interstate commerce. The court opined that the act applies equally to in-state and out-of-state spammers and serves the legitimate local interest of eliminating the cost shifting that occurs when deceptive spam is sent. The only requirement the Act places on spammers, the court held, is truthfulness in the subject lines of email messages.

In September 2002, Heckel was found liable under the anti-spam statute. On October 18, 2002, the court ordered Heckel to pay fines of more than $98,000 for sending the misleading and unsolicited commercial emails. This marked the first time such a fine had been levied by a U.S. court against a defendant under an anti-spam statute.

Ferguson v. Friendfinder Inc., 94 Cal. App. 4th 1255, 115 Cal. Rptr. 2d 258 (Cal. Ct. App. 2002).

The California Court of Appeal ruled that California's original anti-spam statute (Cal. Bus. & Prof. Code § 17538.4, passed in 1998 but repealed by the 2003 California anti-spam law) was constitutional and valid. Among other things, the law required that all unsolicited emails contain a toll-free number that a recipient could use to opt out of receiving future emails, and also required that the subject lines of unsolicited emails contain an "ADV:" or "ADV:ADLT" label. The appeals panel reasoned that the law did not discriminate against out-of-state actors, nor regulate commerce occurring wholly outside the state, nor conflict with other states' laws regulating spam, nor unduly burden interstate commerce. Weighing the costs of unsolicited commercial email to consumers and ISPs against the costs of complying with the law, the court concluded that the statute's affirmative-disclosure requirements did not "impose any appreciable burden" on senders of spam. The court rejected the defendant's claim that it was impossible to determine the residence of an email recipient, and, therefore, impossible to determine when it was necessary to comply with the statute. Instead, the court held that a commercial email sender's decision to comply with the law "all the time" in order to avoid the need for determining the recipient's physical location would amount to nothing more than "a business decision [that] simply does not establish" a constitutional violation. The California Supreme Court denied the defendant's request for review of the appeals court decision.

Application of State Spam Laws

Government Enforcement of State Spam Laws

The attorneys general of a number of states have brought suits against spammers under their respective spam laws, as discussed below:

 Washington v. Haberli, No. 02-2-35691-5SEA (Wash. Super. Ct., filed Dec. 16, 2002).

On December 16, 2002, Washington's attorney general filed a complaint against Ernesto Haberli for using false and misleading information in the subject lines of emails to conceal pornographic material within the body of the email and for misrepresenting the sender's identity. Such actions constitute violations of the Washington Unsolicited Electronic Mail Act and the Washington Consumer Protection Act. Prosecutors seek injunctive relief and a $2,000 fine for each violation (that is, for each email sent).

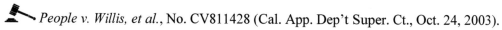 *People v. Willis, et al.*, No. CV811428 (Cal. App. Dep't Super. Ct., Oct. 24, 2003).

California's attorney general filed suit against PW Marketing, a California bulk-mail marketing company that allegedly sent millions of unlawful unsolicited emails to California residents. The principals of the company were also named as defendants. Although the suit was brought under California's 1998 anti-spam statute, on October 24, 2003 the court issued a permanent injunction prohibiting the defendants from sending any unsolicited commercial email in violation of either the 1998 statute or the amended anti-spam statute which wasn't to become effective until January 2004. The court also imposed a $2 million fine on the defendants.

Missouri's attorney general has filed the first two lawsuits under that state's anti-spam statute. The complaints, filed in October 2003, alleged that email marketers violated the state law by sending messages to Missouri email addresses without proper labeling, and also by continuing to send emails after receiving recipients' requests to stop. The violations came to the state's attention because the unsolicited messages were sent to email addresses maintained by the attorney general for the sole purpose of monitoring compliance with the anti-spam law. *See* Stefanie Olsen, "Missouri Files Spam Suit Under New Law," CNET News.com (Oct. 10, 2003), *at* http://news.com.com/2100-1028_3-5089720.html.

In December 2003, Virginia became the first state in the country to level felony charges against email marketers. Virginia prosecutors charged two men with four felony counts of violating the state's spam law. The men are accused of sending thousands of spam emails per day to AOL subscribers that contained false header information. Under the Virginia statute, which took effect in July 2003, it is a felony to send more than 10,000 messages in a 24-hour period or 100,000 messages in a 30-day period. If convicted, each defendant faces up to five years in prison and fines of $2,500 for each of the four felony counts. *See* Jonathan Krim, "Virginia Indicts Two Men on Spam Charges," WASHINGTON POST (Dec. 11, 2003), at E1.

New York v. Synergy6, Inc., et al., (Case No. not available) (N.Y. Gen. Term filed Dec. 18, 2003).

The New York State attorney general filed suit in New York state court against three prolific email marketers. The suit was precipitated by Microsoft, which had set up specific email accounts on its "Hotmail" email system in attempt to catch spammers. Microsoft claims that the defendant marketers sent mass emails using forged sender names, false subject lines, fake server names, inaccurate and misrepresented sender addresses, or obscured transmission paths. The suit was brought under New York's false advertising and deceptive trade practices statutes, and seeks injunctive relief as well as statutory damages. A copy of the complaint is available at http://www.oag.state.ny.us/press/2003/dec/dec18b_03.html.

Private Civil Cases Relating to Spam

A number of private civil cases have also addressed the legality of unsolicited commercial email in various factual contexts, as well as the rights that consumers and businesses have with respect to such messages. These cases have been brought under a number of legal theories, including trespass, privacy, computer fraud, unfair competition, and breach of contract.

Cyber Promotions, Inc. v. America Online, Inc., 948 F. Supp. 436 (E.D. Pa. 1996).

Cyber Promotions, a business that sent millions of emails per day to AOL email accounts, sued AOL because AOL had blocked Cyber Promotions' emails from reaching AOL users. In the first major decision relating to unsolicited commercial email, the court found that Cyber Promotions had no constitutional right to send messages to AOL users. The First Amendment prohibits governmental restrictions on speech. It does not limit AOL's right to control speech within its service. The judge later rejected Cyber Promotions' claim that AOL was an "essential service" to which it had a right of access under antitrust law.

CompuServe, Inc. v. Cyber Promotions, Inc., 962 F. Supp. 1015 (S.D. Ohio 1997).

CompuServe, an Internet service provider, sued Cyber Promotions to stop it from sending unsolicited commercial email to CompuServe users. Cyber Promotions had repeatedly ignored CompuServe's requests to stop spamming CompuServe customers, and CompuServe had been unable to block Cyber Promotions' email messages through technical means. The judge issued a preliminary injunction prohibiting Cyber Promotions from spamming CompuServe users, finding that continued spamming constituted a trespass on CompuServe's computers. The parties subsequently settled their dispute.

Hotmail Corp. v. Van$ Money Pie, Inc., et al., 47 U.S.P.Q.2d 1020, 1998 U.S. Dist. LEXIS 10729 (N.D. Cal. April 16, 1998).

Hotmail, an email service provider, sued defendants claiming that they had sent out thousands of email messages with falsified headers that made it appear as though the messages came from Hotmail addresses. Hotmail also claimed that defendants had created Hotmail accounts through which they sent unsolicited commercial email. Bounceback messages and responses to defendants' emails flooded Hotmail's servers. Hotmail sought injunctive relief, alleging that defendants' use of the "Hotmail" trademark in their emails constituted false designation of origin, trademark dilution under federal and state law, and violation of the Computer Fraud and Abuse Act. Hotmail also alleged some state common law and statutory claims, including trespass to chattels. The court entered a permanent injunction against defendants, finding that defendants' use of the Hotmail mark in the email headers violated Hotmail's trademark rights.

 America Online, Inc. v. Netvision Audiotext, Inc. d/b/a Cyber Entertainment Network, No. 99-CV-1186 (E.D. Va., amended complaint filed Dec. 22, 2000).

America Online sued Netvision Audiotext, an online adult-entertainment company, claiming that Netvision created "incentives" for its affiliated third-party webmasters to send unsolicited commercial email to AOL customers on Netvision's behalf. The lawsuit alleged violations of the Virginia Computer Crimes Act and federal Computer Fraud and Abuse Act, among other statutes. In April 2002, the parties settled pursuant to a court order requiring Netvision to pay an undisclosed amount of monetary damages to AOL and to discontinue soliciting Netvision affiliates to send unsolicited commercial email.

 Classified Ventures, LLC v. Softcell Marketing, Inc., 109 F. Supp. 2d 898 (N.D. Ill. 2000).

Some email marketers have tried to mask the source of their mass email campaigns by using false return email addresses, a practice known as "spoofing." In this case, Softcell Marketing, a company that provides email promotional services, mounted a promotion of various pornographic sites using Classified Ventures' cars.com domain in the return address for their emails. The court permanently enjoined Softcell from using the cars.com domain, finding service mark infringement, dilution, and unfair competition.

 Earthlink Inc. v. Doe, No. 1:01cv02099 (N.D. Ga., complaint filed Aug. 7, 2001); *Earthlink Inc. v. Krantz*, No. 1:01cv02098 (N.D. Ga., complaint filed Aug. 7, 2001); *Earthlink Inc. v. Smith*, No. 1:01cv02099 (N.D. Ga., complaint filed Aug. 7, 2001).

On August 7, 2001, Internet service provider Earthlink filed suit against several defendants alleging that sending spam via Earthlink's systems violated the Electronic Communications Privacy Act, the Computer Fraud and Abuse Act, the Lanham Act, and other federal and state laws. Earthlink maintained that the defendants used stolen credit-card numbers to purchase accounts from Internet service providers, used stolen passwords to obtain access to third parties' email accounts, and used all of these stolen accounts to send spam. Earthlink sought damages, treble damages, punitive damages, attorney fees, and an injunction barring the defendants from sending spam to any Internet user; engaging in the theft or misuse of third-party credit-card numbers, passwords, or email accounts; and using any computer or device to obtain Internet access.

In 2002, the U.S. District Court for the Northern District of Georgia awarded Earthlink $25 million in damages from K.C. Smith, who had allegedly sent more than one billion unsolicited emails through Earthlink's networks. *Earthlink v. Smith*, No. 1:01-CV-2099 (N.D. Ga. 2002). On May 7, 2003, the same court awarded Earthlink $16.4 million and issued an injunction against Howard Carmack, the so-called "Buffalo Spammer." The court found that Carmack had used stolen and/or bogus credit card numbers to purchase dial-up Internet access accounts, which he used to send spam. *Earthlink v. Carmack*, No. 1:02-CV-3041-TWT, 2003 U.S. Dist. LEXIS 9963 (N.D. Ga. May 7, 2003).

Morrison & Foerster, LLP v. Etracks.com Inc., No. 40494 (Cal. Super. Ct., filed Feb. 6, 2002).

Morrison & Foerster LLP, a California law firm, filed a complaint against Etracks, which sent Morrison & Foerster employees unsolicited emails in violation of California's 1998 anti-spam law, Cal. Bus. & Prof. Code § 17538.4, and in violation of Morrison & Foerster's company policy. The law firm alleged that Etracks had actual notice of Morrison & Foerster's policy prohibiting unsolicited email advertisements because it sent an email message to the opt-out address included in Etracks' email messages, email-remove@response.etracks.com. The complaint requested damages of $50 per unsolicited email advertisement received, plus attorney fees and costs. On May 30, 2003, the court granted plaintiff's request to dismiss the case voluntarily.

MonsterHut, Inc. v. PaeTec Communications, Inc., 294 A.2d 945 (N.Y. App. Div. 2002).

A New York State trial court issued a temporary restraining order prohibiting Internet service provider PaeTec from terminating the alleged spammer, MonsterHut, Inc., from its network. The ISP had received complaints that MonsterHut was sending unsolicited emails in violation of its contract, which represented it was a fully consensual, email marketing service. MonsterHut argued that, under the parties' agreement, the spam restriction only would apply if more than 2% of the people who received MonsterHut's emails complained. An appeals court reversed the trial court ruling on May 3, 2002, stating that the parties' agreement prohibited MonsterHut from sending unsolicited commercial emails. On May 8, 2002, PaeTec disconnected MonsterHut from its network.

On May 17, 2002, the State of New York filed suit against MonsterHut for fraudulently advertising that the company's email marketing service was "permission based." The suit alleged that many consumers who did not opt in nonetheless received commercial email from MonsterHut. On January 6, 2003, the New York Supreme Court enjoined MonsterHut from fraudulently, deceptively, and illegally misrepresenting its "opt-in," "opt-out," and "permission based" policies. *New York v. MonsterHut Inc.*, No. 402140-02 (N.Y. Sup. Ct. Jan. 6, 2003).

America Online v. CN Productions, No. 98-552-A (E.D. Va. 2002).

The U.S. District Court for the Eastern District of Virginia awarded America Online nearly $7 million in damages from CN Productions because CN Productions sent AOL subscribers almost one billion emails that advertised adult websites. The court also granted America Online's request for an injunction against CN Productions.

Verizon Online Services v. Ralsky, 203 F. Supp. 2d 601 (E.D. Va. 2002) (denying motions to dismiss); No. 01-432-A (E.D. Va. Oct. 28, 2002).

Verizon sued Ralsky, alleging that he had sent millions of unsolicited commercial emails through Verizon's servers. On October 28, 2002, the parties reached a settlement. Although Ralsky admitted no liability for his actions, he agreed to pay an undisclosed sum to Verizon and to refrain permanently from sending bulk emails over any of Verizon's networks.

Gillman v. Sprint Communications, No. 020406640 (Utah Dist. Ct. 2003) (unpublished).

A class-action suit seeking to enforce Utah's anti-spam legislation was filed against Sprint. The suit sought damages of $10 per day for each unwanted email, plus court costs. In a decision announced February 28, 2003, the court held that "the email at issue in this case does not fit the statutory definition of an 'unsolicited commercial email' under the Utah statute" and granted Sprint's motion for summary judgment.

 Intel v. Hamidi, 71 P.3d 296, 1 Cal. Rptr. 3d 32 (Cal. 2003).

The California Court of Appeal, citing recent spam cases, ruled that the time employees spend reading and blocking electronic mail messages was enough to establish the injury necessary to make out a claim for trespass to chattels, even though the messages did not harm the company's computer network. On six occasions, Hamidi, a disgruntled former Intel employee had sent messages disparaging the company to between 8,000 and 35,000 Intel employees.

On June 30, 2003, the Supreme Court of California reversed the California Court of Appeal's decision and found that Hamidi's emails did not damage Intel's computer systems such that they interfered with the use or possession of Intel's property. The court analogized the lack of productivity that Intel claimed that its employees suffered as a result of having to read Hamidi's emails to the harm that would result from receiving an unwanted letter or telephone call. In such instances, the court held, the harms were insufficient to constitute trespass to chattels.

 UPS v. John Does One-Ten, No. 103-CV-1639 (N.D. Ga. filed June 13, 2003).

On June 13, 2003, United Parcel Service filed a lawsuit against unnamed defendants claiming that they sent unsolicited commercial emails that appeared to originate from UPS email addresses. (Disguising the origin of an email is known as "spoofing.") UPS based its claims on federal and state laws that prohibit computer fraud and racketeering. As of December 31, 2003, the parties were still conducting discovery in the case.

 Featherston v. Lightfoot, No. 02-2-32024-4SEA (Wash. Super. Ct. Aug. 20, 2003).

Lord Nigel Featherston sued Ohio-based spammers under Washington's anti-spam law. Featherston is an anti-spam activist who had shut down some spammers' websites. As retribution, defendants "spoofed" his email address in the "from" line of spam messages, resulting in more than 58,000 messages in his inbox when mis-addressed messages were bounced back. Although Featherston could have sought penalties of about $29 million under the statute, his complaint sought only $250,000 in damages. In August 2003 the court granted his motion for default judgment, awarding him his requested damages.

 Amazon.com Inc. v. Cyberpower Party Ltd., No. CV032620 (W.D. Wash., filed Aug. 8, 2003).

Amazon's suit against Cyberpower is one of eleven lawsuits against named and unnamed defendants recently filed by Amazon.com in six states and Canada. Amazon.com is seeking injunctive relief and as yet unspecified damages against spammers who engage in "spoofing"—that is, altering the "From:" line of an email message to mask the true identity of the sender—using "Amazon.com" in the place of the spammer's name. One of Amazon's claims against the spammers is for trespass to chattels, based on the allegation that by spoofing Amazon's domain name, the spammers caused innumerable bounce-back messages to be routed to Amazon's servers, putting a burden on its systems.

Earthlink Inc. v. John Does 1-25 (N.D. Ga. filed Aug. 27, 2003).

Earthlink Inc. filed suit in federal court against two groups that engage in extensive email marketing, alleging that the groups used stolen and false credit card and bank account numbers to purchase fraudulently hundreds of email accounts from Earthlink. The groups would then use the accounts to send large amounts of unsolicited email to legitimate Earthlink subscribers. The complaint alleges violations of numerous federal laws, including the Electronic Communications and Privacy Act, the Computer Fraud and Abuse Act, and the Lanham Act, and seeks a minimum of $5 million in damages.

Robert Braver, who operates a web-hosting, email and Internet business, became the first person to bring suit under Oklahoma's spam law when he sued three email marketers in December 2003. The statute prohibits the transmission of emails with missing or invalid header or routing information, and also requires that all unsolicited commercial emails be identified as "ADV" in the subject line. It also permits ISPs to recover $25,000 per day for violations. Braver has previously gained notoriety for bringing anti junk-fax lawsuits. *See* Press Release, Robert Braver, "Oklahoma Email Provider Files More Suits Against Spammers" (Dec. 4, 2003), *at* http://www.mail-archive.com/suespammers@spamcon.org/msg01566.html.

A resident of Washington brought suit under that state's spam law against Commonwealth Marketing Group, Inc., a Pennsylvania company, claiming the defendant sent him over 1,200 unsolicited email messages. The plaintiff sought $500 for each unwanted email, for aggregate damages of $600,000. The suit, filed in December 2003, alleges that the messages were false and misleading because they were designed to make the recipient believe he would be applying for a major credit card while they were actually advertisements for defendant's own products and credit services. The defendant has countered that the suit is a scam and that the plaintiff actually solicited the messages. *See* Torsten Ove, "Local Telemarketer Embroiled Again, This Time over Spam," PITTSBURGH. POST-GAZETTE (Jan. 4, 2004), *available at* http://www.post-gazette.com/pg/04004/257517.stm.

FTC Enforcement Efforts

On February 12, 2002, the Federal Trade Commission announced a three-point program designed to crack down on deceptive spam under its general statutory mandate to prohibit false or deceptive trade practices. The announcement reported: (1) the settlement of charges against seven defendants accused of distributing a deceptive email chain letter that promised returns of $46,000 on an investment of $5; (2) the issuance of warning letters to more than 2,000 individuals suspected of continuing to run this same email chain letter scheme; and (3) the launch of a consumer-education effort, co-sponsored by various ISP associations, to warn email users about the dangers of illegal chain mail. *See* Press Release, "FTC Launches Crackdown on Deceptive Junk Email" (Feb. 12, 2002), *available at* http://www.ftc.gov/opa/2002/02/eileenspam1.htm.

As part of its plan to reduce illegal email chain letters, the FTC has targeted open relays for elimination. Open relays are mail servers that forward email for anyone, allowing spammers to send large quantities of email. In a letter to open relay operators, the FTC outlined the problems associated with open relays and requested that the operators close their relays.

Howard Beales, the Director of the FTC's Bureau of Consumer Protection, indicated that the Commission planned to "launch a systematic attack on fraudulent and deceptive spam." Speaking at the Second Annual Privacy & Data Security Summit on January 31, 2002, Beales told conference attendees that his bureau would work on cases involving false opt-out mechanisms and misleading unsubscribe links that only serve to verify and confirm the validity of a spam recipient's email address.

The FTC, in conjunction with other federal agencies, participates in the Department of Justice's ongoing investigation known as "Operation E-Con." The Operation has led to the arrests of more than 130 people allegedly involved in online auction scams, identity theft, business opportunity frauds, and intellectual property theft. As a result, the FTC has seized more than $17 million in assets. See David McGuire, "Gov't Cracks Down on Internet Scammers," WASHINGTON POST (May 16, 2003), *available at* http://www.washingtonpost.com/ac2/wp-dyn/A60804-2003May15?language=html.

In its quest to reduce spam, in 1998 the FTC established a spam database, to which people can forward spam emails they have received. The FTC's database is the most comprehensive spam database in the world. By the fall of 2002, it contained over 20 million messages received at a rate of approximately 70,000 messages per day. "FTC: Where Spam Goes Off to Die" (Nov. 5, 2002), *at* http://www.wired.com/new/politics/0,1283,55972,00.html.

The FTC has taken steps to protect its own email servers from unwanted commercial email by using "blacklists" to filter email. Businesses and individuals employ "blacklists"—lists of suspected spammers from whose email addresses a server will not accept incoming email—to curb the flow of spam. However, the FTC's use of third-party blacklists to filter email sent to its servers raised concerns about First Amendment rights to petition the government. Because the FTC uses email for much of its communication with the public (*e.g.*, for receiving comments for rulemaking proceedings and requests for information under the Freedom of Information Act), critics claim that the FTC's use of a blacklist unconstitutionally interferes with the public's right to communicate with the government. Officials in the FTC, however, defend the use of blacklists as a method of filtering pornography and damaging viruses. Declan McCullagh, "Public Access to FTC Hurt by Spam Lists," CNET News.com (Nov. 26, 2002), *at* http://news.com.com/2100-1023_3-975473.html. As of December 2003, no lawsuit had been filed or action taken to limit or eliminate the FTC's use of blacklists.

Self-Regulation

In March 2003, the Internet Research Task Force convened the first meeting of its Anti-Spam Research Group in San Francisco. The Research Group aims to develop a more systematic and research-based framework for combating spam. Its first step is to formulate a more uniform definition of "spam." At this meeting, termed the "JamSpam Forum," representatives from Yahoo, Dell, Oracle, Microsoft, Sun Microsystems, AOL, and DoubleClick gathered to discuss ways to combat spam. Suggestions put forth at this meeting included email authentication standards, the closing of open relays, and more transparency. *See* Stefanie Olsen, "Tech Firms Tackle Spam," CNET News.com (Mar. 14, 2003), *at* http://news.com.com/2100-1032-992759.html.

The Direct Marketing Association (DMA) has teamed up with the FBI to initiate Operation Slam Spam. Under the program, the DMA will actively assist law enforcement agencies in the investigation and identification of spammers who are violating current spam laws by providing technical expertise and resources. Press Release, Direct Marketing Association, "DMA Statement Re: Operation Slam Spam" (Aug. 22, 2003), *at* http://www.the-dma.org/cgi/disppressrelease?article=484.

The DMA, the American Association of Advertising Agencies (AAAA), and the Association of National Advertisers have also announced guidelines for proper marketing via electronic mail. In October 2003, the three organizations laid out guidelines that they said were meant to distinguish between legitimate marketing messages and spam. Among other things, the set of nine guidelines calls for every commercial email to clearly identify its subject matter in the subject line and to include a valid address for the sender, as well as a notice on how recipients can opt out of receiving future emails. The guidelines are available from the AAAA website at http://www.aaaa.org/downloads/bulletins/6302.pdf.

Also in October 2003, three leading interactive associations announced a joint agreement against the sending of spam. The Interactive Advertising Bureau, Network Advertising Initiatives' Email Service Provider Coalition, and TRUSTe released the "Email Marketing Pledge," which requires the receipt of informed consent from the recipient prior to sending commercial email. The Pledge also establishes concrete definitions of spam, prior business relationships, informed consent, and various forms of opt-in mechanisms for email. It even goes as far as to say that commercial email should not be sent unless there is a prior business relationship or informed consent from the recipient. A full copy of the Pledge is available at http://www.networkadvertising.org/espc/pledge.asp.

Blacklists

Mail Abuse Prevention Systems, LLC (MAPS), maintains a real-time "Blackhole List" of entities it considers to be spammers, and distributes it to ISPs, which use the list to block electronic mail from those listed. MAPS has faced a number of lawsuits from companies that objected to being listed on the Blackhole List. In January 2001, a federal district court in Massachusetts ruled that a plaintiff was unlikely to prevail in a defamation charge because of MAPS's truth defense. *Media3 Technologies LLC v. Mail Abuse Prevention System LLC*, No. 00-CV-12524-MEL, 2001 U.S. Dist. LEXIS 1310 (D. Mass. Jan. 2, 2001).

In August 2000, a federal trial court in New York similarly rejected a motion for preliminary injunction, finding that the plaintiff would suffer no irreparable harm from being listed by MAPS. *Harris Interactive Inc. v. Mail Abuse Prevention System, LLC*, No. 00-CV-6364L(F) (W.D.N.Y. August 8, 2000). However, in November 2000, the U.S. District Court for the District of Colorado entered a temporary injunction preventing MAPS from listing Exactis.com (now Experian Emarketing, Inc.) on the Blackhole List, on the ground that Exactis.com was likely to be able to prove its claim that MAPS's listing unlawfully interfered with Exactis's business relationships. *Exactis.com, Inc. v.*

Mail Abuse Prevention System, LLC, No 00-K-2250 (D. Colo. Nov. 20, 2000). MAPS settled the lawsuit by agreeing not to list the company again without first obtaining leave from the court.

EMarketersAmerica, a group of email marketers, sued Spews.org, a nonprofit organization dedicated to protecting consumers from spam, for causing undue financial harm by publishing the marketers' IP addresses on a publicly available "blacklist." *EMarketersAmerica v. Spews.org*, No. 03-80295 (S.D. Fla., filed Apr. 14, 2003). Internet service providers used Spews.org's blacklist for their email filters. In September 2003 Emarketers voluntarily dismissed the suit.

The Email Service Providers Coalition has established a forum to which people can report email that they believe a filter has mistakenly blocked. One Internet user has sued Earthlink for $2 million after it allegedly terminated his email service after concluding that he was a spammer. *Hall v. Earthlink Network, Inc.* No. 98 Civ. 5489 (S.D.N.Y., filed July 30, 1998), *available at* http://www.epic.org/privacy/internet/ hall-complaint-798.html. The trial court heard arguments on plaintiff's motion for summary judgment on June 27, 2003. As of December 31, 2003, no decision had been rendered by the court.

A hosting company won a temporary restraining order against AOL enjoining it from blocking email from the company to AOL subscribers. CI Host, a Texas-based web-hosting business, sued AOL in state court in Texas for defamation, interference with contractual rights and prospective contractual rights, and unfair competition, alleging that AOL wrongly accused it of promoting the sending of spam to AOL customers. The restraining order prohibits AOL from blocking email to AOL subscribers from CI Host IP addresses, communicating with CI Host customers, and from publishing any information about CI Host. *See* Aman Batheja, "CI Host Says AOL Blocking, Sues," FORT WORTH STAR-TELEGRAM (Aug. 22, 2003), *available at* http://www.dfw.com/mld/startelegram/ news/local/6597267.htm. On August 29, 2003, the suit was removed to federal court on AOL's motion based on diversity jurisdiction. No decision had been reached in the case as of December 31, 2003.

Remedial Measures

Some Internet service providers have been redesigning their systems to meet the challenges of spam. For example, Earthlink has a challenge-response system that is intended to impede a spammer's ability to send automatically generated emails. Earthlink's challenge-response system is designed to filter out emails sent by automated means: when an email is sent to a challenge-response user (who has registered as such a user with Earthlink), Earthlink automatically sends an email back to the sender, requiring that the sender verify that he or she is a live person. Once the sender verifies this by re-typing a word that appears in the email, the original message is sent on to the recipient. The system will also recognize future emails from that sender and not require the sender to verify those future messages. The main problem the challenge-response system faces is that recipients may believe that the verification request is itself spam and not respond, causing legitimate emails to be lost. *See* Jonathan Krim, "EarthLink to Offer Anti-Spam Email System," WASHINGTON POST (May 7, 2003), at E01.

Microsoft and Yahoo have instituted "image blocking," which allows users to turn off images within emails that would otherwise allow the sender to confirm that the user has opened the email. In March 2003, Microsoft also began limiting the number of emails that its Hotmail subscribers may send within one day to 100 messages, to minimize the likelihood that spammers will use its servers to send mass unsolicited emails. *See* Evan Hansen, "Microsoft Unveils New Antispam Tools" (May 7, 2003), *at* http://news.com.com/2100-1025-1000417.html.

Yahoo also announced plans to launch a new spam "scrubber," software that would embed a secure, private key in a message header when an email message is sent. The system receiving the email would check an Internet database for the public key registered to the domain sending the email. If the public key is able to decrypt the private key embedded in the message, the email then would be delivered. If there is no match, the email is blocked. For the program to be effective, it would probably require widespread use by e-marketers because otherwise a legitimate organization that does not use the software would have its emails blocked. Yahoo said it hopes to be able to launch the software some time in 2004. *See* Cynthia L. Webb, "Scrubbing Away the Stain of Spam," WASHINGTON POST (Dec. 8, 2003), *at* http://www.washingtonpost.com/wp-dyn/articles/A45495-2003Dec8.html.

America Online maintains a "report spam" button that its subscribers can use to flag messages that have evaded AOL's email filters. In March 2003, AOL reported that despite the fact that it was blocking more than one billion unsolicited messages per day, the number of unsolicited commercial emails getting through to its subscribers had doubled in six months. AOL has also made technical changes to its network to block spam that uses the Windows "messenger service," a Windows feature intended to allow network administrators to send text-only messages to their users. The messages appear in dialog boxes on users' screens. Some spammers have developed a program that uses the feature to send bulk commercial messages. *See* Robert Lemos, "AOL Blocks Messenger Spam," CNET News.com (Nov. 25, 2002), *at* http://news.com.com/2100-1023-975298.html. Most recently, AOL broadened its definition of "spam" to include unsolicited commercial messages transmitted via instant messaging and chat postings. The revised definition will only affect U.S. subscribers and became effective on August 3, 2003. Those who send spam using instant messaging or chat postings are subject to cancellation of their membership or, potentially, prosecution under applicable laws. *See* Jim Hu, "AOL: Spam and Chat Don't Mix," CNET News.com (July 9, 2003), *at* http://news.com.com/2100-1032-1024010.html.

CipherTrust, an email security company, has developed a spam archive similar to the one that the FTC maintains. Individuals can forward their spam to the archive so that makers of anti-spam tools have samples on which to test their newly developed products. *See* Stefanie Olsen, "Tech Firms Tackle Spam," CNET News.com (Mar. 14, 2003), *at* http://news.com.com/2100-1032-992759.html.

Some ISPs also maintain "Whitelists." These are essentially the inverse of blacklists: they are lists of legitimate mass email senders maintained by ISPs. Email that one of these mailers attempts to send through the ISPs' servers are supposed to be automatically accepted. The purpose of these lists is to allow legitimate emailers (such as publishers of email newsletters) to avoid having their mass emails blocked by ISPs' spam filters. Like blacklists, however, whitelists have their problems. They must be compiled over time, and offer only a partial solution to the spam problem because they are only helpful to those emailers who are able to get the ISP to add them to the list. They are also not maintained centrally, and, as such, the burden is on the email senders to get themselves on the lists of each of the ISPs that maintain them. Nonetheless, they can be a useful tool for legitimate mass mailers to help ensure that their emails are delivered.

International Spam Laws

After two years of lobbying by consumer groups and Internet service providers, in May 2002 the European Parliament passed a strict anti-spam measure, called the Telecommunications Data Protection Directive. *See* "Directive on Privacy and Electronic Communication," Directive 2002/58/EC of the European Parliament and of the Council, 2002 O.J. (L 201) 37, *available at* http://register.consilium.eu.int/pdf/en/02/st03/03636en2.pdf. The Directive adopts an opt-in approach: companies may not send unsolicited emails to prospective customers unless they have previously agreed to receive them. This approach is quite different from the largely opt-out-based U.S. spam legislation. The Directive called for each member state to adopt its own law implementing the Directive by October 31, 2003.

Italy was the first country to adopt an anti-spam law to implement the EU Directive. On September 3, 2003, the Italian government made it a crime to send unsolicited commercial email without first obtaining the informed consent of the recipient. Spammers face fines of up to 900,000 Euros and may be sentenced to prison time as well. *See* "Italy Goes Opt-in, Law States Senders of Unsolicited Bulk Email Now Face Jail" (Sept. 4, 2003), *at* http://www.spamhaus.org/news.lasso?article=10.

Britain has also taken steps to enact anti-spam legislation that complies with the Directive. Parliament passed a law that imposes fines of up to £5,000 on spammers if convicted by a magistrate. Fines that may be imposed in a jury trial are unlimited. Unlike Italy's law, however, the British statute does not provide for jail sentences for offenders. Under the law, as prescribed by the EU Directive, it is unlawful to send unsolicited commercial emails without having first established a consensual customer relationship. The law also prohibits the sending of unsolicited messages to wireless telephones. Some people have been critical of the law, however, because it does not prohibit sending unsolicited emails to businesses. *See* Alok Jha, "Unlimited Fines Threatened for Spam Emails," THE GUARDIAN (Sept. 19, 2003), *available at* http://www.guardian.co.uk/online/spam/story/0,13427,1045330,00.html. As it attempts to curb the spam problem, Britain has announced plans to combat spam on the international level by extraditing mass emailers from overseas for trial in British courts. Britain's Computer Misuse Act makes it illegal to tamper with and damage another's computer, and gives the government the power to extradite violators for trial in the U.K. According to British officials, the F.B.I. indicated that it did not see a problem with such extradition requests from Britain. *See* Bernhard Warner, "MPs Want to Extradite Overseas Spammers," YAHOO! NEWS UK & IRELAND (Oct. 30, 2003), *at* http://uk.news.yahoo.com/031030/80/eckzl.html.

As of the European Parliament's October 31, 2003 deadline, only a handful of EU nations had enacted laws addressing spam under the parameters of the Directive. In December 2003 the EU asked nine of its member countries—Belgium, Finland, France, Germany, Greece, Luxembourg, the Netherlands, Portugal, and Sweden—to explain within two months how they intend to comply with the law. The EU said that a failure on the part of these countries to comply with the Directive could result in legal action in the European Court of Justice. *See* "EU Demands 9 States Add E-Privacy Law," YAHOO!

NEWS UK & IRELAND (Dec. 5, 2003), *at* http://uk.news.yahoo.com/031205/80/egcdc.html.

Sweden responded to the EU's challenge to enact spam legislation by proposing an anti-spam measure in December 2003. Under the proposed legislation, the government would be empowered to issue fines of up to five million kroner (US$673,000) for sending unsolicited commercial email. The law also would prohibit sending messages to wireless telephones. *See* "Sweden Proposes Drastic Fines for Spammers," YAHOO! NEWS UK & IRELAND (Dec. 4, 2003), *at* http://uk.news.yahoo.com/031204/323/eg9gx.html.

One of the toughest stances against spam has been taken by Australia. On December 2, 2003, the Australian Senate, following action in the nation's House of Representatives two months earlier, passed the Spam Bill 2003. The legislation allows for penalties of up to AU$1.1million per day to be imposed on spammers. Among other things, the law requires that: recipients consent to receive commercial email; sender information in emails be accurate; and emails contain a functioning unsubscribe feature. It also contains a ban on email address harvesting, and has a flexible regime for the imposition of civil sanctions. A copy of the law is available at http://parlinfoweb.aph.gov.au/piweb/Repository/Legis/Bills/Linked/18090301.pdf.

South Korea has taken a governmental and self-regulatory approach to combating spam. In February 2003, the Korean Ministry of Information and Communication announced that it would introduce an opt-in system that would require organizations to acquire recipients' consent before sending commercial emails. Prior to this announcement, South Korea had used an opt-out system that allowed organizations to send mass emails as long as the recipient did not indicate a desire to be removed from the mailing list. See Jong sik Kong, "Prior Consent of Receivers Are Required for Sending a [sic] Mass Emails" (Feb. 20, 2003), *at* http://english.donga.com/srv/service.php3?bicode=020000&biid=2003022189018. In addition, three wireless telephone companies in South Korea now offer a service to block unsolicited commercial messages from appearing as text messages on wireless telephones.

In Japan, legislation enacted in July 2002 requires that unsolicited commercial emails be labeled with "unsolicited advertising" in the subject line. Invoking the statute, DoCoMo, a major mobile phone service provider in Japan, obtained a ¥6.57 million (US$54,420) judgment in March 2003 after spammers sent large quantities of email to randomly generated email addresses. Email sent to randomly generated email addresses that did not actually exist cost DoCoMo ¥4 million to return. See "DoCoMo Wins Spam-Mail Fight" (Mar. 25, 2003), *at* http://www.cnn.com/2003/BUSINESS/asia/03/25/docomo.reut.

Taiwan is considering legislation that would crack down on spam. In December 2003, the Taiwan Ministry of Justice submitted an amendment to Taiwan's Law for the Protection of Computer-managed Personal Information that would specifically address spam. The amendment would require that spammers ask for consent from recipients the first time they send an unsolicited commercial email, and would impose fines of between NT$20,000 and NT$200,000 on parties who continue to send spam without having received consent. Under the amendment, ISPs would also be required to provide information about the sender if a recipient requests such information for an email that does not contain the sender's identity or a return email address. *See* Jimmy Chuang, "Internet Spammers, Junk Mailers to Face Stiff New Fines," TAIPAI TIMES (Dec. 18,

2003), at 2, *available at* http://www.taipeitimes.com/News/Taiwan/archives/2003/12/18/ 2003080008.

With the proliferation of global efforts to combat spam, there has been much discussion about the need for international cooperation. European countries have acknowledged the difficulty of enforcing their spam laws, alleging that much of the spam received by their citizens originates from overseas, mainly from the United States. The anti-spam organization spamhaus.org alleges that 90% of spam received by individuals in the United Kingdom originates in the U.S. *See* "United States Set to Legalize Spam on 1 January 2004," Spamhaus.org, *at* http://www.spamhaus.org/news.lasso?article=150.

One approach to improving international cooperation has been proposed by The Organization for Economic Cooperation and Development (OECD), which has drafted Guidelines for Protecting Consumers from Fraudulent and Deceptive Commercial Practices Across Borders. (OECD is an organization made up of 30 leading industrialized nations, including the United States.) The Guidelines are not binding on any of the member nations, but they do recommend how governments can cooperate to combat consumer fraud. While they do not mention spam specifically, the Guidelines were drafted to address problems created by Internet fraud and commercial email. *See* Lawrence J. Speer, "OECD Sets New Consumer Guidelines to Fight Cross-Border Internet Fraud," 8 ELEC. COMMERCE & LAW REP. (BNA) 637 (2003). Guidelines available at http://www.oecd.org/dataoecd/24/19/2956420.pdf.

The United States and the United Kingdom have also acknowledged the need for inter-governmental cooperation at the legislative level. In December 2003, two U.S. Senators and three members of Britain's parliament sent a joint letter to the U.S. Commerce Secretary and British Secretary of State for Trade and Industry, calling for bilateral efforts to eradicate spam. The letter acknowledged the tendency of spammers to target overseas consumers, and encouraged international enforcement efforts to combat fraud, illegal sales of prescription drugs, and child pornography. *See* "U.S., U.K. Call for Spam Pact," News.com.au (Dec. 10, 2003), *at* http://www.news.com.au/common/story_page/ 0,4057,8122770%255E15306,00.html.

National "Do Not Call" List

On June 27, 2003, the Federal Trade Commission launched its national "Do Not Call" registry. Telemarketers are prohibited from making calls to the residential telephone lines of those who have registered for the Do Not Call list. Many people predict that one result of this program will be a marked increase in spam, as direct marketers look to email addresses to replace newly off-limits telephone numbers. The list has been enormously popular; as many as 158 telephone numbers were registered every second on the first day the list was made available to the public. David Ho, "Do-Not-Call List Grows to More Than 10M," A.P. (July 1, 2003). The FTC was to begin enforcement of the list on October 1, 2003; however, legal challenges to the FTC's authority to enforce the Do Not Call list delayed full implementation of the list until October 7, 2003. Press Release, Statement of FTC Chairman Timothy J. Muris, "Court Rules FTC Can Proceed with Do Not Call Registry" (Oct. 7, 2003), available at http://www.ftc.gov/ opa/2003/10/dncgrant.htm. On October 16, 2003, the FTC reported that the Do Not Call list contained 53.7 million telephone numbers, and more than 15,000 consumers had, by that time, already filed complaints against telemarketers for violations. Press Release, FTC, "Consumers on Do Not Call Registry File Over 15,000 Complaints Against

Telemarketers" (Oct. 16, 2003). In December 2003 the FTC issued its first citation to a company for calling individuals whose numbers were registered on the Do Not Call list, although the violator was not immediately fined because it did not hold an FCC license.

Internet Advertising

Since popularization of the Internet began in the mid-1990s, media and marketing companies have sought to tap the power of the Internet to deliver highly targeted advertising that is relevant to consumers and effective for advertisers. But the very strengths that make the Internet a promising advertising medium have raised concerns about fairness from regulators, consumer advocates, and competitors of Internet advertisers. Although it has been relatively easy to see how consumer protection laws of broad application apply in this new medium, it is less clear how other laws that may impact advertising will be applied to online conduct in the coming years.

Policing Fraudulent Advertising

There is no doubt that consumer protection laws of broad application, such as the FTC's mandate to police "unfair or deceptive acts or practices," apply to Internet marketing. The FTC has taken an active role in combating fraud perpetrated through the Internet. As early as 1998, the FTC announced its belief that "it is important to address Internet fraud now, before it discourages new consumers from going online and chokes off the impressive commercial growth now in progress and potential for innovation on the Internet." *Consumer Protection in Cyberspace: Combating Fraud on the Internet: Hearing Before the House Comm. on Commerce, Subcomm. on Telecommunications, Trade, and Consumer Protection*, 105th Cong. 1998 (prepared statement of Eileen Harrington, Associate Director of the Consumer Protection Bureau, Federal Trade Commission).

This goal has been supported by the FTC and similar state agencies that enforce the rights of consumers against fraudulent advertisers. When Congress preempted most state spam laws with the CAN SPAM Act of 2003, it was careful to not to disturb the right of states to police Internet fraud. Specifically, although the CAN SPAM Act preempts state anti-spam laws to the extent they regulate the sending of commercial email, the Act makes clear that state laws that relate to acts of fraud or computer crime remain unaffected by the Act.

Over the last few years, the FTC has taken steps to combat Internet fraud and deceptive online advertising practices in a number of different areas, including:

- Collaborating in a joint effort with other federal agencies and state attorneys general to crack down on various "cyberscams," including curtailing the practices of websites that advertised envelope-stuffing work-at-home opportunities but then did not provide consumers with the materials advertised, as well as shutting down a "discount" web-hosting business that was imposing extra charges on consumers' credit cards after they subscribed to the hosting company's services. *See* FTC Release, "Federal, State, Local Netforce Targets Cyberscams" (July 30, 2002), *at* http://www.ftc.gov/opa/2002/07/mwnetforce.htm.

- Charging online sellers of generic and remanufactured inkjet printer cartridge refills with deceptively representing on their websites that the products were new, brand-name items. *See* FTC Release, "On-line Sellers of Inkjet Printer Cartridge

Refills Agree to Pay $40,000 Civil Penalty to Settle with the FTC" (Aug. 23, 2002), *at* http://www.ftc.gov/opa/2002/08/ebabylon.htm.

- Promoting "Operation Cure.All," an initiative begun in 1997 to target deceptive and misleading Internet promotion of products and services that promise to cure or treat serious diseases or conditions. *See* FTC Release, *FTC Testifies on the Internet Sale of Prescription Drugs from Domestic Web Sites*, Mar. 27, 2003, *at* http://www.ftc.gov/opa/2003/03/onlinepharm.htm.

- Joining forces with the attorneys general of 29 states to undertake "Operation Bidder Beware," which targets fraudulent Internet auction practices, targeting scams in which winning bidders have sent payment but never received the merchandise they paid for, and attempting to close fraudulent escrow services. *See* FTC Release, "Internet Auction Fraud Targeted by Law Enforcers" (Apr. 30, 2003), *at* http://www.ftc.gov/opa/2003/04/bidderbeware.htm.

- Monitoring online retailers that are subject to the FTC's Mail or Telephone Order Rule. The rule requires that sellers ship products to buyers within the time specified in their advertisements. In November 2003 the FTC sent letters to 37 online retailers that were making "quick ship" claims (that is, promises to ship an order within 24 to 48 hours) and rebate offers in connection with Internet sales, reminding them that they need to abide by FTC rules. Under these rules, if a seller will not be able to meet the promised shipping deadlines, it must inform the consumer and provide an opportunity to cancel the order. *See* FTC Release, "FTC 'Surf' of 51 Internet Retailers Designed to Bolster Consumer Confidence in Online Shopping" (Nov. 10, 2003), *at* http://www.ftc.gov/opa/2003/11/holidaysmarts.htm.

- Engaging in collective efforts with other federal agencies, including the Securities and Exchange Commission and the Department of Justice, to stop a wide variety of deceptive Internet schemes and illegal scams, including bogus business opportunities, deceptive money-making scams, illegal advance-fee credit card offers, and identity theft. *See* FTC Release, "Law Enforcement Posse Tackles Internet Scammers, Deceptive Spammers" (May 15, 2003), *at* http://www.ftc.gov/opa/2003/05/swnetforce.htm.

- Charging operators of an Internet-based business that promised substantial income to individuals who invested in an Internet shopping mall with conducting an illegal pyramid scam. In a complaint brought in the United States District Court for the District of Arizona, the FTC alleged that the defendants deceptively represented that consumers who participated in the business would earn a substantial amount of money, when, in fact, most of the investors lost money. The defendants were also alleged to have provided deceptive marketing material to affiliates, thereby providing those affiliates with a way to deceive consumers. *See* FTC Release, "FTC Charges Internet Mall Is a Pyramid Scheme" (July 7, 2003), *at* http://www.ftc.gov/opa/2003/07/nexgen.htm.

Contextual Marketing: Paid Search and Targeted Pop-Ups

Marketers have long sought ways to target their advertisements to those consumers who are most interested in their products. Magazine publishers and cable networks, for example, typically target narrower segments of the population than television broadcasters and daily newspapers. Database marketers have long marketed products and services to consumers based on profiles of individual consumers they have developed over time. Supermarkets regularly give customers who have just bought one product a cash-register-generated coupon for a competing product. Various companies are trying to use the Internet to deliver highly targeted advertising to consumers based on the interests they demonstrate through the search terms they include in search-engine queries, the websites they visit, and the pages within those sites that attract their attention. But the competitors of those who have employed these new ad targeting technologies sometimes object to mechanisms the marketing companies use to target advertising and to the way in which these ads are presented. Their objections have focused on trademark and copyright law, but have also included state-law claims ranging from unfair competition to trespass to chattels. Some of the leading cases are discussed below.

Paid Search: Keyword Triggered Advertising

Marketers can take an educated guess about what a consumer is interested in by observing the search terms that the consumer enters in a search-engine query. Many of the major search engines offer advertisers an opportunity to "buy" particular search terms so that their ads are shown to consumers who use these terms in their queries. When the search terms used to trigger ads are, or include, the trademarks of an advertiser's competitors, those competitors may complain that the process by which these ads are targeted infringes and/or dilutes their trademarks.

Nissan Motor Co. v. Nissan Computer Corp., 204 F.R.D. 460 (C.D. Cal. 2001).

The plaintiff, Nissan Motor, has held several U.S. registered trademarks including the word mark "Nissan" since 1959. The defendant, Nissan Computer Corp., was founded in 1991 by Uzi Nissan, who had used his name in connection with several businesses since 1980. In the mid-1990s, Nissan Computer registered its logo as a trademark in North Carolina and registered the domain names nissan.com and nissan.net, which resolved to Nissan Computer's website. Nissan Motor "purchased" the search terms "nissan" and "nissan.com" from various search engine operators to ensure that users searching for such terms would be directed to its website rather than the website of Nissan Computer. Nissan Computer alleged that this action by Nissan Motor constituted unlawful appropriation of the search terms. The court found that because Nissan Motor had a "valid, protectable trademark interest in the 'Nissan' mark," Nissan Motor could not be held liable for purchasing these search terms even though Nissan Computer held the registrations to the nissan.com and nissan.net domain names.

Google, Inc. v. American Blind & Wallpaper Factory, Inc., No. 5:03-CV-05340-JF (N.D. Cal. filed Nov. 26, 2003).

Internet search engine Google filed a declaratory judgment action seeking court approval of its practice that allows its advertisers to include trademarks of their competitors as keyword search terms to trigger their own advertisements in Google search results. Under Google's "AdWords" program, advertisers purchase advertising links associated with certain keywords. Google then posts links to these advertisers' sites in the margins of its results page whenever a user types a search query that includes the keywords. American Blind & Wallpaper had complained that several of its competitors had purchased advertising keywords from Google that used American Blind's trademarks. American Blind contends that this practice violates the Lanham Act.

Although Google agreed to prohibit the use of some of the American Blind marks, it contends that some other of the American Blind marks are descriptive terms that other advertisers have the right to use. It thus seeks a declaratory judgment that its current policy regarding the sale of keyword-triggered advertising does not constitute trademark infringement.

See also Playboy Enterprises, Inc. v. Netscape Communications Corp., et al., 55 F. Supp. 2d 1070 (C.D. Cal. 1999), *aff'd* 202 F.3d 278 (9th Cir. 1999) (holding that sale by defendant search engines of plaintiff's trademarks "playboy" and "playmate" as keyword search terms to prompt banner advertisements for competitors' adult entertainment websites was not a use in commerce" under Lanham Act because the terms were common, English words in their own right); *Mark Nutritionals Inc. v. FindWhat Services Inc.*, No. SA-02-CA-0085-OG (W.D. Tex. filed Jan. 31, 2002); *Mark Nutritionals Inc. v. Overture Services Inc.*, No. SA-02-CA-0086-OG (W.D. Tex. filed Jan. 31, 2002); *Mark Nutritionals Inc. v. Alta Vista Co.*, No. SA-02-CA-0087-EP (W.D. Tex. filed Jan. 31, 2002); *Mark Nutritionals Inc. v. Innovative Marketing Solutions Inc. d/b/a Kanoodle.com*, No. SA-02-CA-0088-OG (W.D. Tex. filed Jan. 31, 2002) (actions against search engines by company that markets the Body Solutions weight-loss program claiming that search engines' practices of allowing advertisers to purchase the rights to have their websites listed first when users enter the search terms "body" and "solutions" violates the Lanham Act); *Metaspinner GmbH v. Google Deutschland GmbH*, Landgericht Hamburg, No. 312 O 887/03 Nov. 14, 2003 (German court) (granting temporary injunction to stop "preisserver.de" website's use of plaintiff's trademark "preispiraten" as a keyword in a sponsored link to the site).

Targeted Pop-Ups

Pop-up format ads (and their cousins, pop-under ads) are a ubiquitous annoyance on the Internet. Several suits have alleged that when pop-ups are served to users who have shown at interest in the products or services of the advertiser's competitors, or when the ads pop up in front of a website being displayed on a user's computer screen, without permission from the website being displayed, these ads are unlawful. To date, the results of these cases have been mixed.

Washingtonpost.newsweek Interactive Co., LLC, et al. v. Gator Corp., C.A. No. 02-909-A, 2002 U.S. Dist. LEXIS 20881 (E.D. Va. 2002).

The plaintiff news organizations complained that Gator violated their copyright and trademark rights by displaying pop-up format ads to computer users who were visiting the plaintiffs' websites. Gator had developed and deployed software that would track a user's Internet activity and deliver pop-ups that Gator determined would be of interest to the user based on the user's past Internet usage. The publishers claimed that Gator violated their trademark rights because computer users saw Gator's pop-ups at the same time as they saw the publishers' trademarks on their respective websites and were therefore confused about the source of the pop-ups. The publishers claimed that display of the pop-ups in front of their web pages created unauthorized derivative works that violated the copyright rights. A federal judge focused on the trademark claims in concluding that the plaintiffs had established a likelihood of prevailing on the merits of their claims; he entered a preliminary injunction prohibiting Gator from displaying ads to users visiting the plaintiffs' websites. The case was settled in February 2003 without any written opinion evaluating Gator's conduct or the plaintiffs' legal theories. The terms of the settlement were not disclosed.

A number of lawsuits challenging Gator's practices have been consolidated for discovery in federal court in Atlanta. *Gator Corp. v. Gator Corp.*, No. 1:03md01517 (N.D. Ga., filed Aug. 20, 2003), consolidating for discovery: *United Parcel Service v. Gator Corp.*, No. 1:02cv02639 (N.D. Ga., filed Sept. 26, 2002); *Six Continents Hotel v. Gator Corp.*, No. 1:02cv03065 (N.D. Ga., filed Nov. 12, 2002); *Gator Corp. v. L.L. Bean, Inc.*, No. 1:03cv01198 (N.D. Ga., filed May 2, 2003); *Gator Corp. v. PriceGrabber.com*, No. 1:03cv01302 (N.D. Ga., filed May 2, 2003); *Lendingtree, Inc. v. Gator Corp.*, No. 1:03cv01224 (N.D. Ga., filed May 6, 2003); *Extended Stay America v. Gator Corp.*, No. 1:03cv01225 (N.D. Ga., filed May 6, 2003); *Gator Corp. v. Tiger Direct, Inc.*, No. 1:03cv01260 (N.D. Ga., filed May 8, 2003); *Gator Corp. v. Extended Stay America*, No. 1:03cv01303 (N.D. Ga., filed May 8, 2003); *Tigerdirect, Inc. v. Gator Corp.*, No. 1:03cv01273 (N.D. Ga., filed May 9, 2003); *Hertz Corp. v. Gator Corp.*, No. 1:03cv01973 (N.D. Ga., filed July 14, 2003); *True Communication v. Gator Corp.*, No. 1:03cv02297 (N.D. Ga., filed July 30, 2003); *Gator Corp. v. Gator Corp. Wells Fargo & Co. v. Gator Corp.*, No. 1:03cv02709 (N.D. Ga., filed Sept. 11, 2003); *Overstock.com v. Gator Corp.*, No. 1:03cv02810 (N.D. Ga., filed Sept. 17, 2003).

TGC Corp. v. PC Pitstop, LLC, Case No. 5:03-cv-04167 (N.D. Cal. filed Sept. 11, 2003).

Adware company Claria (formerly Gator), owner and distributor of the Gator software program, recently settled a suit against a critic of its Gator program who labeled it "spyware" and sold software tools designed to remove Gator from users' computer systems. Claria has been aggressively suing critics and anti-spyware advocates that have described the software as "spyware," which it contends is defamatory. Claria classifies Gator as "adware." The suit alleged that the defendant, PC Pitstop, was engaging in false advertising, unfair business practices, trade libel, defamation and tortious interference. Although the terms of the settlement were not announced, following the settlement PC Pitstop removed pages from its website that had been entitled "Is Gator Spyware?" and "Gator Boycott List." *See also* Paul Festa, "Gator Foe Bitten, But Still Not Shy," CNET News.com (Dec. 1, 2003), *at* http://news.com.com/2100-1024-5112435.html (discussing PC Pitstop's launch of new "Gator Information Center," which still recommends that computer users uninstall Gator.)

U-Haul International, Inc. v. WhenU.com, et al., 279 F. Supp. 2d 723 (E.D. Va. 2003).

Defendant WhenU.com developed and deployed software that monitors the activity within a user's web browser and serves advertisements to the user's computer desktop based on the URLs of the web pages visited by the user, the search terms the user types in search engine queries, and the content of the web pages the user views. U-Haul sued WhenU on federal copyright infringement, trademark infringement, and unfair competition theories, and on various related state-law theories, based on ads for a U-Haul competitor that WhenU served to users who were visiting the U-Haul website. In granting WhenU's motion for summary judgment on all of U-Haul's federal claims, the court emphasized that: the WhenU ads are served only to users who have installed the WhenU software pursuant to WhenU's license agreement consistent with the user's right to control his/her own computer display; and that the ads open "in a WhenU-branded window that is separate and distinct from the window in which the U-Haul website appears." The court found that the appearance of a WhenU-branded pop-up ad to a user viewing the U-Haul website does not constitute a trademark use of any U-Haul mark because WhenU does not use U-Haul's "trademarks to identify the source of its goods or services." The court analogized the simultaneous appearance of the WhenU and U-Haul marks to comparative advertising, which "does not violate trademark law, even when the advertising makes use of a competitor's trademark." The court also rejected U-Haul's copyright infringement claim. The court found that WhenU did not "display" the U-Haul website, nor did it create a derivative work based on that website when it displayed a pop-up ad in front of the page of the U-Haul site being viewed by a consumer: "To conclude otherwise is untenable in light of the fact that the user is the one who controls how items are displayed on the computer, and computer users would infringe copyrighted works any time they opened a window in front of a copyrighted Web page that is simultaneously open in a separate window." 279 F. Supp. 2d at 731. U-Haul dismissed the related state claims, but appealed the trial court's grant of summary judgment for WhenU on its trademark and copyright claims. However, U-Haul dismissed its appeal before the case was briefed or argued in the Court of Appeals.

Wells Fargo & Co. et al. v. WhenU.com, Inc., No. 03-71906, 2003 U.S. Dist. LEXIS 20756 (E.D. Mich., preliminary injunction denied Nov. 19, 2003).

Wells Fargo and Quicken Loans, which marketed the availability of mortgages on their respective websites, sued WhenU.com for serving pop-up ads for competing mortgage lenders to users who were visiting the plaintiffs' websites. Plaintiffs alleged trademark and copyright infringement and sought a preliminary injunction. In a detailed opinion accompanied by extensive factual findings, the trial court denied plaintiffs' request for an injunction, finding that plaintiffs had failed to establish a likelihood that they would succeed on the merits of their claims. Like the *U-Haul* court, the court found that the plaintiffs had failed to establish that WhenU "used" plaintiffs' trademarks in any manner actionable under trademark law, analogized the pop-ups to permissible comparative advertisements, and rejected the plaintiffs' argument that the appearance of WhenU's ads in front of plaintiffs' web pages constituted creation by WhenU of a derivative work in violation of plaintiffs' exclusive rights as copyright holders.

1-800 Contacts, Inc. v. WhenU.com, et al., No. 02 CIV 8043, 2003 U.S. Dist. LEXIS 22932, 69 U.S.P.Q.2d (BNA) 1337 (S.D.N.Y. Dec. 22, 2003).

1-800 Contacts, a retailer of contact lenses, sued WhenU.com and its advertiser, Vision Direct, complaining of pop-up ads for Vision Direct that WhenU displayed to users who were visiting the 1-800 Contacts website. Like the plaintiffs in the *U-Haul* and *Wells Fargo* cases, discussed above, 1-800 Contacts complained of trademark and copyright infringement. Plaintiff sought a preliminary injunction. Like the *U-Haul* and *Wells Fargo* courts, the trial court rejected 1-800-Contact's copyright claim, finding that the plaintiff was not likely to prevail on its derivative work theory: "to hold that computer users are limited in their use of Plaintiff's website to viewing the website without any obstructing windows or programs would be to subject countless computer users and software developers to liability for copyright infringement and contributory copyright infringement." 2003 U.S. Dist. LEXIS 22932 at *43. But unlike the *U-Haul* and *Wells Fargo* courts, the court found that the pop-up ads infringed 1-800 Contacts trademarks. The court found that WhenU "used" plaintiff's trademark in two ways: "First, in causing pop-up advertisements for Defendant Vision Direct to appear when [WhenU] users have specifically attempted to access Plaintiff's website—on which Plaintiff's trademark appears—Defendants are displaying Plaintiff's mark 'in the . . . advertising of' Defendant Vision Direct's services." 2003 U.S. Dist. LEXIS 22932 at *54. Second, "Defendant WhenU.com includes Plaintiff's URL . . . in the proprietary WhenU.com directory of terms that triggers pop-up advertisements on [WhenU] user's computers. In doing so, Defendant WhenU.com 'uses' Plaintiff's mark to advertise and publicize companies that are in direct competition with Plaintiff." 2003 U.S. Dist. LEXIS 22932 at *55. The U.S. Court of Appeals for the Second Circuit granted expedited review of the trial court's decision. *1-800 Contacts, Inc. v. WhenU.com, Inc.*, Nos. 04-0026-cv & 04-0446-cv (2d Cir., filed Jan. 7, 2004).

FTC v. D Squared Solutions, LLC, et al., No. AMD 03 CV 3108 (D. Md. filed Oct. 30, 2003).

The FTC brought suit in U.S. District Court for the District of Maryland, alleging that defendants engaged in unfair practices in violation of the Federal Trade Commission Act by using the Windows Messenger Service to send pop-up ads to unwitting Internet users. The Windows Messenger Service is a feature of Microsoft Windows that is intended to allow network administrators to provide instant information to network users, such as the need to log off the network due to a malfunction. Because of its intended purpose, the pop-up appears on the user's screen if the user is logged into the network; he or she need not be using an Internet browser. The defendants used this feature to bombard computer users with always-on Internet connections with messages advertising their pop-up blocker software. The messages sent to users would instruct users to visit the defendants' website to purchase the software. On December 15, 2003, the court denied the FTC a preliminary injunction, finding that the government had not demonstrated that the pop-ups were likely to cause substantial injury to consumers. The court set trial for March 2004.

Advertising for Internet Gambling

On June 11, 2003, the U.S. Department of Justice sent a letter to several trade organizations, including the Newspaper Association of America and the National Association of Broadcasters, warning the associations and their members that the DOJ considers it unlawful to publish advertisements for Internet gambling, whether in print, over radio or television, or on the Internet. The letter states that advertisements for gambling may violate various state and federal laws, and that entities and individuals accepting and running such advertisements may be aiding and abetting illegal activities. *See* Letter from John G. Malcolm, Deputy Assistant Attorney General, U.S. Department of Justice, to Newspaper Association of America (June 11, 2003). The letter pointed out that under federal criminal law, any person who aids or abets illegal Internet gambling activities is punishable as a principal. 18 U.S.C. § 2.

The letter to the trade organizations appears to have been just the first step in the DOJ's crackdown on illegal Internet gambling. On September 10, 2003, at the behest of DOJ, the U.S. District Court for the Eastern District of Missouri issued a subpoena for the records of at least one Internet gambling portal site. The subpoena seeks all information in the site's possession since January 1, 1997, relating to advertisements for Internet gambling. Among other things, the subpoena called for the production of information regarding all financial transactions between the site operator and any advertiser, as well as the names and identifying and contact information for each gambling advertiser with whom the site had contact. It also called for the site to produce correspondence, notes, and other planning or policy documents which referred to the letters, described above, that DOJ sent to the trade organizations. *See* "U.S. Court Subpoenas Gaming Portals," INTERACTIVE GAMING NEWS (Sept. 30, 2003), *at* http://www.igamingnews.com/index.cfm?page=artlisting&tid=4553.

Internet Pharmacies

Internet companies offering pharmaceutical products and medical services over the Internet were the target of an FTC action for deceptive trade practices. In July 2000, the FTC brought an action in the U.S. District Court for the District of Nevada against twelve defendants it alleged were falsely advertising the existence of a medical clinic and seeking potential patients' personal information over the Internet. The companies charged consumers a $75 "medical consultation" fee for the services they offered. The complaint alleged that the pharmacies were telling patients that all prescriptions were being filled on site, when it was actually sending the patients' personal information to an out-of-state physician who was filling the prescriptions. Shortly after the suit was filed, the FTC settled the case with the defendants. Among other things, the settlement prohibited the defendants from making deceptive claims and required disclosures about medical and pharmaceutical relationships. *See F.T.C. v. Rennert, et al.*, No. CV-S-00-0861 JBR (D. Nev. July 6, 2000).

In a more recent development, the Food and Drug Administration (FDA) had to ramp up monitoring of online pharmaceutical sales in the wake of the bioterrorism threats that followed the September 11, 2001 attacks on the United States. Websites began selling the drug Cipro (which was used to treat people who may have been exposed to the virus Anthrax) from their websites, but were not requiring individuals to have prescriptions for the drugs. The FDA sent "cyber letters" to these sellers, some of whom were international companies, noting that offenders could be charged $500,000 for selling drugs without prescriptions. *See* Mark Sweet, "Policing Online Pharmacies: Bioterrorism Meets the War on Drugs," 2001 Duke Law & Tech. Rev. 41 (2001), *available at* http://www.law.duke.edu/journals/dltr/articles/2001dltr0041.html.

Congress has also begun to investigate ways to curtail illicit sales of prescription drugs and narcotics by Internet pharmacies. The House Energy and Commerce Committee asked the heads of Visa International, MasterCard International, FedEx Corp. and United Parcel Service to explain how their businesses identify and address Internet pharmacy sites that use their services. The House committee also indicated that it intends to hold hearings on the Internet pharmacies in 2004 and indicated that new legislation will be introduced in an attempt to close the loopholes that allow illegal pharmacies to operate. *See* Gilbert M. Gaul and Mary Pat Flaherty, "Firms Pressed on Internet Drugs," WASHINGTON POST (Dec. 10, 2003), at A4.

'Green Card' Lottery Websites

The FTC filed a complaint against website operators who allegedly deceived consumers into thinking they were offering services of the U.S. government in connection with the State Department's annual Diversity Visa (DV) lottery. The DV lottery makes available 50,000 permanent resident visas to people with at least a high school education or two or more years of work experience in an appropriate trade who are from countries with low rates of emigration to the U.S. According to the FTC, the defendants' sites urged consumers to use defendants' services to register for the DV lottery. The defendants charged a fee for this service. Not all the information provided on the site was accurate, however; the sites invited some consumers who were not even eligible for the DV lottery to apply. There was also no guarantee that by using defendants' site consumers' applications for the DV lottery were satisfying government guidelines and would automatically be included in the lottery. Moreover, in several places on the sites the defendants allegedly expressly or implicitly held themselves out as affiliated with the U.S. government by including telephone numbers for their organization that actually belonged to the State Department.

Among other charges, the FTC charged the defendants with violations of the FTC Act for this conduct, charging them with illegally holding themselves out as a federal government agency and misrepresenting that their services would satisfy the guidelines for the lottery. On October 3, 2003, the court granted the FTC's motion for a temporary restraining order, enjoining defendants from continuing to operate their sites. *See FTC v. Global Web Solutions, Inc.*, No. 03-CV-2031-HHK (D.D.C. filed Oct. 1, 2003), *available at* http://www.ftc.gov/os/2003/10/usaiscomp.pdf.

Attorney Email Advertising

At least one state has ruled that its Rules of Professional Conduct for attorneys require that the legend "attorney advertising" must appear on law firm newsletters, brochures and emails deployed to attract new clients. The label need not be applied to law firm websites, however. The Utah State Bar Ethics Advisory Opinions Committee issued its ruling in February 2003 in response to a law firm's request for guidance as to formulating its client development efforts. The Committee said that because an email from a law firm encouraging the recipient to engage the firm in legal services can be a solicitation, it must contain the "advertising material" label. *See* "'Advertising' Notice Must Be on Material Designed to Lure Clients, but Not Web Site," 7 ELEC. COMMERCE & LAW REP. (BNA) 286 (Mar. 27, 2003).

Chapter 8: Advertising and Marketing
Summary of the Law

- Spam, as unsolicited commercial email is known, is a growing global problem for users of electronic communications; studies indicate that as of December 2003, more than 58% of all email was spam.

- Until recently, spam was regulated only at the state level. That changed with the enactment of a comprehensive federal spam law in December 2003, the CAN SPAM Act of 2003. The CAN SPAM Act preempts conflicting state law; except to the extent that they prohibit false or deceptive content in emails, state laws that otherwise regulate unsolicited commercial email are preempted by the federal Act. The CAN SPAM Act requires senders of unsolicited commercial email to provide recipients with a valid and functional mechanism to opt out of receiving future email. The opt-out mechanism can be an Internet link or working reply email address, but in either case, a consumer's request to opt out must be honored within ten business days. The statute also prohibits falsifying header information or subject lines, and creates a labeling requirement for emails with adult content. Enforcement is primarily vested with the FTC, although state attorneys general have the right to bring civil enforcement actions, as well. The statute does not provide individuals with a private right of action. The Act also requires the FTC to look into creation of a federal Do-Not-Email list similar to the recently implemented federal Do-Not-Call list.

- Since the CAN SPAM Act only took effect on January 1, 2004, it is not surprising that there is, as yet, no judicial gloss on the statute. Suits to combat spam under state laws have been brought by state attorneys general, ISPs, and individuals, with some success. The most notable is a judgment by a California court, awarding the state attorney general $2 million in damages against a spammer. Virginia recently became the first state to file criminal charges against spammers.

- There have been some industry efforts at self-regulation of spam. Several industry groups have announced guidelines for the sending of spam, although the most invasive spammers seem to pay little attention to these nonbinding guidelines. Other industry efforts to control spam include the establishment of private "blacklists" of known spammers made available to ISPs, which, in turn, may block mail from those senders. The providers of these lists have faced some lawsuits from companies claiming their legitimate messages were blocked. ISPs have also become more aggressive in fighting spam, introducing features such as challenge-response systems and Internet "scrubbers," as well as "whitelists" that are lists of legitimate commercial emailers whose messages are not to be blocked.

- Individual and corporate plaintiffs have traditional state law causes of action at their disposal to attempt to fight spam. Causes of action for trespass, invasion of privacy, computer fraud, unfair competition, and breach of contract have all been asserted against spammers, with varying degrees of success.

- International efforts at combating spam are also increasing. The EU Directive on Privacy and Electronic Communications was in effect and supposed to be adopted by all member nations by October 31, 2003, although only a few of the EU member states had adopted legislation in compliance with the Directive by that date. Unlike the U.S. CAN SPAM Act, the Directive takes an opt-in approach to spam, prohibiting unsolicited commercial email without the prior affirmative consent of recipients. Australia has also been proactive in fighting spam, adopting a law in December 2003 that imposed severe penalties for sending spam and included an opt-in regime. Many countries have also called for increased international cooperation to combat the spam problem.

- Under the FTC Act, the FTC has authority to police unfair or deceptive trade practices that occur via the Internet. The FTC has used this power to take an active role in cracking down on fraudulent Internet advertising activities. In carrying out these efforts, the FTC has targeted, among others, the practices of Internet marketers of pharmaceutical products, Internet auction sites, and Internet gambling websites.

- Contextual marketers monitor the Internet activity of computer users (analyzing the search terms they include in search engine queries, the URLs of web pages they visit and/or the words that appear on the pages they visit) and target contextually relevant advertising to users based on their apparent interests, as reflected in their Internet activity. Various website operators have sued contextual marketers on trademark and copyright theories. To date, the copyright claims have been uniformly rejected by the courts, although one federal court has found that contextually targeted pop-up format ads may violate the trademark rights of the website the computer user is visiting when the ad pops up. The first court of appeals ruling on contextual advertising could come as early as the summer of 2004.

PERSONAL JURISDICTION

Personal Jurisdiction Basics

A defendant may be sued in the state in which he or she resides. Generally, when the defendant is not a resident of the state in which the suit is brought, a court may hear the case only where the court properly exercises "personal jurisdiction" over the defendant. *World-Wide Volkswagen Corp. v. Woodson*, 444 U.S. 286, 291 (1980).

The concept of personal jurisdiction, or the power of a court to exercise authority over a defendant, serves to ensure fairness in the judicial system. For example, the requirement that a court have personal jurisdiction over the defendant prevents a plaintiff from filing claims in distant courts just to force the defendant to litigate in an inconvenient location.

Each state has a so-called "long-arm" statute that defines the circumstances under which the state's courts may exercise jurisdiction over out-of-state defendants. The reach of these long-arm statutes is circumscribed by the Due Process Clause of the United States Constitution. If the court does not have personal jurisdiction over the defendant, the court cannot enforce any judgment it may render against the defendant, and the court will dismiss the case.

Assuming the requirements of the forum state's long-arm statute are satisfied, a court may assert personal jurisdiction over a nonresident defendant through the exercise of either "specific jurisdiction" or "general jurisdiction." *Helicopteros Nacionales de Colombia, S.A. v. Hall*, 466 U.S. 408 (1984).

Specific Jurisdiction

When litigation is related to or arises out of the defendant's contacts with the forum state, a court may properly assert jurisdiction over the defendant through the exercise of specific jurisdiction. *Helicopteros*, 466 U.S. at 414. Specific jurisdiction is properly exercised over a nonresident defendant via a state's long-arm statute when the defendant has "minimum contacts" with the forum such that maintenance of the suit does not offend "traditional notions of fair play and substantial justice," and the defendant would reasonably have been able to anticipate being haled into court in the forum state. *World-Wide Volkswagen Corp.*, 444 U.S. at 291-92; *International Shoe Co. v. Washington*, 326 U.S. 310, 316 (1945). If a nonresident defendant has "purposefully directed" his or her activities toward a state's residents or businesses and benefits from the protections provided by that state's laws, then the forum has specific jurisdiction over disputes arising from those contacts. *Burger King Corp. v. Rudzewicz*, 471 U.S. 462, 472 (1985).

General Jurisdiction

When the litigation does not relate to or arise out of the defendant's contacts with the forum state, a court may properly assert jurisdiction over the defendant through the exercise of general jurisdiction. *Int'l Shoe*, 326 U.S. at 318. General jurisdiction is properly exercised over a nonresident defendant only when the defendant is present in the forum state or maintains "continuous and systematic" contacts with the state. *Helicopteros*, 466 U.S. at 414-16.

Personal Jurisdiction and the Internet

The existence of personal jurisdiction has traditionally been analyzed according to territorial concepts by which a nonresident defendant may understand that he or she is expected to abide by the forum state's legal rules. *See Digital Equipment Corp. v. AltaVista Technology, Inc.*, 960 F. Supp. 456, 462-63 (D. Mass. 1997). Commercial activities on the Internet, however, operate outside of traditional territorial boundaries. Though some magazines and a few newspapers have long enjoyed national distribution, the Internet permits immediate distribution to a national and international audience to an extent not available through other media. An online order form permits a retailer to complete sales without ever setting foot in a forum state, while a chat room may make defamatory comments available in every forum in the U.S. with minimal effort or planning on the part of the participants. Courts therefore must determine whether jurisdiction may attach over a nonresident defendant where the contacts involved are primarily (or even exclusively) electronic. In some cases, the existence of a website that is theoretically accessible by residents of a given state may be the only "contacts" the company has within that state.

Although courts have generally analyzed cyberspace jurisdictional issues using traditional jurisdictional principles, certain methods of analysis specific to cyberspace are developing. For example, courts analyzing personal jurisdiction in the web publishing context factor electronic contacts, as well as traditional physical contacts, into their analyses to determine whether they may properly exercise either specific or general jurisdiction. *See EDIAS Software International, L.L.C. v. BASIS International, Ltd.*, 947 F. Supp. 413 (D. Ariz. 1996). Courts also consider the nature of such electronic contacts: jurisdiction is more likely to be asserted in cases involving interactive websites than those involving passive websites. *See Zippo Manufacturing Co. v. Zippo Dot Com, Inc.*, 952 F. Supp. 1119 (W.D. Pa. 1997).

In addition, many courts have used an "effects test" to analyze personal jurisdiction in tort cases, considering whether the forum state is the focal point of both the harmful activity and the harm created, or, similarly, whether the defendant intended to cause injury in (and knew injurious effects would be felt in) the forum state. *See Calder v. Jones*, 465 U.S. 783 (1984).

Finally, some courts have also employed the *Keeton* test, which traditionally has been used in determining whether a court can properly exercise jurisdiction over a print publication. *Keeton v. Hustler Magazine, Inc.*, 465 U.S. 770 (1984). Under the *Keeton* test, continuous and deliberate circulation of a web publication in a forum state can subject the publisher to personal jurisdiction in that state, regardless of whether the publication was targeted to a nationwide audience. *Naxos Resources (U.S.A.) Ltd. v. Southam Inc.*, 24 Media L. Rep. 2265 (C.D. Cal. May 30, 1996). These methods of analysis, which are often used in conjunction with one another, are discussed below.

Totality of the Contacts

In determining whether a state may exercise personal jurisdiction over a nonresident defendant in the context of online communications, courts often use a "totality of the contacts" analysis, taking into account the defendant's electronic contacts (such as sales conducted via a website) as well as its physical contacts (such as attendance at a trade convention in the forum state). *See Telephone Audio Production, Inc. v. Smith*, No. 3:97-CV-0863-P, 1998 WL 159932 (N.D. Tex., Mar. 26, 1998). Some examples of this analysis are described below.

Cases in Which the Totality of the Contacts Was Found Sufficient to Support the Exercise of Jurisdiction

EDIAS Software International, L.L.C. v. BASIS International Ltd., 947 F. Supp. 413 (D. Ariz. 1996).

EDIAS, an Arizona-based company, entered into a contract to distribute software for BASIS, a New Mexico-based company. BASIS subsequently became dissatisfied with EDIAS and terminated the contract. BASIS then posted a press release on its website and sent electronic mail messages to EDIAS customers stating that it had terminated the contract because EDIAS refused to guarantee customers a fair price and failed to provide technical support in selling BASIS software. EDIAS filed suit against BASIS in Arizona for, among other things, libel and tortious interference with contract and prospective advantage.

The court found it appropriate to exercise specific jurisdiction over BASIS because BASIS had purposefully availed itself of the privilege of doing business in Arizona and therefore should have been able to predict that it would be subjected to jurisdiction in the state. In reaching this conclusion, the court not only focused on the fact that BASIS posted allegedly libelous statements on its website and sent allegedly libelous electronic messages into Arizona, but also noted, among other things, that BASIS had entered into a contract with EDIAS—an Arizona corporation; had contacted EDIAS employees via telephone and facsimile in Arizona; had sold products to EDIAS for distribution; had sent invoices to EDIAS in Arizona; and had sent employees to visit Arizona.

See also Telephone Audio Productions, Inc. v. Smith, 1998 WL 159932 (finding exercise of specific jurisdiction was proper because the defendant purposefully availed itself of the laws of Texas by traveling to Texas, selling products to Texas residents and targeting Texas residents in its marketing, which included operating a website that was accessible in Texas).

National Football League v. Miller, 2000 U.S. Dist. LEXIS 3929, 54 U.S.P.Q.2d 1575 (S.D.N.Y. 2000).

The defendant maintained a website, located at nfltoday.com, that was designed so that a visitor could click on a hyperlink and immediately connect to the official National Football League website, framed by the defendant's nfltoday.com site. The defendant's website also contained banner ads for online gambling ventures. The plaintiff, the NFL, claimed that the defendant's website caused damage to the NFL in New York by linking the NFL's trademarks to gambling activities. In denying the defendant's motion to dismiss for lack of personal jurisdiction, the court noted that the defendant must have recognized that, because there were two NFL teams with a major New York presence, it was likely that this site "would ultimately appear on thousands of computer screens in New York." *Id.* at *6. The fact that the defendant earned substantial revenue from the website via advertising directed to New Yorkers was also a factor in the court's decision.

Metro-Goldwin-Mayer Studios et al. v. Grokster, 243 F. Supp. 2d 1073 (C.D. Cal. 2003).

Record labels, film studios, and music publishers brought a copyright infringement action against distributors of software that allows file-sharing of digital works. Defendants' software allowed users to engage in peer-to-peer file sharing; the plaintiffs contend that Grokster, Kazaa, and other similar services violate copyright law because the works shared were often copyright-protected. (A Dutch court ruled that Kazaa was not responsible for the infringing activities of its users when Dutch copyright holders brought a similar action. *See Buma/Stemra v. Kazaa*, Dutch Supreme Court (Dec. 19, 2003), discussed in Chapter 4, Copyright, page 125.)

After U.S. plaintiffs had brought their action in a federal court in California, Sharman, Inc., purchased Kazaa's assets. Sharman is incorporated in the island nation of Vanuatu, with its principal place of business in Australia. Its computer servers operate from Denmark, and the source code for its software is said to be in Estonia. Sharman moved to dismiss the case for lack of personal jurisdiction. It argued that its only presence in California (and in the U.S.) is via its presence on the Internet, which by itself should not subject it to jurisdiction.

In January 2003, the District Court for the Central District of California held that the court had personal jurisdiction over Kazaa. The Kazaa software has been downloaded an estimated 143 million times by Internet users in the United States. The court assumed that at least two million of those users are in California. Additionally, Sharman's distribution of the software is a commercial act. Because of Sharman's significant and commercial contact with California residents, there is a presumption that jurisdiction is proper. The court also noted that Sharman was well aware of the claims that its users infringe copyrights, and reasonably should have been aware that many music and video copyrights are owned by companies based in California. Accordingly, the court concluded that Sharman had purposely availed itself of the right to conduct commercial activity in California, with knowledge that its actions might impact the rights of California entities. Exercise of jurisdiction over Kazaa/Sharman, the court concluded, was appropriate.

Cases in Which the Totality of the Contacts Was Found Insufficient to Support the Exercise of Jurisdiction

 Amberson Holdings v. Westside Story Newspaper, 110 F. Supp. 2d 332 (D.N.J. 2000).

The plaintiff, owner of the "West Side Story" trademark, sued in federal court in New Jersey claiming that the defendant's use of the mark in its newspaper title and domain name constituted infringement. The defendant operated its "Westside Story Newspaper" in Southern California and also administered the content of its website there, but it assigned the website's "westsidestory.com" domain name to a host server owned and operated by a New Jersey corporation. Other than its contact with the host server, the defendant had never advertised, solicited, or conducted any business with New Jersey residents.

The court held that the defendant's contacts with New Jersey were not sufficient to support an exercise of personal jurisdiction because the written contract with the New

Jersey corporation, in the absence of other contacts within the state, did not amount to the necessary "minimum contacts" with the forum. The court noted that the defendant had never made direct sales to New Jersey, solicited or advertised to sell its product there, made any shipment of merchandise directly into or through the state, maintained an office in the state, or owned any real or personal property there. The court found that the defendant's website constituted nothing more than a "passive advertisement"—it provided information about the defendant's company, displayed ads of outside vendors, and gave users the option to contact the company via email.

 Digital Control Inc. v. Boretronics Inc., et al., 161 F. Supp. 2d 1183 (W.D. Wash. 2001).

The defendants, Boretronics Inc. and Willie Lessard of Minnesota, designed and manufactured a transmitter for use in underground drilling. They advertised this transmitter in two industry journals, created a website offering the transmitter for sale, and maintained a toll-free number to handle customer inquiries and orders. The plaintiff, Digital Control Inc., brought suit in federal court in Washington alleging that the defendants had infringed its patents. The defendants sought dismissal of the plaintiff's claims for lack of personal jurisdiction. The court agreed.

The court found that "the defendants' limited contacts with the State of Washington [were] not such that they 'should reasonably anticipate being hauled into court' [there]." 161 F. Supp. 2d at 1185. The court adopted the "website plus" rule, under which something more than nationwide advertising is needed to justify the exercise of personal jurisdiction. Although the industry journals, website, and phone number through which the defendants advertised and sold their product were nationally distributed, the defendants did not receive any inquiries from, nor make any sales to, residents of Washington. Because the defendants only used indiscriminate, nationwide forms of advertising, the court concluded that they had not availed themselves of the privilege of doing business in Washington.

 Nam Tai Electronics, Inc. v. Joe Titzer, 93 Cal. App. 4th 1301 (Cal. Ct. App. 2001).

A Colorado resident posted 246 messages on Yahoo's Internet message boards concerning Nam Tai, a consumer electronic-products manufacturer incorporated under the laws of the British Virgin Islands, based in Hong Kong, and traded on the NASDAQ exchange. To post to Yahoo message boards, the defendant was required to register an alias, or "Yahoo ID," and to agree to Yahoo's terms of service, which state that California law governs the relationship between the person registering and Yahoo. Nam Tai contended that at least three of the messages were false, misleading, or otherwise unlawful.

In the appellate court's view, "the determinative question is whether the websites themselves are of particular significance to California or Californians such that the user has reason to know the posting of a message will have significant impact on the state." The court found that Nam Tai failed to show sufficient contacts between the Colorado defendant and California to justify the court's exercise of personal jurisdiction. Specifically, there was no evidence that the defendant's messages or the message boards on which they were posted were directed at or disproportionately likely to be read by Californians. The court also rejected the plaintiff's argument that the Yahoo choice of law provision created jurisdiction over the defendant, finding that the Yahoo terms of service only governed the relationship between Yahoo and its users, not the relationship between Yahoo and the libel plaintiff, Nam Tai.

Compare Equidyne Corp. v. Does 1-21, 279 F. Supp. 2d 481 (D. Del. 2003), in which the plaintiff corporation sued unidentified defendants, claiming that the defendants posted information about the corporation on Yahoo and Lycos message boards about the corporation in violation of the Securities and Exchange Commission Act, which prohibits dissemination of nonpublic corporate information. Because the suit was brought under the SEC Act, which allows nationwide service of process, the court exercised personal jurisdiction over the defendants. However, the court found that Delaware was not a proper venue for the case because the plaintiff had not introduced any evidence that the messages were targeted at Delaware shareholders.

 Wildfire Communications, Inc. v. Grapevine, Inc., No. 00-CV-12004-GAO 2001 U.S. Dist. LEXIS 18238, (D. Mass. Sept. 28, 2001).

Wildfire Communications, a Massachusetts-based company, was contacted via email by Grapevine, Inc., an Illinois-based Internet service provider, in an effort to market Grapevine's online "business card" product, available for $14.95 a month. Through this contact, Wildfire learned of Grapevine's registration of the domain name "wildfire.net." Although Wildfire did not purchase Grapevine's product, it subsequently agreed to purchase Grapevine's "wildfire.net" domain name for $10,000. When the deal fell through, Wildfire sued Grapevine in federal court in Massachusetts, alleging trademark infringement and unfair competition.

The U.S. District Court in Massachusetts refused to assert personal jurisdiction based on the agreement to purchase the domain name. The court noted that "[t]he sum of defendant's contacts with Massachusetts include three web pages . . . a contract with a Massachusetts corporation for the sale of a domain name . . . and a one-time, unsuccessful solicitation." 2001 U.S. Dist. LEXIS 18238, at *9-10. The court found that these contacts with Massachusetts were not sufficient to satisfy the minimum-contacts test.

See also Hartcourt Cos. v. Hogue, 817 So. 2d 1067 (Fla. Dist. Ct. App. 2002) (defendant's maintenance of a website accessible in Florida, combined with a debt to be paid to a Florida resident for finding investors, did not constitute sufficient minimum contacts).

Standing Stone Media Inc. d/b/a Indian Country Today v. indiancountrytoday.com, 193 F. Supp. 2d 528 (N.D.N.Y. 2002).

Standing Stone owns *Indian Country Today*, a Native American newspaper, with an online version published at www.indiancountry.com. In January 2000, the newspaper's management decided to register additional domain names based on its trademark, "Indian Country Today." Two weeks after the decision to register the additional domain names (but before any action was taken), Miles Morrisseau, the newspaper's editor in chief, was fired. One week after he was fired, Morrisseau registered in his own name the domain names that Standing Stone had planned to register.

Standing Stone filed suit against Morrisseau in the Northern District of New York alleging cybersquatting. Morrisseau resided in Ontario, Canada, and had registered the name from there with Register.com, a domain-name registrar located in the Southern District of New York. The court determined that the controlling statute, the Anticybersquatting Consumer Protection Act (ACPA) (described in Chapter 3, Domain Names, at page 63), did not provide jurisdiction over the defendant in a forum in which neither the domain-name registrar nor the defendant was located.

Machulsky v. Hall, 210 F. Supp. 2d 531 (D.N.J. 2002).

The plaintiff, a New Jersey resident, bought and sold collectable coins on eBay. She sued out-of-state customers for mail fraud, wire fraud, extortion, conspiracy, tortious interference with prospective economic advantage, and other related claims arising from online commercial transactions conducted through eBay. The court determined it could not assert jurisdiction over the defendants. First, the defendants did not have sufficient minimum contacts with the state as a result of their transactions on eBay to allow the assertion of specific jurisdiction. In addition, the email correspondence between the plaintiff and the defendants did not constitute purposeful availment by the defendants of the right to do business in New Jersey. Finally, the negative-feedback statements that the defendants posted on eBay about the plaintiff were considered "passive."

Nature of the Website (the *Zippo* Test)

In determining whether a nonresident defendant's website is sufficient to confer personal jurisdiction over the defendant in the courts of a state in which the website is accessed, courts have looked to the nature of the defendant's website. Generally, the more interactive the site, the more likely a court will exercise jurisdiction over the nonresident defendant. In determining whether a site is interactive, courts consider whether the site exchanges information with a user and is more commercial in nature (such as sites that permit online product orders or allow users to exchange files with the server) or whether the site merely provides general information, much as a traditional print advertisement does.

The "nature of the website" jurisdictional analysis was articulated in *Zippo Manufacturing Co. v. Zippo Dot Com, Inc.*, 952 F. Supp. 1119 (W.D. Pa. 1997). In *Zippo*, the court stated that based on its review of the relevant case law, the likelihood that personal jurisdiction can be constitutionally exercised "is directly proportionate to the nature and quality of commercial activity that an entity conducts over the Internet." 952 F. Supp. at 1124. The court identified three categories of Internet activity:

1. "At one end of the spectrum are situations where a defendant clearly does business over the Internet. If the defendant enters into contracts with residents of a foreign jurisdiction that involve the knowing and repeated transmission of computer files over the Internet, personal jurisdiction is proper." (*citing CompuServe, Inc. v. Patterson*, 89 F.3d 1257 (6th Cir. 1996)).

2. *See also, e.g., Quokka Sports, Inc. v. Cup International, Ltd.*, 99 F. Supp. 2d 1105 (N.D. Cal. 1999) (specific jurisdiction in trademark infringement suit was proper where the court aggregated the foreign defendant's contacts with the U.S. and those contacts were interactive and involved commercial activity targeted at the U.S. market).

3. The "middle ground" along the spectrum "is occupied by interactive websites where a user can exchange information with the host computer. In these cases,

the exercise of jurisdiction is determined by examining the level of interactivity and commercial nature of the exchange of information that occurs on the website." (*citing Maritz, Inc. v. Cybergold, Inc.*, 947 F. Supp. 1328 (E.D. Mo. 1996)).

4. *See also, e.g., People Solutions, Inc. v. People Solutions, Inc.*, No. 3:99-CV-2339-L 2000, U.S. Dist. LEXIS 10444 (N.D. Tex. 2000) (the defendant's website could interact with, sell products to, and contract with residents of the forum, but there was no evidence that the website had done so; therefore, the court ruled there was no personal jurisdiction over the defendant); *Efford v. Jockey Club*, 796 A.2d 370 (Pa. Super. Ct. 2002) (the defendant's website provided general information about The Jockey Club and permitted users to register foals online, but the plaintiff failed to allege how many Pennsylvania foals had been registered on the website; therefore, the court ruled there was no personal jurisdiction over the defendant).

5. The far end of the spectrum involves "situations where a defendant has simply posted information on an Internet website which is accessible to users in foreign jurisdictions. A passive website that does little more than make information available to those who are interested in it is not grounds for the exercise of personal jurisdiction." (*citing Bensusan Restaurant Corp. v. King*, 937 F. Supp. 295 (S.D.N.Y. 1996), *aff'd*, 126 F.3d 25 (2d Cir. 1997)).

See also, e.g., Mink v. AAAA Development, L.L.C., 190 F.3d 333 (5th Cir. 1999) (personal jurisdiction in copyright infringement suit was not proper where the defendant's website merely provided users with a printable, mail-in order form, a toll-free telephone number, a mailing address, and an email address); *American Homecare Federation, Inc. v. Paragon Scientific Corp.*, 27 F. Supp. 2d 109 (D. Conn. 1998) (personal jurisdiction in trademark-infringement suit was not proper where the defendant's website merely provided a toll-free number and did not list any products for sale, provide any downloadable files, or contain any email links); *Jewish Defense Org., Inc. v. Superior Court*, 85 Cal. Rptr. 2d 611 (Cal. Ct. App. 1999) (personal jurisdiction in defamation suit was not proper, in part because the defendant merely contracted via computer with Internet service providers in the forum state and maintained a passive, informational website that did not seek to attract readers to site and did not capture or retrieve information from visitors).

Cases in Which the Nature of the Website Supported the Exercise of Jurisdiction

Blumenthal v. Drudge, 992 F. Supp. 44 (D.D.C. 1998).

White House aide and former journalist Sidney Blumenthal and his wife, who were residents of the District of Columbia, sued Matt Drudge, publisher of the "Drudge Report," and America Online for libel, invasion of privacy, and intentional infliction of emotional distress in federal court in Washington, D.C. The suit complained of statements made in the "Drudge Report," a web publication. Drudge's base of operations for writing, publishing, and disseminating the Drudge Report was California, where he resided. Drudge moved to dismiss or to transfer for lack of personal jurisdiction.

In conducting its jurisdictional analysis, the court applied both the *Zippo* analysis and the "effects test" (discussed below at page 273) and denied the defendant's motion to dismiss. The court focused primarily on the element of the District of Columbia's long-arm statute permitting jurisdiction to be exercised over a nonresident defendant who has "engage[d] in [a]. . . persistent course of conduct [in the District of Columbia]." 992 F. Supp. at 53. The court found that Drudge had engaged in a persistent course of conduct in the District both because he operated "an interactive website that is accessible to and used by District of Columbia residents and, [because] . . . he has had sufficient nonInternet related contacts with the District of Columbia," which included soliciting contributions from District residents. *Id.* at 56. The court further concluded that exercising jurisdiction over Drudge would not violate his constitutional rights because the District's long-arm statute did "not reach the outer limits of due process. . . ." *Id.* at 58.

In analyzing the "level of interactivity" of the "Drudge Report," the court, relying on the *Zippo* test framework, rejected Drudge's contention that his site was "passive." *Id.* at 56. The court concluded that "[t]he constant exchange of information and direct communication that District of Columbia Internet users are able to have with Drudge's host computer via his website is the epitome of website interactivity." *Id.* The court noted that users who access the website may request subscriptions to the "Drudge Report" by emailing their requests to Drudge's host computer; as each new edition of the Report is created, it is sent to every email address on Drudge's subscription mailing list.

For a discussion of this case in the context of service provider immunity under the Communications Decency Act of 1996, *see* Chapter 5, page 144.

Ty, Inc. v. Baby Me, Inc., 2001 U.S. Dist. LEXIS 5761, 64 U.S.P.Q.2D (BNA) 1442 (N.D. Ill. 2001).

The plaintiff, Ty, Inc., a Delaware corporation with its principal place of business in Illinois, sued the defendant, Baby Me, Inc., a Hawaii corporation, for copyright, trademark, and trade dress infringement. Ty owned copyright in various "plush toys," marketed as "Beanie Babies," and also owned numerous federal trademark registrations for, as well as common-law trademark and trade dress rights in, a variety of marks associated with the toys. Baby Me manufactured and sold plush toy bears in Hawaii under the name "Baby Me Bears," and for seven months, the defendant also sold the bears via its website, shipping the bears to purchasers. The Baby Me website included an order form, pictures of the bears, and pricing information. Ty alleged that the "Baby Me Bears" infringed its copyrights and trade dress because they were confusingly and substantially similar to its "Beanie Babies" plush toys, and infringed its trademark rights by including the word "beanies" as a metatag on its website. (For discussion of trademark issues arising out of the use of metatags, *see* Chapter 2, page 39.) According to Ty, an Illinois consumer purchased three "Baby Me Bears" from the website and had them shipped into the state.

Citing *Zippo*, the court found that the exercise of specific jurisdiction over Baby Me was proper because Baby Me's interactive website facilitated product ordering and shipping, indicating to the court that Baby Me intended to conduct business with consumers throughout the entire United States, including Illinois. Also important to the court was the sale of "Baby Me Bears" to at least one Illinois resident, which further indicated to the court that the company conducted business in Illinois over the Internet.

School Stuff, Inc. v. School Stuff, Inc., No. 00 C 5593, 2001 WL 558050 (N.D. Ill. May 21, 2001).

The plaintiff, School Stuff, Inc., an Indiana corporation and holder of the "School Stuff" trademark, sued the defendant, an Arizona corporation by the same name, in an Illinois court alleging trademark infringement and dilution based on the defendant's use of the "School Stuff" mark. Both parties sold educational and school supplies. The plaintiff alleged that personal jurisdiction in Illinois was proper because the defendant did business on the Internet totaling $8,748.61 in sales, of which $447.09 were made to Illinois residents.

After concluding that the defendant's sales in the state of Illinois were not "continuous and systematic" such that general jurisdiction could be asserted, the court applied the *Zippo* analysis and determined that specific jurisdiction was proper. The court concluded that the defendant had conducted business over the Internet with Illinois residents and therefore purposefully availed itself of the privilege of doing business in the state. The court also noted that Illinois' interest in adjudicating injuries such as trademark infringement relating to companies located within its borders outweighed the burden on the defendant in having to appear before an Illinois court.

See also Park Inns International, Inc. v. Pacific Plaza Hotels, Inc., 5 F. Supp. 2d 762 (D. Ariz. 1998) (finding personal jurisdiction proper where the defendants maintained websites through which hotel reservations could be made and through which seven reservations were solicited and completed by residents of the forum state); *Audi AG v. Izumi*, 204 F. Supp. 2d 1014 (E.D. Mich. 2002) (finding personal jurisdiction proper where the defendant's website enabled users in Michigan to place product orders and solicited business from Michigan residents).

 Gorman v. Ameritrade Holding Corp., 293 F.3d 506 (D.C. Cir. 2002).

The plaintiff, David Gorman, a Virginia resident, entered into a contract with Freetrade.com to have Freetrade post a hyperlink on its site to Gorman's website. Defendant Ameritrade.com then bought the Freetrade website and removed the link to Gorman's site. Gorman sued Ameritrade in the District of Columbia, alleging that his prior contract with Freetrade.com barred removal of the link by the new owner. The trial court found that Ameritrade, which had its principal place of business in Nebraska, was not subject to either specific or general jurisdiction in the District of Columbia, and dismissed the case before Gorman could discover the number of customers Ameritrade had in D.C.

The U.S. Court of Appeals for the District of Columbia Circuit disagreed, finding that Ameritrade's highly interactive website may provide sufficient "continuous and systematic" contacts to establish general jurisdiction in the forum. The court noted that Ameritrade's website allows customers to buy or sell stocks 24 hours a day, which would likely be sufficient to satisfy the requirement of D.C.'s long-arm statute that the defendants "do business" in the District. *Gorman*, 293 F.3d at 514. The appellate court rejected Ameritrade's argument that its stock transactions took place in "cyberspace," rather than within the territorial boundaries of the forum. The court stated that "Ameritrade is quite wrong in treating 'cyberspace' as if it were a kingdom floating in the mysterious ether, immune from the jurisdiction of earthly courts." *Id.* at 516. However, the court ultimately affirmed the trial court's dismissal of the case because Gorman had failed to serve the complaint properly on Ameritrade.

In re Ski Train Fire in Kaprun, Austria on Nov. 11, 2000, No. 01-CIV-6554, 2002 U.S. Dist. LEXIS 14563 (S.D.N.Y., Aug. 6, 2002).

The accessibility and interactivity of a website were found sufficient to support assertion of jurisdiction over a foreign corporation that otherwise did not do business within the forum state in a suit that did not relate to website activities. In a lawsuit filed over a fatal accident, New York residents established jurisdiction over a Munich company based on the interactivity of its website. Other defendants in the case, who did not avail themselves of the right to do business in New York by operating an interactive website, successfully moved for dismissal based on lack of personal jurisdiction. *See Ski Train Fire*, 203 F. Supp. 2d 403, No. 01-CIV-6554, 2002 U.S. Dist. LEXIS 17566 (S.D.N.Y., Sept. 19, 2002).

Bird v. Parsons, 289 F.3d 865 (6th Cir. 2002).

The plaintiff, Darrell Bird, an Ohio resident, brought an action for trademark infringement against the co-defendants, Marshall Parsons and Dotster.com, a national domain-name registrar. Bird owned the trademark for his computer software company "Financia." The defendant, Marshall Parsons, registered "efinancia.com" through the co-defendant, Dotster.com.

Dotster.com argued the court lacked personal jurisdiction because Dotster.com is not based in Ohio and does not have its servers there. In an attempt to show Dotster.com had sufficient contacts, the plaintiff simply divided the total number of Dotster.com's clients by 50 states, estimating Dotster.com had registered nearly 5,000 websites in Ohio. The court found that 5,000 figure was sufficient to confer specific jurisdiction over Dotster.com, because it showed Dotster had an interactive website and an intent to do business with Ohio residents, although there was no evidence of the true number of Dotster.com clients in Ohio. "[T]he proffered evidence that Dotster regularly chooses to do business with Ohio residents is sufficient to constitute purposeful availment." *Id.* at 875.

See also Thomas Publishing Co., et al. v. Industrial Quick Search, Inc., et al., 237 F. Supp. 2d 489 (S.D.N.Y. 2002) (website is sufficiently interactive in soliciting business and commercial activity in New York to exercise personal jurisdiction over defendant); *Alpha International, Inc. v. T-Reproductions, Inc., et al.*, 2003 U.S. Dist. LEXIS 11224 (S.D.N.Y. July 1, 2003) (in a trademark dispute, an interactive website that permits purchase of the disputed product is sufficient to exercise personal jurisdiction over the defendant); *Directory Dividends, Inc. v. SBC Communications, Inc., et al.*, 2003 U.S. Dist LEXIS 12214 (E.D. Pa. July 2, 2003) (SBC's website specifically targets Pennsylvania residents by providing an area of the site devoted to the needs and questions of Pennsylvania residents; despite the fact that the website was not the source of the harm alleged in this lawsuit, the website was sufficiently interactive to support exercise of general personal jurisdiction).

Computeruser.com, Inc. v. Technology Publications LLC, No. 02-832, 2002 U.S. Dist. LEXIS 13453 (D. Minn., July 20, 2002).

The interactive features of the "Sexiest Geek Alive" website were sufficient to permit assertion of personal jurisdiction over the site's operators. The plaintiff was Computeruser.com, a Minnesota company and publisher of the nationwide magazine *Computer User*. The defendant, Technology Publications, was a licensee of plaintiff, authorized to produce and distribute the plaintiff's magazine in Texas. Computeruser.com sued Technology Publications for trademark infringement for allegedly continuing to use computeruser.com's mark on its website without authorization after the termination of the license agreement. The defendant's site featured message boards, free email, and regular communication with users, including the "Sexiest Geek Alive" contest. Over 18,000 applications to enter the contest were submitted via the website in two months' time, including, the court presumed, some from Minnesota residents. The exercise of personal jurisdiction was therefore proper.

 Hartoy, Inc. v. Thompson, No. 02-80454-CIV, 2003 U.S. Dist. LEXIS 3185, (S.D. Fla., Jan. 29, 2003).

The court applied the *Zippo* analysis to a dispute in which the plaintiff, Hartoy, a Florida corporation, alleged that the defendant had illegally produced and distributed a toy truck containing components of Hartoy's toy products and components of defendant's toy products. Defendant, a Wisconsin resident, allegedly sold some of these products on his website. The defendant moved to dismiss for lack of personal jurisdiction, arguing that, as a Wisconsin resident, he could not be haled into court in Florida. The court concluded that it had personal jurisdiction over defendant Thompson based on the interactivity of his website. Because Thompson's website allowed users to place orders for his products online, and because there was evidence that some Florida residents had, in fact, made such purchases, the court concluded it could exercise personal jurisdiction over Thompson.

 Brach's Confections Inc. v. Keller, 2003 U.S. Dist. LEXIS 16817, Case No. 03-CV-2032 (N.D. Ill., Sept. 23, 2003).

A website that allowed users to buy bulk orders of candy by clicking on an email link and paying either by check or PayPal payment service was sufficient to create personal jurisdiction over the defendant website operator. The New Jersey defendants registered and operated websites under domain names that included the plaintiff's trademark, including brachs.org and brachsconfections.com. Citing *Zippo*, the U.S. District Court for the Northern District of Illinois found at least four residents of Illinois had made purchases from the defendants' "interactive" website, and ruled those purchases were enough to establish personal jurisdiction to maintain the trademark infringement suit.

 Gator.com Corp. v. L.L. Bean, Inc., 341 F.3d 1072 (9th Cir. 2003).

Defendant L.L. Bean, Inc., which operates a mail-order and Internet-based clothing and outdoor equipment company, was found to be subject to general jurisdiction in California even though the company was not authorized to do business in California, had no agent for service of process in California and was not required to pay taxes in California. The defendant's website accounted for over $200 million, or 16%, of the defendant's total sales. In addition, 6% of the defendant's total sales were to California residents via either its catalogs, toll-free telephone number or website, totaling "millions of dollars." The plaintiff, Gator.com, distributes software that served to users of the L.L. Bean website users a pop-up window displaying coupons for Eddie Bauer, an L.L. Bean competitor. L.L. Bean sent the plaintiff a letter demanding Gator.com "cease and desist" the practice. Instead, Gator.com filed for declaratory judgment in the U.S. District Court for the Northern District of California. The trial court ruled it did not have personal jurisdiction over L.L. Bean.

The Ninth Circuit reversed, finding that L.L. Bean's commercial contacts with California residents via the catalog, telephone and Internet, satisfied the "continuous and systematic" test for general personal jurisdiction. 341 F.3d at 1078. The Ninth Circuit added that L.L. Bean "targets" California residents by electronic advertising and maintains a "highly interactive" website through which California consumers can purchase L.L. Bean products. *Id.* The court ruled, "[t]here is nothing 'random, fortuitous, or attenuated' about subjecting L.L. Bean to the authority of the court as L.L. Bean has deliberately and purposefully availed itself, on a very large scale, of the benefits of doing business within [California]." *Id.* at 1079. Alternatively, the court applied the "sliding scale" test of *ALS Scan, Inc. v. Digital Service Consultants, Inc.*, 293 F.3d 707 (4th Cir. 2002) (discussed further at page 272), and found that general jurisdiction was proper because L.L. Bean had engaged in "something more" than systematic transmission of electronic signals. *Id.* at 1080. In addition to a "highly interactive" and "very extensive" website, L.L. Bean had "millions of dollars in sales, driven by an extensive, ongoing, and sophisticated sales effort involving very large numbers of direct email solicitations and millions of catalog sales," sufficient to find general jurisdiction. *Id.* (citing *Zippo Mfg. Co. v. Zippo Dot Com Inc.*, 952 F.Supp.2d 1119 (W.D. Pa. 1997)).

Cases in Which the Nature of the Website Did Not Support the Exercise of Jurisdiction

Cybersell, Inc. v. Cybersell, Inc., 130 F.3d 414 (9th Cir. 1997).

The plaintiff, Cybersell, Inc., an Arizona corporation and holder of the "Cybersell" service mark, sued the defendant, a Florida corporation by the same name, for service-mark infringement based on its use of the "Cybersell" mark on its website. The plaintiff, which provided Internet advertising, marketing, and consulting services, had no website and had not yet been granted a registration for the "Cybersell" mark when the defendant decided to offer web page construction and consulting services under the Cybersell name. The trial court granted the defendant's motion to dismiss for lack of personal jurisdiction, and the plaintiff appealed. The plaintiff conceded that the Arizona court did not have general jurisdiction over the defendant, but alleged that specific jurisdiction could be properly exercised.

The court held that the exercise of specific jurisdiction was not proper because the defendant's use of the "Cybersell" mark on its website was passive and the defendant conducted no commercial activity in Arizona. The defendant's website merely displayed information about the defendant's services and included an email link for inquiries related to those services. No Arizona resident could contract with the defendant via the website, and there was no evidence that the defendant had entered into any contract or conducted any business with any resident of Arizona. Additionally, with the exception of an email from the plaintiff, there was no evidence of any online communication between the defendant and Arizona residents. Therefore, the court concluded that the defendant had not taken any action or consummated any transaction by which it purposefully availed itself of the privilege of conducting business in Arizona.

 Copperfield v. Cogedipresse, 26 Media L. Rep. (BNA) 1185 (C.D. Cal. 1997).

Magician David Copperfield brought a libel action against the author, publisher, and distributors of *Paris Match* magazine. Copperfield alleged that a story published in *Paris Match* contained false and defamatory information about his relationship with model Claudia Schiffer. Copperfield argued, among other things, that the existence of a *Paris Match* website established general jurisdiction over the defendant in California. The court, although concluding that the website was sufficiently interactive and commercial in nature to fall within the second ("middle ground") category identified in *Zippo*, declined to find personal jurisdiction on that basis, noting, among other things, that the "interactivity [was] limited" and the commercial aspect of the site "consist[ed] almost entirely of advertising." 26 Media L. Rep. at 1188. The court also declined to assert specific jurisdiction under the "effects test" (discussed below at page 276). The court did not state whether the allegedly defamatory statements at issue were available on the *Paris Match* website.

 Mallinckrodt Medical, Inc. v. Sonus Pharmaceuticals, Inc., 989 F. Supp. 265 (D.D.C. 1998).

The defendant, in Seattle, posted an allegedly defamatory message on an AOL bulletin board that resided on a web server located in Virginia. Pointing to that message, the plaintiff claimed that a District of Columbia court had jurisdiction since approximately 200,000 District of Columbia residents are subscribers to AOL with potential access to the posting. In rejecting this argument, the court relied on the long-arm statute of the District of Columbia, which, in relevant part, required that the nonresident defendant "transact. . . business" in the District of Columbia. 989 F. Supp. at 270. The court concluded that the defendant's conduct failed to satisfy this requirement because "[t]he [allegedly defamatory] message was not sent to or from the District of Columbia, the subject matter of the message had nothing to do with the District of Columbia, and neither plaintiffs nor [defendant] reside in, have their headquarters in or are incorporated in the District." *Id.* at 272. The court further noted that the act of merely posting a message on an electronic bulletin board, which users may or may not choose to access, is not sufficient to confer personal jurisdiction over a nonresident defendant.

 Barrett v. Catacombs Press, 44 F. Supp. 2d 717 (E.D. Pa. 1999).

The defendant, an Oregon resident, allegedly defamed the plaintiff, a Pennsylvania resident who ran a well-known website called "Quackwatch," by allegedly posting statements on two websites. In addition, the defendant allegedly posted messages regarding the plaintiff on various national listservs and USENET discussion groups with links back to the defendant's websites. The defendant moved to dismiss the plaintiff's lawsuit for lack of personal jurisdiction.

The court, following the analysis used by the court in *Zippo*, examined the nature and quality of the defendant's contacts over the Internet. The court concluded that the defendant's websites were entirely passive, and that such sites were insufficient to trigger jurisdiction in the forum state absent evidence that the defendant was targeting Pennsylvania residents. In addition, the court stated that although the defendant's posting of messages to listservs and USENET discussion groups differed from passive websites because such "messages [were] actively disseminated to those who participate[d] in such groups," such contacts nevertheless also were insufficient to establish personal jurisdiction over the defendant in Pennsylvania. 44 F. Supp. 2d at 728. The court based its ruling on the fact that the listserv and USENET postings "were accessible around the world and never targeted nor solicited Pennsylvania residents." *Id.*

Desktop Technologies, Inc. v. Colorworks Reproduction & Design, Inc., No. 98-5029, 1999 U.S. Dist. LEXIS 1934 (E.D. Pa. Feb. 25, 1999).

The plaintiff, a Pennsylvania corporation and owner of the U.S. trademark "Colorworks," brought suit against the defendant, a Canadian company that owned the Canadian registration for the same mark, for trademark infringement and unfair competition resulting from the defendant's use of the mark in its domain name. The defendant operated its business exclusively in British Columbia and had never transacted business with residents of Pennsylvania. However, the defendant maintained a website, accessible to all Internet users, including those in Pennsylvania, that displayed general information about the company, advertisements for the company, and a listing of employment opportunities with the company. The site listed local telephone and fax numbers and specifically stated that the defendant serviced clients in the local area. The defendant moved to dismiss the lawsuit for lack of personal jurisdiction.

The court granted the defendant's motion, holding that personal jurisdiction could not be asserted because the defendant's website was merely a passive advertisement. The court first rejected the plaintiff's argument for general jurisdiction, reasoning that the website's email links, which were its only interactive element, were "the electronic equivalents of advertisements' response cards," the use of which was insufficient by itself to establish general jurisdiction. 1999 U.S. Dist. LEXIS 1934 at *9. The court then rejected the plaintiff's argument for specific jurisdiction because the level of interactivity on the defendant's website was such that it could be considered passive under the *Zippo* analysis. The court noted that the defendant had never transacted business in Pennsylvania and its website did not exist for the purpose of attracting or entering into contracts with consumers outside of Canada.

Mid City Bowling Lanes & Sports Palace, Inc. v. Ivercrest, Inc., 35 F. Supp. 2d 507 (E.D. La. 1999), *aff'd without opinion*, 208 F.3d 1006 (5th Cir. 2000).

The plaintiff, Mid City Bowling Lanes, operated a bowling alley in New Orleans, Louisiana, where patrons could bowl while listening to live musical entertainment. Mid City coined the phrase "Rock 'N' Bowl" to advertise this entertainment combination and subsequently was granted a federal registration for the "Rock 'N' Bowl" trademark. The defendant, Ivercrest, used the "Rock 'N' Bowl" mark in association with the Diversey River Bowl, a bowling alley it owned and operated in Chicago, Illinois. Ivercrest used the "Rock 'N' Bowl" mark in Diversey's local advertising campaign, on Diversey's website, and in its domain name. After becoming aware of Ivercrest's use of the mark on the Diversey website, Mid City sued Ivercrest alleging trademark infringement and unfair trade practices. The defendant moved to dismiss the suit for lack of personal jurisdiction.

After noting the local nature of the bowling services being sold by each entity, the court held that the defendant's use of the plaintiff's mark on a website that was available to anyone who had Internet access was an insufficient basis for the exercise of personal jurisdiction. The website merely contained the mailing address and local phone number of the defendant's facility and other information concerning entertainment options at the bowling alley. There was no evidence that the defendant had any contact with Louisiana other than by making the website available to Louisiana residents. Internet users could not make any purchases or engage in any direct communication with the defendant through the website. Therefore, the court found that the plaintiff had failed to establish "minimum contacts" sufficient to support either specific or general jurisdiction.

Callaway Golf Corp. v. Royal Canadian Golf Association, 125 F. Supp. 2d 1194 (C.D. Cal. 2000).

The defendant, the Royal Canadian Golf Association (RCGA), announced publicly through its website and other media that it would not permit the use of certain golf clubs in its regulation tournaments. Callaway, a California manufacturer of one of the prohibited clubs, brought several claims in federal court in California, including defamation, based on the announcement. RCGA filed a motion to dismiss for lack of personal jurisdiction. The plaintiff replied that jurisdiction in California could be established on the basis of the RCGA website, which was accessible in California.

The court held that RCGA had not purposefully availed itself of the privileges and protections of California law through the maintenance of its website. The decision noted that the site was both passive, as it displayed general information about golf and the Association, and interactive, as it allowed users to purchase tickets to RCGA-sponsored golf tournaments and other items. Few Californians had taken advantage of the commercial aspects of the site, and the revenue from the commercial activity as a whole comprised less than 1% of the defendant's sales. The court maintained that even if the site were more interactive, personal jurisdiction still could not be exercised over the defendant. It reasoned that the operation of the website had no relationship to the claims of the plaintiff. Because the press release itself was more like an advertisement (*i.e.*, passive in nature) and not directed specifically at the forum, the court dismissed the suit for lack of personal jurisdiction over the Canadian defendant.

Lofton v. Turbine Design, Inc., 100 F. Supp. 2d 404 (N.D. Miss. 2000).

The plaintiffs, a Mississippi-based aircraft-conversion company that designed and developed engine applications, and several of its shareholders, sued a Florida-based competitor (TDI), for posting allegedly defamatory statements to its website about one of the plaintiff's aircraft designs. The defendant moved to dismiss for lack of personal jurisdiction.

The plaintiff argued that the accessibility of the defendant's website to Mississippi residents was sufficient to establish personal jurisdiction. Using the *Zippo* analysis, the court noted that TDI's website was used solely to advertise its services and was purely passive in nature. The court dismissed the case for lack of personal jurisdiction because "[t]he website [did] not contain a price list for services, contract for engagement of services, or order form."

Bailey v. Turbine Design, Inc., et al., 86 F. Supp. 2d 790 (W.D. Tenn. 2000).

The plaintiff, a resident of Tennessee, brought suit in Tennessee for libel, tortious interference with contract, and conspiracy, based on a website produced by the defendants that contained, among other things, allegations of technical problems associated with the plaintiff's work and the plaintiff's criminal history, and a reference to the plaintiff's company as a group of "con artists." The defendants, a Florida corporation and a Florida resident, moved to dismiss for lack of personal jurisdiction. The court granted the defendants' motion, applying both the *Zippo* analysis and the "effects test" (discussed below at page 276).

The court found that it lacked personal jurisdiction over the defendant under the criteria set forth in *Zippo*: "[h]ere, there is no indication whatsoever that the website is anything other than wholly passive" and that "the allegedly defamatory statements were merely posted on the website to be viewed by whomever cared to do so." 86 F. Supp. 2d at 795. The court further noted that there was "no evidence to suggest that any effort was made to reach out to Tennessee residents any more than to persons residing elsewhere," and, in fact, there was no indication that any Tennessee resident except for the plaintiff ever visited the website. *Id.*

Amazon.com, Inc. v. Kalaydjian, 2001 U.S. Dist. LEXIS 4924, 58 U.S.P.Q.2d (BNA) 1247 (W.D. Wash. Feb. 20, 2001).

The plaintiff, whose principal place of business was in Washington, alleged that the defendant, Kalaydjian, infringed and diluted its trademark through the marketing of his sun-tanning products in California. The defendant marketed his products on a website bearing the domain name AmazonTan.com. On the website, customers could receive information about Kalaydjian's products, but they could not exchange information with the defendant or purchase his products.

After deciding that general jurisdiction over the defendant was lacking, the court dismissed the action for want of specific jurisdiction. Though the defendant's registered domain name was similar to the plaintiff's trademark, the posting of a website bearing that name was not sufficient to indicate that the defendant had taken advantage of the privilege of conducting business in Washington. Similarly, the shipment of a single bottle of suntan lotion to a Washington resident in response to a request from the resident did not constitute purposeful availment of the benefits of doing business in Washington. The website was not sufficiently interactive to confer jurisdiction because, in the court's eyes, it did little more than provide information available to those who were interested in it. Finally, communications between the two parties concerning the alleged trademark infringement did not establish a basis for jurisdiction in Washington.

Remick v. Manfredy, 52 F. Supp. 2d 452 (E.D. Pa. 1999), *aff'd*, 238 F.3d 248 (3d Cir. 2001).

The plaintiff, a Pennsylvania attorney, sued a former client (a boxer), the client's advisers, and an Illinois law firm representing the former client for, among other things, libel. The alleged libel arose out of a letter to the plaintiff (copied to one of the other defendants) from the Illinois law firm, which alleged that the plaintiff had engaged in certain misconduct. The defendants, none of whom resided in the forum state of Pennsylvania, moved to dismiss the lawsuit for lack of personal jurisdiction.

The plaintiff argued that the court could exercise general jurisdiction over the defendant boxer and the Illinois law firm, because they maintained websites that purportedly solicited business in Pennsylvania. The court disagreed, granting the defendants' motion to dismiss. Using the *Zippo* analysis, the court concluded that both websites were "passive" in nature and that "there [was] no evidence that they [were] interactive or offer[ed] anything other than general information and advertising. . . . Advertising on the Internet has been held to fall under the same rubric as advertising in a national magazine and it is well settled law in [the Third] Circuit that advertising in a national publication does not constitute the 'continuous and substantial contacts with the forum state' required to give rise to a finding of general jurisdiction." The Court of Appeals for the Third Circuit affirmed. *See also Resnick v. Manfredy*, 52 F. Supp. 2d 462 (E.D. Pa. 1999) (a companion action, in which the court issued an opinion virtually identical to the opinion in *Remick*).

Robbins v. Yutopian Enterprises Inc., 202 F.Supp. 2d 426 (D. Md. 2002).

The plaintiff, Charles Robbins, a Pennsylvania resident, sued the California-based defendant, Yutopian Enterprises, for copyright infringement in federal court in Maryland. The defendant allegedly placed an unauthorized copy of the plaintiff's software, which allows users to play an online version of the ancient board game "Go," on the defendant's website, Yutopia.com.

The federal trial court found that it lacked personal jurisdiction over the defendant, though Yutopia.com had completed 46 sales to Maryland residents over $10^1/2$ months via the website and telephone orders. The court found those contacts did not provide the "continuous and systematic" presence required for general jurisdiction. The court also concluded that the plaintiff's copyright claim did not arise out of those Maryland contacts, and so could not give rise to specific jurisdiction.

ALS Scan, Inc. v. Digital Service Consultants, Inc., 293 F.3d 707 (4th Cir. 2002), *cert. denied*, 123 S. Ct. 868 (2003).

The Maryland-based plaintiff ALS Scan, a company that creates and markets adult photographs of female models, alleged that the defendant, a Georgia-based Internet service provider, infringed its copyright rights by allowing one of its website customers to copy hundreds of the plaintiff's photographs and place them on his website. The defendant ISP argued that it had no contracts with persons or businesses in the forum state of Maryland, conducted no business in Maryland, had no offices in Maryland, and did not advertise in Maryland other than through its website, which was equally accessible to Internet users everywhere.

The federal trial court in Maryland found that it had no general or specific jurisdiction over the defendant, and the Fourth Circuit agreed. The Court of Appeals adapted a version of the *Zippo* test specifically for websites that target or direct activity at a forum state: "[A] State may, consistent with due process, exercise judicial power over a person outside of the State when that person (1) directs electronic activity into the State, (2) with the manifested intent of engaging in business or other interactions in the State, and (3) that activity creates . . . a potential cause of action cognizable in the State's courts." *Id.* at *11. Under this modified test, nonresidents who operate "passive" websites remain immune from personal jurisdiction in foreign states. *Id.* Applying this test, the court concluded that the defendant's activity was, at most, passive activity and did not subject it to the jurisdiction of the Maryland court.

The U.S. Supreme Court denied ALS's request to review the Fourth Circuit's decision.

See also Newspaper Association of America v. Mancusi, Civ. Action No. 01-1635-A (E.D. Va. May 8, 2002) (the defendant's website, which served as a portal to newspaper websites from across the nation, did not seek any information from users and did not offer sale of any goods or services, so it did not meet the due-process requirement for minimum contacts).

Donmar, Inc. v. Swanky Partners, Inc., No. 02-C-1482, 2002 U.S. Dist. LEXIS 15308 (N.D. Ill., Aug. 19, 2002).

An out-of-state nightclub's website that allowed users to sign up for a mailing list and receive local driving directions did not have sufficient minimum contacts with the forum to support jurisdiction. The court also considered favorably the defendant's attempts to limit the area in which it conducted business by editing its mail list and only providing directions from within its home state. Such acts suggested to the court that the website was not targeting out-of-staters. Accordingly, the court ruled that the defendant nightclub could not be subject to the court's jurisdiction.

Nexgen Solutions, Inc. v. Nexgen Solutions Corp., No. AW-02-736 (D. Md., Aug. 28, 2002).

The plaintiff, Nexgen Solutions, Inc., held a federal trademark registration for NEXGEN SOLUTIONS INC. The company sued the defendant over its use of the trademark in Nexgen Solutions Corp.'s domain name. The court determined that use of a trademark in a domain name is insufficient to establish jurisdiction. The court relied on *Zippo* in characterizing the defendant's site as passive, and therefore not sufficient to subject the defendant to personal jurisdiction in the forum.

Aero Products International, Inc. v. Intex Corp., No. 02-C-2590, 2002 U.S. Dist. LEXIS 17948, 64 U.S.P.Q. 1172 (N.D. Ill. 2002).

In a patent infringement suit over the design of an air mattress, the U.S. District Court for the Northern District of Illinois ruled that an operator of a website that merely advertised the mattress was not subject to specific jurisdiction. The court found that the defendant did not specifically direct its advertising to forum residents because the site involved only a moderate degree of interactivity (under the *Zippo* analysis), did not allow sales, and did not exchange information with its users.

Electronic Broking Services, Ltd. v. E-Business Solutions & Services, No. JFM-03-1350, 2003 U.S. Dist. LEXIS 17897; 68 U.S.P.Q.2d (BNA) 1531 (D. Md. Sept. 30, 2003).

The U.S. District Court for the District of Maryland ruled that the combination of a business "partnership" with a Maryland corporation and a website that contained an email link to contact the operator was not enough to allow personal jurisdiction in Maryland over an Egyptian defendant. The plaintiff, a British corporation, alleged the defendant infringed the plaintiff's "E-Business Solutions" trademark. The plaintiff did not argue that the defendant had enough "continuous and systematic" contacts to provide general jurisdiction over the defendant, but argued that specific jurisdiction was proper based upon the defendant's business relationship with a Maryland corporation and the defendant's "semi-interactive" website, which included a link to contact the defendant via email. Applying tests from *Zippo* and *ALS Scan*, the trial court found no basis for specific jurisdiction over the defendant because there was no indication that the defendant "intentionally targeted residents in Maryland through its website or directed its electronic activity into Maryland with the manifested intent of conducting business within the state." 2003 U.S. Dist. LEXIS 17897 at *12. The court also rejected the plaintiff's argument that a business relationship with a single Maryland corporation, even if established through the defendant's website, provided sufficient contacts to allow personal jurisdiction. Allowing personal jurisdiction over the defendant would violate constitutional fairness principles, the court said, because the defendant had never entered Maryland in creating or maintaining the business relationship, had no other contacts with Maryland, and the burden on the defendant to defend itself in Maryland would be great. *Id.* at *16-17.

Accuweather, Inc. v. Total Weather, Inc., 223 F. Supp. 2d 612 (M.D. Pa. 2002).

The plaintiff alleged that the defendant improperly registered domain names that included the plaintiff's trademark. The court granted the defendant's motion to dismiss based on lack of jurisdiction because the court found that the defendant lacked minimum contacts necessary to subject it to jurisdiction in the forum. The court transferred the action from Pennsylvania to the Western District of Oklahoma, where the defendants resided and where all its Internet activities originated.

Riddell Inc. v. Monica et al., Case No. 03-C-3309, 2003 U.S. Dist. LEXIS 13053 (N.D. Ill., July 23, 2003)

A website that provided information about sports equipment products and allowed users to submit basic contact information, but did not allow online sales, did not create sufficient contacts for exercise of general jurisdiction in Illinois, the U.S. District Court for the Northern District of Illinois ruled. The plaintiff, a manufacturer of sports equipment, sued a former employee who had created a website to market sporting goods allegedly designed during his employment with the plaintiff. Relying on its analysis in *Aero Products International, Inc. v. Intex Corp.*, No. 02-C-2590, 2002 U.S. Dist. LEXIS 17948, 64 U.S.P.Q. 1172 (N.D. Ill. 2002), the court ruled the website provided only limited interactivity, allowing users to submit contact information.. In addition, the plaintiff introduced no evidence that the defendant's website "targeted" Illinois. However, even though the website did not provide sufficient interactivity to warrant the exercise of personal jurisdiction, the court exercised jurisdiction over the defendant because the injury allegedly caused by the defendant's conduct occurred in Illinois.

Toys "R" Us v. Step Two S.A., 318 F.3d 466 (3d Cir. 2003).

Toys "R" Us and Step Two own trademark rights in the name "Imaginarium" in their respective countries. Toys "R" Us, an American company, alleged that Step Two, a Spanish company, had infringed its "Imaginarium" trademark by registering and using website domain names such as www.imaginariumworld.com, www.imaginarium-world.com, www.imaginariumnet.net and www.imaginariumnet.org. The Court of Appeals for the Third Circuit concluded that although Step Two's websites were interactive within the meaning of the *Zippo* test, the sites did not appear to be targeted to U.S. Internet users. Step Two's sites are entirely in Spanish; prices are in pesetas or Euros; and merchandise can only be shipped to addresses in Spain. The court found that it lacked personal jurisdiction over Step Two because Step Two did not purposefully avail itself of the privilege of doing business in the U.S., even though its websites were interactive.

Hitachi Shin Din Cable, Ltd. v. Cain, 106 S.W.3d 776 (Tex. App. 2003).

The Texas Court of Appeals reversed the trial court's finding that exercise of personal jurisdiction was proper over Hitachi, the manufacturer of a clock-radio that had allegedly malfunctioned and caused a fire. Plaintiff had alleged, among other theories, that Hitachi's Internet presence provided a sufficient basis to exercise personal jurisdiction. The court concluded that under the *Zippo* test, Hitachi's website was too passive to provide a sufficient basis for exercise of personal jurisdiction because the site merely provided information, and did not have interactive properties.

Pound v. Airosol Co. Inc., No. 02-2632-CM, 2003 U.S. Dist. LEXIS 15869, (D. Kan. Sept. 11, 2003).

The U.S. District Court for the District of Kansas ruled that a website that solicits telephone purchases, but provides no method of ordering through the website itself, is not sufficient to support exercise of personal jurisdiction. The defendants, who resided in Colorado and Virginia, operated an informational website for reptile hobbyists that included advertisements for their product, called "Black Knight." Although the website did not accept online orders, anyone interested in purchasing Black Knight was invited to order via a Colorado-based telephone number on the website. Applying *Zippo*, the court ruled the website, which invited email contact with the operators but not online purchases, was "minimally interactive," and therefore fell into the middle ground between active and passive websites. The court concluded that the website was commercial in nature, but found that the commercial nature alone was not enough to support exercise of jurisdiction, because no Black Knight products had been sold to Kansas consumers and there was no evidence the website operator targeted Kansas residents. The court ultimately found that exercise of personal jurisdiction was proper on different grounds related to the defendants' business dealings with a Kansas vendor.

See also Snyder v. Dolphin Encounters, Ltd., 235 F. Supp. 2d 433 (E.D. Pa. 2002) (even though defendant's website permitted customers to make reservations and to buy souvenirs, the court lacked personal jurisdiction over defendant because its website did not specifically target users in Pennsylvania); *Hammer v. Trendl*, 2003 WL 21466686 (E.D.N.Y. Jan. 18, 2003) (mere posting of a book review on a website that is available worldwide does not sufficiently target New York residents to justify exercise of personal jurisdiction over the defendant); *Arriaga v. Imperial Palace, Inc.*, 252 F. Supp. 2d 380 (S.D. Tex. 2003) (defendant hotel's ability to accept reservations online was insufficient to support an exercise of personal jurisdiction because actual payment and hotel stay occur in the state where the hotel is located); *Brown v. Grand Hotel Eden, et al.*, No. 00-Civ. 7346, 2003 U.S. Dist. LEXIS 10983 (S.D.N.Y. June 30, 2003) (although users of hotel website could inquire about room availability online, court found this to be an insufficient basis for exercise of personal jurisdiction because users could not book rooms online); *Century Marketing Corp. v. Aldrich, et al.*, 2003 Ohio 1396, 2003 Ohio App. LEXIS 1350 (Ohio Ct. App. Mar. 21, 2003) (in a suit alleging misappropriation of trade secrets, "simply showing that [defendant] Langlie has a website does not establish purposeful availment of the privilege of conducting commerce in the state of Ohio."); *Caterpillar, Inc. v. Miskin Scraper Works, Inc.*, 256 F. Supp. 2d 849 (C.D. Ill. 2003) (passive website that does not list products for sale or even quote prices is an insufficient basis for exercising personal jurisdiction over the defendant); *David White Instruments v. TLZ, Inc., et al.*, 2003 U.S. Dist. LEXIS 8375 (N.D. Ill. May 16, 2003) (in patent infringement suit, court found defendant's website to be passive because disputed tools were merely posted on the site and not for sale; therefore, it could not exercise personal jurisdiction over the defendant).

Effects Test

Many courts looking to decide whether a publisher may be sued in a foreign jurisdiction have used an "effects test" to determine whether the forum state "is the focal point both of the story and the harm suffered." *Calder v. Jones*, 465 U.S. 783, 788 (1984). When confronted with online distribution of a publication, some courts have similarly examined whether the defendant intended to cause injury in the forum state and whether the nonresident defendant knew that the "effects" of such injury would be felt in the forum state.

The courts often place emphasis on whether the forum state was the target or focus of the defendant's activities. For example, in a libel case, the court may look at whether the defendant's comments were directed against the individual in his local capacity, rather than against his national persona. *See Blumenthal v. Drudge*, 992 F. Supp. 44 (D.D.C. 1998) (discussed further at pages 262 and 263). Similarly, some courts have reasoned that the "effects test" is less applicable to international and national corporations, as such companies are not confined to a particular geographic location. *See Conseco, Inc. v. Hickerson*, 698 N.E. 2d 816 (Ind. Ct. App. 1998). In domain-name disputes, the mere posting of a website with a domain name that contains another corporation's trademark will not likely be enough to subject the publisher to jurisdiction in a particular forum absent some purposeful targeting of the forum or knowledge of the plaintiff's whereabouts prior to posting. *See American Information Corp. v. American Infometrics, Inc.*, 139 F. Supp. 2d 696 (D. Md. 2001). However, purposeful targeting of the forum state is not dispositive, and some courts exercise personal jurisdiction even in the absence of targeted activity if the harm itself occurs in the forum state. *See Peregrine Financial Group, Inc. v. Green*, 2001 U.S. Dist. LEXIS 14317 (N.D. Ill. Aug. 28, 2001) (discussed further at page 278).

Cases in Which the "Effects Test" Was Applied and Assertion of Jurisdiction Was Found to Be Proper

California Software, Inc. v. Reliability Research, Inc., 631 F. Supp. 1356 (C.D. Cal. 1986).

Reliability Research operated an Internet bulletin-board service that allowed users to post or view messages. The plaintiffs alleged that Reliability Research had made false and defamatory statements to users residing outside of California about the plaintiffs' right to market certain software.

Citing *Calder*, the court noted that personal jurisdiction may be exercised where the defendant's intentional, out-of-state conduct is directed at the forum state. The court concluded that Reliability Research was subject to personal jurisdiction in California because it had intentionally directed communications over its online service to third parties outside of California with the intent to cause harm in California. "Because defendants intentionally influenced third parties to injure the California plaintiffs, defendants should have foreseen answering for the veracity of their statements and the propriety of their conduct in California." 631 F. Supp. at 1362.

🔨 *EDIAS Software International, L.L.C. v. BASIS International Ltd.*, 947 F. Supp. 413 (D. Ariz. 1996).

In addition to finding specific jurisdiction on grounds that BASIS had purposefully availed itself of the laws of Arizona (in the *Cybersell* case discussion above at page 267), the court found that "BASIS's email messages to Arizona and . . . website which reaches Arizona customers . . . confer jurisdiction in Arizona under the 'effects test.'" 947 F. Supp. at 420. The court determined that "BASIS directed the email, web page, and forum message at Arizona because Arizona is EDIAS' principal place of business." *Id.* Although the court did not mention the number of email messages sent to Arizona or whether evidence showed that any Arizona user had in fact accessed the BASIS website, it nevertheless ruled that exercising personal jurisdiction over BASIS was appropriate because BASIS could have foreseen that its actions might cause a loss of potential customers to EDIAS in Arizona. *Id.* at 422.

🔨 *Blumenthal v. Drudge*, 992 F. Supp. 44 (D.D.C. 1998).

The court, in addition to exercising personal jurisdiction over Drudge because of the interactivity of his website (discussed above at page 263) and because of his nonInternet related contacts with the District, also determined that jurisdiction was appropriate under an "effects test." The court noted that "[b]y targeting the Blumenthals who work in the White House and live in the District of Columbia, Drudge knew that 'the primary and most devastating effects of the [statements he made] would be felt' in the District of Columbia." 992 F. Supp. at 57 (citation omitted). Thus, Drudge "should have had no illusions that he was immune from suit here." *Id.*

🔨 *Panavision International, L.P. v. Toeppen*, 141 F.3d 1316 (9th Cir. 1998).

In *Panavision*, the court of appeals affirmed the trial court's decision to exercise personal jurisdiction over an out-of-state defendant who registered "panavision.com" as an Internet domain name and thereby prevented Panavision International, a California-based business, from using its own trademark as a domain name. The court noted that the defendant had engaged in a scheme to register Panavision's trademark "for the purpose of extorting money from Panavision." Because the defendant's conduct "had the effect of injuring Panavision in California where Panavision has its principal place of business and where the movie and television industry is centered," the "effects test" was satisfied.

For a discussion of this case in the cybersquatting context, *see* Chapter 3, page 63.

🔨 *Blakey v. Continental Airlines, Inc.*, 730 A.2d 854 (N.J. Super. Ct. 1999), *rev'd and remanded*, 751 A.2d 538 (N.J. 2000).

The plaintiff, a pilot with Continental Airlines, alleged that she was libeled by certain online postings made by the defendants on the Continental Crew Management System, which provides Continental crew members, pilots, and flight attendants with flight information, schedules, and a bulletin board on which to exchange information and opinions. Continental Airlines is based in New Jersey. The plaintiff alleged that the defendants, who were Continental pilots, had posted on the Crew Management System bulletin board certain defamatory statements relating to the plaintiff's skills as a pilot and the motives behind a lawsuit that she had filed against Continental Airlines that was pending before a federal court in New Jersey. All but one of the defendants resided outside of New Jersey, as did the plaintiff. Nevertheless, the plaintiff asserted that the

New Jersey court could exercise jurisdiction over the defendants because the alleged defamatory comments were published in the forum state via the bulletin board.

The Supreme Court of New Jersey held that "defendants who published defamatory electronic messages, with knowledge that the messages would be published in New Jersey and could influence a claimant's efforts to seek a remedy under New Jersey's Law Against Discrimination, may be properly subject to the State's jurisdiction." The court said that "traditional principles of jurisdictional analysis" should be applied "irrespective of the medium through which the injury was inflicted" and therefore applied the "minimum contacts" test. The court ruled that if the allegedly defamatory statements were published with the knowledge or purpose of causing harm to the plaintiff in pursuit of her civil rights within New Jersey, then the minimum contacts test would be satisfied and personal jurisdiction would exist. The court stated that it could not determine from the record whether the defendants knew of the plaintiff's pending lawsuit against the airline at the time of their allegedly libelous statements, so it remanded the case to the trial court for further proceedings.

 Peregrine Financial Group, Inc., et al. v. Green, 2001 U.S. Dist. LEXIS 14317 (N.D. Ill. Aug. 28, 2001).

The plaintiffs, Peregrine Financial Group, Inc., an Illinois corporation, and Utrade.com, a Georgia corporation, filed suit in federal court in Illinois against the defendant, David Green, a resident of Arizona, alleging defamation, tortious interference with business expectancy, commercial disparagement, and unfair competition arising from emails sent by the defendant to Utrade.com customers.

The defendant and his company, CTCN, had entered into a contract with Utrade.com to provide a trading system that would take and fill the plaintiffs' trade orders. Within two weeks of signing the contract, the plaintiffs became concerned about the validity of Green's trading system, "the integrity of [d]efendant as one of the purported system developers, and the aggressive advertising utilized by [d]efendant." 2001 U.S. Dist. LEXIS 14317 at *3. As a result of those concerns, the plaintiffs terminated their contract with the defendant. The plaintiffs alleged that the defendant then "began a campaign of defamation against Utrade . . ." in the form of email messages sent to the plaintiffs' customers and "other persons" containing defamatory remarks about the plaintiffs. *Id.* However, none of the approximately 30 customers who received the defendant's emails was a resident of Illinois, and the content of the emails appeared to be targeted not at Peregrine, the only Illinois plaintiff, but at a former partner of Peregrine, and at Utrade.com. In addition, all of the defendant's actions were taken in Arizona and all of his contacts with Peregrine were through Utrade.com in Georgia. The defendant moved to dismiss the suit for lack of personal jurisdiction and improper venue.

The court found the exercise of jurisdiction proper. The court relied on *Janmark Inc. v. Reidy*, 132 F.3d 1200 (7th Cir. 1997), which applied the "effects test" to the Illinois long-arm statute. The *Janmark* court held that "'there can be no serious doubt' after the Supreme Court's decision in *Calder v. Jones* that 'the state in which the victim of a tort suffers injury may entertain a suit against the accused tortfeasor.'" 2001 U.S. Dist. LEXIS 14317 at *7, quoting *Janmark*, 132 F.3d at 1202. According to *Janmark*, this principle holds true "even though the actions taken by the defendant constituting the alleged tort may have occurred wholly outside the borders of Illinois." *Id*. However, the court granted the defendant's motion to dismiss because it found that Illinois was not the proper venue for the case.

In reaching its decision on jurisdiction, the court expressed concern about the defendant's connection with Illinois, stating, "[the] plaintiffs run dangerously close to forcing [the] defendant to defend a suit because of his 'random, fortuitous, or attenuated contacts' with Illinois, or because of the 'unilateral activity of another party or third person.'" 2001 U.S. Dist. LEXIS 14317 at *10, *quoting Burger King Corp. v. Rudzewicz*, 471 U.S. 462, 475 (1985).

 Verizon Online Services, Inc. v. Ralsky, et al., 203 F. Supp. 2d 601 (E.D. Va. 2002).

The defendants, who were Michigan residents, sent millions of unsolicited bulk emails, which allegedly overloaded the servers of the plaintiff's network, causing system delays and customer complaints. Applying the effects test, the court found the defendants knew or should have known that the brunt of the harm from the spamming would fall on Verizon's servers in Virginia. The court found the defendants purposefully availed themselves of the privilege of doing business in Virginia because sending unsolicited emails was a deliberate act to solicit business from Verizon's subscribers for financial gain. As such, the court concluded that the unsolicited emails constituted sufficient minimum contacts with Virginia, and personal jurisdiction over the defendants was therefore proper. At the end of October 2002, Verizon settled the case with Ralsky.

 Northwest Healthcare Alliance, Inc. v. Healthgrades.com, Inc., No. 01-35648, 2002 U.S. App. LEXIS 21131 (9th Cir. 2002) (not for publication), *cert. denied*, No. 02-1250, 2003 U.S. LEXIS 3267 (Apr. 28, 2003).

The plaintiff, a Washington State company, is a provider of home health-care services. The defendant, a Colorado company, operated a website that rated the quality of home health-care providers. The plaintiff sued in federal court in Washington, alleging libel and violations of Washington's consumer-protection statutes. The trial court dismissed the case for lack of personal jurisdiction, applying the "sliding scale" *Zippo* test. The U.S. Court of Appeals for the Ninth Circuit reversed, stating that the appropriate test was *Calder*'s "effects test"; the defendant had "purposely interjected" itself into the Washington forum, and most of the harm occurred in Washington.

Graduate Management Admission Council v. Raju, 241 F. Supp. 2d 589 (E.D. Va. 2003).

Plaintiff GMAC, a nonprofit organization located in McLean, Virginia, administers the Graduate Management Admission Test (GMAT), which is used by graduate business schools to assess applicants. Raju, a citizen of India, registered the domain names "gmatplus.com" and "gmatplus.net" in April and May 2000, respectively. Using these domain names, Raju set up websites from which he allegedly sold, as test preparation materials, actual questions from old GMAT exams that had never been published or available elsewhere. GMAC sued Raju for using the trademarked name "GMAT" on his website and for selling copyright-protected questions without authorization from GMAC. The court ruled that while exercise of personal jurisdiction over Raju could not be justified under the "minimum contacts" analysis, the "effects" test did provide a sufficient basis for exercising personal jurisdiction over Raju. Because Raju directed his website at American residents, and because he directed harm at GMAC, a Virginia corporation, the court concluded that it had personal jurisdiction over Raju.

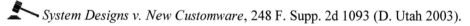 *Amway Corp. v. Procter & Gamble Co.*, No. 1:98-CV-726, 2000 U.S. Dist. LEXIS 372 (W.D. Mich. Jan. 6, 2000), *aff'd* 346 F.3d 180 (6th Cir. 2003).

The defendant, an Oregon resident, operated a passive website entitled "Amway: the Untold Story," on which he posted anecdotal information about individuals' negative experiences with Amway Corporation, a mail-order company located in Michigan. Amway joined the defendant to a suit it had initiated against Procter & Gamble in Michigan federal court for tortious interference with contract, among other claims, based on allegations that Procter & Gamble had facilitated the development of the defendant's website. Amway alleged that the defendant caused harm to Amway in Michigan by publishing on his website defamatory statements about the company and its officers.

The defendant asserted that his website was "passive" and therefore, under *Zippo*, the court could not exercise personal jurisdiction over him. The court acknowledged that for personal jurisdiction to exist there must be "something more" than merely a passive site. The court, however, determined that "'something more' may be satisfied under the 'effects doctrine.'"

Thus, the court analyzed the case under *Calder* and concluded that the plaintiff must show the following to establish jurisdiction over an out-of-state defendant: "(1) the defendant committed an intentional tort; (2) the plaintiff felt the brunt of the harm in the forum such that the forum can be said to be the focal point of the harm suffered by the plaintiff as a result of that tort; (3) the defendant expressly aimed his tortious conduct at the forum such that the forum can be said to be the focal point of the tortious activity." 2000 U.S. Dist. LEXIS 372 at *11. Applying these factors, the court first determined that Amway had alleged that the defendant committed an intentional tort. It then concluded that Amway suffered the brunt of the harm in Michigan, its principal place of business. Finally, the court found that the defendant had an "insider's knowledge" of Amway and specifically targeted his website at the company and its officers in Michigan. *Id.* at *15. Accordingly, the focal point of the harm was in Michigan. Based on these factors, the court determined that it could exercise personal jurisdiction over the defendant.

The U.S. Court of Appeals for the Sixth Circuit affirmed the judgment of the trial court, but did not discuss the jurisdictional issues.

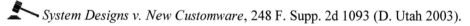 *System Designs v. New Customware*, 248 F. Supp. 2d 1093 (D. Utah 2003).

System Designs, a computer software company located in Utah, sued New Customware, a California corporation, for infringement of the trademark name "Customware." Defendant New Customware operated a website at www.customware.com, where it posted information about its software training programs and offered both online and on-location training. Because the website solicited potential customers nationwide by providing a national toll-free number, and permitted customers to register, set up and pay for classes online, the court concluded that New Customware had effectively aimed its services at the Utah market. The court noted that a simple trademark search of "Customware" would have yielded the result that the name had already been trademarked in Utah, thereby warning the defendant that it might be subject to suit there. Therefore, the court considered any infringing conduct to have been targeted toward, and any harm arising out of infringement to have occurred in, Utah. Based on the interactivity of the website and its intent to attract customers from Utah to participate in the training programs, the court concluded it could exercise personal jurisdiction over New Customware.

⚖ *Wagner v. Miskin*, 660 N.W.2d 593 (N.D. 2003).

Miskin, a University of North Dakota student, allegedly used multiple media to defame her physics professor, Wagner. The court, applying the effects test, concluded that the statements Miskin posted on the Internet were directly aimed at North Dakota and its residents. Miskin posted her statements on a website located at www.undnews.com, a site dedicated to events at the University of North Dakota. Based on this fact, as well as Miskin's use of University of North Dakota email address to allegedly harass Wagner, the court concluded that the trial court had not erred in exercising personal jurisdiction over Miskin.

See also D.C. Micro Development, Inc. v. Lange, et al., 246 F. Supp. 2d 705 (W.D. Ky. 2003) (hacking into a server located in Lexington, Kentucky and emailing 150 Kentucky residents satisfies the "purposeful availment" prong of the effects test; effects in Kentucky were foreseeable).

Cases in Which the "Effects Test" Was Applied and Assertion of Jurisdiction Was Found Not to Be Proper

⚖ *Naxos Resources (U.S.A.) Ltd. v. Southam Inc.*, 24 Media L. Rep. (BNA) 2265 (C.D. Cal. 1996).

Naxos Resources, a wholly owned California subsidiary of a Canadian corporation, sued the Canadian publisher of the *Vancouver Sun* in California over an allegedly libelous article published in the *Sun*. Approximately 500 hard copies of the *Sun* were routinely distributed in California and the article was available to readers on the Internet and through LEXIS and WESTLAW.

The court noted that under the "effects test," personal jurisdiction did not exist unless the plaintiff showed: (1) that the defendant's article was "calculated" to cause injury in the forum state; and (2) that the defendant "knew or intended" that the "brunt" of the injury would be felt in the forum state. *Id.* at 2267.

The court held that the plaintiff failed to meet either prong of the test. First, the article was distributed and read primarily in Canada and therefore did not appear directed at California in particular. *Id.* at 2267-68. Second, it was not at all clear that the article's reference to "Naxos Resources Ltd." was intended to refer to the plaintiff, Naxos Resources (U.S.A.), rather than to its parent corporation, Naxos Resources (Canada). *Id.* Consequently, the court concluded that due process prohibited it from exercising personal jurisdiction over the defendant. *Id.* at 2269. (Application of the *Keeton* test to this case is discussed at page 289).

⚖ *Copperfield v. Cogedipresse*, 26 Media L. Rep. (BNA) 1185 (C.D. Cal. 1997).

In addition to rejecting the plaintiff's argument that the court had general jurisdiction over the defendant (discussed above at page 268), the court, employing the "effects test," also declined to exercise specific jurisdiction over the defendant. The court found that the alleged defamation was not "primarily directed at plaintiffs in California" and that the defendants did not "kn[o]w or intend[] that the brunt of the injury caused by the defamation would be felt in California." 26 Media L. Rep. at 1189. The court noted, among other things, that "[t]he alleged defamation was contained in an article published in France in a French magazine, written in the French language, investigated by French reporters, and with a circulation primarily to readers in France." *Id.*

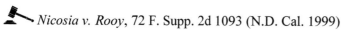 *Nicosia v. Rooy*, 72 F. Supp. 2d 1093 (N.D. Cal. 1999)

The plaintiff, a California resident, brought an action against the defendant, a Washington State resident, for slander and libel in connection with statements the defendant published on her website. The court determined that a nonresident's maintenance of a website is not sufficient by itself to establish jurisdiction. Rather, the court maintained that a nonresident defendant must do "something more" to direct its activities to the forum state.

The court determined that "something more" existed in this case because the defendant "sent at least eleven emails, out of a total 100, to California addresses, inviting the recipients to view the articles on her website." The court rejected the defendant's contention that personal jurisdiction could not be exercised because the emails she sent merely invited people to view her website, and thus did not deliver the defamatory material into the forum state. The court deemed the defendant's argument "a distinction without a difference" because the "email invitations target California residents in a way similar to sending the defamatory materials." 72 F. Supp. 2d at 1095.

 *Millennium Enterprises, Inc. v. Millennium Music, L.P., et al.*, 33 F. Supp. 2d 907 (D. Or. 1999).

The plaintiff, an Oregon corporation that owned retail outlets named "Music Millennium," filed suit against the defendants, Millennium Music, Inc. and Millennium Music, L.P., both South Carolina companies, alleging trademark infringement and dilution, and unfair competition. Both parties sold music through retail stores and the Internet, but the majority of the defendants' business was conducted through their retail stores in South Carolina. The defendants' contacts with Oregon consisted of a website available to consumers in Oregon, the sale of a single compact disc to an Oregon resident via the website, which was orchestrated by the plaintiff through an acquaintance, and limited purchases from an Oregon manufacturer. The defendants filed a motion to dismiss for lack of personal jurisdiction.

The court held that the defendants' one commercial sale in Oregon and their limited purchases from an Oregon manufacturer did not establish the requisite minimum contacts. The court then rejected the plaintiff's argument that the defendants should be subject to jurisdiction under the *Calder* "effects test" because the effects of the infringing activities caused harm in Oregon. The court found there was no evidence that the defendants intentionally directed their activities at Oregon knowing that the plaintiff would be harmed. Finally, the court undertook a *Zippo* analysis and held that although the defendants' website was interactive and had the potential for sales and contacts with all Internet users, "deliberate action" within the forum state was lacking and therefore personal jurisdiction was not proper. 33 F. Supp. 2d at 921. The court stated that the fact that someone who accesses the defendants' website can purchase a compact disc does not render the defendants' actions purposefully directed at the forum.

Search Force, Inc. v. Dataforce International, Inc., 112 F. Supp. 2d 771 (S.D. Ind. 2000).

The plaintiff, Search Force, Inc., owner of the trademark "Data Force," brought an action in federal court in Indiana against the defendant, Dataforce International, Inc., alleging unfair competition and trademark infringement. The defendant moved to dismiss the suit for lack of personal jurisdiction. Search Force maintained its principal place of business in Indiana, while Dataforce conducted business in Florida. Both corporations provided employment services, including personnel recruitment and placement, in the area of information technology. Both companies also used Internet postings, national advertising, and toll-free numbers to reach prospective recruits and employers. They both paid fees to post job openings on two interactive, online-recruiting websites owned and operated by third parties. However, Dataforce only advertised one job position located in Indiana, and the majority of its placements were for positions located in Florida. It did not have any employees, agents, contractors, or offices in Indiana, nor did it circulate any hard-copy advertisements in that state.

The court stated that "something more" than mere Internet presence was required to establish personal jurisdiction over the defendant. In the context of trademark infringement claims in which the mark is used in connection with the defendant's Internet activity, the "something more" is provided by a particularized injury suffered in the forum state. In other words, the court stated, the mere fact that the forum state is the principal place of business for the plaintiff does not form the basis of personal jurisdiction. The court observed that recent precedent had diverged from an earlier trend that presumed personal jurisdiction where a defendant used an interactive website and did not purposefully avoid the forum state. More recent cases supported the conclusion that the defendant must avail itself of the forum state in a manner that is more purposeful than simply including an allegedly infringing mark on an interactive website.

The court found that Dataforce had not entered into or maintained any continuing relationship with any Indiana resident or entity. The injury to Search Force was not concentrated in Indiana except to the extent that the plaintiff's main operations were conducted in that state. Dataforce's Internet activity was not specifically directed to Indiana, and the single listing of an Indiana position placed several years before the suit did not create any marketplace confusion that was particularized to Indiana. Therefore, the court dismissed the suit for lack of personal jurisdiction over the defendant.

CoStar Group, Inc., et al. v. LoopNet, Inc., 106 F. Supp. 2d 780 (D. Md. 2000).

CoStar Group, Inc. and CoStar Realty Information, Inc. (collectively "CoStar"), both Delaware corporations with their principal place of business in Maryland, created, produced, and distributed databases containing photographs and descriptions of real estate. The defendant, LoopNet, a California corporation, provided a web hosting service for users who wanted to advertise real estate over the Internet. Users of the LoopNet service could post information and photographs on the site, which could then be searched by others. Before the photographs were posted, they were reviewed to ensure that the pictures were related to real estate and did not bear any copyright notice. Only after review were the photographs posted, and then they were posted by a LoopNet employee, not the users. The LoopNet site was available to Maryland residents and contained listings of Maryland properties. CoStar filed suit alleging direct and contributory copyright infringement by LoopNet based on its posting of several photographs from

CoStar databases. In response, LoopNet filed a motion to dismiss the suit for lack of personal jurisdiction.

CoStar asserted that the court could exercise personal jurisdiction over LoopNet based on the "effects" test. The court disagreed, stating that "[t]he mere fact that a nonresident defendant's act causes an effect in the forum state, or even that such effect was foreseeable, is not enough by itself to support jurisdiction. . . . Courts have carefully limited the application of the effects test to cases where the nonresident defendant commits an intentional tort knowing the conduct will cause harm to the plaintiff in the forum state." 106 F. Supp. 2d at 785. The court stated that there was no evidence that LoopNet had knowingly posted infringing photographs on its website. At best, the court postulated, the procedure by which the photographs were reviewed before their posting was negligent. The court explained that although the distinction between an intentional and negligent tort is irrelevant for purposes of copyright infringement liability, it is dispositive in the *Calder* "effects" analysis. Because CoStar failed to show intentional infringement on the part of the defendant, personal jurisdiction was not proper.

 Winfield Collection, Ltd. v. McCauley, 105 F. Supp. 2d 746 (E.D. Mich. 2000).

The plaintiff, Winfield Collection, Ltd., was a Michigan manufacturer and seller of home-craft patterns. The defendant, McCauley, was a citizen of Texas who purchased craft patterns from the plaintiff by mail. McCauley made crafts based upon the plaintiff's patterns and sold almost all of these crafts in the Houston area. However, two customers in Michigan purchased the defendant's crafts on eBay. The plaintiff sued for copyright infringement based on McCauley's commercial use of the patterns. The plaintiff claimed that the court had personal jurisdiction over the defendant based on the defendant's sales to the two Michigan residents and the interactive nature of the defendant's website.

The court granted the defendant's motion to dismiss for lack of personal jurisdiction. The court found that the defendant's contacts with Michigan were "random" and "attenuated"; the function of an eBay sale is to award the product to the highest bidder, and the defendant had no control over who that bidder would be. Therefore, she never purposefully availed herself of the privilege of doing business in Michigan. The court also rejected the plaintiff's argument that personal jurisdiction was proper due to the interactive nature of the defendant's website. The court countered that the real inquiry was whether the defendant had sufficient minimum contacts with the forum, and that the mere presence of an interactive website is not sufficient. "The manner of establishing or maintaining those contacts, and the technological mechanisms used in so doing, are mere accessories to the central inquiry." 105 F. Supp. 2d at 750. The plaintiff failed to present any evidence that the defendant targeted Michigan customers through her website. The court also applied the "effects test" and found that the defendant's conduct was not aimed at the forum state, nor did it have an effect there. The defendant's contacts with the forum state were therefore "fortuitous and de minimus" and beyond the defendant's control. *Id.* at 751.

See also Metcalf v. Lawson, 802 A.2d 1221 (N.H. 2002) (finding that the sale of an excavator through eBay by a seller in New Jersey to a purchaser in New Hampshire was not sufficient to create minimum contacts in New Hampshire).

Bailey v. Turbine Design, Inc., 86 F. Supp. 2d 790 (W.D. Tenn. 2000).

In addition to ruling that personal jurisdiction could not be asserted under the *Zippo* test, discussed above at page 262, the court held that personal jurisdiction likewise could not be asserted under the "effects test." The court stated that the "[p]laintiff was not attacked as a Tennessee businessman. Indeed, the alleged defamatory comments had nothing to do with plaintiff's state of residence. Thus, it cannot be said that the defamatory statements constitute actions 'expressly aimed' at Tennessee." 86 F. Supp. 2d at 796. Given these circumstances, the court refused to exercise personal jurisdiction based solely on the fact that "some of the harm caused by alleged tortious conduct occurred in Tennessee." *Id.*

Oasis Corp. v. Judd, et al., 132 F. Supp. 2d 612 (S.D. Ohio 2001).

The plaintiffs, the Oasis Corporation and several of its employees, were located in Ohio; the defendants were residents of Oklahoma. Oasis produced and distributed water coolers. The defendants, tenants of an Oklahoma building that had burned down, sought compensation from plaintiffs, whose product they believed to be responsible for the fire. After they were unsuccessful in their attempts to recover from the plaintiffs, the defendants launched a "gripe site" on the Internet. The gripe site voiced complaints about Oasis and provided the email addresses and phone numbers of several Oasis employees. The site was never used for commercial gain. Oasis and the employees filed suit, claiming that Oasis's trademarks had been damaged, and that the employees had been libeled and their privacy invaded. The defendants responded by filing a motion to dismiss the suit for lack of personal jurisdiction.

Three significant factors contributed to the court's decision to grant the motion to dismiss for lack of personal jurisdiction: (1) the alleged wrongs arose solely from the content of the defendants' website; (2) the site was noncommercial in nature; and (3) neither the defendants nor the website had any inherent connection to Ohio. The first factor was important to the court's determination that several calls, faxes, and email messages from the defendants to the plaintiffs were unrelated to the libel claims of the plaintiffs. The court then turned to the substance and function of the defendants' website. The noncommercial nature of the site led the court to believe that the *Zippo* interactivity analysis did not apply. Finally, the court determined that the website had no connection to Ohio. The computers hosting the site were not located in Ohio, nor had there been meaningful interaction between the site and a significant number of Ohio residents. Applying the "effects test," the court also concluded that Ohio was not the "focal point" of the website's accusations.

Revell v. Lidov, 2001 WL 285253 (N.D. Tex. Mar. 20, 2001), *aff'd*, 317 F.3d 467 (5th Cir. 2002).

The defendant published an article on a Columbia University website implicating the plaintiff in an alleged conspiracy involving the bombing of PanAm Flight 103. The plaintiff, a resident of Texas, sued the defendant for libel in federal court in Texas. The defendant, Lidov, moved to dismiss the complaint for lack of personal jurisdiction, claiming he had never solicited or engaged in any business or entered into any contract with any Texas resident. The defendant also claimed he was unaware that the plaintiff resided in Texas, and that he did not have a commercial purpose in disseminating the article. Though items could be purchased through the website, both parties stipulated that the article itself could not be purchased and could only be viewed by those who chose to access the site.

The trial court held that the plaintiff had failed to establish the minimum contacts necessary to proceed in Texas court. The opinion concluded that the website was passive under the *Zippo* analysis. The mere ability of users to post documents on the portion of the site where articles were displayed did not make the site interactive in the court's eyes. The court reached this conclusion even though other portions of the site were more interactive. It also rejected application of the "effects" test, noting that, in this case, the material was not intentionally circulated in such a manner that the defendant would have known his defamatory statements would have reached the forum state. Additionally, the court stated that the article did not address the plaintiff's role as a resident of Texas, but instead criticized his national persona, further indicating that the defendant did not knowingly direct the Internet posting to the forum state.

The U.S. Court of Appeals for the Fifth Circuit affirmed. The court viewed the *Zippo* analysis as ill suited to the general jurisdiction inquiry, "because even repeated contacts with forum residents by a foreign defendant may not constitute the requisite substantial, continuous and systematic contacts required for a finding of general jurisdiction." But the court had no trouble disposing of the question of general jurisdiction: the defendants' contacts with Texas, even if continuous, were not "substantial."

As to specific jurisdiction, the court considered both the *Zippo* interactivity analysis and the *Calder* effects tests, ultimately concluding exercise of jurisdiction by the trial court would have been "unfair," and therefore would have violated the defendants' due process rights: "This inquiry into fairness captures the reasonableness of hauling a defendant from his home state before the courts of a sister state; in the main a pragmatic account of reasonable expectations—if you are going to pick a fight in Texas, it is reasonable to expect that it be settled there." The court looked to "the geographic focus of article," found that it was not Texas, and affirmed the trial court's dismissal for lack of personal jurisdiction over the defendants.

See also Jewish Defense Organization, Inc. v. Superior Court, 85 Cal. Rptr. 2d 611 (Cal. Ct. App. 1999) (personal jurisdiction in libel suit was not proper, in part because the plaintiff, a New York resident, failed to provide evidence that California was his principal place of business, or that the alleged libel was targeted at California or would cause the brunt of any harm there).

Medinah Mining v. Amunategui, et al., 237 F. Supp. 2d 1132 (D. Nev. 2002).

Medinah Mining, a Nevada corporation, filed suit against numerous defendants for allegedly posting defamatory messages on a website. Defendant James Ingram, a resident of Arkansas, moved to dismiss the lawsuit filed in federal court in Nevada for lack of personal jurisdiction.

Medinah Mining is a publicly traded company that is incorporated in Nevada and headquartered in California, but operates in Chile. Medinah alleged that Ingram posted false and defamatory statements about Medinah Mining and its officers on www.ragingbull.com, an interactive site that reports financial news and permits users to post information about publicly traded companies. Medinah alleged that Ingram's statements drove down the trading price of Medinah stock.

The court applied the "effects" test, pointing out that where the plaintiff's principal place of business is not the forum state, it is difficult to find that messages were directed there. Because Medinah was merely incorporated in Nevada and did not have any contacts or operations within the state, Ingram could not have directed his alleged defamation to Nevada. Furthermore, there must be evidence that harm was suffered in the forum state. The court concluded that because any alleged harm could not plausibly have been directed toward nor felt in Nevada, it could not exercise personal jurisdiction over Ingram. The court therefore dismissed the case.

English Sports Betting Inc. v. Tostigan, et al., Civ. No. 01-2202, 2002 U.S. Dist. LEXIS 4985 (E.D. Pa. March 15, 2002).

The plaintiff, Dennis Atiyeh, a Pennsylvania resident and owner of a Jamaica-based, online gambling enterprise, alleged that the defendant author and website owners libeled him by publishing articles about the plaintiff's legal problems. The plaintiff argued personal jurisdiction over the defendants was proper under the "effects test" because the defendants "purposely targeted a Pennsylvania resident with defamatory comments." *Id.* at *7. The court rejected this argument, ruling that it did not have jurisdiction over the defendants. The court stated that the defendant's audience was targeted based upon a shared interest in off-shore sports gambling, rather than based on a geographic location. *Id.* at *9.

Griffis v. Luban, 646 N.W.2d 527 (Minn. 2002), *cert. denied*, 123 S. Ct. 1483 (2003).

A Minnesota resident posted a message on the Internet challenging an Alabama teacher's credentials, and accusing the teacher of obtaining her degree "from a box of Cracker Jack." The teacher sued in an Alabama court for defamation, and obtained an injunction prohibiting the Minnesota resident from continuing to make such allegations. The teacher filed the Alabama judgment with a Minnesota court and sought to enforce the injunction. A Minnesota trial court found that the Alabama court had personal jurisdiction over the defendant, and the defendant appealed. To determine whether the Minnesota court could enforce the Alabama judgment against the Minnesota defendant, the Minnesota Supreme Court applied the *Calder* effects test. The Minnesota Supreme Court held that the plaintiff teacher had not satisfied the third prong of the effects test: the plaintiff did not show that the defendant had expressly aimed her tortious conduct at the Alabama forum such that Alabama was the focal point of the defamation. That the defendant knew that the teacher lived and worked in Alabama was not sufficient to warrant exercise of personal jurisdiction in Alabama over the defendant. The Minnesota Supreme Court vacated the decision of the Minnesota trial court enforcing the Alabama judgment. The U.S. Supreme Court recently declined to review the case.

Pavlovich v. Superior Court of Santa Clara County, 58 P.3d 2 (Cal. 2002), *order vacating stay*, No. 02A530, 2003 WL 46660 (U.S. Jan. 3, 2003).

Pavlovich, a resident of Texas, knowingly posted to the Internet computer code that could be used to decrypt DVD copy protection controls. The DVD Copy Control Association, Inc. (DVD CCA, the party in interest in the case) sued Pavlovich in California, seeking an injunction requiring removal of the code from the Internet. The plaintiffs argued that California jurisdiction was proper because the industry most harmed by the defendant's conduct, the film industry, is primarily situated in California. The

California Supreme Court rejected that argument. Applying the effects test, the court held that the mere knowledge that an intentional act might have an adverse affect on an industry connected to the California-based plaintiffs was not sufficient to establish that the act was expressly targeted at California. The only contact Pavlovich had with California was via the Internet; he owned no property, had no telephone, and conducted no business in California. His knowledge that his actions might harm a company located in California did not, in the court's view, warrant exercise of personal jurisdiction by a California court.

The DVD CCA requested a stay of the ruling by the U.S. Supreme Court, which granted its request on December 26, 2002. But on January 3, 2003, the Supreme Court vacated the stay, ending DVD CCA's efforts to keep the California Supreme Court's ruling from taking effect.

 Leap Wireless International v. Endesa, 2003 WL 1871100 (Cal. Ct. App. Apr. 14, 2003) (not for publication).

Leap Wireless, a Delaware corporation with its principal place of business in San Diego, California, owns a subsidiary called Inversiones, a Chilean corporation, which in turn owns Smartcom, another Chilean corporation providing wireless telecommunications services in Chile. Endesa, a Spanish corporation, learned that Leap Wireless was interested in selling Smartcom and entered into negotiations with Leap for the purchase of Smartcom. Endesa made an initial payment toward the purchase in 2000, but withheld payment of the balance in May 2001, alleging that Leap had breached the purchase agreement. Leap then sued Endesa in California state court for the balance of the purchase price. Endesa moved for dismissal for lack of personal jurisdiction; the trial court granted the motion.

On appeal, Leap claimed that Endesa had sufficiently targeted California to justify exercise of personal jurisdiction by a California court: Endesa had met with Leap in San Diego to negotiate the sale; it had made telephone calls and sent emails and faxes into California; and it maintained a website that could be viewed in English. The court disagreed, finding that the San Diego meeting was preliminary in nature and insufficient to establish sufficient contacts. The court also concluded that the telephone calls and emails were too attenuated to support a finding of personal jurisdiction. Finally, the court concluded that an English language choice on Endesa's website did not sufficiently target California; rather, "additional evidence of express aiming or intentional targeting" is required to establish personal jurisdiction. *Id.* at 5. Therefore, the trial court dismissed the case for lack of personal jurisdiction over Endesa.

 Falwell v. Cohn, 2003 WL 751130 (W.D. Va. Mar. 4, 2003).

Jerry Falwell, a well-known evangelist, sued Gary Cohn, a resident of Illinois, in federal court in Virginia for registering and operating two parody websites located at www.jerryfallwell.com and www.jerryfalwell.com. Cohn used the sites to post anti-Falwell material, including cartoons, jokes, and articles. Defendant Cohn moved to dismiss the case for lack of personal jurisdiction. Cohn had never lived in Virginia, owned property in Virginia or conducted business in Virginia. But the court found most compelling the fact that Cohn's websites were directed at a national audience, and not specifically at Virginia residents. Because his websites did not specifically target Virginia residents, Cohn could not "reasonably anticipate being hauled into court" there. *Id.* at *3.

The court dismissed the suit for lack of personal jurisdiction. (For a discussion of this case in the context of trademarks, see Chapter 2, page 92.)

B.E.E. International v. Hawes, et al., 267 F. Supp. 2d 477 (M.D.N.C. 2003).

B.E.E., an Israeli corporation with an American subsidiary, sued several former employees and Belovo, S.A., a Belgian corporation, for trademark infringement, breach of contract, and unfair trade practices. Belovo S.A. had previously served as B.E.E.'s exclusive distributor of emulsifying machines in Europe. B.E.E. contended that Belovo's website provided sufficient contacts in the U.S. to warrant the exercise of personal jurisdiction. Belovo's website contained only information about its products, and listed Michael Hawes, another defendant and North Carolina resident, as the point of contact for American inquiries. In granting Belovo's motion to dismiss for lack of personal jurisdiction, the court applied the three-part analysis set forth in *ALS Scan*. (For a discussion of the *ALS Scan* case, see page 272.) The court first held that listing Hawes as a U.S. contact did not rise to the level of interactivity and targeting of electronic activity at the state, so as to justify a finding of personal jurisdiction. Second, the court found that by listing Hawes as the contact person, Belovo did not indicate intent to do business within the state of North Carolina. Finally, the electronic activity of posting an informational website listing Mr. Hawes was not the direct cause of the alleged harm. Based on these facts, the court dismissed the claims against Belovo S.A. for lack of personal jurisdiction. *Id.* at 486.

See also Tamburo v. eBay, Inc., et al., 2002 U.S. Dist. LEXIS 22686 (N.D. Ill. Nov. 22, 2002) (district court lacks personal jurisdiction where defendant's sole contact with the forum state was the deposit of funds into plaintiff's account as part of the eBay payment process).

Keeton Test

In *Keeton v. Hustler Magazine, Inc.*, 465 U.S. 770 (1984), the Supreme Court decided that a nonresident defendant not physically present in the forum state, but who "continuously and deliberately" circulates its publications in such forum, should reasonably foresee answering for the truth of its content in that state. 465 U.S. at 781. In *Keeton*, the publisher produced a national magazine targeted to a nationwide audience, yet with only a small percentage of its overall circulation aimed at the forum state. In the court's mind, however, there was "no unfairness in calling it to answer for the contents of that publication wherever a substantial number of copies are regularly sold and distributed." *Id.* Therefore, under the *Keeton* test, a court might choose to exercise jurisdiction over a nonresident defendant who has posted a libelous publication on the Internet, depending on whether such posting was continuously and deliberately available to a wide audience, including residents of the forum state. The standard for what constitutes a "substantial number of copies" has been subject to various interpretations.

Naxos Resources (U.S.A.) Ltd. v. Southam Inc., 24 Media L. Rep. (BNA) 2265 (C.D. Cal. 1996).

After failing to find a basis for jurisdiction based on the "effects test" (discussed above at page 276), the court found that neither the newspaper's print circulation of 500 copies per week in California nor the newspaper's availability online in California constituted systematic and continuous activity sufficient to allow exercise of general jurisdiction over the defendants. Citing *Keeton*, the court concluded that electronic contacts caused by mere presence on the web could not give rise to general jurisdiction because, if they could, online publishers could be subject to suit in any state for activities unrelated to the state.

 Telco Communications Group, Inc. v. An Apple A Day, Inc., et al., 977 F. Supp. 404 (E.D. Va. 1997).

The plaintiff, a Virginia corporation, alleged that a Missouri corporation posted multiple press releases on the Internet that libeled the plaintiff and depressed its stock price. The plaintiff claimed that jurisdiction attached under Virginia's long-arm statute, which permits jurisdiction over a defendant that causes injury within the state if the defendant regularly conducts business in the state.

The court found that exercising jurisdiction over the nonresident defendants was proper pursuant both to the Virginia long-arm statute and the Due Process Clause. The court noted that, in posting the press releases in question, the defendants were advertising their firm and soliciting investment-banking assistance, and that this advertising and solicitation was available to Virginia residents 24 hours a day. The court ruled that these activities "constitute[d] a persistent course of conduct, and that the two or three press releases rise to the level of regularly doing or soliciting business [in Virginia]." *Telco Communications Group*, 977 F. Supp. at 407. The court emphasized that its ruling did not offend the Due Process Clause because the defendants reasonably should have known that allegedly libelous information posted on the Internet would be circulated or distributed in Virginia and that plaintiff was based in Virginia. Thus, "their activities were sufficient to serve as an analogue for physical presence." *Id.*

 Young v. New Haven Advocate, 315 F.3d 256 (4th Cir. 2002), *cert. denied*, 123 S. Ct. 2092 (2003).

The plaintiff, a warden of a Virginia prison, sued Connecticut-based newspapers *The New Haven Advocate* and *The Hartford Courant* for libel allegedly stemming from articles written about the prison's treatment of Connecticut inmates. The defendants argued that they had a miniscule number of subscriptions in Virginia and that none of the writing, reporting, or editing took place in Virginia, although the reporters performed telephone interviews with Virginia sources and the articles were posted on the newspapers' websites. The plaintiff countered he had never been to Connecticut, but he was able to view the allegedly defamatory articles in Virginia via the Internet.

The federal trial court first applied the "effects test" and found that the harm to the warden's reputation, if any, occurred in Virginia. Then, applying the *Keeton* test, the court concluded that an article regarding Virginia prisons and available in Virginia via the Internet was sufficient to allow personal jurisdiction over the defendant newspapers. *Young v. New Haven Advocate*, 184 F. Supp. 2d 498, 508 (W.D. Va. 2001). The U.S. Court of Appeals for the Fourth Circuit reversed. The court held that a newspaper's presence on the Internet, by itself, was not sufficient to subject the newspaper to personal jurisdiction in every state in which its website was accessible. The court found that the newspaper's content was aimed at a Connecticut audience and that it did not target Virginia readers simply by making its content available online. Therefore, the newspaper did not have sufficient contacts with Virginia to warrant exercise of personal jurisdiction. A Virginia court could properly exercise jurisdiction over defendant newspapers only if they had "manifest[ed] an intent to target and focus on" a Virginia audience. 315 F.3d at 256.

 Carefirst of Maryland, Inc. v. Carefirst Pregnancy Centers, 334 F.3d 390 (4th Cir. 2003).

The plaintiff, a Maryland insurance company, brought an action against the defendant, an anti-abortion advocacy group based in Chicago, for alleged infringement of the plaintiff's "Carefirst" trademark. Defendant's only contact with Maryland was through its website; although the defendant had received more than $1,500 in donations from Maryland residents, it had never solicited funds from Maryland residents or otherwise targeted the forum. The Fourth Circuit Court of Appeals affirmed the trial court's dismissal of the case for lack of personal jurisdiction, citing the effects test and its earlier decision in *Young v. New Haven Advocate*, 315 F.3d 256 (4th Cir. 2002). The *Carefirst* court said three factors were relevant to determining whether specific jurisdiction was proper: (1) the extent to which the defendant has purposefully availed itself of the privilege of conducting activities in the state; (2) whether the plaintiffs' claims arise out of those activities directed at the state; and (3) whether the exercise of personal jurisdiction would be constitutionally "reasonable." The court found the defendant operated a "semi-interactive" website, but that it was directed at Chicago-area pregnant women, and not at Maryland residents. Because the defendant did not act with the "manifest intent" of targeting Maryland residents through its website, the harm to the Maryland plaintiff's trademark was not in itself sufficient to establish specific jurisdiction, the court concluded. *Id.* at 401.

Realuyo v. Villa Abrille., 2003 WL 21537754 (S.D.N.Y. July 8, 2003).

The availability of a "passive" news website to New York residents was not enough to confer personal jurisdiction over Filipino defendants regarding an allegedly defamatory article posted on the website, the U.S. District Court for the Southern District of New York ruled. The plaintiff, a New Jersey resident who practiced law in New York, sued the defendant website publisher for libel based on the article, posted on a defendant's website. The court first found general jurisdiction was lacking because none of the defendants had a continuous presence in New York. The court then ruled that there were no grounds for exercising specific jurisdiction based upon the accessibility of the website to New York residents, even though 332 of the website's 7,000 registered users lived in New York. For specific jurisdiction to attach, the court said the defendant must have "engaged in purposeful activities" in New York and there must be a "substantial relationship" between the activities and the claim asserted. *Id.* at *15. Quoting *Young v. New Haven Advocate*, 315 F.3d 256 (4th Cir. 2002), the *Realuyo* court stated that application of the effects test in the Internet context "requires proof that the out-of-state defendant's internet activity is expressly targeted at or directed to the forum state." *Id.* at *30-31. Finding no evidence that the article specifically targeted New York residents, the court concluded it would be unreasonable for the defendant to expect to be haled into a court in New York.

Lawsuits Brought in Foreign Jurisdictions

Potential liability in defamation suits brought in foreign courts is particularly troubling to U.S. publishing companies that maintain substantial assets abroad. But it also presents a broader societal risk. No legal system in the world is as protective of speech as the U.S. system. If U.S. publishers subject themselves to suit throughout the world every time they publish on the web, financial self-interest will necessarily make them more timid, less willing to take on difficult issues and powerful foreign interests.

For discussion of international defamation issues generally, *see* Chapter 5, pages 154 to 156.

A case involving the government of Zimbabwe illustrates the potential conflict between American free speech rights and restrictions on speech in other countries. Zimbabwe employs intelligence officers to surf the Internet looking for criticisms of the country. When officers found an allegedly false criticism of the government on Guardian Unlimited, the website of London-based newspaper *The Guardian*, prosecutors charged *Guardian* journalist Andrew Meldrum with the crime of "false publication." Prosecutors argued that the statute allows punishment of anyone who publishes an article that is subsequently proven false, no matter how credible the information in the report appeared at the time of publication. One of the issues facing the Zimbabwe court was whether the article was "published" in London, where it was uploaded to the Guardian Unlimited web server, or in Harare, Zimbabwe, where it was downloaded at the Central Intelligence Organization. Meldrum was eventually acquitted of the charge; but the court refused to rule on the jurisdictional issue. *See* Zimbabwe "Reporter Cleared, Then Expelled," BBC News (July 15, 2002), at http://news.bbc.co.uk/1/hi/world/africa/2128651.stm.

For a discussion of this case in the context of defamation, *see* Chapter 5, page 155.

Dow Jones & Co. v. Gutnick, [2002] HCA 56 (Dec. 10, 2002).

On December 10, 2002, Australia's highest court rejected the efforts of Dow Jones & Company to have a libel suit against it transferred from Australia to a U.S. court. The case involved an allegedly libelous article about Australian mining magnate Joseph Gutnick, who lives and works in Victoria, Australia. Gutnick claimed to have been libeled by a February 2000 *Barron's* article that appeared on WSJ.com, the online edition of *The Wall Street Journal*. The court found that Australian courts have jurisdiction to hear a libel claim based on the article, even though few print copies of the article circulated in Australia and the online version of the article was likely accessed by a few hundred readers, at most, in Australia. Dow Jones sought to have the case transferred to a U.S. court, arguing that the online version of the article was "published" in New Jersey where Dow Jones' web servers are located, and, therefore, a U.S. court, not an Australian court, should hear any challenge to the article. Dow Jones contended that subjecting a web publisher to suit in every nation in the world from which its website could be accessed would severely curtail freedom of speech on the web. The High Court of Australia, however, disagreed, finding that "the spectre which Dow Jones sought to conjure up in the present appeal, of a publisher forced to consider every article it publishes on the World Wide Web against the defamation laws of every country from Afghanistan to Zimbabwe is seen to be unreal when it is recalled that in all except the most unusual of cases, identifying the person about whom material is published will readily identify the defamation law to which that person may resort."

The reporter who wrote the article responded by filing a writ with the United Nations Human Rights Commission. The reporter claimed that he has been denied his right to free speech in violation of Article 19 of the United Nations' International Covenant on Civil and Political Rights. He also claimed that because Australia has submitted to the jurisdiction of the United Nations Human Rights Commission, Australia would be obligated to modify its libel laws if the United Nations finds a violation. "Australian Laws Challenged at UN" (Apr. 18, 2003), *at* http://www.smh.com.au/articles/2003/04/18/1050172745955.html. The trial in Victoria is scheduled to take place in early 2004.

For discussion of the defamation aspects of this case, *see* Chapter 5, page 159.

See also Cullen v. White (2003) WASC 153. (Western Australia's supreme court ruled that a California resident defamed an Australian academic by publishing defamatory remarks on the Internet, and the court awarded over $60,000 in damages).

Harrods, Ltd. v. Dow Jones & Co., [2003] EWHC 1162 (QB).

Harrods, a prominent British department store, sued Dow Jones & Co., owners of *The Wall Street Journal*, an American newspaper, for libel. On April 5, 2002, *The Wall Street Journal* published an article that described Harrods as "the Enron of Britain"; it also warned that if the company ever went public, investors should "question its every disclosure." The article referred to a satirical press release that Harrods issued the day before April Fool's Day, which suggested that Mohamed Al Fayed, Harrods' owner, might propose a public offering. The release indicated that all interested parties should contact LOOF LIRPA, April Fool spelled backwards.

After Harrods complained about the article, *The Wall Street Journal* replied that it had published the article as a joke, in response to Mr. Fayed's own prank. Dow Jones & Co. moved to dismiss the action in the English court, but the judge denied the motion. Despite the facts that the article did not appear in the European edition of *The Wall Street Journal*, that only ten American edition copies were sent to the U.K., and that very few readers accessed the article on the newspaper's WSJ.com website, the judge concluded that the English court system was the proper forum to decide the case. As of December 31, 2003, this case remained pending.

Limiting Recourse to Foreign Courts

The discussion below focuses on potential bars to suits brought in foreign jurisdictions. Because the United Kingdom and Canada, as English-speaking countries lacking the speech protections afforded under the U.S. Constitution, have proved attractive forums for defamation suits brought against U.S. publishers, those jurisdictions are the focal point of this discussion.

Jurisdiction and Service of Process

United Kingdom

If an electronic publication is accessed in the United Kingdom, personal jurisdiction over the publisher is presumed, subject to service of process according to the relevant rules. Mark Stephens, "Cyberspace: The Latest Developments in England," *Media Defense in the Twenty-First Century*, Libel Defense Resource Center Conference (1997), at 1. If an ISP is named as a defendant publisher, personal jurisdiction may be asserted even if the ISP's terms and conditions of use indicate a specific choice of law.

Where an action has been commenced against a U.S. defendant, a court in the United Kingdom is competent to hear the case: (1) if the defendant is present within the United Kingdom; (2) if the defendant consents to the court's jurisdiction; or (3) if there has been proper service on the U.S. defendant outside the jurisdiction in accordance with the

British Conflict of Law Rules. *See* P.M. North & J.J. Fawcett, *Chershire and North's Private International Law* 179, 191 (12th ed. 1992).

Some years ago, the High Court in London gave permission for service of process over the Internet in a case concerning anonymous email messages that were being transmitted into the United Kingdom from another part of Europe. *Anonymous v. Anonymous* [1996] (unreported).

The European Union's E-Commerce Directive mandates that proper choice of law is in the "country of origin" (that is, where the originator of the allegedly defamatory statements is domiciled) for its member states; however, the "country of origin" rule does not apply to countries outside the E.U., such as the United States. U.S. entities posting potentially defamatory materials on a website accessed within the E.U. may well be subject to a foreign nation's laws, even if the expression would otherwise be protected in the U.S. *See* Directive 2000/31/EC of the European Parliament and of the Council of 8 June 2000, available at http://europa.eu.int/comm/internal_market/en/ecommerce/2k-442.htm, on certain legal aspects of information society services, in particular electronic commerce, in the Internal Market, OJ L 178, 17.7.2000, p. 1; Thomas C. Vinje & Ann-Charlotte Hogberg, *Whose Law Governs in EU?*, N.Y.L.J., Apr. 30, 2001, p. 3.

Canada

In Canada, the general rule is that personal service will confer personal jurisdiction on the court. Steven M. Siros, *Borders, Barriers, and Other Obstacles to a Holistic Environment*, 13 N. Ill. U. L. Rev. 633, 646 (1993). Personal jurisdiction can be asserted over foreign defendants by service if there are consequences from the defendant's actions in the forum province, even if the damage was caused by activities abroad. *Id.* at 647.

Forum Non Conveniens

If a defendant is properly served and subject to a court's jurisdiction, the action may still be subject to a stay under the doctrine of *forum non conveniens*. In either the United Kingdom or Canada, if the foreign defendant is served inside the forum country, the burden is on the defendant to show that another forum is more appropriate. If, however, the defendant is served outside the forum country, the burden is on the plaintiff to demonstrate that the United Kingdom or Canada is the appropriate forum. Mark Stephens, "Cyberspace: The Latest Developments in England," *Media Defense in the Twenty-First Century*, at 2; *Frymer v. Brettschneider* [1994] 19 O.R. 3d 60, 84-85.

United Kingdom

English courts have developed a list of factors to consider in conducting a *forum non conveniens* analysis in the defamation context.

Berezovsky and Another v. Forbes Inc., [1998] E.M.L.R. 278 (C.A. Nov. 19, 1998).

The Court of Appeal overruled a trial court decision holding that the United Kingdom was not the appropriate forum for a libel action based on an article published in *Forbes* magazine. The court applied the fact-intensive *Spiliada* test (*see Spiliada Maritime Corp. v. Cansulex Ltd.* [1987] 1 AC 460, [1986] 3 All ER 843), which calls for the court to identify the jurisdiction in which the case may be tried most suitably for the interests of all the parties and for the ends of justice.

The trial court found that Russia would be the most appropriate forum because the plaintiffs were from Russia, witnesses were in Russia, and the plaintiffs' connections to England were tenuous. The Court of Appeal disagreed, finding that the plaintiff (a leading Russian businessman who also served as Deputy Secretary of the Security Council of the Russian Federation) had cultivated a reputation in England through years of effort and, as a result, the article accusing him of involvement in organized crime damaged his reputation in England. It further found that the magazine's content was international in scope and noted that the magazine was published worldwide on the Internet. Finally, it found that *Forbes* had about 6,000 readers in England, not including Internet readers. Thus, trying the case in the United Kingdom met the standards of *Spiliada. See also* "Libel Can Be Sued in Many Jurisdictions," *Times Newspapers, Ltd.,* Nov. 27, 1998.

Chada and Osicom Technologies Ltd. v. Dow Jones & Co. Inc., [1999] I.L.Pr. 829 (C.A. May 14, 1999).

The plaintiffs sued defendant for defamation over statements published in defendant's magazine. The Court of Appeal affirmed the trial court's stay of the proceedings on grounds of *forum non conveniens*. The court decided that the United States would be the more appropriate forum because: (1) only 1,257 copies of the magazine were sold in the United Kingdom, as compared to 283,520 copies sold in the United States; (2) the content of the magazine, including articles, advertising, and quotations from stock markets, related to the United States; (3) the plaintiff had a business relationship in the U.K. for only four months; and (4) there was no evidence showing that plaintiffs' reputation in the United Kingdom was harmed by the article. The court also listed eight factors that should be considered when analyzing *forum non conveniens* cases: (1) the personal status of the plaintiffs; (2) the business status of the plaintiffs; (3) the plaintiffs' connections to the U.K.; (4) the status of the defendants; (5) the extent of the publication; (6) the nature of the publication; (7) the meanings which the plaintiffs attach to the article; and (8) the juridical advantages and disadvantages of the case being heard in the U.K. as opposed to the U.S.

Canada

In *Olde v. Capital Publishing Ltd. Partnership,* 64 A.C.W.S. 3d 1138 (July 26, 1996), *appeal dismissed,* 77 A.C.W.S. 3d 970 (Jan. 22, 1998), the Ontario Court of Justice permanently stayed a libel suit against New York-based *Worth* magazine. Where all parties were U.S. citizens, 99% of the magazine's distribution was in the United States, the article focused primarily on business operations in the United States, and the bulk of the plaintiffs' injury, if any, occurred in the United States, the Court determined that "all of the relevant factors . . . point overwhelmingly to the U.S.A. as the appropriate jurisdiction." Ontario Ct. of App. Decision, at 1.

International Choice of Law

Even though a defamation suit is filed in a foreign court, that country's choice-of-law rules may require the court to apply the laws of another jurisdiction. If a foreign court determines, for example, that U.S. law has a more significant relationship to the action, it may apply the laws of the United States, rather than the laws of the forum. *Cf. Desai v. Hersh,* 719 F. Supp. 670 (N.D. Ill. 1989) (suggesting that a U.S. court would apply Indian law, rather than U.S. Constitutional law, where statements published in India were not on matters of public concern in the United States or where defendant intentionally and directly exploited the Indian market), *aff'd*, 954 F.2d 1408 (7th Cir.), *cert. denied*, 506 U.S. 865 (1992). If a foreign court applies U.S. law with its First Amendment protections, the advantages won by the plaintiff's forum shopping are lost.

In *Ellis v. Time, Inc.*, 26 Media L. Rep. 1225 (D.D.C. 1997), the plaintiff, in addition to his American libel law claims, argued that the court should apply English libel law based on the publication in Britain of the allegedly defamatory statements. The court rejected this contention because application of English libel standards would violate the First Amendment's protection of free speech.

Recognition and Enforcement of Foreign Judgments

The states in this country have traditionally relied on principles of "comity" in recognizing and giving effect to judgments obtained in foreign countries. *See Hilton v. Guyot*, 159 U.S. 113, 164 (1895). More recently, many states have codified the rule of comity by enacting the Uniform Foreign-Money Judgments Recognition Act (UFMJRA) available at http://www.law.upenn.edu/bll/ulc/fnact99/1920_69/ufmjra62.pdf. Craig A. Stern, "Foreign Judgments and the Freedom of Speech: Look Who's Talking," 60 Brook. L. Rev. 999, 1020-21 (1994).

Although the applicable law will vary slightly from state to state, generally, under the UFMJRA, other state statutes, or the common-law rule of comity, a state is precluded from enforcing a foreign judgment if the judgment was rendered in a proceeding incompatible with due process and can decline to enforce a judgment where enforcing the judgment would be repugnant to the public policy of the state. *See Uniform Foreign Money-Judgments Recognition Act* § 4, 13 U.L.A. 268 (1986). *See also* Jeremy Maltby, Note, "Juggling Comity and Self-Government: The Enforcement of Foreign Libel Judgments in U.S. Courts," 94 Colum. L. Rev. 1978, 1986-87 (1994). Some U.S. courts have refused to enforce British libel judgments on public policy grounds because the standards of British defamation law are antithetical to protections afforded the press by the U.S. Constitution. *Bachchan v. India Abroad Publications, Inc.*, 585 N.Y.S.2d 661, 664 (N.Y. Sup. Ct. 1992); *Telnikoff v. Matusevitch*, 702 A.2d 230, 239 (Md. 1997). Indeed, in *Bachchan*, the court suggested that where the public policy to which the foreign judgment is repugnant is embodied by the First Amendment, the refusal to recognize the judgment is "constitutionally mandated." 585 N.Y.S.2d at 663. *But see Desai v. Hersh*, 719 F. Supp. 670, 679-81 (N.D. Ill. 1989) (suggesting that the First Amendment can protect speech published in a foreign country only where the speech is on a matter of public concern in the United States, and that a defendant may shed his or her First Amendment protections if the defendant intentionally and directly exploits a foreign market).

However, at least one court has enforced a foreign judgment despite the UFMJRA. In *Reading & Bates Construction Co. v. Baker Energy Resources Corp.*, 976 S.W.2d 703 (Tex. Ct. App. 1998), the appeals court overruled a trial court decision refusing to enforce a Canadian patent infringement judgment on the grounds that it violated the public policy of the United States. *Reading & Bates*, 976 S.W.2d at 704. The appeals court ruled that the applicable public policy under the UFMJRA is state policy, not national policy. *Id.* at 709. Because federal courts have exclusive jurisdiction in patent and trademark actions, the court held that the measure of damages in patent infringement cases does not have an impact on the public policy of Texas. *Id.* at 708-09. The court also held that the judgment should not be denied effect on reciprocity grounds because it is not clear that Canada would automatically refuse to enforce a similar judgment rendered in Texas. *Id.* at 709-10.

In November 2000, a French court ordered Yahoo to stop French users from accessing Yahoo sites over which Nazi memorabilia were sold. Under French law, it is illegal to exhibit or sell objects with racist overtones. Yahoo France barred the sale of Nazi memorabilia, but French users could still access Yahoo.com, where such items were listed for sale. Yahoo subsequently prohibited the sale of Nazi merchandise on its auction sites, but asked a U.S. court for a declaratory judgment that it is not bound to filter out French users or face the $13,000-per-day fine for failure to do so threatened under French law. In 2001, the U.S. District Court in California ruled in *Yahoo, Inc. v. La Ligue Contre Le Racisme et L'Antisemitisme*, 169 F. Supp. 2d 1181, that U.S. law, not French law, governs Yahoo's right with respect to content on U.S.-based servers. The U.S. Court of Appeals for the Ninth Circuit heard argument on the appeal in December 2002. As of December 31, 2003, the appeal remains pending. *Yahoo, Inc. v. La Ligue Contre Le Racisme et L'Antisemitisme*, No. 01-17424 (9th Cir., filed Dec. 7, 2001). Meanwhile, an appeals court in France ruled that neither Yahoo nor its former CEO is guilty of condoning or justifying war crimes or crimes against humanity. *Association L'Amicale des Deportes d'Auschwitz v. Societe Yahoo Inc., Tribunal Correctionnel de Pari*s, case number unavailable (Feb. 11, 2003). *See* "French Court Ruling Ends Long-Term Saga Over Nazi Memorabilia Auctions on Yahoo," ELECTRONIC COMMERCE & LAW REPORT, Vol. 8, No. 7, p. 176 (Feb. 19, 2003); Jon Henley, "Yahoo Cleared in Nazi Case," THE GUARDIAN (Feb. 12, 2003), *available at* http://www.guardian.co.uk/international/story/ 0,3604,893642,00.html; "Ex-Yahoo Chief Acquitted Over Nazi Relics," CNET News.com (Feb. 11, 2003) *available at* http://news.com.com/2100-1023-984148.html.

For discussion of the free speech implications of this case, *see* Chapter 1, page 28.

Chapter 9: Personal Jurisdiction
Summary of the Law

- Personal jurisdiction is the power of a court to render and enforce a judgment against a person or legal entity, such as a corporation. Limitations on when a court may properly exercise jurisdiction over a defendant that doesn't reside in the forum state protect a defendant from being forced to defend himself in a distant state with which he has no real connection.

- Traditionally, a court had personal jurisdiction over those who lived, transacted business, or engaged in harmful conduct within the state's borders. However, the nature of the Internet allows a person easily to transmit information across state lines, and a defendant may not even know where his transmission will be received.

- Web-based contacts between a defendant and a forum state may be enough to warrant a court's exercise of personal jurisdiction over the defendant, even if the defendant never physically entered the forum state. The courts must determine whether exercising personal jurisdiction under the circumstances meets both the requirements of the state's "long-arm" statute and federal constitutional fairness requirements, embodied in the Due Process Clause of the Constitution.

- Personal jurisdiction may be either general or specific. Specific jurisdiction applies when the injury that is the subject of the suit arose directly out of the defendant's contact with the forum state. General jurisdiction applies when the defendant's contacts with the forum state are so pervasive that it's fair to require the defendant to defend himself in the forum state even if the conduct out of which the suit arises occurred elsewhere. The U.S. Supreme Court has ruled that the federal Constitution requires that a defendant have sufficient "minimum contacts" with a forum state before he is subject to the state's jurisdiction.

- In Internet-related cases, courts will often look to the totality of the contacts a defendant has with the forum state to determine whether they are "continuous and systematic." If so, the court may exercise general jurisdiction and determine whether the defendant is liable for a matter that occurred outside the state.

- A defendant's actions that "target" a particular state may result in personal jurisdiction over the defendant in that state. Courts look at the facts of each case to determine whether the defendant "purposefully availed" himself of the benefits of doing business in the state, or whether the defendant "purposefully directed" his activities toward the forum state.

- In evaluating whether a given website is sufficiently connected with the forum state to permit the exercise of personal jurisdiction over the operator of the site, courts often apply a "sliding-scale" analysis, evaluating the nature and quality of the contacts the website has with the state. At one end of the spectrum are highly interactive websites that invite interaction by residents of the forum state. Courts often find such interactivity sufficient to permit the court to exercise jurisdiction over the website even if the website is not, in any physical sense, located within the state. At the other end of the spectrum are purely passive websites that display information but invite no real interaction. Courts often find that the ability of state residents to access such a site is insufficient to convey the state's courts jurisdiction over the site. Many websites fall between these two ends of the scale.

- Courts also may apply an "effects test," which determines whether a defendant knew the focal point of any harm that might result from his conduct would be felt in the forum state. This test is often applied in the defamation, trademark infringement, and copyright infringement contexts.

MISCELLANEOUS

Unauthorized Access to Websites

Traditional protections against trespass and wiretapping have been applied in recent years to prohibit unauthorized access to websites.

Application of Trespass Law

Courts have had little difficulty finding that trespass law, despite its ancient roots, is relevant in the virtual world. But there has been considerable disagreement about the degree of interference the trespass must have caused to the plaintiff's computer system to be actionable.

eBay, Inc. v. Bidder's Edge, Inc., 100 F. Supp. 2d. 1058 (N.D. Cal. 2000).

Bidder's Edge conducted automated searches of more than 100 websites and aggregated their auction listings. eBay sued Bidder's Edge, alleging that its use of search "bots" to search the eBay site constituted trespass on eBay's website. According to eBay, the automated searches being conducted by Bidder's Edge took up an estimated 1.11% to 1.53% of eBay's server capacity, resulting in irreparable harm to eBay. A federal court in California found the concept of trespass applicable to computer systems and held that the defendant's unauthorized searches intentionally interfered with the plaintiff's possessory interest in the computer system, proximately causing damage to the plaintiff. The court enjoined Bidder's Edge from using bots to search the eBay site for listings, reasoning that if other aggregators did the same thing, eventually eBay's servers would be overwhelmed. Bidder's Edge appealed, but before the appeal was heard the parties settled the case, with Bidder's Edge paying eBay damages and agreeing to drop the appeal. *See* Troy Wolverton, "eBay, Bidder's Edge End Legal Dispute," CNET News.com (March 1, 2001), *available at* http://news.com.com/2100-1017-253443.html?tag=prntfr.

Register.com, Inc. v. Verio, Inc., 126 F. Supp. 2d 238 (S.D.N.Y. 2000).

A federal court in New York granted the plaintiff's motion for a preliminary injunction prohibiting the defendant's search engine from accessing registrant contact information contained in the plaintiff's database and from using that information for mass marketing. The plaintiff, Register.com, a domain-name registration service, brought a trespass suit against Verio, an Internet service provider, seeking to enjoin it from marketing its services to individuals who had recently registered domain names through Register.com. Verio had been using search bots to search Register.com's database of individuals who had recently registered domain names, and used this information to solicit business from the individuals through telemarketing and email. The court found that the plaintiff was entitled to the injunction, as it had demonstrated a likelihood of success on the merits and irreparable harm on its trespass and other claims. The court followed the *eBay v. Bidder's Edge* rationale and held that Verio's search bots had presented and would continue to present an unwelcome interference with Register.com's computer system. The court also expressed the concern that if the court denied the injunction, other companies would be encouraged to deploy search bots and further diminish Register.com's server capacity.

Oyster Software, Inc. v. Forms Processing, Inc, No. C-00-0724 JCS, 2001 WL 1736382 (N.D. Cal. Dec. 6, 2001).

The plaintiff, Oyster Software, is a California company that develops forms-processing software for companies. The defendant, Forms Processing, Inc. (FPI), is a Florida company offering document management services. FPI hired a web design company, Top-Ten, to create and promote its company website. Using data-scraping robots, Top-Ten designers appropriated metatags from Oyster's site and incorporated them into the FPI site. Oyster sued FPI in federal court in California, arguing that FPI's scraping of Oyster's metatags constituted a trespass.

The court refused to dismiss Oyster's trespass claim, even though Oyster could show only a "negligible" load placed on its computer systems by Top-Ten's bots. The concept of trespass, the court held, does not require anything greater than *use* of the complaining party's property. 2001 WL 1736382 at *13.

EF Cultural Travel BV v. Explorica, Inc., 274 F.3d 577 (1st Cir. 2001).

The plaintiff and the defendant companies compete in providing global tours for high-school students. The Court of Appeals for the First Circuit upheld a lower-court injunction against the defendant's use of an electronic agent that combed through the plaintiff's database for pricing information. The court found that the plaintiff would likely succeed on the merits of its claim under the Computer Fraud and Abuse Act (CFAA). In particular, the court found that the plaintiff could make out a claim under the CFAA even if the unauthorized intrusion did not, in and of itself, cause damage to the system, because the alleged $21,000 that the plaintiff said it had spent assessing the effect of the defendant's data scraper on its web server was sufficient to meet the minimum threshold set by the statute.

On April 25, 2002, Homestore.com, an online real-estate services company, filed suit in federal court in Los Angeles against Bargain Network, an online classified service, claiming that Bargain Network was unlawfully scraping listings off one of Homestore's websites and that the site had been deep-linking to Homestore's real-estate listings without consent. The complaint alleged trespass, breach of contract, and tort claims. *See* "Linking, A Fundamental Premise of the Web, Is Challenged," Siliconvalley.com (June 9, 2002), *available at* http://www.siliconvalley.com/mld/siliconvalley/news/editorial/3435606.htm. In July 2002, the parties settled, with Homestore agreeing to drop the suit in exchange for Bargain Network's agreement to permanently refrain from collecting and displaying Homestore's data.

Ticketmaster Corp. v. Tickets.Com, Inc., No. CV99-7654-HLH(VBKx), 2003 U.S. Dist. LEXIS 6483 (C.D. Cal. March 7, 2003).

Ticketmaster, an online entertainment-events ticket seller, brought suit to prohibit Tickets.com, an online events-referral agent, from deep-linking its customers directly to Ticketmaster's interior web pages, bypassing Ticketmaster's home page, resulting in less advertising revenue for Ticketmaster. Ticketmaster alleged that this deep-linking, as well as Tickets.com's use of electronic "spiders" to retrieve information from the Ticketmaster website, constituted trespass and copyright infringement, as well as false advertising and passing-off. After initially denying Ticketmaster's motion for a preliminary injunction to prohibit Tickets.com from deep-linking to the Ticketmaster website, the court proceeded to grant summary judgment to Tickets.com on plaintiff's trespass and copyright claims.

The court recognized that trespass law applied to computer systems, but held that to prove a trespass plaintiff had to show "some tangible interference with the use or operation of the computer being invaded by the spider." 2003 U.S. Dist. LEXIS 6483 at *12. Because there was no evidence that the spider caused physical injury to Ticketmaster's computers, there was not sufficient injury to find for the plaintiff. In addition, the court held that there was no copyright infringement because Tickets.com's spiders were just collecting factual information from the Tickets.com website. (Facts themselves, as opposed to the expression of facts, are not subject to copyright protection.)

For discussion of this case (and of deep-linking in general) in the context of copyright and trademark infringement, *see* Chapter 2, page 37, and Chapter 4, pages 104 and 106.

EF Cultural Travel BV v. Zefer Corp., 318 F.3d 58 (1st Cir. 2003).

The U.S. Court of Appeals for the First Circuit ruled that the injunction upheld in *EF Cultural Travel v. Explorica, Inc.*, 274 F.3d 577 (1st Cir. 2001), barred Zefer Corporation from using a data scraping tool it designed for Explorica to scrape travel pricing information from the EF Cultural Travel website. The court reasoned that the injunction against Explorica also prevented any third party from providing services that would allow Explorica to circumvent the injunction. The court found that CFAA liability is not triggered when a user merely exceeds a website operator's "reasonable expectations" of how information from its website is to be used. Rather, a CFAA violation occurs when a user knowingly, and with intent to defraud, violates a website's explicit terms of use.

Intel Corp. v. Hamidi, 71 P.3d 296, 1 Cal. Rptr. 3d 32 (Cal. 2003).

Kourosh Kenneth Hamidi was employed as an engineer at Intel for fifteen years. He was fired in 1995. After his dismissal, Hamidi circumvented Intel's electronic security system to gain access to Intel's confidential list of employee email addresses. He then sent six separate emails criticizing the company to as many as 35,000 employees at a time. Hamidi persisted in sending these emails after receiving a written demand from Intel that he stop. Intel filed a trespass claim against Hamidi, alleging that Hamidi's emails slowed productivity, distracted employees from their work, and required the company to invest time in attempting to rid the system of Hamidi's messages. The trial court found that Hamidi's emails constituted a trespass because they disrupted Intel's business by using its property: "Intel has the right to exclude others from speaking on its property. Intel is not required to exercise its right in a 'content-neutral' fashion. Content discrimination is part of a private property-owner's bundle of rights. Intel does not welcome Hamidi." The California Supreme Court disagreed:

> After reviewing the decisions analyzing unauthorized electronic contact with computer systems as potential trespasses to chattels, we conclude that under California law the tort does not encompass, and should not be extended to encompass, an electronic communication that neither damages the recipient computer system nor impairs its functioning. Such an electronic communication does not constitute an actionable trespass to personal property, i.e., the computer system, because it does not interfere

with the possessor's use or possession of, or any other legally protected interest in, the personal property itself. The consequential economic damage Intel claims to have suffered, i.e., loss of productivity caused by employees reading and reacting to Hamidi's messages and company efforts to block the messages, is not an injury to the company's interest in its computers—which worked as intended and were unharmed by the communications—any more than the personal distress caused by reading an unpleasant letter would be an injury to the recipient's mailbox, or the loss of privacy caused by an intrusive telephone call would be an injury to the recipient's telephone equipment. *Hamidi*, 71 P.3d at 300.

In other words, the California Supreme Court held that any damages resulting from the effects of unwanted emails do not amount to damage to property under California's trespass laws. For a discussion of the *Hamidi* case in the privacy context, see Chapter 8, page 234.

American Airlines, Inc. v. Farechase, Inc., No. 067-194022-02 (Tex. Dist. Ct. 2003).

Farechase developed and licensed to commercial users in the travel industry a "web automation" application that enabled users to access American Airlines' flight schedule, availability, and fare information that resided on the airline's website, AA.com. American Airlines had not authorized Farechase or its users to access the data on AA.com. American Airlines brought a claim against Farechase, alleging trespass as well as a violation of the terms and conditions of the User Agreement posted on the AA.com website. A Texas trial court agreed with the airline that Farechase's unauthorized "scraping" of information from the AA.com website violated the User Agreement, and suggested that Farechase's unauthorized access to AA.com might have constituted an unlawful trespass. Accordingly, in March 2003, the court issued an order temporarily enjoining Farechase from accessing AA.com or scraping data from the site without written authorization from American Airlines. In June 2003, American Airlines and Farechase announced they had reached a settlement. Under the terms of the settlement agreement, American Airlines agreed to license Farechase's software and to consent to "special access" to its AA.com website by Farechase. *See* "American Airlines, Farechase Settle Suit," DALLAS BUSINESS JOURNAL (June 13, 2003), *available at* http://dallas.bizjournals.com/dallas/stories/2003/06/09/daily55.html.

Amazon.com Inc. v. Cyberpower Party Ltd., No. CV032620 (W.D. Wash., filed Aug. 8, 2003).

Amazon's suit against Cyberpower is one of eleven lawsuits against named and unnamed defendants recently filed by Amazon.com in six states and Canada. Amazon.com is seeking injunctive relief and as yet unspecified damages against spammers who engage in "spoofing"—that is, altering the "From:" line of an email message to mask the true identity of the sender—using "Amazon.com" in the place of the spammer's name. One of Amazon's claims against the spammers is for trespass to chattels, based on the allegation that by spoofing Amazon's domain name, the spammers caused innumerable bounce-back messages to be routed to Amazon's servers, putting a burden on its systems. As of December 31, 2003, Amazon's cases remained pending.

Application of Wiretapping Law

 Konop v. Hawaiian Airlines, Inc., 302 F.3d 868 (9th Cir. 2002), *cert. denied*, 537 U.S. 1193 (2003).

The U.S. Court of Appeals for the Ninth Circuit held that gaining unauthorized access to a password-protected website does not violate the Wiretap Act. Accessing a website does not constitute the sort of "interception" of a communication necessary to establish a violation of the Act. Only a transmission can be intercepted, not a file in temporary or permanent storage, such as a web page.

Konop, a pilot for Hawaiian Airlines, created a website on which he posted criticisms of the Airline, its executives, and its employees' union. Access to the site was limited to users with passwords. Konop asserted that the Airline violated the Wiretap Act when it obtained a password and used it to access the site without Konop's permission or knowledge. The court rejected his Wiretap Act claim on the ground that accessing stored files (the pages of a website) was not the interception of a communication.

Insurance

For many businesses in our increasingly information-based economy, information, and the software used to manipulate it, are among the most valuable assets. Not surprisingly, disputes have arisen over whether particular insurance policies cover injury to such assets.

 America Online Inc. v. St. Paul Mercury Insurance Co., 347 F.3d 89 (4th Cir. 2003).

In 1999, AOL released version 5.0 of its popular Internet access software, only to discover numerous bugs and glitches in the program that caused serious interoperability problems with other programs on the computers of many consumers. As a result, AOL faced multiple class-action lawsuits and sought to have its insurance carrier indemnify it for the class-action claims it settled with its customers. The insurance company refused to indemnify AOL on the grounds that "damage" caused by computer software did not qualify as "tangible" property damage under the terms of the insurance policy. The Court of Appeals for the Fourth Circuit agreed with the insurance company. The court reasoned that the computer hardware could be brought back to full operability once the software was adequately fixed. Therefore, according to the court, the temporary inability of the class action plaintiffs to use their computers while the problem software was running did not equal the kind of damage to tangible property covered by the insurance policy because the damage within the software had no physical effect on the hardware itself.

One judge dissented, observing that corruptions in software must cause at least *microscopic* physical changes to the structure of the hardware if they are written permanently to the computer's hard drive. Despite the smaller size of the physical changes, the judge found no appreciable conceptual difference between damage to a computer hard drive and a dent on the hood of a car.

 Cincinnati Insurance Co. v. Professional Data Services, Inc., No. 01-2610-CM, 2003 U.S. Dist. LEXIS 15859 (D. Kan. July 18, 2003).

Like the Fourth Circuit in *St. Paul Mercury Insurance*, discussed above, a federal court in Kansas found that data was not tangible property within the meaning of the applicable insurance policy. The defendant, Professional Data Services, provided software support services for medical clinics. A customer brought suit against Professional Data Services, alleging that the software did not perform as represented, and that, as a result, the customer had suffered loss in the use of the software, as well as the loss of customer data. Professional Data Services submitted a claim to its insurer, which, in turn, filed an action seeking a declaratory judgment that the losses incurred were not covered by Professional Data Services' insurance policy.

The court ruled that the loss of a software program and the associated data did not qualify as a loss of "tangible" property covered by the policy. The court stated that the damaged property must be capable of being touched or otherwise perceived by human senses to qualify as "tangible." A computer program, according to the court, is not "tangible" in this sense. The court also noted that damage resulting from a negligent software vendor's misrepresentation as to what the program was capable of doing could not be deemed "accidental" for the purposes of the insurance policy. *See also Compaq Computer Corp. v. St. Paul Fire and Marine Insurance Co.*, No. C3-02-2222, 2003 Minn. App. LEXIS 1078 (Minn. Ct. App. Sept. 2, 2003) (holding that computer data does not qualify as "tangible property" for the purposes of an insurance policy, and that allegations of criminal wrongdoing under the CFAA are beyond the scope of the insured's coverage where the policy excludes coverage for criminal, fraudulent or dishonest acts).

 State Auto Property and Casualty Insurance Co. v. Travelers Indemnity Co. of America, 343 F.3d 249 (4th Cir. 2003).

The U.S. Court of Appeals for the Fourth Circuit ruled that an insurance company was obligated to defend its insured against a claim of trademark infringement arising out of registration of the domain names "www.nissan.com" and "www.nissan.net." The policyholder argued that the use of the trademark in the domain name qualified as an "advertising injury," a claim that was covered under the insurance policy. The insurer refused to defend the policyholder, arguing that the registration of the domains was not a misappropriation of advertising ideas or of a business plan, and was therefore not covered. The trial court agreed with the insurer, and granted summary judgment. On appeal, the Fourth Circuit reversed and vacated the lower court's decision, finding that because the domain names were chiefly used for directing potential customers to the policyholder's site (and, therefore, its posted advertisements), the use of the trademark was "in the course of advertising" and was covered by the policy.

UCITA—The Uniform Computer Information Transactions Act

General

The National Conference of Commissioners on Uniform State Laws (NCCUSL) voted to approve the Uniform Computer Information Transactions Act (UCITA) on July 29, 1999. Just as the Uniform Commercial Code (UCC) was designed to govern the sale of tangible goods, UCITA is a commercial code that applies to computer information transactions—that is, transactions involving information that can be processed or received by a computer. *See generally* Mary Jo Howard Dively, *The New Laws that Will Enable Electronic Contracting: Survey of Electronic Contracting Rules in the UETA and the UCITA*, 38 Duq. L. Rev. 209 (2001). Like the UCC, UCITA provides the default rules for transactions while allowing contracting parties to opt out of these rules. Despite the enthusiasm of the uniform law commissioners, only two states, Maryland and Virginia, have adopted UCITA.

Application of UCITA: Examples

UCITA is a broad statute that addresses a variety of commercial issues that arise in the context of computer information transactions, including warranties, perfect tender, manifesting assent to a contract, mass market licenses, choice of law and forum, and shrinkwrap licenses.

UCITA only governs transactions that include an agreement to create, modify, transfer, or license computer information. If a contract involves both computer information and another product, UCITA applies only to the part of the deal that involves computer information. For example, if an individual buys a computer, the sale of the computer falls under Article 2 of the UCC because the computer is a good; however, licenses for the software pre-loaded on the computer would be governed by UCITA. *See, e.g., M. A. Mortenson Co. v. Timberline Software Corp.*, 998 P.2d 305 (Wash. 2000); *but see Advent Systems Ltd. v. Unisys Corp.*, 925 F.2d 670, (3d Cir. 1990) (pre-UCITA holding that software is a "good" under the UCC). The Official Comments to UCITA emphasize that the distinguishing factor between computer information transactions and sales of goods is whether the primary subject matter of the transaction, about which the purchaser or licensee has the most interest, is a tangible good. For example, in a computer information transaction, the information exchanged may be contained on a CD-ROM or some other physical medium, but the licensee "has little interest" in the CD itself once the information on that CD is transferred to the buyer's computer.

Examples of contracts covered by UCITA: Contracts to create or develop computer information; contracts for Internet access; agreements to create or distribute multimedia works; contracts for data processing or analysis of computer information; contracts involving distribution of computer programs; and contracts involving the grant of rights to use computer programs.

Examples of contracts not covered by UCITA: Contracts that do not significantly involve computer information; contracts for the sale of computers, televisions, DVD players, and the like; contracts for print media; contracts for sound recordings; contracts for motion pictures, or for broadcast or cable programming; contracts for airline transportation, even if they involve electronic ticketing; contracts to create and publish print books, even where the author delivers the manuscript in electronic form; contracts for digital-signature certificates (the product is identification services, not computer information); and personal services (except contracts for computer information development or support).

The Status of UCITA

In August 2002, the NCCUSL approved 38 new amendments to UCITA in response to criticism leveled at the statute by the American Bar Association.

The Committee report that resulted in the amendments is available at http://www.nccusl.org/nccusl/ucita/UCITA_Standby_Comm.htm. The amendments are largely designed to clarify the language of certain UCITA provisions. Substantive changes will allow consumers to criticize software companies without the risk that their licenses could be revoked and also to reverse-engineer some software.

As of December 31, 2003, Maryland and Virginia are the only states to have passed UCITA (with some amendments). The Maryland statute took effect in October 2000; the Virginia statute took effect in July 2001. Versions of UCITA have been introduced in at least eleven other states, namely Arizona, Delaware, Hawaii, Illinois, Louisiana, Maine, New Hampshire, New Jersey, Oklahoma, Oregon, and Texas, as well as the District of Columbia and the U.S. Virgin Islands, but none has been enacted. Iowa has not only rejected UCITA, but has enacted legislation to protect Iowa residents and businesses from its effects. Iowa Code § 554(D).101 (2003). If a contract signed by an Iowa resident or business contains "a choice of law" provision stating that the contract is to be interpreted under the law of any state that has enacted UCITA, the choice-of-law provision will be "voidable" and the contract will, instead, be interpreted under Iowa law. Iowa Code § 554(D).104 (2003).

Support for UCITA seems to have waned. *See* Joseph Menn, "Support for Software Law Eroding," L.A. TIMES (Nov. 20, 2000). Like Iowa, North Carolina, West Virginia, and Vermont have enacted laws that prohibit application of UCITA to their states' residents. Recent attempts to adopt UCITA were thwarted in Nevada and Oklahoma.

At a recent conference, the NCCUSL acknowledged that because of political and other forces it would be an inefficient use of the conference's resources to continue to pursue the adoption of UCITA. NCCUSL therefore withdrew the statute from consideration for endorsement by the American Bar Association (ABA). *See* Statement of K. King Burnett, President of NCCUSL (Aug. 1, 2003), *available at* http://www.nccusl.org/nccusl/ucita/KKB_UCITA_Letter_8103.pdf.

Detailed information related to UCITA is available on the NCCUSL website, www.nccusl.org.

The Converging Voice and Data Networks

The Telecommunications Act of 1996 mandated that telephone companies allow their competitors to offer services over their networks. As cable companies have come to compete with telephone companies in providing broadband Internet access, competitors of the cable companies have sought similar "open access" to the cable "pipes." And telephone companies, long accustomed to being regulated and taxed, want to see their cable competitors subjected to a similar scheme of regulation and taxation.

To date, the Federal Communications Commission has viewed traditional telephone services as tightly regulated "telecommunications services," while treating cable modem services as more loosely regulated "information services." The FCC has done so even though Internet-based networks can carry high-quality voice communication using voice-over-Internet-protocol (VoIP) technology.

 Brand X Internet Services v. Federal Communications Commission, 345 F.3d 1120 (9th Cir. 2003).

The United States Court of Appeals for the Ninth Circuit held in October 2003 that the FCC had erred in concluding that cable modem service is properly characterized as an information service. Instead, a three-judge panel ruled that cable modem service has attributes of both an information service and a telecommunications service and that it therefore should be classified as both. On December 3, 2003, the FCC asked the Ninth Circuit to rehear the case, arguing that, under Supreme Court precedent, the three-judge panel should have been more deferential to the considered views of the FCC. As of December 31, 2003, the Ninth Circuit had not decided whether to grant the requested *en banc* review.

At least two courts have refused to apply rules applicable to telephone service to Internet services. A Tennessee state appeals court ruled that online service provider Prodigy was not obligated to pay a Tennessee tax assessment because its services could not be classified as "telecommunications services". *Prodigy Services Corp. v. Johnson*, No. M2002-00918-COA-R3-CV (Tenn Ct. App., Aug 12, 2003), *appeal denied*, 2003 Tenn. LEXIS 1270 (Tenn. 2003). A federal trial court judge in Minnesota ruled against public utilities regulators in that state who wanted to subject VoIP provider Vonage to telephone operator license requirements and to mandate that Vonage, like traditional telephone service providers, collect and remit fees to support the operation of 911 services. *See* Ben Charny and Evan Hansen, "Court's Call: Hands Off VoIP," CNET News.com (Oct 8, 2003), *at* http://www.news.com.com/2102-7352_3-5088158.html?tag=st_util_print.

Internet Taxation

In states that impose a sales tax, buyers are obligated to pay the tax and sellers that operate within the state are obligated to collect the tax and remit it to the government. There has been much debate about whether states should be allowed to force out-of-state companies to collect taxes on their behalf for online purchases. For example, when a customer in North Dakota buys a sweater online from L.L. Bean in Maine, should L.L. Bean apply the appropriate North Dakota sales tax to the purchase and remit the tax to North Dakota? State governments want the transaction taxed because a purchase online instead of at a local store means less tax revenue for the government. Many traditional retailers do not think it is fair that their goods are taxed while those sold online are not.

The Internet Tax Moratorium, which was enacted in 1998 and expired in October 2003, did not prohibit states from taxing Internet sales, though many believed that it did. The moratorium prohibited taxation of Internet access fees and imposition of taxes that discriminated against Internet transactions, for example, by taxing them more heavily than other transactions.

Assessing Sales Tax on Internet Purchases

Though few realize it, consumers in the 45 states that tax retail sales owe tax on their online purchases even if the merchants they buy from do not collect those taxes. Consumers owe a use tax on purchases they make from out-of-state merchants that corresponds to the sales tax they pay on purchases made in-state.

Of course, states would be happy to obligate out-of-state merchants to collect sales taxes on their behalf, but under existing law, they cannot. The Commerce Clause of the U.S. Constitution gives Congress the authority to regulate interstate commerce. The courts have interpreted this power to be exclusive to Congress. Individual states may not "burden" interstate transactions in ways that would interfere with Congress's exclusive authority. Accordingly, in 1992, the Supreme Court made clear that a state cannot compel an out-of-state seller to collect tax on sales made to consumers in the state, unless the seller has a substantial physical presence in the state. *See Quill Co. v. North Dakota*, 504 U.S. 298 (1992). As a result, states cannot require collection of sales tax by "remote vendors" that sell their products via the Internet, telephone, or mail order, absent an authorizing act of Congress.

Several states have begun education campaigns to inform citizens about their tax obligations, and some states, such as California, Washington, Iowa and Wisconsin, have begun to send tax bills to residents who do not pay a use tax on out-of-state purchases. These notices, however, have been limited primarily to online sales of tobacco where states have had moderate success in obtaining the customer lists of online tobacco sellers via the federal Jenkins Act. For other online sales, the states may lack an effective means of discovering which of their citizens are making online purchases and in what amounts, making tax collection difficult.

Dozens of states recently joined forces to make their tax codes simple and uniform in an effort to get Congress to grant them the authority to require out-of-state web and catalog merchants to collect sales taxes on sales made in their states. *See* Jon Hart and Kevin Brandon, "The Long Arm of the Tax Man," WSJ.com (Oct. 28, 2003), *at* http://online.wsj.com/public/resources/documents/SB106424236255857700.htm. As of December 31, 2003, 37 states and the District of Columbia are participants in this Streamlined Sales Tax Project, a confederation of state tax authorities that have crafted the Streamlined Sales and Use Tax Agreement ("SSUTA").

The agreement lays the groundwork for voluntary sales-tax collection by vendors lacking a physical presence in a given jurisdiction, typically retailers conducting business transactions through the Internet or by mail. The agreement will take effect when at least ten states representing at least 20% of the total population of all states that impose a sales tax pass legislation in conformity with the Project's rules. (Forty-five states and the District of Columbia impose sales tax.) In the meantime, compliance with the Agreement remains voluntary. Under the Agreement, states establish uniform definitions of taxable goods and services, and maintain a single tax rate statewide for each product or service.

In California, Governor Gray Davis signed a bill that allows California to join the Streamlined Sales and Use Tax Project as a voting member, clearing the way for California to adopt the SSUTA. An early version of another bill (S.B. 103) would have required online vendors with bricks-and-mortar counterparts in the state to collect sales tax from California customers. The final version of S.B. 103, as passed by the California legislature was stripped of its provisions relating to Internet purchases before it was sent to the Governor and signed into law in October 2003. *See* the California Legislature record of the history of the bill, *available at* http://info.sen.ca.gov/cgi-bin/postquery?bill_number=sb_103&sess=CUR&house=B&site=sen; Associated Press, "California Senate Approves Collection of Internet Sales Taxes" (June 4, 2003), *available at* http://www.siliconvalley.com/mld/siliconvalley/news/editorial/6017306.htm.

Many national retailers have begun to collect sales tax for online purchases. Brian Krebs, "Major Dot-Com Retailers Begin Levying Sales Tax," WASHINGTON POST (Feb. 6, 2003), *at* http://www.washingtonpost.com/ac2/wp-dyn?pagename=article&node=&contentId=A31210-2003Feb5&notFound=true. The online counterparts of stores such as Walmart, Target, Toys R Us, and Marshall Fields volunteered to collect sales tax as part of the Streamlined Sales and Use Tax Agreement. As a result, these sites will receive amnesty from state efforts to collect back taxes from sites that did not charge such taxes in the past. States that are not parties to this agreement, however, are free to pursue back taxes. Illinois has initiated lawsuits seeking back taxes for online purchases from 32 businesses, including Target and Walmart. *See* "Illinois Joins Lawsuits Seeking Back Taxes for Online Sales by Several Large Retailers," 8 ELECTRONIC COM. & L. REP. (BNA) 237 (2003).

Lawmakers in both the House and Senate have offered bills designed to give states direct authority to require out-of-state merchants to collect sales taxes on their behalf. Congressmen Ernest Istook of Oklahoma and William Delahunt of Massachusetts proposed the House version of the legislation (H.R. 3184) that would work in conjunction with the Streamlined Sales and Use Tax Agreement to help states collect tax revenues from online transactions. The Senate version (S. 1736), introduced by Senator Mike Enzi of Wyoming, is substantially similar to the House version. Lawmakers have been careful to point out that the two bills would not actually *create* new taxes, but rather aid enforcement of existing tax obligations. Both versions of the bill exempt companies doing less than $5 million per year in business from the reach of the proposed law. Online retailer Amazon.com has reportedly been working with legislators on the details of the bill. Brian Krebs, "Internet Sales Tax May Get Amazon.com's Support," WASHINGTON POST (Sept. 25, 2003), http://www.washingtonpost.com/ac2/wp-dyn/ A63763-2003Sep25.html.

Recognizing the difficulty that states face in collecting taxes on online purchases of tobacco products in particular, the U.S. House of Representatives is processing new legislation that grants additional powers to state attorneys general to enforce state taxes on online tobacco sales. The proposed legislation would allow the attorney general of a state to sue tobacco sellers in federal court for violating state tax and sales regulations. The bill (H.R. 2824) also puts reporting burdens on tobacco sellers, including vendors operating on Indian reservations, to disclose to the state its monthly sales of tobacco products. Roy Mark, "House Panel Moves Against Web Tobacco Sites," http:// www.internetnews.com/ec-news/print.php/3086641. Some states, including Massachusetts, New Jersey, and Rhode Island, have begun to send invoices directly to residents for the payment of taxes for online tobacco purchases. "Web Tobacco Buyers Get Taxed" (Feb. 19, 2003), *at* http://www.wired.com/news/business/0,1367,57657,00.html.

States have continued to find ways to collect taxes from online transactions. The Kansas Department of Revenue recently issued rulings that require online retailers, regardless of their location, to collect state and local taxes from Kansas customers for software and website design services. Under the Kansas law, the location of the web server itself is not relevant in determining whether such taxes must be collected. Galit Allemeier, "Sales Tax Imposed on Web Design When Customers Located in State," 8 ELECTRONIC COM. & L. REP. (BNA) 168 (2003).

In *Westcott Communications, Inc. v. Strayhorn*, 104 S.W.3d 141 (Tex. App. Mar. 20, 2003), the Texas Court of Appeals ruled that training programs that originated in Texas and were either broadcast on the Internet or recorded on videotape and shipped to consumers across the country should be taxed as "services performed within [Texas]." Previously, Westcott Communications, which maintains its broadcast equipment, production facilities, and corporate headquarters in Texas, apportioned its subscription revenues based on the location of its customers. However, following an audit, the state's Comptroller of Public Accounts determined that such revenues should be reapportioned to Texas because that is where the programs originated. The Texas Court of Appeals upheld the Comptroller's decision. The court reasoned that Westcott "is paid to provide training to its customers. This training . . . [is] all done by employees from its Texas facilities." 104 S.W.3d at 147.

Moratorium on Internet Access Taxation

Enacted in 1998, the Internet Tax Freedom Act expired October 31, 2003. The tax moratorium created under the Act covered Internet access fees, as well as multiple or discriminatory taxation of electronic commerce, such as a state taxing a transaction already taxed by another state, or taxing electronic sales at a higher tax rate than other sales. Included in the original moratorium was a grandfather clause that permitted some states to retain existing taxes on Internet access.

Despite numerous proposals that came before Congress in late 2003 to make the moratorium permanent, the Senate ultimately could not agree on the scope of the proposed ban—in particular, the definition of "Internet access," which can be accomplished though a wide range of mechanisms. The ban also faced strong opposition from the states, which argued that their budgets require them to seek additional revenue wherever possible. States also worry that a broad definition of "Internet access" would limit existing state authority to collect taxes for general telecommunications services, as the convergence in voice and data networks continues.

For a further discussion of these issues, *see, e.g.*, Declan McCullagh, "Ban on Net Tax Dead Till 2004," CNET News.com (Nov. 26, 2003), *at* http://news.com.com/ 2100-1028-5112140.html; Carl Bialik, "Efforts to Expand Net-Tax Ban Make Senate Passage Uncertain," WSJ.com (Nov. 6, 2003), *at* http://online.wsj.com/article_print/ 0,,SB106765247277140000,00.html; "Temporary Ban on Internet Service Taxes Runs Out as Move for Permanent Ban Bogs Down," SiliconValley.com (Oct. 31, 2003), *at* http://www.siliconvalley.com/mld/siliconvalley/news/editorial/7150575.htm; Grant Gross, "States Protest Congressional Internet Tax Ban," Infoworld.com (Sept. 24, 2003), *at* http://www.infoworld.com/article/03/09/24/HNinternettax_1.html.

State Efforts to Protect Sales Tax Interests

In January 2003, the Massachusetts Revenue Commissioner announced that its state income tax forms will include a new line item, asking taxpayers to estimate and pay sales tax on items they purchased out of state, including items purchases over the Internet. The sales tax itself is not new; it has been required since 1967, but the Commonwealth, like most states, has done little to enforce it. Now that Internet sales are increasingly depriving states of tax revenue, states such as Massachusetts are taking steps to minimize the losses.

The State of Washington passed legislation that exempts online vendors that neither own nor operate stores within the state from collecting sales and use taxes from Washington residents. Part of the legislature's intention in passing this Act was to relieve sellers with very limited connections to Washington from the obligations of collecting sales and use taxes. Wash. Rev. Code §§ 82.08050 & 82.12.040 (2003).

In March 2001, Arkansas passed a law requiring an online seller to collect taxes on sales made to customers in Arkansas if the seller is affiliated with a brick-and-mortar retailer located in the state. The law is predicated on a sales tax nexus theory that has already been rejected by the courts in the context of mail-order sales. *See, e.g., SFA Collections, Inc. v. Bannon*, 217 Conn. 220 (1991), 585 A.2d 666; *Quill Corp. v. North*

Dakota, 504 U.S. 298 (1992) (holding that physical presence of company or its agent is required to collect use tax).

Barnesandnoble.com must now collect sales taxes on goods purchased by California customers. Even though the Barnes & Noble bricks-and-mortar stores and barnesandnoble.com website are separately incorporated, the California Franchise Tax Board issued a ruling requiring the website to collect sales tax because the bricks-and-mortar stores often distributed coupons that were redeemable on the barnesandnoble.com website. For a copy of the Board's decision, *see* http://www.boe.ca.gov/legal/pdf/bncom.pdf.

Minnesota also requires bricks-and-mortar retail stores to collect sales tax from customers when the stores accept returns or exchanges of items that customers purchased over the stores' Internet sites. Brian Krebs, "Major Dot-Com Retailers Begin Levying Sales Tax," WASHINGTON POST (Feb. 6, 2003), *at* http://www.washingtonpost.com/ac2/wp-dyn?pagename=article&node=&contentId=A31210-2003Feb5&notFound=true.

The New York State Department of Taxation and Finance stated that the sale of a gift certificate by an Internet merchant resulted in income to that merchant, taxable in New York, when the customer who purchased the gift certificate accessed the merchant's website from a location in New York. According to the department's Advisory Opinion, the sale would result in taxable income in New York regardless of where the merchant's website servers were located. See NY State Dep't of Taxation and Finance, Office of Tax Policy Analysis Technical Services Division, Advisory Opinion TSB-A-02(3)C (Apr. 18, 2002) *at* http://www.tax.state.ny.us/pdf/Advisory_Opinions/Corporation/A02_3c.pdf.

Tobacco

Under a New York law that took effect in November 2000, tobacco can only be shipped to authorized New York dealers. This law effectively prevents online retailers of tobacco products from selling to individual consumers in New York, indirectly protecting the State of New York's tax interest in tobacco sales. In November 2000, several tobacco companies brought suit in federal court to challenge the constitutionality of the law. The trial court found that strict scrutiny should be applied to the statute because it discriminated against interstate commerce on its face. *See Santa Fe Natural Tobacco Co., Inc., et al. v. Spitzer*, Nos. 00-7274, 00-7750, 2001 U.S. Dist. LEXIS 7548 (S.D.N.Y. June 8, 2001), *rev'd sub nom. Brown & Williamson Tobacco Corp., et al. v. Pataki*, 320 F.3d 200 (2d Cir. 2003). Applying strict scrutiny, the court held that the statute was unconstitutional, noting that although the state had a legitimate interest in enacting the law (attempting to curtail the sale of cigarettes to minors), the state had failed to demonstrate that the law was narrowly tailored to achieve that goal, and, moreover, had not shown that the statute was the least restrictive means of promoting the state's interest. *Id.* at *87. The court also found that the law would not have survived under the balancing test set forth in *Pike v. Bruce Church*, 397 U.S. 137 (1970). *Id.* at *93. Under the *Pike* test, "where the statute regulates evenhandedly to effectuate a legitimate local public interest, and its effects on interstate commerce are only incidental, it will be upheld unless the burden imposed on such commerce is clearly excessive in relation to the putative local benefits." *See id.* (quoting *Pike*, 397 U.S. at 142).

The Court of Appeals for the Second Circuit reversed. Analyzing the factors that the trial court had concluded rendered the statute unconstitutional, the Second Circuit found that that statute applied evenhandedly to both in-state and out-of-state businesses and did not impede the flow of goods in interstate commerce. The statute therefore did not discriminate against out-of-state entities or unjustifiably burden interstate commerce. 320 F.3d at 216. As a result, the statute would survive strict scrutiny. The court also analyzed the statue under the *Pike* test. It found that because the statute only incidentally burdened interstate commerce, the effects on interstate commerce were not clearly excessive in relation to the putative local benefits so as to render the statute unconstitutional. *Id.* at 217.

In another ruling regarding the shipping of tobacco products from out-of-state, Texas's Comptroller recently published a letter ruling stating that under a recently passed Texas law, tobacco vendors selling cigarettes by mail order and Internet are prohibited from shipping the goods into Texas unless they pay Texas's excise tax and place a tax label on each pack. *See* "Internet, Mail-Order Cigarette Sellers Face New Regulations to Import Product," 8 ELECTRONIC COM. & L. REP. 951 (2003).

Wine

Several state laws banning the sale of wine over the Internet are also being challenged throughout the country. In July 2003, the Federal Trade Commission (FTC) released a report that encouraged states to repeal laws that restrict residents from making catalog and online purchases of wine from out-of-state vendors. *See* FTC, "Possible Anticompetitive Barriers to E-Commerce: Wine" (2003), *at* http://www.ftc.gov/os/2003/07/winereport2.pdf. The report found that "e-commerce offers consumers lower prices and more choices in the wine market, and that states could expand e-commerce by permitting direct shipping of wine to consumers." Press Release, FTC, "E-Commerce Lowers Prices, Increases Choices in Wine Market" (July 3, 2003). The report criticized restrictive laws by pointing out that in-state vendors may not carry wines that are desired by local consumers and that there are more effective means of achieving states' goals of preventing minors from buying wine from out-of-state vendors. *Id.*

Nexus for State Tax Purposes

In July 2002, the Court of Appeals of Tennessee reversed a trial court's grant of summary judgment in favor of America Online on the tax commissioner's claim that AOL's activities in Tennessee provide a sufficient nexus to subject it to state taxes. The court found that a reasonable finder of fact could conclude that AOL has a nexus with the state by virtue of the many in-state businesses, including network service providers, that help make AOL services available to Tennessee residents. *See America Online, Inc. v. Johnson*, No. M2001 00927 COA R3 CV, 2002 Tenn. App. LEXIS 555 (Tenn. Ct. App. July 30, 2002).

Proposed Federal Legislation

The Jurisdictional Certainty Over Digital Commerce Act, H.R. 945, 108th Cong. (2003), which was reintroduced in February 2003, was referred to the House Subcommittee on Telecommunications and the Internet in March 2003. As of December 31, 2003, no further action has been reported. The bill would reserve to Congress the right to regulate commercial transactions of digital goods and services over the Internet, including sales of software, e-books and digital music files.

State Internet Taxation Decisions

 In re Borders Online Inc., Cal. State Bd. of Equalization, No. SC OHA 97-638364 (Sept. 26, 2001).

Borders.com's policy of giving its customers the option of returning items for cash refunds at Borders retail stores made Borders (the corporation that operated the retail stores) the authorized representative of Borders.com (the separately incorporated website) and demonstrated that Borders.com was doing business in California. Consequently, Borders.com was required to collect tax on sales made in California, even though Borders.com, unlike Borders (the retail store) had no physical presence in California. This case is available at http://www.boe.ca.gov/legal/pdf/borders.pdf.

Bans on Online Sales of Certain Products

Courts are divided over the constitutionality of bans on online sales of alcohol and tobacco products.

Alcohol

 Swedenburg v. Kelly, 232 F. Supp. 2d 135 (S.D.N.Y. 2002).

The U.S. District Court for the Southern District of New York ruled that New York State's ban on the shipment of wine from out-of-state vendors was an unconstitutional violation of the Commerce Clause. The court found that the "statutory ban on the direct shipment to New York of out-of-state wine is not 'evenhanded' and constitutes a *per se* violation of the Commerce Clause." *Id.* at 147. In discussing the discriminatory nature of the law, the court noted that, unlike remote vendors, "in-state vendors . . . are currently able to sell their products over the Internet and to ship directly to homes in New York state." *Id.* at 148. The Second Circuit heard oral arguments in this case in September 2003. Dana Nigro, "Appeals Court Hears New York Wine-Shipping Case," WINE SPECTATOR ONLINE (Sept. 5, 2003), http://www.winespectator.com/Wine/Daily/News/0,1145,2182,00.html.

Laws in other states have also been struck down. For example, in Virginia, a federal trial court struck down a statute prohibiting the direct shipment of alcoholic beverages from out-of-state vendors to Virginia consumers while allowing direct shipment from in-state vendors to Virginia consumers. Virginia appealed the decision. While the appeal was pending, the Virginia legislature amended the statute to allow direct shipments of alcohol so long as the out-of-state shipper purchases a $50 license and limits shipments to two cases per month, per customer. Additionally, each shipping carton must be conspicuously labeled as alcohol and delivery agents must verify the recipient is over the age of 21. In light of the change in Virginia law, the Fourth Circuit vacated the trial court's order and remanded the case to the trial court for consideration of the amended statute. *Bolick v. Roberts*, 199 F. Supp. 2d 397 (E.D. Va. 2002), *vacated and remanded*, 330 F.3d 274 (4th Cir. 2003).

Similarly, the U.S. Court of Appeals for the Fourth Circuit struck down a North Carolina law restricting the shipment of wine from out-of-state online vendors to North Carolina residents as a violation of the Commerce Clause. *Beskind v. Easley*, 325 F.3d 506 (4th Cir. 2003).

On the other hand, courts in Indiana and Michigan have upheld prohibitions against the shipment of alcohol into their respective states. *Bridenbaugh v. Freeman-Wilson*, 227 F.3d 848 (7th Cir. 2000); *Head v. Engler*, 00 Civ. 71438, slip op. (E.D. Mich. Sept. 28, 2001).

As of December 31, 2003, a suit challenging a Florida law prohibiting the direct shipment of alcohol to Florida consumers remains under consideration. *Bainbridge v. Turner*, 311 F.3d 1104 (11th Cir. 2002) (vacating and remanding the trial court's decision upholding Florida's ban on direct shipping of alcohol because the state had not sufficiently demonstrated that the prohibition was closely related to its goals of temperance and revenue collection). Other cases challenging similar provisions in other states have also been filed in federal courts. *See Parker v. Morrison*, D. Ariz., CV-03-1948-EHC (filed Oct. 7, 2003); "Ban on Interstate Commerce Shipment of Wine Violates Commerce Clause, Complaint Alleges," 8 ELECTRONIC COM. & L. REP. 985 (2003).

Tobacco

As noted above at page 313, New York's law prohibiting direct online sales of tobacco products to New York consumers survived a constitutional challenge in *Brown & Williamson*. A second lawsuit challenging the New York law was brought by the Online Tobacco Retailers Association, two Native American online tobacco sellers, and two disabled consumers. In addition to making the same Commerce Clause arguments made by the *Brown & Williamson* plaintiffs, the plaintiffs contend that the law violates various treaties with Native American tribes, tribal sovereignty, and the Indian Commerce Clause. The plaintiffs sought a preliminary injunction to prevent enforcement of the ban, but only on the grounds that the law violated the Dormant Commerce Clause. Citing the Second Circuit's decision in *Brown & Williamson*, the judge denied the injunction request. "Judge Upholds Ban on Internet Cigarette Sales" (June 23, 2003) *at* http://1010wins.com/topstories/winstopstories_story_174131205.html. As of December 31, 2003, the litigation was still in progress.

California, Washington, and Oregon have filed suits against online vendors for selling tobacco products to residents of their respective states. Paul Queary, "State Sues Over Online Cigarettes," SEATTLE TIMES (Nov. 1, 2002), *available at* http://archives.seattletimes.nwsource.com/cgi-bin/texis.cgi/web/vortex/display?slug=netcigs01m&date=20021101&query=online+cigarette; Reuters, "California Sues Net Firms Over Cigarette Sales" (Apr. 2, 2002), *available at* http://uk.news.yahoo.com/030402/80/dwsb5.html.

Other Products

Some states have enacted laws restricting the online sale of other products to their residents. For a time, Tennessee maintained a law that prohibited the sale of funeral caskets to residents by vendors that were not licensed by the state. This law, however, was struck down by the U.S. Court of Appeals for the Sixth Circuit. *Craigmiles v. Giles*, 312 F.3d 220 (6th Cir. 2002). Similar laws restricting Internet sales of items ranging from cars to contact lenses have been enacted in other jurisdictions. Declan McCullagh, "Courts Spurn State Laws on Caskets, Wine," CNET News.com (Dec. 11, 2002), *available at* http://news.com.com/2102-1017-976900.html.

International Taxation Efforts

On May 7, 2002, the European Union approved a plan to begin requiring payment of the European VAT (Value Added Tax) by U.S. firms selling products over the Internet to

European consumers. European companies selling to nonEuropean consumers will not have to pay the VAT. *See* "EU Taxes U.S. E-Commerce," WIRED (May 6, 2002), *available at* http://www.wired.com/news/business/0,1367,52325,00.html. The plan is seen by some Europeans as necessary to level the playing field between U.S. and European competitors. *See* Owen Gibson, "EU Clamps Down On Tax Loophole," THE GUARDIAN (UK) (May 7, 2002), *available at* http://media.guardian.co.uk/Print/58,4408610,00.htm (discussing the European perspective). U.S. industries, however, complain that the VAT is an attempt to add barriers to trade and will ultimately be impossible to enforce. *See* Joanna Glasner, "U.S. Not Happy About EU Tax," WIRED (May 8, 2002), *available at* http://www.wired.com/news/business/0,1367,52378,00.html (describing U.S. industry reaction to the tax measures).

The VAT went into effect on July 1, 2003. This tax, which applies to online purchases by European consumers of products such as software, downloaded music, and e-books, will add 15% to 25% to the cost of products. Reuters, "EU Ends Free Internet Tax Ride," CNET News.com (June 9, 2003), *available at* http://news.com.com/2100-1019_3-1014519.html. In determining the customer's country of residence and the corresponding amount of tax to be charged, online sellers must rely on information provided by the consumer. However, "geolocation technology" may help vendors identify their customers' locations with greater accuracy. This technology uses the online shopper's IP address to identify his or her location within a 50-mile radius. The technology has certain limitations; "anonymizers" and the inconsistent assignment of IP addresses may limit its utility. Information Technology Ass'n of America, "Ecommerce Taxation and the Limitations of Geolocation Tools" (Nov. 10, 2002), *available at* http://www.itaa.org/taxfinance/docs/geolocationpaper.pdf. The implementation of the VAT forces U.S. online retailers either to begin taxing their European customers based on their country of residence or to establish an office in an EU-member country and receive an exemption. Deterred by the burden of complying with the tax codes of 15 different countries, some companies, including America Online and eBay, have moved their European division headquarters to EU-member countries in order to qualify for an exemption. Brian Krebs, "EU Stirs Up Internet Sales Tax Debate," WASHINGTON POST (June 9, 2003), *at* http://www.washingtonpost.com/ac2/wp-dyn/A36150-2003Jun9?.

On the other hand, a British businessman named Nigel Payne took out full-page ads in Washington, D.C., newspapers in an effort to persuade the United States government to *allow* him to pay taxes on his online gambling business. Payne wants Congress to allow Internet gambling companies to operate in the United States, emphasizing the direct financial benefits the U.S. government could reap by legalizing (and taxing) an online gambling industry. *See* "Let Me Pay £7.5m Tax, Begs Chief," THE GUARDIAN (UK) (May 14, 2002).

The Americans with Disabilities Act (ADA)

The Americans with Disabilities Act (ADA), 42 U.S.C. §§ 12101, *et seq.*, was passed in 1990 to provide "a clear and comprehensive national mandate for the elimination of discrimination against individuals with disabilities." The statute prohibits discrimination "on the basis of disability in the full and equal enjoyment of the goods, services, privileges, advantages, or accommodations of any place of public accommodation by any person who owns, leases, or operates a place of public accommodation." 42 U.S.C. § 12182(a).

Places of Public Accommodation

Places of public accommodation typically include physical locations, such as inns, restaurants, theaters, schools, parks, retail stores, and recreational facilities. Whether the ADA applies to nonphysical environments is a subject of debate.

 Carparts Distribution Center, Inc. v. Automotive Wholesalers Ass'n of New England, 37 F.3d 12 (1st Cir. 1994).

The U.S. Court of Appeals for the First Circuit found that the ADA applied to nonphysical structures when it held that an AIDS patient's employer-provided health plan could be a public accommodation under the ADA.

See also Doe v. Mutual of Omaha Insurance Co., 179 F.3d 557, 559 (7th Cir. 1999), *rehearing en banc denied*, 1999 U.S. App. LEXIS 18360 (7th Cir. 1999), *cert. denied*, 528 U.S. 1106 (2000) (recognizing that websites and other "electronic space[s]" might be deemed public accommodations for purposes of the ADA); *Morgan v. Joint Administration Board*, 268 F.3d 456, 459 (7th Cir. 2001) (indicating that the ADA would apply to a health plan if it were sold over the Internet).

 Rendon v. Valleycrest Products, 294 F.3d 1279, *rehearing en banc denied*, 2002 U.S. App. LEXIS 27593 (11th Cir. 2002).

The U.S. Court of Appeals for the Eleventh Circuit determined that the automatic "fast finger" device used to advance contestants on the television game show *Who Wants To Be A Millionaire?* was within the scope of the ADA, but only because of its relation to the physical space of the game-show studio.

Websites as Places of Public Accommodation

Because the Internet is not a physical place, there has been considerable debate about whether the ADA applies to websites, and if so, to what extent.

Both Congress and various courts have been asked to decide whether a website is a place of public accommodation subject to ADA compliance. In 2000, the House of Representatives held a hearing on whether the ADA should apply to private Internet sites, but to date Congress has not sought to amend the ADA to address this issue.

In 1999, the National Federation of the Blind sued America Online, claiming that AOL violated the ADA by failing to make its service accessible to blind persons. The Federation dropped its suit when AOL agreed to offer software that makes its system compatible with devices used by visually impaired computer users. *See National Federation of the Blind v. America Online, Inc.*, No. 99-CV 12303EFH (D. Mass., filed Nov. 4, 1999). The National Federation of the Blind/America Online Accessibility Agreement is available at http://www.nfb.org/Tech/accessibility.htm.

Various advocacy groups continue to press to make websites accessible to the visually impaired. The National Federation of the Blind has introduced a seal of approval to identify websites that provide easy access to visually impaired users. To earn the seal of approval, a site must provide easy navigation for blind users and be compatible with technologies that magnify content or read it aloud. The websites of Wells Fargo Bank, Hewlett Packard Co., and the Social Security Administration are among the websites that have received this recognition. "New Seal of Approval Rewards Accessible Web Sites" (June 23, 2003), *at* http://www.contentbank.org/news_item.asp?news_item_id=78.

Meanwhile, the American Foundation for the Blind (AFB) is reportedly considering filing lawsuits against some Internet service providers that require users to type a word displayed to them in characters that are not machine readable to register for email and other services. Paul Festa, "Spam-bot Tests Flunk the Blind," CNET News.com (July 2, 2003), *at* http://news.com.com/2100-1032_3-1022814.html. While this verification system successfully deters software bots from accessing protected portions of websites, it also blocks access to visually impaired users because the codes cannot be read by audio programs that recite web content to users. To remedy this problem, some companies have replaced the visual test with an aural test that reads the content; however, according to AFB, the audio output is unintelligible to many users. Members of the Web Accessibility Initiative of the World Wide Web Consortium (W3C) are working to develop and promote a more efficient and universal means of accommodating visually impaired Internet users.

Some courts have also considered the issue of whether websites can be considered places of public accommodation for the purposes of the ADA.

Hooks v. Okbridge, No. 99-50891, 2000 U.S. App. LEXIS 23035 (5th Cir. Aug. 24, 2000).

In an unpublished opinion, the U.S. Court of Appeals for the Fifth Circuit affirmed the trial court's ruling that a commercial website was not a place of public accommodation subject to the ADA.

Access Now, Inc. v. Southwest Airlines, Co., 227 F. Supp. 2d 1312 (S.D. Fla. 2002).

On October 18, 2002, the U.S. District Court for the Southern District of Florida ruled that the ADA does not apply to commercial websites.

The plaintiff, Access Now, sued Southwest Airlines, alleging that its website violated the ADA because it did not enable access by blind persons using screen-reader technology. Without the technology, blind Internet users are unable to access many of the site's features. The plaintiff argued that the website was a place of public accommodation, characterizing it as a "place of exhibition," like theaters, movie houses, and stadiums; as a "display," like museums, libraries and galleries; and as a "sales establishment," like bricks-and-mortar retail stores. The court, however, held that the ADA applies to physical structures only. "To expand the ADA to cover 'virtual' spaces would be to create new rights without well-defined standards." 2002 U.S. Dist. LEXIS 19795 at *14. Access Now appealed the decision to the Eleventh Circuit, which heard oral arguments in the case in November 2003. As of December 31, 2003, the Eleventh Circuit had not yet ruled on the appeal. *Access Now, Inc. v. Southwest Airlines, Co.*, No. 02-16163-BB (11th Cir. filed Mar. 17, 2003). Access Now also sued American Airlines in a separate action before the same Florida court and on the same legal theory. That case is on hold pending the Eleventh Circuit's ruling in the *Southwest* case. *Access Now v. American Airlines*, No. 02-CV-22076 (S.D. Fla., filed July 12, 2002).

Access Now has also reportedly settled suits with retail bookseller Barnes & Noble and clothing retailer Claire's Stores, ending suits in which Access Now had alleged that the merchants' respective websites violated the ADA. *See* Matthew Haggman, "The

ADA and the Internet," MIAMI DAILY BUS. REV. (Oct. 17, 2002), *available at* http://www.adaaccessnow.org/internet.htm.

⚖ *Martin v. Metropolitan Atlanta Rapid Transit Authority*, 225 F. Supp. 2d 1362 (N.D. Ga. 2002).

The plaintiffs, a group of disabled individuals, sued the city of Atlanta's metropolitan transit authority (MARTA) under the ADA and moved for a preliminary injunction. As part of their complaint, the plaintiffs alleged that MARTA's website was not equally accessible to persons with and without disabilities. On October 7, 2002, a federal trial court granted the plaintiffs' motion for a preliminary injunction, in part, and directed the parties to confer in good faith toward agreeing on appropriate remedies for the ADA violations. MARTA officials had already been working toward making the website more accessible, including schedules available in Braille output, and content that is easily detectable by plain-text reading software for visually impaired users.

Even if Congress were to legislate (or a court were to rule) that a website is a public accommodation, website operators nevertheless would not necessarily be required to alter the content of their sites to provide access to disabled persons. The regulations implementing the ADA indicate that a public accommodation is not required "to alter its inventory to include accessible or special goods that are designed for, or facilitate use by, individuals with disabilities." 28 C.F.R. § 36.307(a). Cases in which courts have suggested that a website might be deemed a public accommodation have not gone so far as to say that a website must therefore provide access to its contents to disabled persons. For example, in *Doe v. Mutual of Omaha Insurance Co.*, 179 F.3d 557 (7th Cir. 1999), although the court suggested that a website could be considered a public accommodation, it stated that the ADA "does not regulate the content of the products or services sold." 179 F.3d at 564. Likewise, in *McNeil v. Time Insurance Co.*, 205 F.3d 179 (5th Cir. 2000), the court stated that a place of public accommodation, which includes a health insurance plan, a nonphysical entity, "need not modify or alter the goods and services that it offers in order to avoid violating [the ADA]." 205 F.3d at 188.

Self-Regulation Initiatives

The World Wide Web Consortium (W3C) has been promoting web accessibility through its Web Accessibility Initiative (WAI), which it started in 1997. The W3C encourages voluntary compliance with ADA provisions and provides guidelines and recommendations for software and web content providers and publishers.

On December 17, 2002, W3C issued its User Agent Accessibility Guidelines, representing consensus among developers and the disability community on accessibility features needed in browsers and multimedia players to allow disabled users to access the web. The guidelines urge designers to make websites more accessible to disabled users. For example, designers are encouraged to provide commands that operate through the keyboard as well as a mouse, and to design applications with screen readers or refreshable Braille output.

To comply with the Web Accessibility Initiative, a website must include:

- text equivalent for every nontext element in a site;

- auditory descriptions of the important information in visual content;

- tables that identify row and column headers;

- if all else fails, a link to an alternative website that has adopted the WAI-recommended technologies.

Information about the WAI is available at http://www.w3c.org/WAI/.

Chapter 10: Miscellaneous
Summary of the Law

Unauthorized Access to Websites

- Ancient principles of trespass law have been found to apply to unauthorized access to websites and databases. Though some courts have required a plaintiff to establish that the defendant's unauthorized access caused damage to, or imposed a substantial burden on, the plaintiff's computer system, more recent cases have required only that the plaintiff establish "some tangible interference with the use or operation" of the plaintiff's computer system.

- The California Supreme Court has held, however, that sending email, even email the sender knows to be unwelcome, does not constitute a trespass on the recipient's computer system.

- A federal court of appeals has found that unauthorized access to a password-protected website does not violate the federal Wiretap Act, because accessing stored files does not constitute the sort of interception of a communication proscribed under the Act.

UCITA

- In 1999, the National Conference of Commissioners on Uniform State Laws (NCCUSL) approved UCITA, the Uniform Computer Information Transactions Act, an effort to standardize state laws affecting computer information transactions.

- Support for UCITA appears to be waning. Only two states, Maryland and Virginia, have passed statutes based on UCITA, while four states, Iowa, North Carolina, West Virginia, and Vermont, have explicitly prohibited application of UCITA to residents of their states. In August 2003, NCCUSL withdrew UCITA from consideration for endorsement by the American Bar Association.

Taxation

- The federal moratorium on Internet access taxes expired in the fall of 2003. Efforts to renew the moratorium have met with resistance in Congress.

- The moratorium has never prohibited states from collecting sales taxes on transactions consummated over the Internet. But such taxes are hard to collect. The courts have interpreted the Commerce Clause of the U.S. Constitution to prohibit a state from requiring an out-of-state merchant to collect sales tax on sales made to state residents, unless the merchant has a substantial physical presence in the state. Even though the buyer may owe sales tax on the purchase, few recognize this tax liability and even fewer pay the tax. The states, strapped for cash, are trying to change this. Legislators at the state and federal levels are considering legislation that would make it easier for states to collect tax revenues from online transactions.

- Thirty-seven states and the District of Columbia recently banded together under the Streamlined Sales and Use Tax Agreement to simplify their tax codes and make them more uniform in the hope that Congress, will, in turn, permit the states to require out-of-state merchants to collect sales taxes on their behalf.

Index